SYMPHONY
FOR THE CITY
OF THE DEAD

SYMPHONY FOR THE CITY OF THE DEAD

Dmitri Shostakovich and the Siege of Leningrad

M. T. ANDERSON

CANDLEWICK PRESS

First edition 2015

Library of Congress Catalog Card Number 2015936915
ISBN 978-0-7636-6818-1

15 16 17 18 19 20 BVG 10 9 8 7 6 5 4 3 2 1

Printed in Berryville, VA, U.S.A.

This book was typeset in Octavian MT.

Candlewick Press
99 Dover Street
Somerville, Massachusetts 02144

visit us at www.candlewick.com

To all young musicians.

Thank you for what you give the rest of us.

CONTENTS

PART THREE

Eugene Weintraub of the Am-Rus Music Corporation inspects the microfilm of Shostakovich's Seventh Symphony (*Leningrad*), op. 60.

PROLOGUE

An American agent met with a Russian agent one bright summer morning when the world was collapsing in the face of Nazi terror. It was June 2, 1942; the Second World War was not going well for the Allied forces. Most of Europe had already been conquered by the Nazi German onslaught. France had fallen, and so had Norway, Denmark, Poland, Belgium, and Czechoslovakia. Now the Germans were deep inside Russia, clawing away at the country's innards.

The American agent and the Soviet agent may have spoken of these things when they met. They may have talked about the need for cooperation between their countries, which were now allied against the Nazi threat. All we know is that after they spoke, the Soviet agent passed a wooden box to the American, who took the box and left the building.

Inside the wooden box was a strip of microfilm that, when unrolled, would stretch over a hundred feet long. It contained hardly any words: just lines and dots and ancient monastic symbols in complicated arrangements.

The Russians hoped it would help change the course of the war.

The microfilm had taken a long route to get all the way from Russia to Washington, D.C. It had been flown by plane to Tehran, then driven across the deserts of the Middle East and North Africa to Cairo. From Cairo, it had been put back on a plane and flown to Brazil, and from there, to the United States. Now it was about to embark on the final leg of its journey — to New York City.

First the American agent stopped for lunch at a cafeteria. He got up from the table to go to the bathroom. When he came back, the table was empty. The box with the microfilm was gone.

He had just lost one of the most widely discussed documents of the war.

Panicked, he scanned the room: People ate. Knives scraped across plates. A busboy retreated toward the trash cans with a tray full of garbage.

There, on the kid's tray, tipping toward the peelings and rinds, was the box.

After a journey of ten thousand miles across steppe, sand, sea, and jungle, the microfilm almost ended its trip in the trash.

The agent stopped the kid short of dumping the microfilm. He retrieved the box. The stupid accident was averted.

The agent set out for New York City. There was a lot to be done. In the next few weeks, hundreds of copies of the documents encrypted on that strip needed to be made, and people were already clamoring for it to be made public.

By the day the Soviet agent and the American agent met to pass along the microfilm, the Germans had conquered most of Europe and then had poured east into Russia. They seemed unstoppable. Their tanks had swarmed across the fertile fields of Russia's southern provinces, destroying villages as they went. And in the north of Russia, the city of Leningrad, once the country's capital, had been surrounded for nine months, locked within its rivers and its trenches, blasted daily by air raids and long-range artillery.

The document on the microfilm concerned the city of Leningrad.

The U.S. Air Transport Command carried the microfilm of Shostakovich's symphony from Payne Field, near Cairo, Egypt, across the deserts of North Africa. Touching down occasionally to refuel, the cargo plane crossed the Atlantic, landed briefly in Brazil, and finally made its way to Washington, D.C.

More than a million people trapped inside the city were blocked off almost entirely from the outside world. Over the winter, they had been without electricity, without running water, without food, without firewood, and almost without hope. Families ate wallpaper paste and sawdust. Women prowled basements for corpses to eat, and there were rumors that gangs of men who had turned cannibal went out at night to hunt for victims in alleys. Germans rained down incendiary bombs on the roofs and strafed the squares and avenues during nightly air raids. Adolf Hitler had demanded that the city and all its inhabitants be utterly destroyed.

Secret Directive No. 1a 1601/41: "The Führer has decided to erase the city of [Leningrad] from the face of the earth. I have no interest in the further existence of this large population point after the defeat of Soviet Russia."

German high command felt it would be too costly to feed all the prisoners of Leningrad if they were captured, and Hitler considered the Russian Slavs, like the Jews, to be an inferior race, fit only for slavery or extermination. His vision was to make "room to live" for his Aryan cohorts. Russia would become breadbasket, oil field, and Teutonic playground in the thrilling gymnastic future of the triumphant Nazi Reich.

In New York, on June 3, the microfilm was unspooled and stretched across an illuminated table. Men inspected it with magnifying glasses. Contained on the film was not, peculiarly, the plans for some technological secret — a submarine or the atomic bomb. It was not some fragment of Enigma code or unscrambled German battle order.

Instead, the microfilm contained 252 pages of the musical score for the Seventh Symphony of a nervous Russian composer named Dmitri Shostakovich. Its codes and symbols would be translated by an orchestra of more than a hundred and would be broadcast to millions sitting by their radios — but we are still arguing today about what secret messages the piece contains, what cries for help.

The score included few words: a few typical performance directions in Italian, as was the tradition. And, on the first page, an inscription in Russian: "Dedicated to the city of Leningrad." For this reason, it was called the *Leningrad* Symphony.

Why had the Soviet government arranged so carefully for this piece to be shipped to the West across battle lines, across a Middle East that was swarming with Fascist tanks, across seas festering with enemy subs? How could it possibly be worth it?

And who was the composer of this desperately sought-after score? Dmitri Shostakovich spent the first several months of the Siege of Leningrad trapped in that city under fire, writing much of his Seventh Symphony in breaks between air raids. He had first announced that he was working on the piece over the radio in September 1941, just a few weeks after the Germans had started shelling the city. He had explained his intentions to an audience of thousands.

The day of his radio broadcast, Shostakovich almost missed his appointment to speak on the air. As he was walking through the streets of the city, the Germans started their daily assault. Sirens howled. An urgent voice barked over the loudspeakers, "This is the local defense headquarters! Air raid! Air raid!" Shostakovich scampered to a bomb shelter. Planes roared over the city's spires and canals. Explosions echoed through the Classical avenues. The composer hid until the all-clear sounded.

As a result, by the time he got to the radio studio, he was almost late. The staff rushed him in front of a microphone, and he delivered his message in his high, tense tenor. It buzzed out of radios all over the city where buildings burned and windows gaped without glass.

"An hour ago I finished scoring the second movement of my latest large orchestral composition," he told his fellow citizens.

> In spite of the war and the danger threatening Leningrad, I wrote the first movements quickly.

Why am I telling you this? I'm telling you this so that the people of Leningrad listening to me will know that life goes on in our city. . . .

Leningrad is my country. It is my native city and my home. Many thousands of other people from Leningrad know this same feeling of infinite love for our native town, for its wonderful, spacious streets, its incomparably beautiful squares and buildings. When I walk through our city a feeling of deep conviction grows within me that Leningrad will always stand, grand and beautiful, on the banks of the Neva, that it will always be a bastion of my country, that it will always be there to enrich the fruits of culture.

We still have the piece of paper on which he typed out the message he read on air. Shostakovich must have left it on a desk at the radio station when he was finished with the announcement. It was used for scrap paper. On the other side, the studio director scribbled his notes about the lineup of radio shows for the next day's broadcasts: instructions on how to construct barricades, suggestions for how to defend your home against German troops, and, finally, the recipe for Molotov cocktails. This was not a drink but a homemade explosive, a bottle of gasoline stuffed with a rag, named after the Soviet foreign minister Vyacheslav Molotov.

Everyone in Leningrad was on the front line.

Shostakovich's attachment to his native Leningrad is more complicated than it might seem from his brave and defiant declaration. In the course of his short life, he had been named both a Soviet hero and an enemy of the people. And similarly, Leningrad itself had been renamed several times since Shostakovich's birth, seen as both Russia's prize jewel and a canker on the hide of the body politic. The Communist government had celebrated Leningrad as the cradle of Soviet Russia—and had punished its citizens viciously for supposed crimes against the Soviet state. As the people of Leningrad fought to defend their city from the Germans, they could not forget that their own army had recently been decimated by Joseph Stalin, their own nation's terrifying dictator. Supposedly, Shostakovich once said that the *Leningrad* Symphony was about "the Leningrad that Stalin destroyed and that Hitler merely finished off." To understand Shostakovich and his music, we must also understand how he was caught up in these struggles for power, these murders and assassinations.

For much of the war, Dmitri Shostakovich worked by day writing kick-line tunes for the homicidal secret police's dance band. At night, he sat huddled at a table in a friend's apartment, smoking cheap cigarettes, playing cards with a man who would later denounce him. They played poker. They drank vodka, when they could get it. Food was extremely scarce at this time. They ate pancakes made out of coffee grounds.

We can imagine him there, in the smoke of that kitchen, throwing down cards. It is late at night. He is, supposedly, a poker fiend. His face is gentle and kind and birdlike behind his round, owlish glasses. Though he is in his late thirties, it is the face of a boy. And that face twitches almost ceaselessly. As he plays, he cannot stop touching his lips with his hands or adjusting his glasses. He pats the back of his hair, but his cowlick won't stay down.

He may have looked frail, but he survived greater assaults and catastrophes than most of us can imagine. And though he seemed nervous, his music would change the lives of thousands and give hope to millions.

This is a tale of microfilm canisters and secret police, of Communists and capitalists, of battles lost and wars won. It is the tale of a utopian dream that turned into a dystopian nightmare. It is the tale of Dmitri Shostakovich and of his beloved city, Leningrad. But at its heart, it is a story about the power of music and its meanings—a story of secret messages and double-speak, and of how music itself is a code; how music coaxes people to endure unthinkable tragedy; how it allows us to whisper between the prison bars when we cannot speak aloud; how it can still comfort the suffering, saying, "Whatever has befallen you—you are not alone."

PART ★ ONE

Russia on the eve of the Revolution was a mixture of the modern and medieval. Electric trams rattle past the ancient walls of Moscow's Kremlin.

THE DEATH OF YESTERDAY

The fate of Dmitri Shostakovich was bound up with the fate of Leningrad from the time he was a child. In 1906, when he was born, the city was called St. Petersburg. It was known as "the Venice of the north" for the canals and rivers that ran beside its grand avenues and beneath its many bridges. It was called "the Window on the West," because it was the most European of Russian cities. It was a city of the arts, a city of poetry, a city of music, a city of the sciences.

Like a fairy tale, it had risen up out of the swamps of the river Neva, called forth by Tsar Peter the Great, the emperor of Russia. Like many fairy tales dreamed up by the mighty, the magic involved in summoning it into existence was years of slave labor in murky ditches.

From a small, muddy village, St. Petersburg grew into the shining capital of the vast Russian Empire, the seat of the tsars. The Romanov dynasty ruled the nation from this city and its many nearby palaces for two hundred years.

As Russia entered the twentieth century, a new modern age, it was still, in many ways, a medieval kingdom. Most of its population were peasants, living in villages in the countryside much as they had for centuries. The peasantry had only recently been freed from slavelike servitude, and they were crushed with debt. The economy was stagnant. The country was hardly industrialized; there were not many factories. Though in St. Petersburg itself, nobles and sophisticates attended balls in Parisian gowns and discussed the poetry of the French, this ramshackle empire also included huge, frigid wastes of fir tree and tundra, deserts where the only inhabitants were nomadic families with their herds, and mountain towns that had never even heard the name of their distant ruler.

During Dmitri Shostakovich's childhood, the last tsar of Russia, Nicholas II, ruled aggressively but not particularly well from his Winter Palace in St. Petersburg. He led the country into one disastrous military engagement after another — first a war against the Japanese, then the First World War against the Germans. There were times when the tsar and his family seemed to ignore all the demands of his counselors and the elected government and listen only to the advice of an infamous Siberian wizard named Rasputin, who had supposedly ensorcelled the tsarina.

This sounded, even to the Russians of the time, like a fairy tale out of some opera in St. Petersburg's gilded theaters; but the hunger, the poverty, and the desperation were real. The powerful were frustrated with their monarch; the middle class was angry that they did not have a representative voice in the government that would always be heard; the peasantry could barely make ends meet.

The Russian intelligentsia looked to the West — to England, France, the United States, and Germany — and there they saw huge factories, efficient railway networks, and new, scientific methods of farming. They saw the future. By comparison, Russia seemed backward — a sprawling nation of remote hamlets where peasants struggled to work the land for powerful landowners; a failing, disorganized empire ruled by a dense prince and his poisonous Siberian monk.

The St. Petersburg of Dmitri Shostakovich's youth was ready to wake up from its ancient, monarchic dream and, blinking and bewildered, confront the new world of the twentieth century.

Many Russians, especially the sophisticated citizens of St. Petersburg, longed for opportunities to modernize their country. But on the other hand, when radical thinkers looked to the West, they saw not only the factories but also the slums that girdled them. They read stories of the rioting in the streets of the great American and English industrial cities; they witnessed the terrible boom-and-bust cycles of unregulated economies. St. Petersburg intellectuals discussed different plans that would hustle Russia forward into the new century without the suffering and wild inequality they saw both in their own country and in the nations of the West. They wanted to create a new society.

They also saw that their tsar, Nicholas II, would not lead the Russian Empire in the direction of modernity and equality. The Revolutionary leader Vladimir Lenin wrote:

> In Russia there is no elective government, and she is governed not merely by the rich and the high-born, but by the worst of these. She is governed by the most skillful intriguers at the tsar's Court, by the most artful tricksters, by those who carry lies and slanders to the tsar, and flatter and toady to him. They govern in secret. . . . These officials tower above the voiceless people like a dark forest — a mere worker can never make his way through this forest, can never obtain justice.

Discontent and economic strangulation plagued everyone from the nation's few industrialists and investors to its millions of rural peasants.

In 1905, the year before Dmitri Shostakovich's birth, his father supposedly joined a mass march on the tsar's Winter Palace to support striking workers and demand justice and bread. Huge crowds gathered, hoping to stir the heart of Nicholas II, the so-called father of their people. Instead, as the thousands congregated, confusion and panic ensued and the tsar's Cossack guardsmen fired into the crowd. People fled in terror and were trampled underfoot. Guardsmen slashed at them with sabers. When it was over, the bodies of hundreds lay bloodied in the snow.

This massacre—as much an example of incompetence as tyranny—pushed many in the country toward radicalism and thoughts of overthrowing the tsar. The day was called Bloody Sunday; the gore on the snow watered the seeds of revolution.

Dmitri Dmitrievich Shostakovich grew up in the midst of this fracturing fairy tale. On the one hand, he was surrounded by the city's gracious parks and pastel palaces, by its quiet canals and its bridges, like the bridges from some fable, guarded by stone lions, griffins, wild horses.

On the other hand, stark realities glared through the mists of fantasy: Shostakovich's mother, Sofia, sheltered Jews who were fleeing from the bloody anti-Semitic pogroms that wracked the countryside. Shostakovich's aunts, like many of the Russian intelligentsia, were revolutionaries. One had married a student radical who'd been thrown in prison. One pecked out Communist articles on a typewriter that she hid, along with her codebooks, in the family's stove. One night the tsar's secret police kicked open their door and searched the apartment for incriminating documents. The aunt, by chance, was away; only Shostakovich's father was home. The police ransacked the place but found nothing.

As Shostakovich's father told the little boy and his two sisters stories about events like these and the chaos on Bloody Sunday, the children started to understand how deep their country's unrest really was.

At the same time, Shostakovich's mother and father brought up the three children—Dmitri (whom they called Mitya); his older sister, Maria; and his little sister, Zoya—in the best traditions of the Russian intelligentsia. They were surrounded by music and literature.

Zoya, Dmitri, and Maria Shostakovich (c. 1912) pose in the woods at Irinovka, where their father worked as manager on a peat farm near Lake Ladoga.

Shostakovich's father, Dmitri Boleslavovich Shostakovich, managed a peat moss farm at Irinovka, a couple of hours outside the capital. The family went out to join him for the summers. They stayed in a huge, cold, strange house. The builder had mistaken the measurements, confusing centimeters and meters, so the rooms were huge and the windows were tiny.

Shostakovich's father was a kind man with an excellent sense of humor and a strong Siberian accent. "He never seemed to take anything seriously," said Zoya. "He was never worried and always full of fun. He had a passion for gadgets — new cigarette-lighters, tiny knives, fancy boxes for all purposes, and any wire or ring puzzles he could find; these he worked over for hours, with his children sitting on the floor around him."

While Mitya's father worked during the day, the boy and his two sisters ran through the woods barefoot and picked mushrooms and berries. They played with the estate's dogs, read adventure novels, and helped the handyman with chores.

Shostakovich's aunt recalled that he was a dreamy boy. "I think you would say he was very alone. He was always alone, really, even when he was gathering berries with his sisters in the country. They would be the ones to find the berries, the quiet Mitya would be the one to eat them."

Others found him shy, too. One of his childhood friends, Boris Lossky, remembered meeting him for the first time at school: "The nine-year-old boy, with fragile, sharp features, looked somewhat like a small sparrow. He sat at the window looking blank-faced through his spectacles while his schoolmates played and amused themselves. Probably his introspection was due to his being under the spell of his inner hearing."

His little sister, Zoya, saw another side of Dmitri Dmitrievich, however: "He was somewhat absent-minded," she said. "Yet he was a wonderfully kind and cheerful child. He was full of mischief and good spirits in the first years of his life, and indeed he remained so until they started beating the fun out of him."

The "they" she spoke of had not yet come into power.

* * *

The three children were also tutored in piano and dance. When Mitya was very little, he was not particularly interested in music. He saw that piano lessons made his older sister, Maria, cry. The young composer preferred blocks.

When the family was in St. Petersburg for the winter, however, he could hear the neighbors — a cellist and a children's book writer — play music through the wall of their apartment. The thin wall introduced him to the music of the old Viennese masters and Russian composers like Peter Tchaikovsky and Alexander Borodin.

Hand in hand with his parents, Shostakovich walked through the streets where these composers had lived. He saw the house where Borodin — not just a composer but also a chemist — had written his splendid quartets and conducted his research on aldehydes and urine. The boy and his parents passed the concert halls where Borodin and the rest of the "Mighty Fistful" of St. Petersburg composers had premiered their works. He strolled on the embankments of the Neva River and the Winter Canal, where a famous heroine in an opera by Tchaikovsky met her lover and jumped to her death. (Tchaikovsky himself, composer of magical ballets, had tried to do the same thing by wading into a frigid river one night, hoping for fatal pneumonia.) It was a city full of music.

Mitya's parents took him to see one of the great fairy-tale operas of St. Petersburg composer Nikolai Rimsky-Korsakov. Shostakovich claims it did not change his life. On the other hand, it did include a princess in a barrel, a man who transformed into a bee, and a whistling squirrel who ate emeralds.

The next day, though he could not even read music, the boy remembered the opera perfectly and sang through much of it in its entirety.

The political and economic situation got worse. Terrorism was on the rise. In the first year and a half of Shostakovich's life, roughly 4,500 government officials were injured or killed in assassination attempts by radicals. In his toddler years, the government recorded 20,000 terrorist acts across the empire, with more than 7,500 fatalities.

By the time he was eleven, the country was trapped in the midst of World War I—a disastrous conflict that many Russian soldiers on the front line did not even understand. Violence overtook the city, and this time, there was no turning back. Millions were starving to death. The country's economy was falling apart. Anger at the regime extended from those living in abject poverty to some of the wealthiest families. The capital did not seem like the city it had once been. Its name had even been changed from St. Petersburg to the much more Russian Petrograd (*gorod,* or *-grad,* being Russian for "city," versus the German *-burg*). The once grand capital now seemed chaotic, angry, hungry.

In February 1917, the people of Petrograd took to the streets. Industrial workers walked out of their factories. Women marched through the avenues, demanding bread and the end of war.

The government called out armed guards to force the mob to quiet down.

The mob was not going away.

On the morning of February 27, 1917, Sofia Shostakovich was eating breakfast when the janitor appeared at the door of their apartment and told her that the whole city was on the march. The government had sent out platoons of fierce Cossack horsemen to control the crowd. The news was terrifying: this was precisely how the massacre on Bloody Sunday had started.

In a few minutes, the cook came in with more news. The tsar's police had panicked and had roared the order, just as in 1905, for the Cossacks to fire into the crowd—to shoot to kill.

But the Cossacks hadn't fired. Instead, a Cossack officer had raised his saber and hacked off the police captain's arm while the order to fire was being given. The Cossacks were siding with the crowd.

Sofia muttered, "This looks like revolution." She ran downstairs and out onto Nevsky Prospect, the great central avenue of the city.

It was mobbed, but the mood was one of triumph. The Cossack horsemen rode along through the crowd, smiling, joking, and laughing. The guards and the army, it seemed, were on the people's side, not the tsar's.

Sofia Shostakovich went back into her building and called Dmitri senior at work. He told her that the tsar's police had lost control of the city. The city's most famous prison had been attacked, and the prisoners had fled. Everything was in an uproar.

The cook, Sasha, went to fetch young Mitya from school. As they pushed their way through the crowds, Mitya was anxious. He kept saying to himself, "There's no revolution. It's all nonsense. It's all nonsense." He held tightly on to Sasha's skirt so he wouldn't be swept away by the tide of people surging around them.

Elsewhere in the city, the mood was not as festive. The tsar's police, crouched on roofs and in doorways, shot at the protesters. Machine-gun fire rattled down avenues as people fled or threw themselves into snowbanks.

Soldiers told to take up arms against their fellow Russians refused. They turned on their officers. Many just handed their guns to the Revolutionaries.

All over the city, as people marched, they sang:

> Let's denounce the old world!
> Let's shake its dust from our feet! . . .
> The rich, the exploiters, the greedy mob
> Deprive you of your hard, hard work. . . .
> The tsar, the vampire, takes from your veins.
> The tsar, the vampire, drinks the blood of the people.

And then:

> Arise, arise, working people!
> Arise against the enemies, hungry brother!
> Forward! Forward!

Dmitri senior ran up the steps to the Shostakovich apartment and burst in, full of excitement. He shouted, "Children — Freedom!"

It seemed as if the tsar's tyranny was toppled. The past seemed to be dying in a single day.

Young Dmitri demanded a length of ribbon, the red of revolution, to tie around his arm.

For the rest of the afternoon, he and his sisters wore their scarlet sashes, parading back and forth in front of their building like soldiers.

They played at rebellion.

Things happened quickly in the days that followed. The old order was breaking down. Unpopular factory bosses who had made their workers' lives miserable were thrown in burlap sacks and rolled through the streets in wheelbarrows. In the countryside, peasants raided their landlords' immense Classical houses. The army and the police were locked in battle with each other on the streets of the capital. Machine-gun emplacements fired into the surging crowds, leaving many dead on the cobbles. All authority seemed to have crumbled to nothing.

On March 2, 1917, Nicholas II, the last tsar of Russia, realized that he could no longer rule, and he abdicated. Officially, he had already been dismissed. The three-hundred-year-old dynasty of the Romanovs was at an end. (The tsar and his family were exiled to a remote town; the next summer, they were all secretly murdered in their basement by their guards.)

There was a new Provisional Government, and there were promises of a universal vote, of universal education, of industrial reforms, of judicial reforms.

The red flag of the Revolution was hoisted up over the tsar's Winter Palace. All over the city, the tsar's two-headed imperial eagles were draped with red cloth.

In one of Petrograd's theaters, a ballet company put on Tchaikovsky's *Sleeping Beauty.* Up in the imperial box, which had previously been reserved only for the tsar's family, who would look down royally at the performance below, normal ticket-holders now lounged and slouched in the seats. In the magical kingdom onstage, the king and queen still wore crowns, but between the acts, the orchestra struck up Revolutionary tunes.

At the end of the ballet, people from the audience jumped up onto the stage to mingle with the dancers. All the old lines between ruler and ruled, between those who paid and those who performed, between the worker and the watcher, seemed to be breaking down.

Together, cast and audience, they all sang out: "Arise, arise, working people! Forward! Forward!"

The Shostakovich children witnessed the celebratory joy of the February Revolution of 1917 — and its violence. Shostakovich later claimed he had seen a boy steal an apple, then, in the ensuing fight with the tsar's police, get slashed to death. His older sister, Maria, and her classmates, spilling out of the doors of their school, saw a policeman brutally kill a young protester from the Bogdanov tobacco factory. There were trucks all over the city, Shostakovich later remembered, "filled with soldiers, who were shooting. It was better not to go out in those days."

In March, a funeral procession for the victims of the Revolution wound through the slushy streets of Petrograd, watched solemnly by millions as a bitter snow and rain fell. The coffins were covered with red flags, and the throngs sang a dirge: "You fell victims in the fatal struggle of selfless love for the people. . . . The people will rise, great, mighty, and free." The Shostakovich children climbed up onto an iron fence by an old churchyard so that they could see.

As the coffins were lowered into the pit where they would be covered with cement, the cannons on the grim, gray walls of the Peter and Paul Fortress across the Neva River fired a final salute. It was, said Leon Trotsky, one of the radicals, "a concluding chord in the symphony" of the February Revolution.

We are told that when young Mitya got home from the mass burial, he played the piano quietly for a long time. There, sitting at the keyboard,

Young Dmitri Shostakovich and his family were among the crowds of thousands who lined the streets of Petrograd in March 1917 to witness the burial of the victims of the February Revolution. Bolshevik Leon Trotsky wrote: "The funeral procession—in its mood a procession triumphant with the joy of life—was a concluding chord in the symphony of the [February Revolution]."

he composed a "Funeral March for the Victims of the Revolution." When guests would come to visit his mother, he would play them this piece and a "Hymn of Freedom" he had written.

Years later, when his hair was flecked with gray, he would remember the songs he heard in the streets on the day of that funeral and the music he wrote right after. He would use them in symphonies recalling the revolutions of 1905 (when his father marched on the Winter Palace) and this year, 1917, the year of two revolutions, the year Russia changed forever.

The houses of the wealthy and the middle class — the bourgeoisie — were ransacked for goods that could be requisitioned for the people's fight, or simply looted in the name of the Revolution.

One day Mitya and his mother were on their way home from his school. They drove through the city's squares and avenues in the car that had come with Dmitri senior's job. A hired driver was at the wheel. In those days, the Shostakoviches lived a life of relative luxury.

As they made their way toward their apartment, two soldiers armed with rifles ran along beside the car. They jumped onto the running boards and held on. It was startling — the Shostakoviches didn't know what was going on.

The soldiers leaned into the windows and said that they were requisitioning the car for the Revolution.

The driver started to argue. It was an outrage.

Sofia Shostakovich quieted him gently. She asked the soldiers if they would drop the family off at home first.

Once they were back at the apartment, she gave the car to the soldiers. They got in and drove off in it.

In those days, most of the civilian automobiles in the city were seized. Family cars now careened around the streets decked with red flags, with guns bristling from the windows and soldiers stuffed in the seats, swaying on the running boards, and gripping the fenders. One diarist talks about the surprise of seeing luxury limousines that were spiky with bayonets.

Cars also rattled down the streets with activists hurling pamphlets out the windows, trying to publicize their party or point of view. Shostakovich's aunt remembered roads being thick with political litter.

That year, it was as if the city was built of ideas and argument: People walked across a pavement of propaganda, and the walls were plastered with posters. Buildings were coated in debates. Type ran in every direction. Newspapers sprang up, printed a few issues in flurries, then died.

Some argued for victory against the Germans. (The country, after all, was still at war.) Some argued for peace at any cost. Some argued for the rule of the industrial workers. Some argued for the rights of the peasants. Some argued for a republic. Some argued for Communism.

Factions split into smaller factions, committees gave rise to other committees, and all of them fought about the shape of the future.

Out of this political turmoil rose a man who called himself Vladimir Ilyich Lenin. That was not his name, but revolutionaries often didn't call themselves by their names.

In April of 1917, the story runs, Mitya Shostakovich and his friends from school heard that this radical, Lenin, was returning to Petrograd by train from his exile in western Europe. They ran in a group to see him when he arrived.

Lenin was the head of the Bolshevik Party. The Bolsheviks argued for the rise of the workers to a long-delayed position of power. Lenin wrote:

> The only way to put an end to the poverty of the people is to change the existing order from top to bottom . . . to take the estates from the big landowners, the factories from the factory owners, and money capital from the bankers, to abolish their *private property* and turn it over to the whole working people throughout the country. When that is done the workers' labor will be made use of not by rich people living on the labor of

others, but by the workers themselves and those elected by them. The fruits of common labor and the advantages from all improvements and machinery will then benefit all the working people, all the workers.

He believed that Russia was only the first country of many that would soon overthrow its government and the control of the bourgeoisie (the middle class — which, incidentally, included the Shostakoviches) in favor of rule by the working class, the proletariat.

Shostakovich and his friends were eager to see this man who, as it happened, would soon change history and plunge his country into yet another bloody revolution. As the boys got near the train station, the crowds got thicker. Lots of people had shown up to see Lenin return to the capital. The kids slipped into a column of workers crossing a bridge. They were part of the jostling.

There was the train, sitting at rest. There, over the heads of adults, up on a platform, was Lenin: a distant smudge with a bald head and a smart little beard. He shouted out to the crowds.

Shostakovich could not hear a word he said, but he did hear, all around him, the roar of the people.

Over the mob, Lenin called out, "The world-wide Socialist revolution has already dawned. . . . Any day now the whole of European capitalism may crash. . . . Long live the worldwide socialist revolution!"

To many people, it was a thrilling idea. As Karl Marx had written at the close of his *Communist Manifesto,* they had nothing to lose but their chains. But many others — including the Shostakovich family, as it turned out — had plenty to lose. Members of the Provisional Government, trying to forge a new democratic republic out of a broken-down monarchy, were very worried by Lenin's radicalism.

Few suspected that this was the direction of Russia's future.

Still, a Soviet biography of Shostakovich declares: "The spectacle of a billowing sea of people, the elemental force of the events taking place, and the figure of Lenin—all this was imprinted forever in the young composer's memory, to pour out later in sweeping symphonic canvases."

We need to examine this story. Shostakovich's biographers write that Lenin's appearance in the city was "imprinted forever" in his memory. His sister Zoya claimed to remember Mitya jogging back from the train station "in raptures."

In his supposed memoir—which may be forged—Shostakovich merely said, "They say that the major event of my life was the march down to the Finland Station in April 1917, when Lenin arrived in Petrograd. The incident did take place. . . . But I don't remember a thing."

There are definitely problems with the story. For one thing, Lenin did not arrive at the train station during the day, but in the middle of the night. Shostakovich could not have simply scampered over from the schoolyard.

The composer was ten years old at the time, in a city where the streets had recently been scoured with machine-gun fire. Did his parents really kiss him on the head and send him out at midnight to join the Revolutionary mob?

Or was this story of him viewing the future leader of Russia from afar something made up later when he—or others—wanted to create, in retrospect, a direct connection to the Bolshevik cause?

At the time when Shostakovich would have seen Lenin at the station, so shortly after the February Revolution, the Bolshevik leader would have only been one Revolutionary extremist among many. No one could have foreseen that he would rise so quickly to power. Moreover, Shostakovich's parents, though they were in favor of the Revolution like many, were certainly not radical Bolsheviks. It's doubtful they would have taken much notice of Lenin at the time. Would their ten-year-old son have gone out of his way to see this man step off a train? It's not impossible, but we also can't take it for granted.

Reconstructing a Soviet life is often difficult. Many of the details of

Shostakovich's youth we know only because his aunt Nadejda Galli-Shohat collaborated on a biography years later, against his wishes. She is not an entirely reliable source; an American interviewer called her "one of those wonderfully frank Russians who can drop into fantasy as easily as most of us find our way into the subway." When the Shostakovich children were young, she loved telling them fairy-tale fibs about her youth in Siberia. We should be cautious of believing absolutely the testimony of a natural story-teller who claimed that in her infancy, she was nursed by a bear.

In the summer of the Revolutionary year 1917, the Shostakoviches decided to send the children out to the peat farm at Irinovka where Dmitri senior worked. While, in the capital, the wobbling Provisional Government sus-tained attacks from the left and from the right, Mitya and his sisters wan-dered through the fir groves, picked mushrooms, read spy novels, and played waltzes on the piano.

As always, it was Zoya who found the mushrooms, and her dreamy brother, Mitya, who picked them.

Zoya later commented, "He could stand right on top of a mushroom and not notice it."

In the midst of the country's political struggles, it was clear to Lenin and the Bolsheviks that they could not win control of the government through a legitimate vote of the nation's new Assembly. As a result, they launched the year's second rebellion.

On October 25, 1917, Lenin and the Bolsheviks seized power. The battleship *Aurora* chugged into position beside the Winter Palace, which was now the headquarters of the Provisional Government. The ship lowered its guns and fired off a terrifying rally of blanks. It was a warning.

Bolshevik forces attacked the palace. It was defended by only a few military cadets, a small division of the Women's Battalion of Death, and forty of the Knights of Saint George under the command of a staff captain on a cork leg. The government's defenders crouched with machine guns behind piles of firewood. The Bolshevik Red Guard swept in and ransacked the place.

This second uprising was called the October Revolution. As the February Revolution had overthrown the tsar, the October Revolution brought the Bolsheviks—the Communists—to power over all the other possible parties.* One revolution had just been toppled by another. The heads of the Provisional Government stepped aside, surrendered, or fled.

Still, when elections for the nation's legislative body, the Assembly, were held, the Bolshevik Party didn't get even a quarter of the votes—so Lenin simply dissolved the Assembly. Now the Bolsheviks, who just a few months earlier had been considered a fringe group of radicals, were in sole control of Russia. Lenin said that he had seized power in the name of the people—though the people had not voted him into power and, as the Bolsheviks knew well, their rebellion was "not popular": "The masses received our call with bewilderment," they reported with frustration. Nonetheless, for roughly the next

---

* A note on terminology: The terms *Bolshevik, Communist, socialist, Marxist,* and *Soviet* are related and often used as if they mean the same thing, but they all have different shades of meaning. Lenin's party was the Bolsheviks. They were a Communist party, that is to say, they believed that eventually, after a series of transformations, all government would fall away and be replaced by utopian communes. They believed that one of the stages government had to go through to reach true Communism was complete government control of industry and commerce—a totalitarian form of socialism. Socialism can refer to the government ownership of any industry or service, from things we take for granted like the fire department, the postal service, railroads, and the highway department to health care, banking, or manufacturing. Different nations make different decisions about what should be owned and provided by the government. Lenin and the Bolsheviks believed that the regime should own *all* industries and services. In general, the Communists drew their philosophy from the political economist Karl Marx and so were also called Marxists. Finally, in the early stages of the revolution, they found their power in the workers' councils, or "soviets," and so the country they eventually gave their name to was called the Soviet Union (or the Union of Soviet Socialist Republics). While these terms—*Bolshevik, Communist, Marxist, socialist,* and *Soviet*—are sometimes used interchangeably, many people have died to make distinctions among them.

Vladimir Lenin returned from exile to lead the Bolsheviks to victory in the October Revolution of 1917.

Having driven the tsar and his family out of the Winter Palace during the February Revolution, members of the Provisional Government now miserably wait among the palace's splendors for their own overthrow by the Bolsheviks in the October Revolution. Outside the windows to the right, the battleship *Aurora*, in the hands of a Bolshevik captain and crew, has aimed its guns at the palace walls and fired off warning shots. The palace is about to fall to Revolutionaries for the second time in a year.

seventy years, Lenin's party would rule the sprawling empire that had once been the tsars'.

Immediately after the Bolsheviks took power, they made good their promises to the working class of Russia: they gave over the factories to the control of the urban workers, and they confiscated all of the great land-owners' country estates in the name of the peasants. The whole notion of private property was in question. Russia had embarked on one of the boldest social experiments in human history.

In the unrest after Lenin dissolved the Assembly, Bolshevik thugs killed two of the previous members of the Provisional Government in cold blood. The city's intelligentsia was shocked.

Dmitri Shostakovich was asked to play the piano for a memorial service held at his sisters' school. He played his "Funeral March for the Victims of the Revolution."

But who at this point were the "Victims of the Revolution"? He had written the piece earlier in the year to lament the death of Revolutionaries killed by the tsar's police. Only a few months later, he played it to lament these two men killed by the Revolutionaries. Two opposing forces, one piece of music.

So Russia proceeded into its uncertain future — as Dmitri Shostakovich played its solemn march of victimhood or victory.

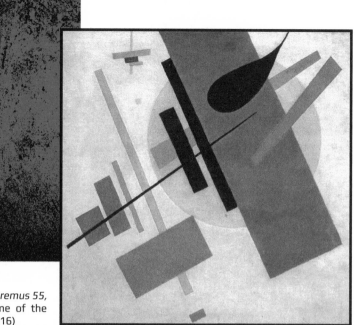

Kazimir Malevich's *Supremus 55,* painted about the time of the Russian Revolution (1916)

THE BIRTH OF TOMORROW

The future had arrived.

Petrograd was full of it.

Dmitri Dmitrievich Shostakovich entered his teenage years just as the capital of Russia also exploded into a strange new youth.

Lenin, in toppling the first Revolutionary government with his own Bolshevik Revolutionary government, had unleashed civil war on the country. This bloody conflict between the Communists and their many enemies would rage for years across the vast territory of Russia. Yet later, Shostakovich claimed, "Despite all the difficulties, I remember that time with a warm feeling."

He was not alone in this. The old world had been tossed away, and a new world beckoned. In this new world, supposedly everyone would be educated—everyone would work—everyone would have enough to eat. The Bolsheviks promised equality for all races and equality for the sexes. Workers and peasants would walk the streets of Moscow and Kiev wearing fine suits and hats. War would, eventually, disappear. In nation after nation, the working class, the proletariat, would rise up and toss aside their masters. National boundaries would no longer matter. This seemed like a wonderful dream. The world would be a lush, industrial utopia.

Bolshevik leader Leon Trotsky predicted, "Man in Socialist societies will command nature in its entirety, with its grouse and sturgeons. He will point out places for mountains and for passes. He will change the course of rivers, and he will lay down rules for oceans."

There was nothing humankind was not capable of.

A lot of young Shostakovich's pleasure came from a warm and happy home. His mother doted on him. His father cracked jokes. His older sister, Maria, played piano duets with him. His younger sister, Zoya, was growing into an angular, eccentric girl with a huge amount of energy and verve.

She insisted on hanging all the pictures in the house at a slant.

Sofia Shostakovich loved to hold parties, and so these years were filled with loud gatherings and evening salons. When Mitya was younger, he would hide under the piano, listening to the sounds thrumming down through the latticework of wood. When he was older, he took part himself, playing dances while the guests and the rest of his family swirled around the apartment. "We invited up to thirty people," his sister Zoya remembered. "There was nothing much to feed the guests on, but we would dance until six in the morning. . . . Life was quite fantastic in those days. Mitya enjoyed himself with the rest of us, and he didn't miss out on the dancing either."

Already, young Mitya's power on the piano astonished people. "It was wonderful to be among the guests," one remembered,

> when the bony boy with thin lips pressed together, a small, narrow, faintly Roman nose, and old-fashioned spectacles with bright metal frames . . . entered the large room and, rising on tip-toe, sat down at the huge piano. Wonderful, for by some obscure law of contradictions the bony boy was transformed at the piano

into a bold musician with a man's strength in his fingers and an arresting rhythmic drive. . . . His music talked, chattered, was sometimes quite outspoken. . . . Then the boy got up and went quietly to join his mother, who blushed and smiled as if the applause were for her and not her wordless son.

Sometimes the Shostakoviches would go to parties at which the great musicians and poets of the city gathered. Alexander Glazunov, the stout director of the Petrograd Conservatory, would be there smoking his cigars and talking about music. When he played the piano, he kept the cigar between his fingers, and the ash waggled up and down the keyboard. The poet Anna Akhmatova, as striking as an idol and carrying herself as if she were already a statue in a ruined temple, would stalk through the crowds of guests, engaged on her strange affairs.

It was through Glazunov that Sofia Shostakovich somehow got her Mitya into the Petrograd Conservatory to study piano at the very young age of thirteen. (As with many musical prodigies, a mother's demands were part of his success.) The boy took the entrance examinations and was found to be very gifted. He left school at thirteen to focus completely on music.

His door to the future was open.

Shostakovich went to the Conservatory to study piano in 1919. There often was not much food or heat in the place in those years, because the Civil War was still disrupting the life of the country in countless ways — but Mitya seemed to feed on music.

The classrooms were freezing. The students trudged to their piano classes in long coats, hats, felt boots, galoshes, and fingerless gloves. On the way to the Conservatory, they'd pick up bits and pieces of wood — a slat from a chair or a broken picture frame. They needed them for heat. During the lesson, they wouldn't take off their coats or hats. There was a small tin stove in the classroom, and they all fed their kindling, scrap by scrap, into the flame. They'd swap seats during the class. Whoever was about to play the piano next would sit by the stove, stretching their fingers. They'd warm their hands and prepare to play. The piano keys were freezing. The ivory was so cold it burned.

In the Conservatory's concert hall, the cherubs on the ceiling had ice on their cheeks.

One of Shostakovich's friends, Leo Arnshtam, remembered the faculty's glee when cabbages were delivered. Round Glazunov tiptoed into a classroom and announced that the cabbages were being unloaded — and, Chopin be damned, the teachers were off like a shot.

"The Conservatoire of my youth smelled of cabbage," said Leo Arnshtam, "but despite everything it breathed inspiration!"

Shostakovich and his friends walked back and forth across the city, across bridges and icy squares, just to hear concerts. They didn't have any money, so they sneaked into rehearsals to listen. They heard symphonies, operas, sonatas. Sitting side by side at the piano, pounding on the keys, breathing steam in the cold of the morning, they played versions of the pieces they'd heard the night before.

Learning these duets, Shostakovich taught himself composition from inside the scaffolding of music, where its wheelworks and gears lay hidden.

Shostakovich's friend Arnshtam called those years "hungry, but nevertheless happy." He remembered Shostakovich:

> This thin and apparently fragile adolescent was exceptionally animated and always in rapid motion. His sharp profile, crowned by a jaunty lick of hair, would flash past me at different corners of the Conservatoire. His outward appearance and behavior did not lead one to suspect the artist in him. . . . Like the rest of us, he waited his turn for the cabbage soup in the Conservatoire queue. And he too, before touching the icy keyboard, had to warm his hands, frozen to the point of numbness.

His teachers certainly noticed him. "An excellent musician, despite his young age. Such early development is remarkable," they wrote in 1921. In 1922, they wrote, "Exceptional gifts which have blossomed early." By 1923, Glazunov announced that Shostakovich was already musically mature.

In those times, said Leo Arnshtam, "Music triumphed. And not just the music we played on our instruments, but the music of revolution!"

The Bolshevik government did not want music and the other arts simply to be for the wealthy anymore. Lenin wrote, beautifully and thrillingly:

> Art belongs to the people. It must have its deepest roots in the broad masses of the workers. It must be understood and loved by them. It must be rooted in, and grow with, their feelings, thoughts, and desires. It must arouse and develop the artist in them. Are we to give cake and sugar to a minority when the mass of workers and peasants still lack black bread? . . . So that art may come to the people, and the people to art, we must first of all raise the general level of education and culture.

Russians of all classes had always been particularly drawn to poetry and music. In the early 1920s, the government tried to promote these enthusiasms. The Commissar of Enlightenment — in charge of spreading education throughout the whole workforce — arranged music schools near factories to teach students of any age and any background how to play instruments and sing. He also arranged for the Conservatory students to go out into the world and make music for the people.

Pianos heaved out of the homes of the bourgeoisie were rolled up onto flatbed trucks. Singers, cellists, and violinists would climb onto the backs of the trucks and they'd bang and rattle out into the countryside to give concerts and dances for the Red Army or for factory workers during their breaks. Shostakovich played in fields and in dining halls.

The audiences, delighted with the free music, would sometimes give him soup or half a sandwich. It made a huge impression on the young composer.

Petrograd, the city of the arts, was wild with frenzied experimentation.

"The streets are our brushes, the squares are our palettes," declared the great Russian Futurist poet and painter Vladimir Mayakovsky. "Drag the pianos out onto the streets."

And art did move onto the streets.

Lenin needed word of Communism to be spread to the people, and creative artists, excited by the idea of this new world, were thrilled to take part in the transformation of art for the masses. Not only were there roving bands of musicians like Shostakovich in his clanking music wagon. There were now great artistic and musical spectacles staged on the avenues of Petrograd. Parades featured effigies of capitalists with top hats and monocles; behind them puttered modern threshing equipment with banners reading, "Machines and Tractors for the Peasants!"; and behind them, to keep everyone interested, leaped acrobats dressed as cucumbers and turnips.

On the anniversary of the October Revolution, a cast of ten thousand acted out "The Storming of the Tsar's Winter Palace" while more than a hundred thousand people looked on, awed, moved, and delighted. Experimental theater troupes set off into the countryside to perform news stories, absurdist clown acts, science-fiction dramas. The Futurist Mayakovsky created bizarre propaganda plays like his *Mysterium-Buffo*, a postapocalyptic extravaganza in which a few working-class survivors of a great biblical flood kick their way through heaven and hell and arrive, instead, at the new Communist utopia — Machine World! — where a glorious new Russia arises, full of electricity and manufacturing.

Many artists thought that this was the moment to destroy the arts of the past. "The thunder of the October cannons helped us become innovative," declared artist Kazimir Malevich. "We have come to burn the brain clean of the mildew of the past."

"Blow up, destroy, wipe from the face of the earth all the old artistic forms," cried the head of the Petrograd Committee of Enlightenment. "How can the new artist, the proletarian artist, the new man not dream of this?" New art, new music, and new drama had to be found for a new world where workers ruled. What would music sound like now that it was no longer being played in the salons of the rich? What would painting look like when it did not have to adorn the Rococo walls of Russian palaces?

As a result, Petrograd swarmed with new art movements: Cubo-Futurists and Neo-Primitivists, Constructivists and Suprematists, Rayonists and Productivists.

For some years, schools of artists all over the globe had been excited by the idea of the future. The poets of the past had flinched from the roaring of automobiles and the screeching of braked trains — but these new artists embraced the strength and dynamism of movement, metal, whistles, cogs. Now these Futurists became a loud voice in the new Bolshevik order — literally shouting on street corners.

They believed that the Revolution needed them, and it was thrilling. "Inside us we had youth and joy," wrote one Futurist. "We lived on art. Those were times of hope and fantasy."

Gone were the landscape paintings of the past, the pictures of ancient Greek heroes, the portraits of women in their silks and feathers. Painters began to reduce everything to simple squares and circles, the intersection of triangles. They were thrilled by geometry. They talked about achieving weightlessness, of painting pictures that were no longer mired in the world. They wanted to leave the earth behind. (Some of them literally achieved weightlessness: Painter Peter Miturich designed blimps. Constructivist Vladimir Tatlin designed a flying machine named after him, the *Letatlin*. Vasily Kamensky's career as a painter started after he stopped working at his previous job: stunt pilot. He crashed into the ground, walked away from the wreckage, and decided he'd better choose a safer profession.)

Composers, too, wanted to celebrate Russia's new modernity. The most avant-garde among them now created pieces full of dark, knotted chords and thunderous declarations, or music like sculptures of crystal: sharp,

A Malevich portrait of a soccer player, entitled *Color Masses in the Fourth Dimension*

An exhibition of the new, geometric art. Hanging in the corner, where a religious icon would normally go in a Russian household, is a painting by Kazimir Malevich entitled *Black Square* (1915). It is of a black square.

hard structures with jutting spikes and dazzling surfaces. Caught up in the frenzy of Futurism, they also forged many pieces specifically illustrating the roar and repetition of machinery. The names of these pieces suggest their brutal, mechanical energy: Mosolov's "Iron Foundry" (a hypnotically violent piece in which, eventually, the percussionists start slamming huge pieces of metal with rods), Prokofiev's *Leap of Steel,* Deshevov's *Rails,* and Ornstein's *Suicide in an Airplane.* The Russian Association of Proletarian Musicians demanded, "The orchestra must become like a factory." To make music even more relevant to the average industrial worker, a manufacturing plant in Petrograd hooted and blasted out a "symphony" on factory whistles and motorized turbines. In the city of Baku, the naval fleet assembled an "orchestra" of artillery, sirens, machine-gun choirs, and, for good measure, a few hydroplanes. The audience sang along.

Many artists of all kinds wanted to make their artistic work useful to people in everyday life — and so the new, geometrical visual style was turned into plates, clothing, furniture, and, most famous of all, posters that revolutionized the world of art and brought the new art to the people. Russia suddenly was on the forefront of the future.

This science-fiction emphasis was politically necessary. The present was bleak. The Revolution and Civil War had catastrophically disrupted agriculture and trade. Industrial output in 1921 was only a fifth what it had been in 1913. The economy was in a shambles, despite Lenin's best efforts to fix it. So the Communist Party demanded that people look forward and remember that their own sacrifices would one day flower in the perfect society for their children or their children's children.

Young Mitya went to see the Futurist writer, artist, and actor Vladimir Mayakovsky perform when he was in town. He already admired Mayakovsky's bizarre and startling verse, his absurdist love poems and declarations with names like "The Spine Flute" and "A Cloud in Trousers."

Mayakovsky was quite a figure. He was a tall man, frighteningly handsome, with a deep, braying voice. By the gentle age of twelve, he had already been stealing his father's sawed-off shotguns to give to Revolutionaries. By the age of sixteen, he had been imprisoned by the tsar's police. By the time he turned twenty, he and fellow Futurists had published *A Slap in the Face of Public Taste,* in which they declared that the past should die to make way for the future. Mayakovsky crowed, "Spit on rhymes and arias and the rose bush and other such mawkishness from the arsenal of the arts. . . . Give us new forms!"

He would yell at his audiences, make fun of them, provoke them, flirt with wives in front of their husbands.

Now he stood before young Mitya and the rest of the café crowd, dressed (if we can believe contemporary reports) in a top hat and a ragged coat, with a wooden spoon sticking out of his jacket pocket like a boutonniere—and he bellowed his poetry of youth through a megaphone:

> No gray hairs streak my soul,
> no grandfatherly fondness there!
> I shake the world with the might of my voice!

Young Dmitri was impressed. He did not imagine he would soon be working side by side with this "clumsy-footed angel," this "singer of gutter miracles," this "thunderbolt of cobbles," who acted as the brash bard of the Revolution.

The conception of art as propaganda was only part of Lenin's program of control. In the years following the Revolution, he needed every means at his disposal to sway the opinions of the population. He wrote, "The state is an instrument of coercion. . . . We desire to transform the state into an institution for enforcing the will of the people. We want to organize violence in the name of the interests of our workers."

"In the name of the interests of our workers"—for Lenin believed that the people themselves often did not understand what they truly needed. As a result, many times in the first years of its history, the Communist government was in conflict with the workers they claimed to serve. In the cities,

Vladimir Mayakovsky, Futurist poet, painter, actor, and handsome brute

workers discovered that they did not, as promised, run their own factories — the state soon did. In the countryside, peasants did not always want to give up their grain stores to the Communists. Lenin made an already tense situation worse by condemning all religion as superstition. The far-flung populations of the Soviet republics were often deeply pious and were aghast when their churches, synagogues, and mosques were ransacked, when their mullahs, rabbis, and priests were killed or forced to flee. Ancient church bells were knocked from their steeples and melted down amid the jeers of Communist cadres. The bodies of Orthodox Christian saints were ripped out of their tombs and put on display in the new Museum of National Hygiene. This horrified the peasantry, already often hostile to the Bolsheviks.

Even after the Civil War was over, there was still violence as the government subdued the uneasy population. There had to be some way to convince the citizens of the good of the Communist cause. The arts were supposed to be part of this coercion. For this reason, Lenin particularly liked film, which he thought had tremendous power to sway the masses.

He was not very fond of music. Not because it didn't move him — but because it did. "It makes me want to say kind things, stupid things, and pat the heads of people," he admitted. "But now you have to beat them on the head, beat them without mercy."

The teenage Shostakovich did not take politics very seriously. At one point he had to take an examination in "Marxist methodology." He and four other students were called into a room and asked questions about politics and music, to determine whether they were counterrevolutionary in their thought.

The examiners asked one student "to explain the difference, from the sociological and economic standpoints, between the work of Chopin and Liszt," two composers of the nineteenth century.

Shostakovich could not keep a straight face. He burst out howling with laughter. He could not stop himself.

An advertisement for baby pacifiers by Vladimir Mayakovsky and Alexander Rodchenko. The poster reads: "No better pacifiers! Never have been! You'll suck on them until you're old! Sold everywhere."

In the 1920s, with the era's emphasis on Soviet artists and writers being useful to society, many took up poster and slogan work like this. Ironically, this meant that for a while, both Communism and its opposite, consumer capitalism, pushed creators toward the same fields: advertising and product design.

Still, Mayakovsky's firecracker personality comes through in this bold, modernistic vision, where pacifiers look like artillery shells and the baby's hands look like pistol shots. There is nothing about these pacifiers that looks remotely pacifistic.

He was sent out of the room.

Later, he was sorry. He asked to be given another chance to take the test and requested that the student he had interrupted be given another chance, too. This time, they both passed.

A few years later, to laugh at a test like that would have been fatal. And by then, Shostakovich would be administering those tests himself.

Though young artists may have been excited by this new world, many people were finding it hard to make ends meet. Most substantial private property had been seized by the government. The value of money fluctuated wildly. People lived by bartering their goods.

Shostakovich's aunt recalled people swapping complaints on the street about what they'd sold so they could eat: "We are living now on our grand piano," and "*We* are living on the bedroom curtains and father's old watch!"

Shostakovich's father had to sell many of their possessions to keep food on the table. He would take items of furniture, jewelry, or clothing on a freight train that went out to the market towns, where he could barter for milk, eggs, and kasha for the family. In the winter, these trains could be frigid, and on one such trip, in February of 1922, he caught a cold.

He came home complaining of a headache. It did not get better. His lungs filled. He had pneumonia.

A few days later, Dmitri Boleslavovich Shostakovich died.

Though the Bolsheviks discouraged religion, six monks came to sing the coffin on its way, and a priest said the ancient rites. Young Mitya and his sisters pressed their faces desperately to the hands of their dead father.

But according to another onlooker, by the time the lid was on the coffin and the dirt hit the lid, Shostakovich had already started to grip his sorrow inwardly. "Mitya and Zoya stood a little off to one side on a mound of newly dug earth. Zoya's distraught little face was wet with tears and her coat was unfastened. Mitya stood, his cap crushed under his arm, slowly wiping his spectacles. His eyes looked especially defenseless without them, but his entire face was filled with inward concentration and composure. No need to go to him with condolences!"

People muttered to Sofia Shostakovich that they were so sorry for her loss.

She replied, "Now I feel like a stone."

Shostakovich left us a document of his mourning: his "Suite for Two Pianos." It is a set of pieces to be played by him and his sister Maria. Together, they rehearse their sadness. It opens with a dark, relentless tolling of bells, a grief that will not cease. It is as if brother and sister, by playing this piece, find a way to summon the sadness itself to be with them in the family parlor, staring at them, silent and aghast.

It is a remarkable piece for a fifteen-year-old composer. He and Maria played it for salons of musicians, dedicating their performances to their father.

One of the pieces in the set, a fantastical dance, may be a morsel for Zoya — she wanted to be a dancer (as well as a painter and, sometimes, a singer). Dmitri often wrote eccentric dances for her, in which one can almost hear her knees and pointy elbows. But even in this light dance, with hints of Zoya's pranks, there is, woven through it, the echo of the mourning bells.

That is perhaps the most moving thing of all about the suite: no matter what mood follows, it is occasionally interrupted by those urgent chimes — just as, often, in the wake of a death, at odd moments, when we are thinking about something else entirely, our grieving takes us unawares.

After the death of Shostakovich's father, the family had no income. Mitya offered to drop his studies and get a job, but his mother wouldn't hear of it. Maria, three years older, gave piano lessons. To make ends meet, Sofia Shostakovich got a job as a cashier at the Workers' Union. She worked from nine in the morning until ten at night.

One evening, a man followed her home from work, perhaps thinking she was carrying money from the register. He caught up with her on the stairs of their apartment building and hit her over the head with a metal rod or a wrench.

She saw stars and thought she'd been shot. She screamed and started ringing all the doorbells on the landing. The man ran for it.

Zoya bounded down the stairs and found her mother splattered with blood. A friend who was a doctor raced over and searched her skull for fractures.

She was fine, but the experience rattled her. A few weeks later, a hundred rubles were stolen from her register at work. No one blamed her out loud, but she was fired. After that, she got a job as a typist in the Palace of Weights and Measures.

This income still was not enough. The family rented out four of their apartment's seven rooms. Shostakovich's mother insisted on keeping the parlor and two bedrooms, but they shared the kitchen and bathroom with their lodgers, who eventually included Shostakovich's aunt Nadejda and her new husband.

This was not unusual in Petrograd. Displaced by the Civil War, at first, and later by the brutal grain requisitions of the Communist government, people were moving in droves into the city to get new manufacturing jobs. Apartments that once had housed a single family and their servants, surrounded by their comfortable settees, their ferns, and their china, now were broken up and subdivided, with each room housing a whole family. Writers of those years often describe the tense unpleasantness of communal living: people sneaking bites of one another's food in the crowded kitchens, people arguing about who used more electricity, people hanging laundry dripping in the common hallways, people waiting in long lines for the toilet or hammering on the bathroom doors, hollering insults at each other. People also listened through the walls to hear if neighbors they particularly hated were speaking out against the regime. That was an easy way to get rid of a neighbor. In those times, people either shouted or spoke in whispers.

Things were not easy within the Shostakovich family, either. Dmitri was often silent and sullen. Zoya, on the other hand, was loud and impassioned. She appears to have argued with everyone, principally herself. Reading her letters, it is impossible not to love her feisty proclamations. "My character," she wrote, "hasn't got the slightest stability. Let's take, for instance, art. What haven't I studied?"

Her mother and older sister rolled their eyes at her inability to commit to one thing or another. Her mother told her that if the ceiling of the apartment fell in, out of all of them, Dmitri was the one who should be saved; he, after all, was the genius.

After the family's setbacks, Sofia Shostakovich sank very deeply into depression. She suggested to the children that she should kill herself. Perhaps, she said, she should kill the three of them, too. "They spoke of it in the calm way one decides to take a trip or a long-wanted rest."

We do not know what they said. We only know that they lived.

In September of 1922, eight months after the death of his father, Dmitri Dmitrievich Shostakovich turned sixteen.

His mother, determined to make his birthday a happy one, threw a huge party for him. Glazunov, the grand old man of Russian music who had done so much for the boy already, was there to toast him. Sofia found some vodka to serve to the guests, and she asked young Dmitri to serve the drinks.

Dmitri wanted to try vodka; now that he was the man of the family, perhaps he felt it was time to take up drinking. He hit the bottle hard that night. Every time he poured out a glass for Glazunov, he sneaked some for himself. Glazunov raised a toast to the boy and drank. So did the boy.

The toasts went on.

A woman raised her glass toward Glazunov and toasted "to the composer of *Scheherazade*!"

Glazunov had not written *Scheherazade* — a dead man named Rimsky-Korsakov had. But Glazunov didn't care. He smiled, raised his glass, and drank anyway.

And so did the boy.

Glazunov was a pretty heavy drinker.

That night, so was the boy.

Eventually, he and his friends ended up in another room, somewhat in a fog, deciding they were all going to start a secret fraternal society. It is unclear what this "united brotherhood" hoped to accomplish. The important thing was the initiation ceremony, which apparently involved them walking past one another in various hieroglyphic poses. Crouched like figures on Assyrian or Egyptian friezes, they paced toward one another, heads turned to the side and arms crooked. They were supposed to do this three times.

The third time was the charm, as the saying goes; after three mystic passes, Shostakovich reeled, toppled over, and boozily passed out on the floor.

Sofia Shostakovich charged in and grabbed her son's friend Boris, glaring at him. Her son could do no wrong; she assumed Boris was responsible for everything. She demanded to know what was going on. Boris tried to explain about the secret society. It suddenly didn't seem very convincing. Boris was exiled from the Shostakovich house forever.

Though Shostakovich perhaps did not make it into any Egypto-Assyrian secret societies that night, he was at least initiated into the old Russian mysteries of vodka.

The family's condition went from bad to worse. Swellings began to appear on Dmitri's neck. They took him to the doctor.

He was suffering from lymphatic tuberculosis. He needed an operation. They sold a piano so he could be treated.

Sofia Shostakovich, sick with anxiety, having lost her husband and fearing the loss of her son, made things impossible in the overflowing apartment. In a passion, she lashed out at her sister Nadejda, blaming her and the Bolsheviks (Nadejda's husband was a Bolshevik) for Dmitri senior's death and Dmitri junior's illness. "You!" she screamed at her sister. "You and those like you are responsible for the revolution! And your marriage was complete nonsense. You did it only because you don't love your own family."

Nadejda stammered out some response to these unfair accusations, but

Sofia demanded sharply, "If both Mitya and your husband were drowning, which one would you save?"

It was a ridiculous question. Nadejda didn't know how to answer. She stammered, "I would save them both."

"No!" shouted Sofia. "No! Suppose only one could be saved."

There was no response that would satisfy Sofia's rage. Through tears, at a loss for an answer, Nadejda wept that she would just drown herself. Scenes like this became more common as the family grew more miserable.

Mitya was studying hard for his final piano examinations, but he had to take a break for the removal of a gland infected by the disease. During his recitals — when he had to play the music of Bach and Beethoven before the faculty of the Conservatory — he wore a bandage around his neck where the incisions had been made. He still played well, though, and passed.

In the summer of 1923, his doctor sent him to a treatment center by the ocean in the sunny south. His sister Maria went with him. They played concerts all along the way to pay for their train fare.

It is a grim-sounding truth that some of the happiest days of Dmitri Shostakovich's life were spent in a tuberculosis sanitarium in the Crimea.

Between arsenic injections, his interest in life was revived. He and Maria swam and played tennis. They enjoyed walks on the grounds. And for the first time, Dmitri fell in love.

Maria, who was supposed to be taking care of her younger brother, wrote back to their mother that he was getting soppy over some popular girl who was always surrounded by admiring boys. The girl was "small, slim, with thick dark hair and a round, pretty face." Her name was Tatiana Glivenko. She was not actually sick, like the others at the sanitarium, but had been sent to Crimea to enjoy the summer sun. She had a small following of admirers who trotted around after her to the cafeteria and the seaside. "Amid these confident, patronizing young people," wrote one of Shostakovich's Russian biographers, "he felt like an ugly duckling with his bandaged neck and big round spectacles."

He did not need to worry. Tatiana Glivenko found him shy and charming. She fell for him, too. Years later, when she was old and he was dead, she remembered him: "How could anybody not have loved him? Everybody did. He was so pure and open and always thought about other people — how to make things better and easier and nicer for them. He never thought or worried about himself. If there are saints on this earth, he was one. He was like that when he was young, when we met, and he remained like that to the end of his life."

It is unclear whether his sisters would have always agreed with her that he was a saint on earth.

Tatiana and Dmitri went for walks and challenged each other to games of tennis. For them, the sanitarium was like a country club. Everything was in flower.

But the summer had to end. They went home to their separate cities — Petrograd and Moscow. Though they lived many miles apart, for years they were in love.

When Dmitri returned to Petrograd, he went to work playing the piano in a movie theater called the Bright Reel.

In the 1920s, movies did not have sound, so in order to have a sound track, the theater owners had to hire live musicians. The musicians either improvised music to fit the scene on screen or played out of books of piano pieces with general titles like "Love Theme," "Chase Scene," "She Is Abandoned," and "The Building Burns Down."

Shostakovich was not fond of his job at the Bright Reel. He worked long hours and didn't always find the movies particularly interesting — for example, *Swamp and Water Birds of Sweden*. He got so bored with this cinematic trudge that he started to imitate birdsong on the piano. He thought he was enlivening the picture. The audience thought he was drunk.

Spending so much time playing the piano for money, he found it difficult to work on his own compositions. To graduate from the Conservatory, he

Scenes and a poster from the 1924 Soviet science-fiction film *Aelita, Queen of Mars* (based on a book by Shostakovich's later supporter Alexei Tolstoi): a silent movie about space-traveling Soviets who start a Bolshevik revolution on the Red Planet. Notice how the geometrical designs of the great Russian experimental artists of the period are used to envision an alien future.

had to complete a whole symphony in place of a dissertation. That was going to take some time.

He did sometimes use his job at the movie theater as an opportunity to practice difficult pieces on the piano, if they fit the action on the screen. When he wrote a piano trio for his distant beloved Tatiana, he invited a couple of friends—a violinist and a cellist—to come to the movie theater so they could practice it together. While the film ran, they pretended his piece was the sound track. We can only hope the movie was a romance. His trio is undoubtedly music by a boy in love—sweet and drunk on adoration. It would not have played well with a crime flick.

The boss at the Bright Reel didn't want to pay him.

Shostakovich pointed out that his pay was already two weeks late.

> He asked me, "Young man, do you love art? Great, lofty, immortal art?" I felt uncomfortable, and I replied that I did. That was a fatal mistake, because [the boss] put it this way: "If you love art, young man, then how can you talk to me now about filthy lucre?" . . . I tried to tell him that I needed the money. He replied that he couldn't imagine or understand how a man of the arts could be capable of speaking about such trivial aspects of life. He tried to shame me. But I held my own.

Shostakovich sued the owner of the Bright Reel for back pay, quit the job, and started to work playing the piano at the Piccadilly.

On November 7, 1924, Shostakovich wrote to a friend, "Now I'm writing a symphony (Conservatory task for this year), which is quite bad, but I have to write it so that I can have done with the Conservatory."

It took him a long time and a lot of anguish to finish his first symphony. While he worked on the piece, he went several times to Moscow—where we might assume he met up with Tatiana. Perhaps around the same time, she came to visit him in Petrograd.

She sat by him while he composed music at the piano. She watched him lovingly. Then Shostakovich's mother would arrive, furious with the girl. She didn't like anyone interfering with her son. She snapped to Tatiana, "Go out and leave Mitya to finish his work."

Shostakovich stood up for Tatiana. He said, "No, I want her to stay here. It helps me."

Sometimes their apartment must have felt very small.

As an old woman, Tatiana remembered that in the Shostakovich family, young Mitya "was the center of life and the idol. His mother was so devoted that she constantly petted and spoiled him. . . . He was automatically freed from any household worry, and it made him impractical to a degree. He always bore the imprint of his mother's influence."

He may have resented his mother's interference, but he could not stand her unhappiness. When he was sending her a little money he had made playing the piano in Moscow, he urged her to recall, "The main thing in life is good cheer, joy, energy, creativity, art, and soul. We are rich in soul. Our spiritual life is second to none. . . . Hold on, Mother dear, to all that is joyful. For there is so much joy that sometimes we don't see it. Joy must be everywhere. For example, I gave a concert and got at least twenty rubles — joy! I took the train without a ticket — joy! Everywhere there is joy."

The relations between the cities of Moscow and Petrograd were changing. When Shostakovich was a child under the tsars, St. Petersburg — Petrograd — was the capital. After the Russian Revolution, Lenin decided that distant Moscow — with its medieval fortress and its ancient roots in older Russian government — should be the capital of the new Soviet Russia. Petrograd was too close to the West, both geographically and culturally. To the Bolsheviks, there was something dangerous and seductive about the capitalist countries of Europe. They wanted their new nation's capital to be as far away from Western decadence as possible.

So in 1918, Lenin had made Moscow the capital.

At the beginning of 1924, Lenin died. Just a few days after his death, a decree went out: the name of Petrograd was going to change once again. Forget Saint Peter, forget Tsar Peter the Great. There was no need anymore for tsarist memories or the blessing of Christian saints. Communism had its own heroes, its own haloes. Petrograd would henceforth be called Leningrad, "Lenin's City," in honor of the greatest hero of the Revolution.

When Shostakovich wrote to Tatiana and his Moscow friends, he slyly put his address down as "St. Leninburg."

May 12, 1926, was a date Shostakovich called his "second birth." He celebrated it for the rest of his life. It was the day his First Symphony was performed by a full orchestra, the Leningrad Philharmonic. He was only nineteen years old.

The conductor thought the kid was very calm during the rehearsals, sitting silently in the auditorium, watching through his round spectacles, saying not a word.

In fact, he was desperately agitated. His composition teacher wrote that young Dmitri was "in a state of such indescribable excitement from hearing the sound of his own music that I only restrained him with difficulty from gesticulating and displaying his agitation."

After the rehearsal, Shostakovich called his mother to tell her it had gone well. She was relieved. She had not been able to think about anything else.

The night before the performance, Shostakovich couldn't sleep, and the next day, he couldn't eat. That evening, at half past eight o'clock, the Shostakovich family all showed up to hear the piece: "Mrs. Shostakovich outwardly reserved . . . ready to stand by her son come what may; quiet, smiling Maria, already convinced that everything would go well; and Zoya—the tomboy, as they thought of her—who was mischievous and wry and took nothing seriously, but was still anxious for her brother."

In 1918, Moscow became the capital of Soviet Russia, and the ancient fortress called the Kremlin became the seat of government. The move away from Petrograd, "the Window on the West," and into the Russian heartland deliberately emphasized the country's bold new self-confidence.

At age nineteen, Dmitri Shostakovich had already gained international fame for his First Symphony.

Sofia Shostakovich later recalled: "By nine o'clock the hall was completely packed. I cannot describe my emotions on seeing the conductor, Nikolai Malko, about to pick up his baton. I can only say that even the greatest happiness is very hard to bear!"

The symphony began.

It is a youthful piece. It sings of young joys and young sorrows. The second movement[*] even includes a theme that would be excellent for an Egypto-Assyrian secret society's nighttime rituals—complete with a part for a collapsing young pianist. Shostakovich had been writing the symphony between sessions in the cinemas, and, in the best possible fashion, it's a piece that sounds like ingenious images on film—and not just the clowning, the scampering. Even in the moments of great sorrow later in the work, there's a sense of whiteface and of kohl around the eyes.

The first audience loved it. They demanded that the frisky second movement—the one with the Egypto-Assyrian dance in it—be played all over again.

As Mrs. Shostakovich wrote: "Everything went off brilliantly—the magnificent orchestra, and the superb execution! . . . It was over, and Mitya was called out again and again. When our young composer came out on stage, seemingly still only a boy, the audience expressed its joy and enthusiasm in a long and tumultuous ovation."

Dmitri Shostakovich had made his first mark on music.

Word about the symphony quickly spread. Soon, the young composer's piece was being played by orchestras in the West—in Vienna, in Berlin, in Philadelphia and Chicago. Crowds all over the world were delighted by its playfulness and pathos.

---

[*] Symphonies traditionally have several movements, each of which typically has its own moods, its own shape, and (most important) its own melodies and musical themes. In the Russia of Shostakovich's day, there were very traditional expectations about how each of those symphony movements should work, and Shostakovich usually played by those rules. One of the reasons that his Second and Third Symphonies, discussed later, seemed so revolutionary is that they weren't organized on any expected plan.

Shostakovich was clearly a talent to be watched.

He didn't know yet how closely some would watch him.

After he graduated from the Conservatory, Shostakovich waded into the ultramodernism of Leningrad. Though he never went as far as some of the extremists, his music of the next several years had many of the same elements of the wider artistic revolution: a joy in angularity; a pleasure in surprising effects; an addiction to the grotesque; irony, sarcasm, and satire; an emphasis on bright color and flat, hard surfaces. His author friends and acquaintances were writing science-fiction romps like mechanized folktales, clownish stories with no direction and no point, fables with no morals. They defied common sense. If music without words can have "characters," then Shostakovich's characters are like those in the absurdist stories of his Leningrad writer friends: broad and bizarre and almost cartoonish at times, full of vivid eccentricities.

Shostakovich's Second and Third Symphonies (1927 and 1929, respectively) are built like the street-corner spectacles of the Futurists, complete with bellowed Communist songs at the end. The Second Symphony was written for the tenth anniversary of the October Revolution; its dedication read, "Proletarians of the World, Unite!" It uses all the musical vocabulary of ultramodernity to depict the masses laboring in darkness—rising out of that darkness into heroic combat. It supposedly even depicts the death of the boy Shostakovich saw slashed on Nevsky Prospect. And then, at the end, it bursts into triumphant song. A chorus enters and chants a rousing hymn for the workers:

> Nobody will ever deprive us
> of the victory over oppression
> and darkness. . . .
> May the name of this victory be October!
> October is labor, joy, and song.
> October is happiness

in the field and at the work bench.
This is our slogan,
the name of the new age:
October, the Commune, and Lenin.

We do not know whether Shostakovich believed in the sentiments of the poem he set for the chorus at the end, though there is no reason to think he didn't believe in the promise of Communism. We do know that he secretly thought this particular poem was awful. He told Tatiana the poetry was "quite disgusting."

In keeping with the vogue for factory music, young Shostakovich included a part in the symphony for a factory whistle to announce the opening of the new workers' utopia. He went to manufacturing plants and soberly listened to the shrieks of their lunchtime sirens, taking notes. He chose his favorite to blast the audience into Revolutionary wakefulness.

In good Communist form, Shostakovich tested the score on "four workers and one peasant" to see if they liked it. They were not so fond of some of the ultramodern entanglements — but they apparently loved his work song at the end, and even joined in.

Shostakovich also wrote for the stage. He clearly loved the sleazy dance tunes of the era. The Soviets loved American jazz, even though it was supposedly wicked and Western. (An article called "The Foxtrot — A New Kind of Pornography" argued, "We should forbid the performance of these disgusting dances. There is no place for them in the revolutionary republic.") When writing music for ballets and plays, Shostakovich delighted in the foxtrots and waltzes and cancans of the evil, capitalist characters. He enjoyed the hungry energy of their greed, even as he mocked it.

Audiences loved his "Tahiti Trot."

He even wrote a ballet about soccer, in which crooked capitalist soccer players face off against clean-living Soviets who perform startling slow-motion gymnastics.

Shostakovich loved the brutal Russian form of soccer. He did not play it—he watched it like a fiend. He spent a lot of his free time at the stadium, cheering for Leningrad's Dynamo team. He was an ardent fan. Friends could ask him any question about the team's past trials and successes, and he would rattle off stats.

He and his friends screamed at the field and jumped up and down like little boys. Afraid of jinxing his favorite team, Shostakovich thought it was bad luck to say that Dynamo would win. Therefore, he always said that he thought the team was in bad shape. He would bet dinner that Dynamo would lose. His friends took advantage of this peculiarity. If Dynamo won the game, then Shostakovich lost the bet and he would have to take them out to dinner. If his beloved Dynamo lost, then he would have no appetite. He'd turn down their invitation to dinner and would slink home without collecting on his bet.

It was very profitable to bet against Dmitri Shostakovich.

At the age of twenty-two, Shostakovich got the chance to work with two of the greatest experimentalists of his age: Mayakovsky and Meyerhold.

Vladimir Mayakovsky was the Futurist poet Shostakovich had gone to watch when he was a boy. Vsevolod Meyerhold was one of the country's most famous (or infamous) stage directors. Everything he did was new and cutting-edge. In his tremendously popular productions, the sets no longer looked like houses or forests; they looked like machines. Every production had a new, futuristic twist: the walls moved, or they were made out of swaying bamboo stalks, or slogans from Lenin and Marx and the Association for Chemical Defense were projected overhead. Meyerhold began one play with a convoy of automobiles roaring over a bridge onto the stage. When he was directing some comedies by the revered nineteenth-century Russian playwright Chekhov, he started to notice how often people in nineteenth-century Russian plays faint—very often—so he called the production 33 Swoons and focused on all the fainting. Whenever someone fainted, a band played a fanfare. There was a different fanfare for men and women. There was no end to Meyerhold's gleeful reenvisioning of the theater.

One writer slyly predicted that sooner or later, Meyerhold would die crushed to death under a stage of naked thespians.

In late 1927, the visionary Meyerhold phoned Shostakovich and said he needed an assistant to organize and perform music for productions at the Meyerhold Theater.

In January 1928, Shostakovich went to Moscow for several months and lived with the craggy, wild-haired director and his family while producing music for plays. It was an exciting time for him. He loved Meyerhold's vision. He even got to act in one production: Meyerhold needed a pianist for a party scene in a play by the famous nineteenth-century Russian writer Gogol. Shostakovich went onstage in white tie and tails and pretended to be a Russian of the nineteenth century, though one who was, apparently, attending a party held in a large system of metallic valves.

The Meyerhold apartment was lively, crammed with antiques and jumble-sale treasures Meyerhold's wife, the actress Zinaida Raikh, had picked up around Moscow. Zinaida Raikh was very beautiful, but not necessarily a particularly good actress. The rumor muttered in the wings was that Raikh only got parts because she was married to Meyerhold.

As it turned out, Raikh was not easy for Shostakovich to stay with. She got irritable at the young composer haunting her apartment and yelled at him as though he were a child. To make things worse, Meyerhold's nanny (who also lived in the apartment) took an uncomfortable interest in the young Shostakovich and kept groping him.

He also got tired of Meyerhold and Raikh boasting about their children, Tanya and Kostya, and how brilliant they were. He wrote to a friend, "Here I am living surrounded by brilliant people (a brilliant theater director, a 'brilliant' actress—'Oh, Zinaida! What a performance you gave yesterday! It was brilliant')."

"Well done, all of you," Meyerhold gushed to his family. "You're all great. Eh, Shostakovich? Aren't they great? Don't you think so?"

"Yes, indeed."

Raikh said archly, "I'd like your opinion, Mitya. Obviously our daughter Tanya has inherited her talent as a poet from her father, but where can our son Kostya have got his tremendous musical talent from?"

Meyerhold intervened and said, "From you, of course."

Raikh fluttered, "Why me? I'm an actress after all, not a musician."

"Yes, you are indeed an actress," Meyerhold pronounced. "You have profound cogitation of the Word. And where the Word comes to an end, there begins Music. Don't you think so, Mitya?"

Shostakovich "maintained a sullen silence and nodded agreement."

It was sometimes difficult to be around the brilliant.

But it was exhilarating. Inspired at least in part by Meyerhold's production of the Gogol play, Shostakovich worked on his first opera, based on Gogol's short story "The Nose." This classic tale was the grandfather of all the absurdist stories written by Shostakovich's friends and acquaintances. It's about a nose that leaves a man's face and runs around St. Petersburg, applying for government jobs.

Shostakovich wrote the script of the opera, the libretto, with two friends of his. They had to write in the morning, since one of his friends was a night watchman at a candy factory (or, as his Soviet job title read, an "agent in conserving nonliquid property"). Shostakovich's friend was often tired, slogging to the apartment after a night standing guard at the candy factory, but he quickly woke up and the three of them turned out a fun and energetic script.

Sitting on Meyerhold's couch, Shostakovich set their words to music. The opera score is bright and loud, full of pranks, honks, and grotesquerie. By the time the nose's owner finds the nose, it is grand and condescending; it wears a plumed hat. It's surrounded by the hymns of an angelic choir. When

Experimental theater director
Vsevolod Meyerhold

Meyerhold's production of *The Magnanimous Cuckold*. The set, by Constructivist artist and designer Liubov Popova, transformed the stage into a machine for drama.

Actress Zinaida Raikh, Vsevolod Meyerhold's wife, playing "The Phosphorescent Woman," who, in a later science-fiction play of Mayakovsky's, returns from the future to lead worthy bureaucrats in a "time train" to the coming Communist paradise.

Meyerhold's production of Gogol's *The Government Inspector,* in which Shostakovich played the piano. In this bizarre scene, we can see the visual emphasis on rhythm, repetition, and design.

an old-fashioned opera aria starts to get off the ground and a girl sings about love, she's smacked down quickly by some squeal or the weird wobbling of a metal saw.

It is a piece full of anarchic joy.

Meyerhold had worked before with Shostakovich's childhood hero the Futurist poet Mayakovsky. (Together, for example, they staged the play about the flood and the workers who find utopia in Machine World.) Now Mayakovsky had written a play called *The Bedbug,* a satire in which a loud, obnoxious con man is frozen accidentally during his wedding and wakes up generations later — in the far future (1973) — to discover that the world is a sterile, mechanical totalitarian state. There's no alcohol, there are no cigarettes, and dreams are considered to be a disturbed psychological abnormality.

Meyerhold wanted Shostakovich to do the music for this odd fable. Shostakovich was excited to be working with the great Mayakovsky, famed Communist playboy and hooligan. From a distance, Mayakovsky had looked to the young Shostakovich like a great man: loud and strong and certain. Their first meeting, unfortunately, did not go well.

The massive modernist stood, staring down at the shrimpish boy composer in front of him. Shostakovich, at that time, looked "very thin and scrawny, pale, with a thick head of hair; he created the impression of being very modest and shy. His light-colored myopic eyes looked out in bewilderment through his spectacles at all that surrounded him. His gait was nervous and rapid, as were the constant movements of his hands."

The Futurist poet was not impressed.

When they went to shake, Mayakovsky only held out two fingers, as if he couldn't be bothered to offer the kid a whole hand.

Meyerhold was embarrassed by Mayakovsky's behavior. He said quickly to Shostakovich that Mayakovsky had developed pains in his hand.

Shostakovich nodded. He held out one finger in return. He said, "I've developed a pain in my hand, too."

* * *

Their discussion about the music for the play didn't go well, either. Shostakovich remembered, "Mayakovsky asked me what I had written, and I told him symphonies, an opera, and a ballet. Then he asked me whether I liked firemen's bands. I said that sometimes I did and sometimes I didn't. Then Mayakovsky said, 'I like firemen's bands the best and I want the music for *The Bedbug* to be just like the kind they play. I don't need any symphonies.' Naturally, I suggested that he get a band and fire me. Meyerhold broke up the argument."

In the final scene of *The Bedbug*, the con man trapped in the future is thrown into a zoo, where he can be observed with disgust by the new world's shining citizens. For this scene, Mayakovsky asked Shostakovich to write something "as simple as mooing."

Shostakovich got to work.

As Shostakovich shuttled back and forth between Moscow and Leningrad, working on the music for *The Bedbug*, he liked Mayakovsky less and less.

The poet was full of himself and very Western. His suits were from Germany, his shoes were from France, and every day, he wore a different American silk tie to rehearsals. It was no secret to Shostakovich or the rest of the cast that the only reason Mayakovsky had written the play was to get money to buy a Renault sports car in Paris. It was one of the only private cars on the streets of Moscow.

This was an odd motive for a Communist writer, the "drummer of the Revolution." A friend of Shostakovich's, the writer Zamyatin (who had created a dystopian world similar to Mayakovsky's in *The Bedbug*), said snidely that Mayakovsky "wrote revolutionary verses — not because he truly loves the proletariat and wants revolution, but because he loves and wants a car and public stature. [He] is in my opinion a prostitute."

Mayakovsky was clearly getting sick of the Communist government — and of the increasingly drab social scene in Soviet Russia. In Paris, he was dating a counterrevolutionary woman who had fled to the West

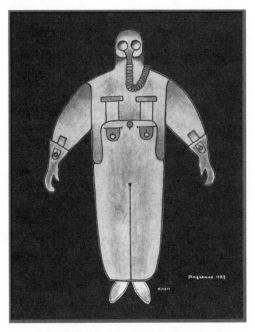

Costume designs for *The Bedbug* drew heavily on the geometrical elements of Futurist art.

Discussing the music for *The Bedbug:* Shostakovich and director Vsevolod Meyerhold (both seated), author Vladimir Mayakovsky and artist Alexander Rodchenko (both standing). Rodchenko designed the sets for the second half of the play, which takes place in the future.

during the Civil War. He loved fine clothes and nights spent gambling on the French coast. Though he would have denied this, *The Bedbug* itself seems to be about a refracted version of Mayakovsky, stuck in a dull, strict Communist future he can't stand.

Snobbery about the West was not the only thing that was difficult about Mayakovsky. There was his way with women. He had, for example, driven a teenage girl to suicide and then, after her death, had written a film scenario in which he mocked her for killing herself.

Shostakovich later remembered: "I can readily say that Mayakovsky epitomized all the traits of character I detest: phoniness, love of self-advertisement, lust for the good life, and most important, contempt for the weak and servility before the strong. Power was the great moral law for Mayakovsky."

And Shostakovich thought the script for *The Bedbug* was "fairly lousy."

Mayakovsky himself was frightened the play wouldn't get enough laughs. He came up with a detestable suggestion: a money-grubbing character in the play should speak with a strong Jewish accent. He told the actress to try one on.

Meyerhold was disgusted by this cheap anti-Semitism. He argued with Mayakovsky. Mayakovsky stayed firm: keep the woman Jewish.

Director Meyerhold took the actress aside. He told her to keep the accent for the rehearsals but drop it for the performance.

This ploy worked perfectly. Mayakovsky was so nervous and so wrapped up in worrying about whether the audience was admiring his work (they weren't) that he didn't even notice.

Shostakovich's music for *The Bedbug* is energetic and satirical. Though his tunes in the human zoo don't exactly "moo," they do capture some of the *oom-pah-pah* idiocy of Soviet-era parades and celebrations. Some of the audience thought the music was pure, obnoxious noise. Meyerhold was delighted: "That'll clean out brains!"

It didn't matter. Though this play is now considered a classic of the

Soviet theater, it did horribly at the time. It flopped. Soviet officials felt they had been mocked by Mayakovsky and Meyerhold.

And theater critics wrote that the music was not the music of the common man. "We must advise Comrade Shostakovich that he should reflect more seriously on questions of musical culture in the light of the development of our socialist society according to the principles of Marxism."

This was a threat.

Increasingly, there were questions of what kind of music composers should be writing. What music should the working class, the proletariat, be listening to? (There was very little sense that they should just be able to decide for themselves.) Should music for "the people" be complex and experimental — the music for a new world — or should it be as simple as possible?

Or to put it another way: Should "the people" be raised up through education and literacy so that they were full participants in the Revolutionary experiment? Or should music, writing, painting, and drama be simplified to the point where anyone could understand them?

An even stranger question came up: Should "the people" be forbidden to listen to the light music they loved? Should jazz (and Shostakovich's music that imitated jazz) be banned? Should the working citizens of Russia instead be belting out simple mass songs about the motherland and joyful labor? That was the attitude many were taking.

"The people" themselves were often not particularly enthusiastic about mass songs. Here, for example, from the grumbling diary of a man at a woodworking factory: "The new songs are sung over and over, with great enthusiasm: 'He who Strides Through Life with a Song on His Lips' and 'I Know no Other Such Land Where a Man Can Breathe so Free.' But another question comes up: can it be that people under a different regime don't sing or breathe? . . . We will continue to stride through life: it's not that far to the grave."

In contrast to *The Bedbug*, Shostakovich's opera *The Nose* opened in Leningrad and played to packed theaters and delighted crowds. Critics, however, were no longer as excited about experiment as they had been a couple of years earlier; now they complained that the crazed music was too bizarre, and even worse, "irrelevant to students [and] metal- and textile-workers." A survey was taken of workers in the audience—100 percent of them said they'd enjoyed it. But that made no difference.

No one knew it yet, but the age of experimentation in Soviet Russia was over. *The Bedbug*, as it turned out, was one of its last manifestations.

Experiments of all kinds were coming to an end. Lenin, in his later years, had experimented with freedom of expression and even with a limited form of capitalism. Now he was dead, and all that was at an end.

At the same time that Meyerhold and Mayakovsky were working on *The Bedbug* and Shostakovich was scribbling *The Nose*, the Soviet Politburo was making preparations to stage their own major event. It was called the Five-Year Plan, and it was supposed to complete the work of Russia's modern industrialization. It was designed to install everyone—from workers in the cities to peasants in the countryside—into one mechanized whole. A new age of regulation and uniformity had begun.

Mayakovsky's play imagined a future in which humans acted like cogs, gears, and levers in a cold, totalitarian factory mechanism. At the same time that his ultramodern stage sets were being built, the Politburo was sending armored trains out into the countryside. When the doors slid open, secret-police units marched out into the muddy lanes to bully the peasantry into giving up much of what they owned and joining huge collective farms. Members of the Communist Youth League, dressed in knickers and military tunics, with brown belts strapped across their chests, enthusiastically joined the hunt across the countryside for wealthier peasants, who were to be "liquidated as a class." Villagers anxious to save themselves accused their personal enemies of hiding money, grain, or a bourgeois past. The accused were stamped as "anti-people." Some were sent off to concentration camps. Thousands of families guilty of nothing more than owning an extra cow were shipped into the wilderness in cattle cars. Some were shot. Farmers watched their livestock being dragged away to the collective farms. If they resisted, their houses were burned. The government requisitioned millions of tons of grain to sell overseas so they could buy the heavy industrial machinery that would make Soviet Russia hum. Peasants could often not grow enough to eat.

Even those who had never farmed were forced into farm collectives. Millions of Kazakh nomads were ordered at gunpoint to give up their herding and their ancient way of life and settle down. They were told to grow crops in soil that was too dry to yield much beside rocks and grasses. They had no idea how to farm, and in the course of forced collectivization, about one and a half million of them starved to death.

Peasants tried to stand up to this farm collectivization. Within a few years, roughly 2,200 small rebellions broke out in villages across the USSR. The peasantry fought with sawed-off shotguns, axes, or whatever came to hand. Farmers hid their grain; they burned down barns that were being taken away from them; they slaughtered their own animals so the government couldn't get its hands on them. But the Five-Year Plan was relentless.

In this new age of regulation, factories as well as farms received their orders from the top. The Five-Year Plan specified production goals workers could never meet—and when they fell short of those goals, they were accused of sabotage. Just as wealthy peasants were hunted in the countryside, in the factories, bourgeois employees and experts on factory production were chased out of their jobs because supposedly they were enemies of the common working people. Firing all experts (sometimes even having them arrested or killed) was a disaster for industrial production. It meant more mistakes on the assembly lines, more delays, more lying about the volume of work being done, more accusations of "wrecking," more arrests, and so, in turn, more mistakes.

The Five-Year Plan was launched in 1928, just before *The Bedbug* had its brief run onstage and *The Nose* took its first bow. The program's effects were not yet clear. But it was absolutely clear that the thrilling experiments of the twenties were over and a new era had begun.

The future had just become a lot colder, a lot more like Mayakovsky's nightmare vision. Lenin had used Mayakovsky's poetry, but he had never liked it. ("Rubbish, stupid, stupid beyond belief and pretentious.") Now Mayakovsky's Communist Party liaison was complaining about the poet's rampant individualism, his income, and his affair with a tsarist noblewoman. They denied him a travel visa and forced him to tone down his satirical work. The poet was shocked to discover that the Party was watching him as closely as they watched ordinary citizens in the countryside.

Perhaps the end of the age of Communist experiment was finally signaled this way:

On April 14, 1930, Mayakovsky spent the morning as he often did, haranguing a girlfriend and trying to convince her to leave her husband. He bickered until she agreed to move in with him later that day. He said he would call her at five. The poet kissed her tenderly and she stepped out of his apartment.

When she was gone, he picked up a loaded Mauser pistol, aimed it at his chest, and shot himself in the heart.

Mayakovsky could not stand to live in the world he had helped to create. He was an individualist who had paradoxically fought for a collective, communistic society.

The rogue in *The Bedbug*, thawed to live in a cold Soviet society of the future, wails, "What is all this? What did we fight for? Why did we shed our blood, if I can't dance to my heart's content—and I'm supposed to be a leader of the new society!"

These words could have been Mayakovsky's, astounded that he was not master of the future he had built.

The writer Boris Pasternak, a friend of the Futurist's, went to the poet's apartment to view the body shortly after the suicide:

> Already people from the town and tenants packed all the way up
> the staircase wept and pressed against each other. . . . A lump
> rose in my throat. I decided to cross over to [Mayakovsky's]
> room . . . to cry my fill. . . . He lay on his side with his face to
> the wall, sullen and imposing, with a sheet up to his chin, his

mouth half open as in sleep. Haughtily turning his back on all, even in this repose, even in this sleep, he was stubbornly straining to go away somewhere. . . . This was an expression with which one begins life but does not end it.

Even in death, Mayakovsky "was sulking and indignant."

The corpse was taken away by the authorities.

At eight o'clock the evening of his death, the Futurist's brain was removed surgically from his skull. The State Institute for the Study of the Brain put it on a scale to determine the precise weight of genius. They found that it weighed 1,700 grams, whereas the standard human brain weighed 1,400. They stored the brain near Lenin's in the Institute's "Pantheon."

The rest of Mayakovsky's body was placed in a coffin on a red cube. Later it was taken to a cemetery on a flatbed truck. Beside it stood a wreath made of sledgehammers, screws, and gears.

Everything was calculated and precise, as it should be when the future arrives.

In late 1923, when Lenin had lain dying, he had looked at the men around him and wondered who would succeed him. He particularly mistrusted the man he had installed as general secretary of the Communist Party Central Committee—an "unpleasant Georgian with . . . wicked yellow eyes."

The man called himself Joseph Stalin. His face was pockmarked from smallpox; his mustache was famous; he appeared on posters smoking a pipe like someone's grandfather. He had risen through the ranks during the Revolution and the Civil War, fighting on the front lines, executing enemies as he needed.

After Lenin's death, Stalin quietly moved to take power.

By 1930, Stalin's foes seemed to melt away.

His name meant "Man of Steel," and his fist began to close.

In an iconic photo, Stalin receives a hug and a bouquet from young Gelia Markizova, daughter of a Communist Party official. Shortly afterward, her parents were arrested and her father was shot for treason.

LIFE IS GETTING MERRIER

In March 1934, two of Russia's most famous poets—Boris Pasternak and Osip Mandelstam—ran into each other while crossing a bridge in opposite directions. Mandelstam seized Pasternak's arm and yanked him close. He apparently told Pasternak that he had just been down to the Ukrainian countryside and had seen with his own eyes the terrifying effects of farm collectivization: unimaginable suffering, mass starvation. He hissed a poem into Pasternak's ear.

It was a song of disgust at Stalin's cruelty:

> His fingers are as fat as grubs
> And the words, final as lead weights, fall from his lips.
> His cockroach whiskers leer
> And his boot tops gleam. . . .
> And every killing is a treat
> For the broad-chested [Stalin].

Hearing this whispered, Pasternak reared back. "I didn't hear this, you didn't recite it to me," he snapped. "You know, very strange and terrible things are happening now: they've begun to pick people up. I'm afraid the walls have ears, and perhaps even these benches on the boulevard here may be able to listen and tell tales. So let's make out that I heard nothing."

They continued on their separate ways.

Pasternak, for his part, decided to see for himself what was going on in the countryside. He requested a pass to visit Ukraine so that he could write a heroic ode on farm collectivization. As he traveled through the southern fields, he saw nightmare images. He discovered that Mandelstam was right — almost no one in Leningrad or Moscow knew the horrors that were going on in their name. Roughly six million people starved to death during the implementation of the Five-Year Plan. In 1933, more than four million people starved in Ukraine alone as their food was taken from them to pay for foreign factory equipment. The Soviet president of Ukraine admitted, "We know millions are dying. That is unfortunate but the glorious future of the Soviet Union will justify it." Pasternak was appalled. "There are no words to describe what I saw there. It was such an inhuman, unimaginable misfortune, such a terrible calamity . . . the mind simply could not take it in." When the poet returned home from his sojourn, he found he could not sleep for a year afterward.

At around that time, Mandelstam recited his squib about Stalin to a circle of his friends.

They were apparently not all his friends: one informed on him. He was arrested by the secret police on May 13, 1934, and charged with "committing a terrorist act against the ruler."

As Mandelstam once said, Russia took poetry more seriously than any nation in the world: "There's no place where more people are killed for it."

The gathering gloom of the USSR in the early 1930s does not seem to have affected Shostakovich immediately. For one thing, as Pasternak and Mandelstam discovered, some of the most disastrous effects of Stalin's

Writer Boris Pasternak, once best known as a poet, is now known in the West for his novel *Doctor Zhivago*, which was published illegally in Italy over the protests of the Soviet government. The following year (1958), Pasternak was awarded the Nobel Prize.

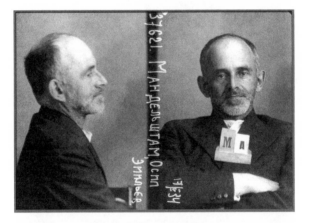

Mug shots of poet Osip Mandelstam from his two arrests, in 1934 and 1938

Five-Year Plan were concealed. The government's newspaper, *Pravda* ("Truth"), was full of lies. Propaganda songs smugly celebrated the triumphs of the Five-Year Plan: "The March of the Happy-Go-Lucky Guys" gloated, "We are taming space and time! We are the young masters of the earth!" Another mass song gushed dreamily, "We were born to make fairy tales come true."

The news that reached the cities was the good news: Industrial production was up, growing by 10 percent annually; collective farmers now had access to modern machinery (though no one mentioned that only one in twenty-five collective farms had electricity); and, perhaps the best news of all, literacy was flourishing in a country that, until the Revolution, had been widely illiterate. As the papers pointed out, the capitalist West, throttled by the Great Depression, appeared to be falling to its knees.

It is unclear how much Shostakovich knew about what was really going on. It appears that at the time, Shostakovich thought he was doing what was expected of him as a composer. Speaking to a *New York Times* interviewer at the end of 1931, he said, "I think an artist should serve the greatest possible number of people. I always try to make myself as widely understood as possible, and, if I don't succeed, I consider it my own fault." This was in stark contrast to modernist composers of the West like Arnold Schoenberg, who claimed, "If it is art, it is not for everybody, and if it is for everybody, it is not art." Shostakovich told the American interviewer and her translators, "I am a Soviet composer, and I see our epoch as something heroic, spirited, and joyous."

He said this sitting nervously in his apartment, "a pale young man, with the lips and hands and the manners of a bashful schoolboy." We do not know if he meant what he said; sitting around him on his mother's sofa were not only the American interviewer but also an official government translator and a Soviet press attaché, who would have reported anything questionable to their superiors. As one Shostakovich scholar has pointed out, this was not the best atmosphere for the free and easy exchange of ideas.

Still, his music of the period really does set out to speak directly to the people — to be "heroic, spirited, and joyous." Just as writers were increasingly being convinced, one way or another, to write novels about scenes of everyday life, about triumphant assembly-line workers, about beautiful milkmaids on collective farms falling in love with handsome tractor drivers, Shostakovich wrote music for ballets and popular films on healthy topics of labor.

He wrote the score for the movie *The Counterplan* (1932), a tale of turbine factory workers scrambling to install new machinery. The movie's theme song, "The Song of the Counterplan," with lyrics by the poet Boris Kornilov, swept across Russia and became a huge hit. In Shostakovich's ballet *The Bolt* (1931), a lazy, malcontented factory worker sabotages machinery by literally throwing a wrench in the works. He is caught, and the ballet ends with the march of triumphant socialist labor. Nothing could be closer to the spirit of Stalin's Five-Year Plan — except perhaps Shostakovich's next ballet, *The Bright Stream* (1935). It is a pretty, even trivial, tale about the love life of a student agronomist at a collective farm in the Caucasus. There is no hint of suffering. The collective farmers spend their time in celebration and dancing.

In projects like these, Shostakovich adhered to the demands of the new style that was sweeping the arts in Soviet Russia, later called Socialist Realism. The "realism" was not necessarily realistic. Yes, writers and composers and painters were no longer supposed to depict the dreams, fables, absurdities, and science-fiction concoctions of the twenties. They were urged to depict real life — keeping in mind that real life in a Soviet state was supposedly leading to universal perfection. As the Composers' Union wrote in their guidelines (1934), "The main attention of the Soviet composer must be directed towards the victorious progressive principles of reality, towards all that is heroic, bright, and beautiful." When Shostakovich wrote *The Bright Stream*, he could not depict the unrest, starvation, and desperate hiding of grain that was going on in the collective farms. That would have been too dangerously real for Soviet Realism.

In a society that was supposed to be understood as a huge machine,

Joseph Stalin, general secretary of the Communist Party, with his iconic pipe

Pageantry after a Leningrad training session in gas-attack preparedness for young scouts. In 1931, Shostakovich provided music for *Declared Dead*, a similar chemical warfare training session, but combined with a vaudeville show. It featured simulated air raids, clowns, trapeze acts, performing horses, a trained German shepherd, and the Twelve Apostles playing in a jazz band. The old Russian anthem "God Save the Tsar" was played as a slinky fox-trot. *Declared Dead* was just one example of the attempts by Soviet musicians and artists to be useful to the public as well as entertaining.

literature and the arts were supposed to be the "gear and screw" of the propaganda mechanism, allowing the government to manipulate people, who were mere "levers" in the intricate clockworks. Stalin had urged writers and artists to be "engineers of human souls." Perhaps without the young Shostakovich even realizing it, his two ballets reflected the two great prongs of attack in Stalin's Five-Year Plan: collectivization in the countryside (*The Bright Stream*) and the arrest of "wreckers" in the city's factories (*The Bolt*). His friends and colleagues were also working on propaganda symphonies about the joys of collective farming and on film scores for wholesome instructional movies with titles like *Communist Youth — The Boss of Electrification*.

If Shostakovich objected to all these stage works and film scores for hire, it was not because he resisted writing about Soviet labor but because he also wanted to work on his own, private projects. He did finally draw the line at writing music for a lively-sounding movie called *The Cement Hardens*.

He wanted to work on his next masterpiece, an opera called *Lady Macbeth of Mtsensk District*. In it, he would capture all the passion of his youth, and because of it, his life would be in danger.

The opera *Lady Macbeth of Mtsensk District* was written over several years. It is a tale of stormy love and murder — a wife who conspires to slay her husband so she can be with her lover and ends up dying in a Siberian chain gang.

Shostakovich's own love life was tempestuous during these years, though hardly homicidal.

One evening, Shostakovich called Tatiana Glivenko and told her he was going to be in Moscow. He asked her to meet him at his hotel. She came to his room. She had difficult news: She was tired of negotiating the distance between Leningrad and Moscow. She was tired of Shostakovich being unable to commit to her. She was tired of Shostakovich's mother. Sofia Shostakovich worshipped her son like a little god and hated it when other women were near him. Tatiana had made up her mind: she was getting married to someone else the next day. Another boyfriend had issued an ultimatum. "Either you marry me or I'll stop coming to your house." Tatiana had decided he was the better bet.

Shostakovich couldn't believe what he was hearing. Tatiana was not wrong: there were other women in his life. In particular, he'd met a young physicist named Nina Varzar in Leningrad, and he'd started to go in the evenings to parties at her family's apartment, where he'd play dances on the piano and make stupid puns to get her to laugh. He felt, however, that he was truly in love with Tatiana.

After years of visits back and forth, their relationship was over.

The next day, Shostakovich miserably called Tatiana's apartment. In the background, he could hear people celebrating. Evidently, the marriage had just happened. Shostakovich was too late. Someone pulled Tatiana away from the wedding party and she picked up the phone.

He said, "It's me — Shostakovich. . . ."

"Yes, I'm listening. . . ."

Was there a silence then? Did he hang up the phone? Did she have to insist that it was over? We don't know how the conversation ended, and it's best that some things remain private. Tatiana herself remembered: "No more was said, and that was that. He returned to Leningrad. According to Zoya, when he walked into his flat his first words were, 'Tanya's got married.' Thereafter my name wasn't mentioned for some time in their house."

Shostakovich's mother watched him like a hawk, though he was now a man well into his twenties. She would call a friend of theirs, a conductor named Nikolai Malko, and gripe, "Mitya wants to marry."

"Well," said Malko. "What then? Let him."

"How can you say that? He's still a child."

The next day, she would call back. She'd say, "It is not so bad." She was no longer worried about a surprise wedding.

"Why?"

"I looked through his diary and found a note, 'Find a room.' I know him. He will never start looking. He does not even know how to start."

She was sure he was too unworldly to be able to move out on his own.

He was, at the time, working on the score for *Lady Macbeth,* with all its passion and tragedy. One of his ex-girlfriends, Galina Serebryakova, visited him at around this time and later recalled:

> [Shostakovich] was thirsting to recreate the theme of love in a new way, a love that knew no boundaries, that was willing to perpetrate crimes inspired by the devil himself. . . .
>
> In the murky room he was writing this new work on a large desk. He would play bits of it through on the piano. I was entertained to tea by two beautiful light-haired girls, Shostakovich's sisters, and his charmingly simple and affectionate mother. The young composer admitted to me that he was about to get married. He was unable to hide his agitation, and, gulping down his words, he told me about his fiancée, trying to remain cool and objective about her, an impossible feat for those in love!

We do not know which fiancée he might have been talking about. The situation was a little complex.

For a long time, Shostakovich still tried to wheedle Tatiana Glivenko away from her husband. She almost agreed to leave her spouse, move to Leningrad, and marry Shostakovich. When he heard this, he acted skittish. Then, in May 1932, she had her first child.

Two weeks later, Zoya wrote to Tatiana and told her that Shostakovich had suddenly, impulsively, married Nina Varzar, the young physicist.

The marriage had happened this way:

Shostakovich announced to his family that he was going to Moscow for business. His mother said she'd walk him to the train station. He waved her away. "There's no need to accompany me."

The second he left, his mother ducked out after him and followed him at a distance.

When she came back in a little while, she was crying. Zoya asked her what had happened, what was wrong.

"I saw the silhouette of Nina [Varzar] in the window of the train compartment," she blubbered. Her son and the Varzar girl were sneaking off to get married secretly.

Zoya Shostakovich and her mother sat next to each other and wept all night long. Later, Zoya couldn't remember why she had been weeping. She actually liked Nina Varzar.

It was important that they all liked each other. Once Nina and Dmitri got married, Nina had to move into the apartment with the Shostakoviches and their tenants. Sofia Shostakovich slept on the couch.

At first, Sofia Shostakovich was no more pleasant to Nina than she had once been to Tatiana. Relations around the apartment were apparently strained. Shostakovich, however, was desperate to enjoy time alone with his new wife. She later remembered, "No sooner would I arrive at the laboratory and get started on an experiment than Mitya would ring up and ask when I would get home." In these close quarters, with his family crowded around him, Shostakovich worked on his ballets, on his film scores, and on the project of which he was proudest, *Lady Macbeth.*

He dedicated the score to Nina.

Lady Macbeth of Mtsensk District was launched in January 1934 at two theaters at once — one in Leningrad and one in Moscow. Though the plot was old — based on a nineteenth-century short story by Nikolai Leskov — the music was passionate, bold, and direct. It contained few of the crazed experiments of *The Nose,* despite slashes of savage humor. There is a touching nobility and deep sadness to its homicidal heroine.

To be safe, Shostakovich invited the People's Commissar of Enlightenment to a run-through, after which the government declared that

Lady Macbeth was "the start of the brilliant flowering of Soviet operatic creativity."

The opera met with immediate success. After the first public performances, the applause was so wild that Shostakovich had to go onstage to take bows not only at the end of the performance but in between individual scenes. Fellow composers wrote that the piece was "a remarkable, deep, and brilliantly orchestrated composition," "the apex of Shostakovich's creative work." Leningrad newspapers trumpeted that the opera would soon become "one of the most beloved of the mass viewer."

Quickly, demands came from opera houses all over the world. The piece was staged in North America, in South America, in England, Sweden, and Czechoslovakia. Leningrad factories staged excerpts of the piece during lunch hours and held discussions of the music among the workers. It was a huge success. Not even thirty years old, Shostakovich was becoming the most famous composer in the Soviet Union.

Even amid the clapping of audiences around the world, however, he could not have helped but notice the murderous hand of history slipping toward Leningrad. In late 1934, the same year Lady Macbeth and her lover first strangled her husband onstage, Leningrad's Communist Party boss, Sergei Kirov, was walking down the hall in Party Headquarters when an assassin who had slipped past the guards pulled out a revolver and shot him in the neck.

Kirov was one of Joseph Stalin's closest friends. He would often stay at Stalin's rooms in the Kremlin when visiting Moscow; Stalin was a coffin bearer at his funeral. The dictator demanded quick action to find and punish whoever was responsible for his friend's death. An emergency order was passed on the day of Kirov's murder, December 1, specifying that anyone arrested for terrorism against the state had to be tried within ten days of their arrest and that, if found guilty, they could be executed summarily, without benefit of appeal. What was later to be called the Great Terror had begun. The purges that convulsed the countryside a few years earlier now hit the urban population. Thus began, in a sense, the first siege of Leningrad.

The secret police began their arrests. Stalin had always hated the city, with its troublesome intelligentsia and its windows on the West. He tried to avoid the place and had not even set foot there during the decade between Lenin's death and the assassination of Kirov. He growled that Leningrad was rotten with traitors waiting to kill off the Communist Party leadership and gave orders that anyone deemed even remotely suspicious should be rounded up and tried for treason. Spreading through the streets and squares, the secret police grabbed everyone they heard had a dubious past: a former baron who was working at an industrial meal-service, an ex-general who was a geography teacher, another ex-general who sold cigarettes in a kiosk. Within a few months, thousands of innocent Leningraders had been pulled out of their homes and delivered to "the Big House"—the headquarters of the secret police in the city. They disappeared. Most were sent to remote work camps; some were shot.

Everyone whose family had not been working class and Bolshevik was in some danger of arrest. People began "masking" themselves, as it was called—hiding their identities and their family histories. The Shostakoviches were in a complicated position. Many of the family had been Revolutionaries and Party members, but Sofia, in particular, had many of the marks of the middle-class intellectual: She had attended an elite girls' school, the Irkutsk Institute for Noblewomen. She had once even been presented to Tsar Nicholas II and, with a troupe of other girls, had danced a mazurka in the royal presence. If attention was turned on her, the family would not be safe from accusation.

The secret police pulled up in front of Leningrad apartments in long black cars, the Black Marias. Everyone listened for the footsteps on the stairs, the knock on the door. Residents' diaries describe the horror of the arrests: A mother watches the secret police search her apartment. They find no evidence; they call their headquarters to report, "Nothing here." They are instructed to arrest the mother anyway. She knows her innocence will not

Dmitri Shostakovich, his wife Nina Varzar, and his closest friend for many years, musicologist Ivan Sollertinsky. It is from Shostakovich's letters to Sollertinsky that we know many of the details of the composer's life before the Second World War.

Friends: Young Joseph Stalin with Sergei Kirov, who became Leningrad's Communist Party leader

protect her from a sentence of years in a northern work camp. Before they take her, she embraces her four-year-old daughter one last time and whispers, heartbroken, "When I come back, you'll be all grown up."

Her neighbors watch her being bundled into the Black Maria and driven away.

Prisoners were usually sent to work camps in frigid northeastern Siberia or in the deserts of Kazakhstan. They felled trees, worked as slave labor on construction projects, and, most dreaded sentence of all, they toiled in the arctic Kolyma goldfields, where the temperature could drop well below −50°F. Death from exhaustion, starvation, or exposure was common, even desired.

On April 7, 1935, Stalin announced that children as young as twelve could be tried and executed as adults. This gave the secret police even more leverage during questioning. Parents who wanted to save the lives of their kids had to provide names of supposed traitors and conspirators. They strained their memories to recall neighbors or coworkers who had made some frustrated comment or cheap joke about the regime. They named names — the Black Marias spread out through the suburbs — and so the net of arrests was spread even wider.

Meanwhile, undercover officers listening in on conversations across the city reported fearfully that people were speaking more openly about their hatred for the Communist Party. "I am not sorry for Kirov," said a sailor. "Let them kill Stalin. I will not be sorry for him." His spite was not unusual.

So who actually was responsible for Kirov's murder? An astounding rumor was making the rounds in Leningrad: that the assassination had been ordered by Stalin himself. Recently revealed documents suggest that this is almost certainly true. Members of the Communist Party Central Committee were horrified at the mass destruction wrought by Stalin and his Five-Year Plan. They were muttering about the possibility of Kirov replacing Stalin as general secretary. Comrade Stalin made sure that would not happen.

Shortly afterward, Kirov's bodyguard said that he wanted to testify regarding the murder. He knew some information that would shed import-ant light on the case.

As he was being driven to Leningrad Party Headquarters to speak his secrets, there was an unfortunate car crash. Someone riding with him in the car grabbed the wheel and yanked it to the side. The car careened toward a house, skidded sideways, and smashed into the wall. The bodyguard was killed on impact. Surprisingly, no one else was injured. The bodyguard's secrets disappeared with him. Was this done deliberately? We will never know: Shortly thereafter, the two secret policemen who had been escorting him were shot. So the case was officially left open.

Stalin supposedly once said, "To choose one's victims, to prepare one's plans minutely, to slake an implacable vengeance, and then to go to bed . . . there is nothing sweeter in the world."

Shostakovich felt the accusations creeping toward him. Raya Vasilyeva, the screenwriter of a movie he was working on (*Girlfriends*), was arrested very publicly in 1935; her name appeared in *Pravda* on a list of fourteen people who had allegedly planned Kirov's murder. He was worried he might be implicated next: "Now, you might ask: What does a screenwriter have to do with the composer? And I'll reply: And what did Raya Vasilyeva have to do with Kirov's murder? Nothing. But she was shot nevertheless."

The arrests continued. After only a few months, some thirty or forty thousand people from Leningrad and its surrounding towns had been exiled to camps in Kazakhstan and Siberia.

At around the same time, Shostakovich was elected deputy of Leningrad's October District — a part-time post that demanded he sort out various bureaucratic disputes in the neighborhood. We do not know pre-cisely what he heard or saw in this position — he left no diary, no record of his duties — but he must have seen paperwork that reflected the disappear-ances, the empty apartments, the children moved to orphanages set up for enemies of the people.

In the midst of this growing terror, Nina and Dmitri's young marriage was falling apart. The strain of living with Sofia Shostakovich was wearing on Nina. There were huge fights in the apartment. After arguing with his wife, Shostakovich would flee to the apartment of his poker buddy Zoshchenko, a writer who specialized in stories about cramped communal living. Zoshchenko would keep working while Shostakovich paced anxiously in circles, arguing with himself. Zoshchenko just ignored him. After a while, Shostakovich would thank him for the conversation and leave. The situation was bad.

As a result of these ruptures, during an international music festival in Leningrad, Shostakovich developed a crush on a young translator and kept writing her desperate letters. He went out to the theater with her on his arm. Nina couldn't take it any longer. She suggested a separation; eventually they decided on a divorce. While in Moscow for work, Shostakovich started to talk to government officials about getting permission to move there, away from the city of his youth, away from beleaguered Leningrad.

The divorce from Nina came through.

Shostakovich returned to Leningrad one last time, to pack his belongings and leave forever.

When he got there, things evidently didn't go as he had planned.

A couple of days later, he telegrammed a friend in Moscow: "Remaining in Leningrad. Nina pregnant. Remarried. Mitya."

Still, they clearly couldn't continue to live with Sofia. The couple started to go through the considerable paperwork to get their own home. As they prepared for their first child, Shostakovich wrote, "There can be no question of a divorce from Nina. I have only now realized and fathomed what a remarkable woman she is, and how precious to me."

She *was* remarkable: physically athletic, intellectually brilliant, and emotionally strong enough to stand up to Mitya. This second marriage between them was an affirmation. It was only at this point that Nina Varzar changed her name officially to Nina Shostakovich. Their marriage was unorthodox — for one thing, she spent each summer up in the mountains of

Armenia, studying cosmic rays — but it is clear that their love and support for each other was total.

Easing their marriage even more, in fall of 1935 word came through that the couple could move into a vacated apartment in a building reserved for Soviet composers. Shostakovich and his pregnant physicist were delighted to move out of his childhood home. Their new apartment was on Kirovsky Prospect — an avenue named after the murdered Kirov.

This is how things stood when, in January of 1936, Joseph Stalin decided it was time to see what the celebrated Dmitri Shostakovich was all about.

On the evening of January 26, 1936, Shostakovich was in Moscow on a concert tour, having left his pregnant wife at home in Leningrad. He got a call: Comrade Stalin was going to be attending *Lady Macbeth* at Moscow's most famous theater, the Bolshoi. Shostakovich should be there on hand, in case the Great Leader and Teacher wished to call him up to his private box afterward and speak to him about the opera.

Shostakovich scurried to the theater, "white with fear."

When most of the audience was seated, Stalin and his entourage filed in and took their places amid whispers of awe and respect. Stalin sat behind a curtain in a steel-plated opera box designed to repel bullets shot from the orchestra pit. He had a bowl of hard-boiled eggs set next to him to crack and eat at intermission. Clumps of plainclothes guards spread throughout the audience.

As Shostakovich's friend the writer Mikhail Bulgakov envisioned the scene, here is what happened next:

> Melik [the conductor] furiously lifts his baton and the overture
> begins. In anticipation of a medal, and feeling the eyes of the
> leaders on him, Melik is in a frenzy, leaping about like an imp,
> chopping the air with his baton, soundlessly singing along with

the orchestra. Sweat pours off him. "No problem, I'll change shirts in the intermission," he thinks in ecstasy. After the overture, he sends a sidelong glance at the box, expecting applause — nothing. After the first act — the same thing, no impression at all.

Shostakovich, sitting in the audience, was in torment. In particular, he was furious that the conductor, to make a bigger impression, to make the whole thing louder, had called in extra brass players. The brass section was blaring away right under Stalin's opera box. Shostakovich looked up to see how Stalin's entourage was receiving the production.

Every time the brass and percussion exploded with a new tune, Stalin's ministers reared back in surprise and turned to look at the hidden Leader behind his curtain. Occasionally, they sneered. Shostakovich was slick with sweat. He sank back in his chair and covered his face with his hand.

Then — a disaster: Stalin and his aides stood up in the middle of the piece and filed out.

Supposedly, as Stalin was making his way out of the theater, a reporter asked him what he thought of Shostakovich's music. "*Eta sumbur,*" he growled, "*a ne musyka.*" — "That's a mess, not music."

No one could pay attention to the second half of the opera.

Afterward, as Shostakovich and a friend walked through Moscow's frigid streets, the composer could not stop talking about the social catastrophe. "Tell me, why did they have to over-increase the sound of the [orchestra]? The people in the government box must have been deafened by the brass section." He grumbled, "I have a feeling that this year, like all leap years, will be a bad one for me."

The next day, he left for the next city on his concert tour, Arkhangelsk, "with a sorrowful soul."

On January 28, the day of his concert in Arkhangelsk, he stopped at the train station to get a morning paper. The day was cold. The line at the newspaper kiosk was long and slow. When he reached the front, Shostakovich bought a copy of *Pravda*. He was leafing through it when he spotted an article about him. The headline was "A Mess Instead of Music: About the Opera *Lady Macbeth of Mtsensk District.*"

Shostakovich stared in horror at the page. His eye ran down the column. "Coarse, primitive and vulgar . . . bourgeois . . . bestial." To be criticized in *Pravda* was a sure sign that a government attack was about to follow. He felt frozen to the spot. He started to shiver. "Nervous, convulsive, and spasmodic . . . fidgety, neurotic." Someone waiting behind him in the line shouted, "Hey, brother, you already drunk this morning?"

The unsigned article pronounced:

> From the first minute, the listener is shocked by deliberate dissonance, by a confused stream of sound. . . . The singing on the stage is replaced by shrieks. . . .
>
> [The composer] scribbles down his music, confusing all the sounds in such a way that his music would reach only the effete "formalists" who had lost all their wholesome taste. He ignored the demand of Soviet culture that all coarseness and savagery be abolished from every corner of Soviet life.

The article compared Shostakovich to his friend the director Meyerhold and accused them both of complexity, clowning, and having betrayed the people.

The article threatened: "It is a game of clever ingenuity that may end very badly."

This was not just a bad review. It was unsigned, and in *Pravda*. That meant it was official Party doctrine. Rumor would soon whisper that the article had been written by Stalin himself. This was a catastrophe for Shostakovich. Arrest seemed inevitable.

The eyes of those in line were on him.

* * *

While (despite claims to the contrary) there is no evidence that Stalin actually wrote "A Mess Instead of Music," it is certain that he approved it. Why did he want to persecute young Dmitri Shostakovich? Especially after *Lady Macbeth* had been running for two years, wildly popular, seen as the great hope of Soviet opera? The answer is unclear. It is likely, for one thing, that Shostakovich's worldwide fame bothered Stalin. It is also possible that Stalin was repelled by the sexual eruptions in Shostakovich's opera. (One American critic called the opera a "pornophony.")

Most important, it seems Stalin wanted to use the example of Shostakovich to scold and worry all of the Soviet Union's cultural leaders, rebuking them for turning away from "real art, real science, and real literature." He wanted to assert the infinite power of his regime and to show them that no one was safe.

A week later, as Shostakovich hurried to Moscow to try to make peace with the government bureaucracy, *Pravda* fired off a second attack on him, called "Balletic Falsehood." It tore into Shostakovich's collective farm ballet, *The Bright Stream*. It complained that the costumes did not look like the real traditional dress of the Caucasus and that the music was not like real Cossack music. The collective farmers in the ballet were as sweet and false as "painted peasants on the lid of a candy-box." The article griped, "According to the ballet's authors, all our difficulties are behind us. Onstage everyone is happy, cheerful, and joyous."

Shostakovich was in a bind. Did the Communist Party Central Committee actually want him to depict the realities of life on a collective farm? Of course not: Six million people had died during the famines and uprisings that followed forced collectivization. Depicting that in a ballet would be suicide; it would definitely "end very badly."

His opera was condemned for showing a life that was coarse and brutal; at the same time, his ballet was condemned for showing the opposite: an idealized and joyous life. These were, a third article declared, both "*lies and falsehood* — the formalistic trickery in *Lady Macbeth* and the sickly sweetness of *The Bright Stream*."

Now Stalin's regime fired off a series of similar articles using Shostakovich as an example and attacking falsehood and anti-people "formalism" in all the arts: film, architecture, theater, and painting ("On Mess-Making Artists"). Everyone realized that "A Mess Instead of Music" marked a new phase in Stalin's Great Terror: he had turned his attention to the intellectuals of Leningrad and Moscow.

Artists, composers, architects, and writers, terrified of being singled out themselves, gathered together and yammered out their agreement with *Pravda*'s historic pronouncement on Shostakovich's *Lady Macbeth*. They sent public letters howling at Shostakovich for his "formalist" crimes against art and fell all over themselves to ask what the wise decrees of the Great Leader and Teacher might mean for the other arts — and even the sciences.

What was this formalism? It literally means music, art, or writing that pays more attention to form and technique than to content. This definition seems vague and confusing, but perhaps that was the point. No one knew what it meant, any more than they knew exactly what its opposite, Socialist Realism, meant. They could mean anything. Under the title of formalism, Shostakovich was attacked at different times for: being too simple, being too complex, being too light and trivial, being too gloomy and despairing, being too emotional, being too unemotional, including popular dance tunes, neglecting the music of the people, tossing out the old ways of the great composers, and following the old ways of the great composers from the pre-Revolutionary past. Decades later, shortly before Stalin died, someone supposedly asked him what formalism and Socialist Realism actually were. He shrugged and replied, "The Devil alone knows."

The Devil alone may have known, but Stalin, increasingly, was willing to kill on the Devil's behalf. No matter what an artist did, no one was safe.

The newspapers were filled with denunciations of Shostakovich, accusing him of being elitist and anti-people. "When I hear Shostakovich's symphonies on the radio, I switch to a different program," an electrician from the

Red Labor Factory wrote in to *Pravda*. "We need the kind of music that can be understood by all Soviet people." There was no acknowledgment that Shostakovich had written two of the most popular Russian hit songs of the 1930s ("The Song of the Counterplan" and "How Beautiful Life Will Be"). The newspapers relentlessly attacked him. He remembered miserably, "I was called an enemy of the people quietly and out loud from podiums. One paper made the following announcement of my concert: 'Today there is a concert by enemy of the people Shostakovich.'"

As he stalked nervously through the streets, he watched as friends crossed the road so they wouldn't have to greet him. Many of them had just denounced him at meetings or in print. They were afraid of being seen with him.

On the way home from his concert tour, Shostakovich stopped in Moscow to plead with the government's Committee for Artistic Affairs. The chief of the committee suggested gently that Shostakovich should take himself into the hinterlands and spend his time recording the folk songs of Belorussia and Ukraine. It was not particularly helpful advice.

Shostakovich went to talk to his one friend high up in the government: military genius Mikhail Tukhachevsky, one of the five marshals of the Red Army. Tukhachevsky, a music lover, had met Shostakovich years before. They had many friends in common. Rumor had it, for example, that Tukhachevsky was having an affair with an ex-girlfriend of Mayakovsky, the bellowing Bolshevik author of *The Bedbug*.

When Tukhachevsky was visiting Leningrad, he and Shostakovich would spend afternoons wandering through the vast Hermitage Museum (part of which was once the tsar's Winter Palace), talking about art. Tukhachevsky was an amateur violinist, and they occasionally played music together. On other days, Tukhachevsky would have his chauffeur drive them out of Leningrad, deep into the woods, and they would stroll there, where they could talk more openly.

Shostakovich arrived at Tukhachevsky's apartment looking "dispirited, confused." Tukhachevsky let him into his study and locked the door behind them. There was quite a contrast between the two men. As Shostakovich described it,

> I was a sickly youth while Tukhachevsky could put a man on a chair and then lift the chair, yes, lift the chair and its occupant by one leg with his arm outstretched. His office in Moscow had a gym with beams, a horizontal bar, and other incomprehensible equipment. . . . He turned off his phones. We sat in silence. And then we started talking very softly. I spoke softly because my grief and despair wouldn't let me speak in my normal voice. Tukhachevsky spoke softly because he feared prying ears.

Tukhachevsky promised to intercede for Shostakovich with Stalin. Shostakovich was enormously relieved to hear this. When he and Tukhachevsky walked out of the study, the composer sat down at the piano and began to play wild improvisations.

He stayed in Moscow and waited anxiously for a call from Stalin. He had heard stories about the Great Leader reaching out to condemned writers to suggest ways they could save themselves. Shostakovich hoped that Tukhachevsky could convince Stalin to reconsider his case. He sat in his room for days, hardly seeing anyone, waiting for the phone to ring.

But Stalin did not listen to Marshal Tukhachevsky's plea for his musical friend. Though the Red Army officer and the composer did not know it, Stalin was already concocting a complicated plot to arrest and execute Tukhachevsky himself.

Finally, Shostakovich gave up waiting and went home to Leningrad, to his pregnant wife. Nina met him at the train station. He embraced her. "Don't worry," he said. "In our family, when somebody cuts a finger, we are worried, but when we are in big trouble, nobody panics," and he murmured again to her, "Don't worry."

He said this to soothe her, but in fact he himself was intensely anxious. He tried to bury himself in his work. At the time, he was in the middle of composing a huge, sprawling Fourth Symphony. He said defiantly to a friend, "Even if they cut off both my hands and I have to hold the pen in my teeth, I shall still go on writing music."

But the section of the new symphony that he worked on when he got home was a funeral march.

The Leningrad Composers' Union held a special session to discuss the formalism of Dmitri Dmitrievich Shostakovich and what it meant for the future of Soviet music. Four hundred people showed up; Shostakovich himself was not among them. He knew that repentance was expected of him; he was supposed to get up onstage and admit wrongdoing. Instead, he was conspicuously absent.

A friend of his described the scene with disgust: "One after another, composers, directors, and critics who had all previously praised the opera [*Lady Macbeth of Mtsensk District*], got up to the podium and took back their earlier judgments." They all admitted that "they had made an error, and only now had the *Velikiy Vozhd,* the Great Leader Stalin, opened their eyes."

Lev Knipper, spy for the secret police and composer of a famous song-symphony about the militants of the Communist Youth League, stood up and called Shostakovich "anti-People." The room broke out into fierce muttering. Someone yelled at Knipper, "You bastard!" The growl of the assembly now was too loud for Knipper even to be heard.

The chairman called the room to order. The meeting — and the accusations — went on. It had hardly concluded when a group of reporters perched themselves on Shostakovich's front stoop, waiting to catch his reaction to being condemned.

He did not appear in public to respond. Years later, he supposedly said,

> If you are smeared with mud from head to toe on the orders of the
> leader and teacher, don't even think of wiping it off. You bow and
> say thanks, say thanks and bow. No one will pay any attention

to any of your hostile rejoinders anyway, and no one will come to your defense, and most of all, you won't be able to let off steam among friends. Because there are no friends in these pitiable circumstances.

We know now from the files of the secret police, the NKVD,* that they were having Shostakovich watched and were reporting the substance of his phone conversations. Doubtless he knew it at the time. The secret police often did not conceal their surveillance, finding it more effective if their targets were uncomfortably aware of scrutiny. At about the same time, for example, composer Sergei Prokofiev's phone was wiretapped. The NKVD made no attempt to hide the fact. There was crackling on the line, and sometimes calls were simply disconnected. Eventually, disembodied voices on the line started laughing out loud at Prokofiev and his wife. During one call, Prokofiev's voice faded and his wife shouted, "I can't hear you!" An eavesdropper spoke up: "You were perfectly audible, I just decided to cut you off."

Leningrad poet Anna Akhmatova was also being watched. When she returned to her apartment after being out for a few hours, she would find magazines she hadn't read spread around the table, or someone else's cigarette butts in her ashtray. This was part of the torment. Shostakovich, similarly, must have known he was being watched.

That spring, Shostakovich considered suicide. The NKVD reported to Stalin that Sofia Shostakovich had made calls to her son's friends, begging them to help him before he fell apart, pleading, "What will happen to my son now?" A friend wrote, "They are driving Shostakovich to the point of suicide; people are saying that they have put a ban on playing Shostakovich over the radio."

Russia's most celebrated author, Maxim Gorky, wrote to Stalin warning him that Shostakovich was a "highly nervous" person and that there would

---

*The acronym stands for the People's Commissariat for Internal Affairs. This agency was the predecessor of the KGB.

be an international outcry if the composer killed himself. His death would reflect badly on the Communist government. Gorky warned, "The article in *Pravda* struck him like a brick in the head. The fellow is completely depressed."

We have no knowledge of whether Stalin listened to Gorky's plea. Regardless, a few months later, Maxim Gorky himself was dead. The head of the secret police admitted in court to having killed him with an overdose of injected heart stimulant.

In Shostakovich's apartment, the composer waited for the midnight knock on the door. He "paced the room with a towel and said he had a cold, hiding his tears." His friends, fearful he would take his own life, "did not leave him and took turns keeping watch."

Why didn't Shostakovich and his family just flee the country?

The borders were closed. There was strict regulation of anyone going in and out of the Soviet Union. The government had announced in 1935 that anyone attempting to flee abroad would be executed. People had to get permission to travel from one Russian city to another, let alone travel to the West. When Soviet officials let a citizen visit Europe or the United States, they invariably kept members of the traveler's family back in Russia to use as hostages. The government decree stipulated that in case of a defection, all "the remaining adult members of the traitor's family," whether they had known about the escape or not, would be arrested and sent into internal exile.

We don't know whether Shostakovich ever considered fleeing. (He does not seem to have had any special fondness for or interest in the capitalist West.) But if he had decided to cross the border illegally, he would have had to live with the awful knowledge that Maria, Zoya, and Sofia, as well as Nina's extended family, would suffer grinding hardships for years as a result of his flight.

There was no way to run.

* * *

Nationally, conditions were getting worse. The Great Terror was spreading far beyond the streets of Leningrad. Late in the spring, *Pravda* and the other newspapers announced that the regime was preparing to stamp out a conspiracy of antirevolutionaries and spies in the pay of foreign powers across the whole width and height of the Soviet Union. German Fascist conspirators and enemies of the people supposedly were everywhere. They had murdered Kirov, and now they planned to destroy the whole Soviet state.

In reality, there was no conspiracy except Stalin's; he had decided to purge his own government of anyone who offered resistance to his rule. Now the net was spread nationwide. Moscow was hit particularly hard. Many of Stalin's old comrades were arrested. Late in the spring of 1936, they were tortured in the basements of the NKVD until they confessed to staggering and even impossible crimes. The typical interrogation protocol was called the conveyor belt. Prisoners were pushed from room to room, being repeatedly questioned by different agents for days at a stretch without sleep. They were beaten by hired thugs. They were forced to stand against walls on their tiptoes for hours. They were told to name more names of others who took part in this imaginary conspiracy.

Torture is a good way to get people to talk but a poor method of finding out the truth; people confess whether there is any reality to the confession or not. The notorious Lavrentii Beria, head of the NKVD during the Second World War, boasted that he could get a prisoner to tell any story required: "Let me have one night with him and I'll have him confessing he's the King of England." The NKVD, however, was not looking for the truth of guilt or innocence. As another NKVD head snapped to his officers, "Better that ten innocent people should suffer than one spy get away. When you chop wood, chips fly." And so the bizarre descriptions of impossible secret plots kept tumbling out.

A torture survivor remembered, "It was impossible to tell who would be killed next. People died in delirium, confessing to a series of outrageous crimes — spying, sabotage, terrorism and wrecking. They vanished without a trace, and then their wives and children, entire families, disappeared as well."

When people disappeared, the neighborhood gossips would always ask, "What was he arrested for?" ("Most people," said the poet Mandelstam's wife, "crazed by fear, asked this question just to give themselves a little hope: if others were arrested for some reason, then they wouldn't be arrested, because they hadn't done anything wrong.") When confronted by this question—"What for?"—poet Anna Akhmatova cried, *"What for? What do you mean, what for?* It's time you understood that people are arrested *for nothing!"* Nonetheless, the state had to make it appear that there was a reason for each and every arrest.

In high-profile cases, the inquisitions were closely managed by Stalin and his cronies. When one of the accused sent a repentant letter to the Politburo, babbling that he had indeed been responsible for Kirov's killing, it was sent back to him with a memo demanding that he try writing it again, this time with "greater sincerity." Stalin made his suggestions like a movie director giving notes, coaxing the best performances out of his bleary-eyed, bloodied, and swollen cast.

Books by the accused disappeared silently from the shelves of libraries. Once these people had been some of the greatest and loudest voices of Bolshevism. Now their voices were heard only by their captors, who waited patiently at their sides with pens, listening for the right story, the right plot twist, the right betrayal.

Day followed day. Shostakovich was a pariah. Hardly anyone would agree to play his music. He saw his earnings diminish just as he faced the prospect of a new child in the family.

"I was completely in the thrall of fear. I was no longer the master of my life, my past was crossed out, my work, my abilities, turned out to be worthless to everyone. The future didn't look any less bleak. At that moment I desperately wanted to disappear."

Leningrad poet Anna Akhmatova's cycle of poems about the Great Terror, too dangerous to circulate in print, instead was memorized by friends and passed on in whispers. "Speechlessness became my home," Akhmatova later wrote, "and my capital—muteness."

Shostakovich reviews his work at the piano.

His friend Meyerhold tried to console him. He spoke warmly about him at an open lecture in Leningrad, defending him publicly. ("He is an original among us — for he thinks.") In private, Meyerhold wrote, "Dear friend! Be brave! Be cheerful! Do not give in to your sadness!" The director tried to convince Shostakovich to write some new music for another production of *The Bedbug*, but the composer miserably "said he was incapable of doing anything."

At times, the thought of suicide overwhelmed him. Then he remembered the words of his writer friend Zoshchenko — that suicide is a "purely infantile act." Killing himself would have been particularly cruel, selfish, and infantile with his own infant on the way.

It was this thought that saved him.

On the morning of May 30, 1936, his daughter, Galina, was born. The celebration was riotous: by coincidence, he had a houseful of conductors coming over to listen to him bang out his Fourth Symphony on the piano. Intoxicated with the clamoring music and with the champagne he was drizzling in their glasses, several of them demanded that they wanted to play this new masterwork by the enemy of the people.

Eventually it was determined that the premiere would be given by the Leningrad Philharmonic Orchestra.

When a friend of his warily raised the question of what *Pravda* would think of the sprawling, bizarre work, Shostakovich angrily leaped up from the piano. "I don't write for the newspaper *Pravda*, but for myself. I basically don't think about who will say what about my work, but write about what moves me, what has sprouted in my soul and mind."

He was fierce again in his own defense. He had found his way through his despair. Years later, he remembered, "After 'A Mess Instead of Music,' the authorities tried everything they knew to get me to repent and expiate my sin. But I refused. I was young then, and had my physical strength. Instead of repenting, I composed my Fourth Symphony."

Experimental composer Alexander Mosolov, who had created some of the most famous factory-machine music of the clanging twenties, was arrested for supposed "counterrevolutionary activity" and sentenced to the gulag—imprisonment in a work camp.

Shostakovich's friend Gavriil Popov, another one of the Futurist composers of the twenties, had his First Symphony banned after its premiere by the Leningrad Philharmonic because it "was a reflection of the ideology of the class enemy." The symphony was not performed again during Popov's lifetime. Both he and Mosolov turned away from their boldest experiments in music. Years later, when they felt it was safe to compose again, they wrote big, splashy tunes and garish finales. They both drank a lot.

The great Sergei Prokofiev retreated from the spiky deviltry of his youthful style and escaped into the bright-colored worlds of fairy-tale ballet, adaptations of the classics, pieces for children (*Peter and the Wolf*), mass songs, and an abjectly fawning cantata in praise of Stalin:

I sing as I cradle my son
in my arms: "You grow up
like a little ear of corn
among the blue cornflowers.
Stalin will be the first words
on your lips.

You will understand from whence
this brilliant light streams.
In your exercise-book
you will draw Stalin's portrait."

. . . .

We are happy to follow you, happy to follow.
Stalin, Stalin!

The whole generation of ultramodern composers who had made the twenties so clamorous and exciting had dissolved. Some had fled. Some had been forced to renounce their earlier work or to hide it in a drawer, to "step on their own song's throat," as Mayakovsky had once said.

Shostakovich was the only one left composing in the bold style of the 1920s, and he was determined that he would make himself heard.

That summer, as Nina nursed and Shostakovich cradled the newborn Galina, the high-ranking Bolsheviks who had been arrested and tortured that spring came up for public trial. The newspapers were full of exclamations of disgust at the prisoners for their treason.

These were not like the tens of thousands of secret trials that were going on around the country, condemning people quietly to years in work camps or to unexplained deaths. The show trials were very public and were carefully stage-managed. Stalin wanted everyone to see proof of guilt, proof of the conspiracy that threatened to bring down the whole nation. This conspiracy, the prosecutors insisted, was the reason for the mass deaths, the millions plowed under, during the otherwise victorious First Five-Year Plan.

When the accused came to trial, they were confronted by rows of their interrogators and torturers sitting in seats right in front of them, leaning forward, staring them in the face. It was important, now that they were on the stand, that they remember their lines. If they went off script, the NKVD ranks in the courtroom were expected to start shouting, to kick up a ruckus so the foreign press couldn't hear what was being said. If any of the prisoners denied even part of their guilt while they were under oath, they were taken out of the courtroom for a brief recess, perhaps a drink of water. It was remarkable: After even a half hour alone with their former interrogators, when they returned to the trial, their former complaints had disappeared miraculously. They all admitted they were guilty. The state prosecutor pronounced, "They blow up mines, they burn down workshops, they wreck trains, they mutilate and kill hundreds of our best people, sons of our country." The shortages of food and clothing across the country, the long lines that people in Moscow and Leningrad had to stand in to get the simplest items, and even pieces of broken glass in the butter—all this was due to these wreckers.

The state prosecutor ended his speech on the final day of the trial by crying out, "I demand that these mad dogs should be shot—every one of them!" In a row, they were sentenced to death, and yet one of the condemned still cried out, "Long live the cause of Marx, Engels, Lenin, and Stalin!"

These high-profile prisoners were all executed on August 25, 1936. The NKVD continued its search for more conspirators, more wreckers and spies in the pay of the Germans.

After the trials, people pointed out that there had been some strange mistakes in the evidence. One alleged conspirator confessed to having recently met a foreign agent at the Hotel Bristol in Copenhagen. But there was a problem: the hotel had been demolished back in 1917.

Supposedly, Stalin was livid at these bumbles in his grand show. He roared, "What the devil did you need the hotel for? You ought to have said 'railway station.' The station is always there."

In this atmosphere, the musicians of the Leningrad Philharmonic Orchestra were wary of playing a symphony by an enemy of the people. This was particularly true of Shostakovich's bizarre Fourth Symphony. It is a big, loud, angry piece. Though its general shape is sprawling and obscure, one thing is very clear: whenever there's a moment where the symphony gets small and conversational, something huge and ghastly swells up and pounces.

People have tried to hear fanciful scenarios in the music—for example, a depiction of the NKVD thudding up steps and banging on Shostakovich's apartment door. But that's far too simple. The piece does not so much seem to be an autobiography as a demonology. It is a parade of grotesque portraits, some playful, some clumsy, and some malevolent. It is as if the composer, having been brutalized, now turns and enacts this savagery upon the audience.

Perhaps most worrying for the orchestral players was the way the symphony ends. By the tenets of Socialist Realism, at the end of a work, there should be a sense of the sunlit Communist future. In the Fourth, after all the sneers and blows and japes, after the assaults and the post-apocalyptic birdcalls and a poky funeral march that sounds as if the hearse is being led by a donkey — after almost an hour of kaleidoscopic travail — it seems as if finally, joy has been achieved. In a series of instrumental solos, Shostakovich takes earlier melodies and makes them dance, darlingly, like puppets. It resembles the music being written at the time for early cartoons — a tea party of woodland creatures, light and bumbling.

And then, towering over all of it, a blaring and satanic anthem spreads its wings, obliterating everything.

This is the spot where, in Shostakovich's previous symphonies, a choir would have burst in, singing the victories of labor. Instead, there is this calamitous brass chorus of triumph, this dissonant bellow that crushes everything beneath it.

After that, the symphony ends, not with a vision of future hope through massed singing, but rather with whispered, eerie, shell-shocked numbness. It is music for a child huddled in broken ruins, clutching his knees after something terrible has passed by, hoping that if he looks up, he will find it has stalked onward — but certain that, in fact, it stands over him, waiting to pounce.

At a rehearsal of the symphony, a friend of Shostakovich's "detected a strong sense of wariness in the hall; rumors had been circulating in musical circles . . . that Shostakovich had not heeded the criticism to which he had lately been subjected, but had persisted in writing a symphony of diabolical complexity and crammed full of formalist tendencies."

Then the final blow fell: While the orchestra was rehearsing, two men walked into the hall. One was the secretary of the Composers' Union. The other was from Communist Party Headquarters. A few minutes later, the director of the Philharmonic appeared and asked Shostakovich to accompany him for a chat in his office.

About fifteen minutes passed.

When Shostakovich came out, he got his friend Isaak Glikman and left. They walked back toward the composer's apartment. Glikman later wrote, "My companion seemed thoroughly downcast, and his long silence only added to my sense of anxiety. At last he told me in flat, expressionless tones that there would be no performance of the symphony." Shostakovich had been forced to cancel its premiere.

A notice was published in the magazine *Sovetskoe iskusstvo* (*Soviet Art*): "Composer Shostakovich appealed to the Leningrad Philharmonic with the request to withdraw his Fourth Symphony from performance on the grounds that it in no way corresponds to his creative convictions and represents for him a long outdated phase."

He was furious and ashamed—but he had a wife and a newborn daughter to think of. It was not the moment to take a stand.

The Fourth Symphony, one of his most fascinating and ingenious works, both brutal and intricate, would go unheard for a quarter of a century, silenced by fear.

It is worth pausing for a moment and asking how music speaks ideas. Shostakovich said,

> Meaning in music, that must sound very strange for most people. Particularly in the West. It's here in Russia that the question is usually posed: What was the composer trying to say, after all, with this musical work? What was he trying to make clear? The questions are naïve, of course, but despite their naiveté and crudity, they definitely merit being asked. And I would add to them, for instance: Can music attack evil? Can it make man stop and think? Can it cry out and thereby draw man's attention to various vile acts to which he has grown accustomed? to the things he passes without any interest?

How does a symphony — especially one as colossal and ramshackle as Shostakovich's Fourth — tell a story?

Of course, some music has words, and they shape our understanding. Shostakovich's Second and Third Symphonies both break out into triumphant workers' choruses ("Listen, workers, / to the voice of our factories: / in burning down the old, we must kindle a new reality. / Into the squares, revolution, / march with a million feet!"). That seems to be a straightforward way of reconstructing what the composer wanted to get across.

This assumption is made a little more complicated by the fact that Shostakovich privately thought that the poems he set in these symphonies were awful. ("Shostakovich did not like them and simply laughed at them," a conductor remembered.) That doesn't necessarily mean he disagreed with their sentiments, but he wished, at least, that the words weren't so lousy.

Most symphonies, however, are wordless. They are built only of tones, nonlinguistic sounds vibrating in the air, and somehow, we take them to heart and feel that they speak to us more deeply than words ever could. Cultures make up certain rules for music that we learn without even recognizing them; for example, in the West, we have decided that music in minor keys tends to sound sad or anxious, while music in major keys conveys confidence, triumph. Other cultures have made other decisions.

Symphonies also sometimes include abstract musical forms such as the waltz, the polka, the minuet, or the fugue. The Fourth Symphony makes use of these forms, which people of Shostakovich's day would have recognized, to tell its story.

One way to understand symphonies is to think of them as movie music without the movie. This is particularly apt in Russia, where composers were often explicitly trying to tell a story through orchestral music (and were sometimes even adapting film scores to symphonic form). There was a long tradition, for example, of Russian symphonies and suites spinning tales of swords and sorcery, of monstrous enemies and swashbuckling barbarian lords. To these were now added symphonies sketching scenes in the life of Revolutionaries, laborers, and Soviet heroes of aviation. In such symphonies — as in many movie scores — melodies could act the part of characters. Tunes and themes could appear in different moods, in different scenes, cloaked cleverly and diversely. They could be sped up, slowed down, or warped grotesquely out of shape. In a moment of sadness, a character melody might be played softly by woodwinds and strings; after a victory, it might be declared by brass.

Through the transformation of tunes, symphonies like Shostakovich's Fourth can tell stories without describing any specific events at all. For example, several themes from the work's first movement that seem groping, wounded, or incompetent reappear as characters at the end of the symphony, now played as cheerful little street dances. Then they are squashed — silenced. It is clear they are acting out some drama. There is no need for us to know names or to demand that these absolutely must be images of NKVD jackboots on the stairs or prisoners tapping out messages on hot-water pipes. It is the emotional narrative that is important.

There are other ways that composers can encode stories and messages, making music more like a spoken language. Some use musical quotations. In one of the most famous pieces of Russian symphonic music, for example, Tchaikovsky's "1812 Overture," the composer depicts the French invasion of Russia under Napoleon and the final defeat of the French by pitting the French national anthem ("La Marseillaise") against a Russian Orthodox hymn and the Russian national anthem ("God Save the Tsar") in a sort of battle royale, complete with cannon shots.

Shostakovich used musical quotation like this to encode a sort of secret message in his Fourth Symphony. The demoniac anthem that blares out at the end of the piece actually contains a quotation from *Oedipus Rex*, an opera by Igor Stravinsky. In the opera, the fragment is sung by a chorus calling to their queen: "Glory, glory, glory! Praise to Queen Jocasta in pestilential Thebes!" They do not realize that the king and queen's own sins have brought a plague down upon them all.

There clearly is some irony in Shostakovich using this fragment right at the moment when, in previous symphonies, he would have included a workers' hymn of praise to the Bolsheviks. Instead, his shout of acclamation comes from a city dying of sickness, calling out to a ruler responsible for the scabs.

Shostakovich would often use quotation like this to signal meanings for his listeners. In the case of this passage from *Oedipus Rex*, it is unlikely that many of the people in the audience had ever heard the Stravinsky opera or could recognize the fragment. In later symphonies, however, Shostakovich often quoted the Revolutionary songs of his youth, songs he would have heard at funerals for Bolsheviks killed in action, songs his father would have sung as he marched on the tsar's Winter Palace. These were tunes known by everyone in the audience.

But we can never be certain exactly what he meant by them. Is he celebrating the Revolutionary cause or pleading for those who suffered later under the Russian Communist yoke—or both? And if we assume that every recognizable tune carries a valuable secret message, then what precisely does Shostakovich mean when, in his intense Second Cello Concerto, he quotes an Odessan jingle called "Pretzels, Buy My Pretzels"?

Later in his life, he used another form of musical code: reducing specific names to notes. For example, he worked out a musical monogram for himself: the letters of his initials, D-S-C-H (in Cyrillic, Д. Ш.), transformed into a four-note motif. He built his very personal Eighth String Quartet around this signature, repeated again and again in different forms, wound around quotations from his own earlier work, and culminating in a quotation from the Revolutionary song "Tormented by Grievous Bondage." At the time, people did not know that this brief motif encrypted Shostakovich's own name; to us now, the piece seems to speak privately of his own feeling of grief and entrapment.

But as the musicologist Richard Taruskin warns us, "There is more to an artwork, one has to think, than there is to a note in a bottle." What are we to make of the fact that in another symphony—one that some argue is supposed to depict Stalin—Shostakovich made a melody out of the name of a woman he had a crush on? Is it necessary to know that in order to "understand" the symphony? No one had any idea the reference was there until years after Shostakovich's death.

People often claim that Shostakovich's music is absolutely clear in its meaning — but then slam their fists on tables at conferences and bicker about what it actually means. For a long time, the Soviets said the music meant one thing, the Americans said it meant something else — and a few lonely souls (Igor Stravinsky among them) complained that music really should mean nothing at all.

What did Shostakovich himself say about musical meaning? According to a friend, "Shostakovich hated being asked questions about his music and whether this or that theme represented something or had any particular meaning. When asked, 'What did you want to say in this work?' he would answer, 'I've said what I've said.'"

This made sense in a society where everyone assumed music had a meaning — but where saying the wrong thing could get a person killed.

The attack on cultural figures — many of them Shostakovich's friends — was going full force. The shadow of the Great Terror fell upon writers particularly grievously.

Osip Mandelstam, the poet who had whispered his squib about Stalin's cockroach mustache to fellow poet Pasternak on the bridge, tried to placate the Great Leader and Teacher by writing a groveling hymn of praise from his exile:

> I would sing of him who shifted the axis of the world. . . .
> How I weep as I draw the portrait of the Leader. . . .
> In the friendship of his wise eyes
> One suddenly sees — a father! . . .
> (His *powerful* eyes — sternly kind.)

Mandelstam thought flattery might do some good. He was, in fact, released from his internal exile and allowed to move back within the orbit of

Moscow. He was even given a travel voucher for an all-expenses-paid vacation at a government resort. He and his wife were given a quaint hut stocked with books and spent several weeks skiing through the forests.

Toward the end of his holiday, on a day when all the guests were thrilled that ice cream was on the menu, the NKVD took the opportunity to arrest Mandelstam on the way to the dining hall. He never got a chance to say a real good-bye to his wife. Mandelstam was sentenced to the gulag and sent to Siberia. He died on the way there, interred at a transfer station, raving piteously that Stalin was going to change his mind and save him.

Mandelstam's wife, Nadezhda, wrote in her harrowing memoir of the Great Terror, "We were capable of coming to work with a smile on our face after a night in which our home had been searched or a member of the family arrested. It was essential to smile — if you didn't, it meant you were afraid, then you must have a bad conscience. The mask was taken off only at home, and then not always — even from your children you had to conceal how horror-struck you were; otherwise, God save you, they might let something slip in school."

Elena Konstantinovskaya, the young translator Shostakovich had almost left Nina for, was arrested.

Another one of his ex-girlfriends from his youth (Galina Serebryakova) was arrested and imprisoned for seventeen years. Two decades later, she spoke out about her imprisonment. In front of a crowded hall, she unfastened a couple of buttons and pointed to the torture scars on her back. Shostakovich was in the audience. Upon seeing the flesh he had once touched so tormented, he collapsed onto the floor.

The man who had written the story of Shostakovich's ballet *The Bright Stream* was arrested and disappeared. The head of the Moscow Composers' Union was executed.

Boris Kornilov, the lyricist for Shostakovich's hit "Song of the Counterplan," was arrested and shot. During Kornilov's interrogation, his ex-wife, the poet Olga Berggolts, was dragged in for questioning. She was pregnant. The NKVD thugs beat her so brutally that she miscarried on the torture-room floor.

We can only imagine the outrage and fear Shostakovich felt when he heard this, looking at his own wife and his newborn daughter.

Nina's mother was arrested and sentenced to a work camp in Kazakhstan.

Shostakovich's uncle was arrested and disappeared.

Shostakovich's sister Maria and her husband were both arrested. Maria was exiled to Central Asia. Her husband was accused of terrorism and imprisoned in a work camp, where he died.

Shostakovich left no written record of his emotions during this time.

Why would he? Diaries got people imprisoned. Letters got people shot.

Mass rallies were held to celebrate Stalin. Troops of athletes strode through the streets of Moscow, carrying portraits of Communist Party leaders, as they once had carried painted icons of saints on religious holidays. Everywhere, Stalin's picture appeared, with its kind smile and his hand raised in welcome.

His slogan for the age was on everyone's lips. "Life is getting better, comrades!" he said. "Life is getting merrier!"

Planes spelled out his name in the sky.

One night late in the Great Terror, Shostakovich and his friend Isaak Glikman came back from a soccer match, perhaps a little tipsy. They were going to have a cup of tea at Shostakovich's apartment. When they got there, the composer couldn't get the door to unlock. He fumbled with his keys.

His friend Meyerhold appeared on the staircase. He happened to be passing by, visiting someone else in the building. Meyerhold helped Shostakovich with the lock. They got the door open.

Shostakovich was delighted to see Meyerhold. They were talking about collaborating on a new project. Shostakovich invited him in for a cup of tea. Meyerhold said no — but maybe they could get together the next day.

They said good night.

It was the last time Shostakovich saw the director alive.

Early the next morning, Meyerhold was arrested by the NKVD. The warrant was signed in blue pencil, which meant that he was probably slated for execution. He was taken by train back to Moscow. There, he was imprisoned in the Lubyanka, the NKVD's headquarters right in the center of Moscow, across the square from the Child World department store. He was imprisoned there for six months.

In public, at lectures, Meyerhold had defended himself and Shostakovich against the charges of formalism. "Where once there were the best theaters in the world, now — by your leave — everything is gloomily well regulated, averagely arithmetical, stupefying, and murderous in its lack of talent," he insisted. "In hunting down formalism, you have eliminated art!"

His pride and stubbornness may have led to his arrest. Now, deep within the Lubyanka, they led to his torture.

In a pleading letter to a government official, he wrote:

> They beat me. . . . They laid me face-down on the floor and beat the soles of my feet and my back with a rubber truncheon. When I was seated on a chair they used the same truncheon to beat my legs from above with great force, from my knees to the upper parts of my legs. And in the days that followed, when my legs were bleeding from internal haemorrhaging, they used the rubber truncheon to beat me on the red, blue and yellow bruises. The pain was so great that it was like boiling water being poured on the tenderest parts of my legs. (I screamed and wept with the pain.) . . . Lying face-down on the floor, I discovered the capacity to cringe, writhe and howl like a dog being whipped by its master.

Meyerhold had to be transferred to the Lubyanka prison hospital so he would not die before they were done with him. As he was being carried off, his torturer threatened him. "If you refuse to write [a confession], we shall beat you again, leaving your head and right hand untouched but turning the rest of you into a shapeless, bloody mass of mangled flesh."

Indeed, they broke his left arm, but he could still hold a pen in his other hand to sign his name.

Under torture, Meyerhold confessed to being in the pay of both the French and the Japanese. He agreed that for years he had been the head of a group of conspirators who "coordinated all anti-Soviet elements in the field of the arts." He was forced to name names.

He named Shostakovich.

At the same time, the writer Isaac Babel was being interrogated. Babel implicated Shostakovich, too. When he was being asked about the supposed conspiracy among the intelligentsia, he said, "We all had in common holding the humiliated Shostakovich as a genius."

Shostakovich's NKVD file now listed him as a "saboteur."

We do not know what saved him from being arrested at this point.

One thing might have helped: A few months after Meyerhold listed the names of Shostakovich and other friends of theirs, the battered director demanded to sign another statement. This time, he agreed that he was in the pay of foreign governments and revolutionaries — but he insisted that there was no anti-Soviet conspiracy in the arts. He said that Shostakovich, and everyone else he had listed, was innocent. It was an incredible act of bravery.

Shostakovich, for his part, never knew he had been implicated. At the pleading of Zinaida Raikh, Meyerhold's wife, he wrote and signed a letter asking for Meyerhold's release.

It did no good.

The court tried Meyerhold in secret. There was no defense lawyer. No witnesses were allowed. He was found guilty.

The next day, he was taken down to the cellar. There was a killing room there. The floor was concrete and slanted so it could be easily hosed down. He was met by an executioner in a leather butcher's apron.

When he was dead, his body was cremated. The remains were thrown in a ditch marked "Common Grave Number One—unclaimed ashes 1930–42 inclusive."

If there is one mercy to Meyerhold's death, it is that he probably heard no news from outside.

A few months after he was arrested, during his period of torture, his wife, Zinaida Raikh, was called and told to return to Moscow because she might be able to get word about him. She stayed at their old apartment. That night, two thugs climbed up onto the apartment balcony. They broke in and found Raikh in the living room. In happier days, Shostakovich, sitting in this room, had rolled his eyes at the doting love talk of Meyerhold and Raikh as they cooed and called each other geniuses.

The murderers grabbed Raikh. She began screaming for help. They stabbed her seventeen times with a knife.

The maid, hearing shouts, ran into the room. The men grabbed the maid and beat her unconscious. She collapsed.

One of the killers ran back to the balcony and leaped off. The other ran out the door of the apartment and galloped down the steps. Raikh's blood was smeared on the wall of the stairwell.

Outside, the murderers ran to a black car waiting at the corner. They drove off into the night.

Raikh was dead by the time someone got her to a hospital. The attack was savage. Both of her eyes had been gouged out.

According to Russian superstition, the last thing a dying man sees is imprinted on the eyes. Apparently, the killers wanted to erase any record of who they were.

At this time, even the unseeing eyes of the unspeaking dead had to be silenced.

Here, supposedly, is Dmitri Shostakovich's epitaph on Vsevolod Meyerhold and Zinaida Raikh:

Meyerhold loved her madly. I had never seen anything like it. It's hard to imagine that such a love could exist in our day. There was something ominous about it — and it did end badly.

It makes you think: the best way to hold on to something is to pay no attention to it. The things you love too much perish. You have to treat everything with irony, especially the things you hold dear. There's more of a chance then that they'll survive.

When we read tales of atrocity, we all want to be the one who stood firm, who would not bend, who shouted the truth in the face of the dictator.

Vsevolod Meyerhold came as close as anyone to achieving this. It is important to know of the full horror of his sacrifice.

It is easy for us all to imagine we are heroes when we are sitting in our kitchens, dreaming of distant suffering.

Party members were purged. Futurist painters were purged. Leningrad factory bosses were purged. Train operators were purged — so many that one railway line had no one left working on it. When the NKVD had finished purging other groups, then Stalin purged the NKVD itself. He decided they were getting too powerful. He had the head of the NKVD replaced, tried, and shot. About twenty thousand secret-police officers were rounded up and exiled or executed. Some officers, knowing all too well what happened when people were imprisoned, shot themselves or threw themselves out of their office windows before they could be arrested. No one was safe.

Scientists who taught strict Darwinian evolution were purged because genetic inheritance didn't always sit well with Stalin's notions of social change. This crippled Soviet science for decades.

Historians were purged. Diplomats were purged.

Collective farmers were purged because during the harvest, the crops were crawling with ticks. The regime claimed that the ticks had been spread by antirevolutionary masterminds. Meteorologists were purged;

supposedly, their weather predictions were wrong because they were trying to sabotage Soviet agriculture.

Stalin purged the other Soviet Republics in the USSR ruthlessly, too. The government of Ukraine was replaced entirely. The government of the Tatar Republic was completely liquidated.

"Better too far than not far enough," exclaimed NKVD head Yezhov before his own arrest. "Beat, destroy without sorting out."

In July 1937, Stalin ordered arrest quotas for each region in the USSR. He didn't provide names of people to be arrested; he provided numbers. According to this schedule, a total of 259,450 people had to be arrested and sentenced to slave labor in the camps; 72,950 had to be shot. It did not matter who they were; all that mattered was that each region fulfilled its quota. Members of Stalin's Politburo spread out across the country to oversee the bloody harvest.

The only way to save oneself and one's family was to admit guilt and give names of other "coconspirators." People blurted out the names of their personal enemies, past lovers, people who'd told jokes at Stalin's expense. In this way, the pool of suspects snowballed, grew. Before long, half the USSR's urban population was listed in the NKVD's records of possible anti-people saboteurs.

To conceal the unimaginable reach of the purges, victims were driven through the streets in trucks marked MEAT and VEGETABLES. At night, they were taken to remote killing fields outside the cities. They were never seen again.

Stalin was not merely trying to remove political enemies. He was not merely trying to terrorize the country into submission. He was trying to break down all social structure that did not emanate from him, and to create a new people, no longer *Homo sapiens*, but *Homo sovieticus*, the New Man of Communism. "Everything that divides the many from each other, that fosters the illusion of the individual importance of man, especially the 'soul,' hinders this higher evolution, and must consequently be destroyed," wrote a horrified onlooker. "Only the 'collective man,' freed from the evil of the soul, mechanically united by external interests with all others, is strong. To him alone belongs the empire of the future; only he will be able to reign therein 'in the millennium.'"

Even the family as a unit was breaking down. Shostakovich watched the accusations rapidly spread farther and farther, tearing families apart. "Son denounced father, wife informed on husband," he remembered miserably. "The papers were full of announcements like 'I, So-and-so, announce that I have nothing to do with my father, enemy of the people So-and-so. I broke off with him ten years ago.' Everyone had grown accustomed to such announcements, they didn't even pay attention. So you broke off with him. It was like reading, 'Selling my furniture,' or 'French lessons, also manicure, pedicure, and electrolysis.'"

One boy who supposedly denounced his father to the government for forging documents was killed by his uncles because of it. This child, Pavlik Morozov, became a famous Communist martyr. Children all across the country read his story and were told that they should follow his example and turn their parents in.

Parents could not even talk freely in front of their own kids.

When one little boy saw his father dragged off by the secret police, he immediately assumed the man was guilty. "Look what those enemies of the people are like," he sobbed, heartbroken. *"Some of them even pretend to be fathers."*

A friend of the Shostakoviches, writing in her diary about the exile of Shostakovich's sister Maria and her husband, and about the execution of countless others:

> The nausea rises to my throat when I hear how calmly people can say it: He was shot, someone else was shot, shot, shot. The word is always in the air, it resonates through the air. People

pronounce the words completely calmly, as though saying, "He went to the theater." I think that the real meaning of the word doesn't reach our consciousness — all we hear is the sound. . . .

God forgive the living and give rest to the dead.

The final touch of ghastly cruelty in the midst of this bloodshed was the infantile humor of Stalin and his band of merry psychopaths. They delighted in their games like children. They played pranks on one another. The head of the NKVD threw the minister of foreign trade's hat up into the trees; he shoved rotten tomatoes into the man's suits so they exploded wetly like blood. At state banquets, Stalin flirted with ladies by throwing pellets of bread and orange peel at their heads. His favorite NKVD interrogators would entertain his giggling court by acting out the groveling of famous prisoners. "Oh, Comrade Stalin will save me — call Comrade Stalin," they would whimper, crawling on the floor.

Stalin roared with laughter until he cried.

(Life is getting better, comrades! Life is getting merrier!)

Life was becoming more like the ultramodern stories and music of the dead 1920s, like Shostakovich's own forbidden score to the Fourth Symphony: violent, arbitrary, absurd, and devilishly dreamlike. One innocent prisoner protested, "I am a victim of an Enemy's lies. Sometimes I think this is a silly dream." It was not unusual for innocents dragged before the NKVD to look around themselves, startled, and say they felt like they must have fallen into some kind of nightmare.

When Shostakovich drank with friends, he would raise his glass in a toast: "Here's to life not getting any 'merrier.'"

One day Shostakovich went to visit a friend. When he got there, his friend was gone. The man had disappeared. A family of strangers was living in the apartment. No one could tell him what had happened to his friend.

Everything the man owned had been thrown out onto the street.

As he watched people vanish, Shostakovich was sure that he would be next. He packed a suitcase with extra clothes and warm underwear and left it by the door. Eventually he started sleeping on the landing outside his apartment.

He did not want Nina and the baby to be disturbed when, inevitably, the NKVD came for him.

Shostakovich hoped that his friendship with Red Army marshal Tukhachevsky would keep him safe until the purges were over. Unfortunately, Tukhachevsky had made many enemies in the regime.

Tukhachevsky was a brilliant military thinker. He wanted to modernize the Red Amy so it would be prepared in case of a war with Germany. Like the rest of the country, he was watching the rise of the Nazis warily. He predicted that Hitler would soon try to attack Germany's neighbors and snatch territory. Gently, he began discussions with officials in England, France, and Poland about the idea of forming an alliance to contain the Germans. He also tried to prepare the Red Army technologically so it would be ready for the onslaught. He wrote a book, *The Future War,* discussing the prospects of modern conflict and how the USSR should prepare for it. He was a strong proponent of tank warfare and the air force.

This did not always make him popular among the Red Army high command. Several of Stalin's closest military advisers had been cavalrymen in the First World War. They believed that the horse was always going to be the most important military device. "What the hell do we need rocket artillery for?" one of them protested. "The main thing is the horse-drawn gun." They believed that tanks were overrated.

Stalin himself was worried that Tukhachevsky and his supporters in the Red Army might become too powerful and challenge the regime. Stalin had already purged the Communist Party. The Red Army was the one organization left that could still topple him. Accordingly, Stalin set out to destroy Marshal Tukhachevsky.

He quietly instructed the NKVD to create a case against the marshal—something damning that would prove that Tukhachevsky was already plotting the government's downfall. The NKVD, in strictest secrecy, began to make inquiries. As Lavrentii Beria, the wartime head of the NKVD, later admitted to his son, "Tukhachevsky had done nothing against Stalin and the party, or at least nothing that would justify his arrest." Evidence of a conspiracy would have to be forged.

What followed must be one of the most bizarre stories in the history of espionage.

In France, there lived a Russian refugee named Nikolai Skoblin. He was a double or perhaps triple agent. He worked for both the Soviets and the Germans. He himself wanted to see Stalin and the Communists overthrown.

Oddly, both the Germans and the NKVD knew that he was a double agent. The NKVD sent someone to explain to him that they were very interested in any evidence that might prove that Tukhachevsky was secretly a German spy. Skoblin agreed to look into it.

The NKVD didn't trust him, so they arranged to have him watched. With the kind of grotesque, *Tintin*-esque whimsy that somehow always dogs espionage like a puppy hot on the heels of a murderous thug, they ordered two spies to stake out Skoblin's house: one named Ivan, Son of Pantelei, and the other named Pantelei, Son of Ivan. One wore a monocle. They usually worked as sandwich-board men, stumping up and down the boulevards of Paris wearing giant signs advertising cheap dinners at restaurants, wine included.

Skoblin, closely monitored by Ivan and Pantelei, contacted the German secret service. He suggested that, one way or another, it might be in Hitler's interest to discover proof that Marshal Tukhachevsky had long been in the pay of Germany.

Late in 1936, Adolf Hitler met with Heinrich Himmler, the head of the Nazi Security Squadron (SS), and they discussed the Tukhachevsky situation. They both agreed that the liquidation of Tukhachevsky and his supporters would be of great use. It would cripple the Red Army. Hitler was already making long-range plans to eventually invade the Soviet Union. He was happy to provide the falsified evidence Skoblin requested.

Through the staged capture of a spy and some dubious submarine plans, Skoblin "leaked" the word that Tukhachevsky was a German agent. Soon, the president of Czechoslovakia had heard rumors that Tukhachevsky was planning to overthrow the Russian government and welcome a German invasion. The president was anxious about the rise of the Nazis. He quickly passed the information on to Stalin. He could not have known that Stalin was the one who had originally seeded this story.

Meanwhile, the Germans had set about forging a set of fake letters from Tukhachevsky to various German generals. They took Tukhachevsky's signature off some military correspondence of the 1920s. They had an engraver copy the marshal's handwriting. They produced a whole string of letters going back ten years, in which Tukhachevsky regularly sent the Germans top-secret reports about the Red Army's troop deployment, their equipment, their strategic ideas, and their production capabilities. Then the SS sent word to the head of the NKVD that this clutch of treasonous letters was for sale for half a million German Deutschmarks. Stalin agreed to buy.

The transfer happened at a meeting between NKVD agents, SS agents, and Skoblin, the double or perhaps triple agent. The Germans handed over their parcel of forged letters. The NKVD handed over the money. It seems likely that Stalin knew perfectly well that the letters were counterfeit. That was okay; so was the stack of bills he used to pay for them.

With these documents in hand, Stalin made his next move against Russia's most exceptional military genius.

On May 10, 1937, Tukhachevsky received word that he was being removed from his job as deputy commissar of defense and being given the command of a distant, provincial region, the Volga Military District. He must have known that this signaled Stalin's displeasure. Friends who saw him at this time said he did not look well.

On May 20, Marshal Tukhachevsky got on a train to travel to his new provincial post, in Kuibyshev. He shut himself in his sleeping berth and went to bed. The train rumbled into the night.

Olga Berggolts was arrested and tortured in 1937 during the investigation of her ex-husband, Boris Kornilov. Later, during the Second World War, she was to become the poetic voice of besieged Leningrad, much as Shostakovich was to become its musical voice.

Mikhail Tukhachevsky, one of the five marshals of the Soviet Union and a notable reformer of the Red Army

In this unsettling photo, Stalin appears to be enjoying the company of an ambassador from another world, a phantom, a visitor from the realm of the dead. This is not inaccurate: The figure to the left of Stalin is someone who has been purged. Unsatisfied simply with obliterating the future of his enemies, Stalin also erased their past. Their names were removed from history books. Their faces and features were burned out of photos like this one, so they were unrecognizable. Other photos were doctored so it appeared the enemies of the people had never even been there. (In the background, Tukhachevsky grins, unaware that he himself will become one of the vanished.)

When he woke, the train was not moving. Everything was silent.

Tukhachevsky got up and looked out the window. He found himself in the middle of a great forest. Tracks stretched into the distance. There was a pile of lumber on a platform. Nothing else.

He went into the other compartments on the train car. They were empty. No one was there. His carriage had been decoupled; the rest of the train was gone. It seemed he was alone in the silent woodland.

When he opened the door to the train carriage, he saw that there were NKVD agents standing guard.

"Where are we?" he demanded.

The officer answered, "At the halt called 'The Bandits.' Your carriage was detached by order of the Commissar-General for Security. I don't know how long it will remain here. Anyway we've got four days' supplies."

Tukhachevsky must have known the end had come. He was probably surprised when he was not murdered immediately.

Instead, an engine pulled up a day later, and on May 23, Tukhachevsky was taken back to Moscow and deposited there, now under guard. He was taken to prison, where he soon found himself surrounded by all his supporters, except one who had committed suicide when the agents went to arrest him.

Tukhachevsky was allowed to see his wife once more. He was not allowed to see his daughter, and never said good-bye to her.

Shortly thereafter, he was handed over to the head of the NKVD for questioning.

The complete records of his interrogation remain in the state archives. Several of the pages are speckled brown with blood spattered from a falling body.

At around this time, Shostakovich got an order to meet with an investigator at "the Big House," the NKVD's grim, modernist headquarters in Leningrad by the river Neva.

Shostakovich went as commanded. He was always punctual. He did not know what the conversation was going to be about. The investigator invited him to sit down, then began the interview by asking chatty questions: "What are you working on now? How are your professional affairs?" And then: "Are you acquainted with Marshal Tukhachevsky?"

Shostakovich admitted, "Yes, I know him."

"Tell me, how and when did you make his acquaintance?"

Shostakovich told him that they had met after a concert and that sometimes they played music together.

"And who else was present at these gatherings?"

"Only members of the family circle."

"Any politicians there, by chance?"

"No, no politicians."

"And what did you talk about?"

"About music."

"And politics?"

The conversation was getting dangerous, Shostakovich could tell. He answered, "No, there was never any talk of politics in my presence."

"Now, I think you should try to shake your memory. It cannot be that you were at his home and that you did not talk about politics. For instance, the plot to assassinate Comrade Stalin? What did you hear about that?"

Shostakovich was panicky. He did not answer. The investigator pressed him. Shostakovich kept repeating, "No, there was never any such talk in my presence."

The investigator insisted, "Think harder. Try to remember. Some of the other guests have verified it already."

Shostakovich denied having ever heard anything about a plot.

The investigator sat back. He said that it was Saturday and that he would give Shostakovich the weekend to remember. "You must recall every detail of the discussion regarding the plot against Stalin of which you were a witness."

They made an appointment for Monday. By then, clearly, Shostakovich either had to make up a story that would betray Tukhachevsky and satisfy the NKVD or he would be arrested himself.

"I understood this was the end," he later told a friend. "Those two days until Monday were a nightmare. I told my wife I probably wouldn't return. She even prepared a bag for me — the kind prepared for people who were taken away. She put in warm underwear. She knew I wouldn't be back."

He destroyed any papers that might possibly be incriminating. He spent the weekend saying good-bye to Nina and his baby daughter.

On Monday, he took his suitcase and went to the Big House. He showed his summons to the guards and went in to wait on a chair to be called by the investigator. He waited for hours. Finally, he timidly spoke to a security guard. The guard thumbed through the list of appointments and couldn't find Shostakovich's name. "What is your business? Whom have you come to see?"

Shostakovich explained he was there to see an investigator called Zakovsky. He had an appointment.

Ah! Now the guard understood what was going on. He apologetically told Shostakovich that over the weekend, Zakovsky had been condemned and arrested. His appointments had apparently been canceled. They were not going to be rescheduled.

Shostakovich left the building. For the moment, he was free. As in some absurdist fable, his executioner was in line for execution. He wandered home across the Neva River, befogged and bewildered by his tenuous reprieve.

Under torture, Tukhachevsky confessed to being an agent in the pay of the German military, the Reichswehr. He admitted to planning a coup to overthrow Stalin's regime. He claimed he had cooked up his scheme with a German general while they'd been walking in a funeral procession behind the coffin of the king of England. After weeks of interrogation, he implicated other officers in the imaginary junta. All of these details were specially tailored by Stalin himself in daily meetings with the head of the NKVD.

The trial of Tukhachevsky and his supposed coconspirators took place on June 11, 1937. It was held in secret.

Tukhachevsky, hearing his comrades accuse him of crimes he had never committed, hearing of a whole alternative world in which he was a villain, said wonderingly, as so many had before him, "I feel I'm dreaming."

He was attacked not just for his treason but also for his supposed incompetence. He was scolded for wasting time and money on tanks when it could have been spent on training horsemen, who were clearly the future of warfare.

There was no question of innocence. Tukhachevsky and all those on trial with him were declared guilty and sentenced to death.

They were shot in the courtyard of NKVD headquarters. Parked trucks revved their motors to hide the noise of gunfire. One of the victims had time before he died to scream, "Long live the Party! Long live Stalin!"

It is likely he was trying to ensure his wife and children were protected.

After Tukhachevsky's death, most of his family was hunted down and liquidated. His wife went mad.

The cleaning up of odds and ends did not stop there. One of the judges miserably told his friends, "Tomorrow I'll be put in the same place." He was not wrong. Soon, five of the eight judges in the Tukhachevsky case were executed. The three NKVD agents who had gone to the West to purchase the forged letters were also killed.

So Stalin got what he wanted: Mikhail Tukhachevsky was no longer a threat. But Stalin did not know how high the price really was: The Leader had just participated in a plot with Hitler to cripple his own army. Meanwhile, Hitler trained one of the world's most fearsome fighting forces — the German Wehrmacht — for war.

It was only after Tukhachevsky was actually sentenced that *Pravda* and the other newspapers even announced his trial to the Russian people. Most people only heard of the trial after Tukhachevsky had been executed.

On July 12, the paper *Izvestiya* declared:

The spies Tukhachevsky, Yakir, Uborevich, Kork, Eideman, Feldman, Primakov and Putna, who sold out to the sworn enemies of socialism, had the audacity to raise a blood-stained, criminal hand against the lives and happiness of the people. . . . The whole country, which had unanimously demanded that the band of eight spies be wiped off the face of the earth, welcomes the decision of the court. Execution by shooting! Such is the sentence of the court. Execution! Such is the will of the people.

It may or may not have been the will of the people. Everyone was agog.

"It was a terrible blow for me when Tukhachevsky was shot," said Shostakovich many years later. "When I read about it in the papers, I blacked out. I felt they were killing me, that's how bad I felt."

He was panicked. That day, he hastily wrote a letter to his government contact: "I have known Tukhachevsky for about eight years. . . . It could not be considered a close comradely acquaintance. . . . He was a great music lover, and all of our conversations touched exclusively on this subject." Tukhachevsky was gone. There was nothing Shostakovich could do for him anymore. He had to save himself.

Once Marshal Tukhachevsky was dead, Stalin unleashed a mass purge of the armed forces. He wanted to make sure there was no possibility of a military coup. Only nine days after Tukhachevsky's body had fallen in that courtyard, Stalin's forces had already rounded up 980 Red Army officers. They were accused of plotting and spying. The purges hit the tank units and the air force hardest. They had been Tukhachevsky's special pride. Only two of the five marshals of the Red Army remained alive, and they both thought tank warfare was overrated.

In just a few months, the purge liquidated or imprisoned about 60 or 70 percent of the officers in the Soviet military. Ninety percent of the generals had disappeared. Thirteen out of fifteen commanders of the army were gone. Then, a few months later, those who replaced them were also purged. In all, around twenty-seven thousand officers and soldiers vanished into concentration camps or mass graves.

In the dark of the night, people in Shostakovich's neighborhood were awakened by gunfire. Otherwise, the city was silent at that hour: no trams, only occasional cars.

Shostakovich's acquaintance and neighbor Lyubov Shaporina lay awake in her bed, listening to the shots, as she described next morning in her diary: "The shooting continued in bursts every ten, fifteen, or twenty minutes." Shaporina opened her window and tried to hear where the gunfire was coming from. "After all, between 3 to 5 in the morning it couldn't be a drill. Who were they shooting? And why?"

The shooting was coming from the gray battlements of the Peter and Paul Fortress. There, in the gloomy shadow of the church where the tsars were entombed, hundreds of soldiers and officers accused of collusion with Tukhachevsky were being executed by firing squad, one after the other.

At around five, the shooting ceased. The sun rose. The trams started moving on their tracks. A new day was beginning.

Shaporina scribbled in her diary: "To spend all night long hearing living people, undoubtedly innocent people, being shot to death and not to lose your mind. And afterwards, just to fall asleep, to go on sleeping as though nothing had happened. How terrible."

The fortress's church spire, needle-thin and dangerously sharp, glimmered gold in the dawn.

Shostakovich had to produce something. Soon, his silence itself would be read as a comment on the cultural revolution going on around him. Silence was becoming dangerous.

He had started writing his Fifth Symphony in the spring. He didn't talk about it with others. Almost no one had heard any of it. He had played a few of its movements on the piano for a musicologist, a mutual friend of his and

As part of the infamous gulag system, prisoners in a work camp dig out the basin of the White Sea Canal. (The term *gulag* is actually an acronym for "Main Administration of Correctional Labor Camps and Colonies.")

Built by forced prison labor, this canal leading from the White Sea to the Baltic was a showpiece of Stalin's Five-Year Plan. It was rushed to completion, and thousands died in the harsh conditions of its construction. Soviet propaganda films (like the one this image is taken from) trumpeted the achievement.

Ironically, however, the speed of construction worked against it. It was not dug deep enough for most modern cargo ships, so it was not of much use as a canal. Instead, Soviet tourist boats drifted up and down its waters, celebrating this project that had cost so many lives.

Tukhachevsky's, but during the investigations into the Tukhachevsky plot, the man had been dragged away and was never seen again.

In the month after Tukhachevsky's death, Shostakovich wrote the symphony's tragic slow movement. Supposedly, it took him only three days to write.

He was well aware that another failure, another public accusation of being "anti-people," could easily lead to death or life imprisonment in a Siberian work camp.

At the beginning of the fall, as he put the finishing touches on the symphony, he discovered that Nina was pregnant again. (It would turn out to be a boy: Maxim.) In these times, pregnancy was not entirely news for rejoicing.

He always had before him the example of the poet Kornilov; the poet's ex-wife, Olga Berggolts; and the unborn baby who had died, battered to death in her womb.

As Shostakovich worked on the last details of the new symphony and considered what face he would put on for the waiting world, a great carnival was held in Moscow. (Life is getting better, comrades! Life is getting merrier!) There was a grand masquerade. Crowds thronged the Park of Culture and Recreation dressed as devils, Russian puppets, and giraffes with their necks tied in knots.

"You don't want to take the mask off," the newspaper *Izvestiya* giddily declared. "You want to maintain your cheerful, festive appearance. . . . A carnival mask is essentially a cap of invisibility. Comrades, acquaintances, relatives and coworkers walk past without seeing you." Fireworks exploded over the river embankments crammed with cardboard grins and leers.

The newspaper concluded: "Now tradition takes over, masks are the rule, and the carnival begins."

On November 21, 1937, Dmitri Shostakovich's Symphony no. 5 in D minor, op. 47, was presented to the world by the Leningrad Philharmonic Orchestra.

"The significance was apparent to everyone," writes one biographer. "Shostakovich's fate was at stake."

The hall was full, and the crowds were alert with nervous anxiety. Two of Shostakovich's friends met in the chaos. Gavriil Popov — whose own First Symphony had been declared forbidden a few years before — gabbled to Lyubov Shaporina, "You know, I've turned into a coward, I'm a coward, I'm afraid of everything." She, for her part, was no better off. "I wake up in the morning and automatically think: thank God I wasn't arrested last night, they don't arrest anyone during the day, but what will happen tonight, no one knows. . . . Every single person has enough against him to justify arrest and exile to parts unknown. . . ."

The orchestra tuned up. The young conductor, Evgeny Mravinsky, walked out and the audience applauded. He had taken on the dangerous challenge of presenting the new symphony. Years later he said, "Until this day I cannot understand how I dared to accept this proposal unhesitatingly."

The first part of the concert was old music, Tchaikovsky's *Romeo and Juliet.*

Shostakovich sat in agony in the audience, waiting for his piece to start. He felt like a gladiator about to die in the imperial arena or like a fish in a fry pan. Over the throbbing strains of Tchaikovsky, a little ditty rang in his ears: "Tiny little fishie, fried little smelt, where's your smile from yesterday, remember how you felt?"

Then, with a bold, bleak declaration, Shostakovich's symphony began. He could not go back now.

Those in the hall who knew his music well (especially those who'd heard some version of the suppressed Fourth Symphony) recognized certain moods from his earlier work: the hints of some pensive character crushed and beaten by brutal marches — the orchestra warding off the blows . . . cruel, clumsy waltzes, like some Russian dancing bear willing to maul a partner . . . And perhaps most chilling of all, they recognized the moments after these assaults, when stillness arrives, and it does not feel like peace, but a stunned, appalled hush . . . as if someone, in the wake of a beating, first opens their eyes to a cold and crystalline new world in which they do not know how to feel.

But what surprised people in the symphony was a new discipline, a new sobriety, a clear use of antique forms to describe new anguish.

By the third movement, a slow lament, Shostakovich's friend Isaak Glikman looked around the hall and saw that the faces of the men and women around him were wet with tears. This was a song for all their dead.

Shostakovich later said,

> Even before the war, in Leningrad there probably wasn't a single family who hadn't lost someone, a father, a brother, or if not a relative, then a close friend. Everyone had someone to cry over, but you had to cry silently, under your blanket, so that no one would see. Everyone feared everyone else, and the sorrow oppressed and suffocated us.

This requiem allowed them to mourn together, in public. In this threnody, there are fragile solos, weak shoots or tendrils of a theme that might easily get crushed underfoot. The full string orchestra takes up those thin melodies and tries them, too, as if, after a great shock, they all are teaching themselves to feel again. They are learning to sing of their own sorrow.

The largo lament came finally, gently, to a last resting place, a resolution. And then, almost terrifying in their brutal joy, the drums and brass began to blast out the symphony's grand finale. It was a huge, lumbering celebration of some kind, thrilling in its explosive energy, its hymns of praise, its screaming triumph.

Some who listened thought that here was the hope they'd been looking for. This was a vision of future freedom without terror.

Others were uncertain. The joy seemed forced.

One thing that everyone agreed on, however, was the symphony's power. As the finale thundered toward its conclusion, members of the audience, in a trance, began to rise out of their seats one by one. "The music had a sort of electrical force," said one.

The last chord sounded.

"The whole audience leapt to their feet and erupted into wild applause—a demonstration of their outrage at all the hounding poor Mitya has been through," wrote Lyubov Shaporina in her diary that night. "Everyone kept saying the same thing: 'That was his answer, and it was a good one.' D. D. [Shostakovich] came out white as a sheet, biting his lips. I think he was close to tears."

Another audience member reported: "A thunderous ovation shook the columns of the white Philharmonic Hall, and Evgeny Mravinsky lifted the score above his head, so as to show that it was not he, the conductor, or the orchestra who deserved this storm of applause, these shouts of 'bravo'; the success belonged to the creator of this work."

The applause would not stop. The audience was practically hysterical.

The cheering went on without abating for half an hour. The authorities were worried it would turn into a demonstration. For the audience, this symphonic victory was not simply about Shostakovich—it was about them. Everyone in the hall that night was a survivor. Everyone there had suffered what the composer had suffered, each in his or her own way. They had just been given a chance to grieve—to mourn together all that had been lost.

Shostakovich was still stiffly bowing in front of the delighted mob. Two of his friends realized it might be a disaster if he were caught standing there when there was any trouble—a spontaneous protest, a riot, anything that might attract attention to him.

They whisked him away.

It appeared that, so long as the regime didn't intervene and arrest him, his symphony was a tremendous success.

The next day, a conductor and friend of the Shostakoviches, Alexander Gauk, who had been at the symphony's premiere, returned to Moscow.

Shostakovich with Evgeny Mravinsky, who conducted the world premiere performance of the Fifth Symphony

He overheard a conversation between two government officials. They were talking about the crowds at the premiere the night before. One — in charge of censoring and approving music — was saying that "it had been a put-up job" and that the audience had been stuffed with Shostakovich's friends.

Gauk interrupted. He said that he had also been at the concert. He pointed out that there had been twenty-five hundred people in attendance. He didn't think a few friends of Shostakovich had made that much difference.

Still, as the weeks went on, there was worry in high places about the crazed ovations the Fifth Symphony was getting all over the USSR. (After one performance, the whole audience demanded to send Shostakovich a congratulatory telegram en masse!) The chairman of the Composers' Union spoke out about the mania for the Fifth: "Unhealthy instances of agitation — even of psychosis to a certain extent — are taking place around this work. In our circumstances this might do both the work and its composer a bad turn." Eventually, the government's Committee for Artistic Affairs sent two representatives to see what the hullabaloo was all about.

After the performance, once again, the audience went wild. One of the officials stood silently. The other "made a constant stream of snide remarks, shouting to make himself heard over the noise in the hall: 'Just look, all the concert-goers have been hand-picked one by one. These are not normal concert-goers. The Symphony's success has been most scandalously fabricated.'"

They demanded a continuing investigation. The Leningrad District Party Committee observed a special performance of the piece to judge whether it was formalistic and secretly anti-people. The director of the Leningrad Philharmonic had to fill out forms about ticket sales and the piece's success. "And in the meantime," he said, "the symphony continued its life, and was widely performed, invariably exciting a lively and enthusiastic response from its audiences."

So what were people getting so excited about? What was this symphony *saying* to them?

We are still arguing about that a whole human lifetime later. Audiences are still trying to decipher the codes in Shostakovich's symphonies, trying to see under the masks he wore to the true face we expect to find beneath. "It's very difficult to speak through a mask," as the writer Viktor Shklovsky said, but "only a few can play themselves without it."

Was the symphony hopeful or tragic? Was the symphony a protest? Or was it exactly what Socialist Realism demanded: a work that ends in triumph, delighted in the faith that life is getting better, that life is getting merrier?

A couple of months after the Leningrad premiere, Shostakovich spoke up. He broke the long silence he had kept since "A Mess Instead of Music." He published several articles describing what the Fifth Symphony was "about." What could be clearer than that?

In an article called "My Creative Response," he laid out exactly what he'd been picturing while he wrote the symphony: "I saw man with all his sufferings as the central idea of the work. . . . The finale resolves the tragedy and tension of the earlier movements on a joyous, optimistic note." The article even implied that the symphony was perhaps about his own turmoil after being criticized by *Pravda*. It was about the spiritual victory when government criticism led him to repent of his doubts, his formalism, and his neurosis in favor of a new faith, a new hope. He wrote that of all the reviews, "one that particularly gratified me said that 'the Fifth Symphony is a Soviet artist's practical creative answer to just criticism.'"

This phrase—"a Soviet artist's practical creative answer to just criticism"—was repeated again and again when the symphony made its way across the oceans to America.

So there we are. Our answer.

Except we don't know if Shostakovich actually meant what he said in this article. We don't even know if it was by him. Especially later in his life, the regime would send Shostakovich articles already written and tell him just to sign his name at the bottom.

Soviet literature and cinema were full of stories of anti-people individu-
alists who, after healthy contact with the Communist cadres around them,
repent, join the masses, and are joyful. It was a trope, a cliché, a well-known
path. Shostakovich had just spent years writing film music for movies that
featured characters who went through precisely this transformation. So in
these articles, was Shostakovich just playing this familiar role? Putting on a
smiling mask to avoid government censorship?

Certainly, some of his friends believed this. "He described his music to
the Party as joyous and optimistic, and the entire pack dashed off, satisfied,"
said soprano Galina Vishnevskaya. "Yes, he had found a way to live and
create in that country. . . . But he learned to put on a mask he would wear for
the rest of his life."

Many in the audiences at the time did not think the finale was optimistic at all. For example, a writer who attended the premiere of the symphony
in Moscow wrote in his diary: "A work of astonishing strength. The third
movement is beautiful. But the ending does not sound like a resolution (still
less like a triumph or victory), but rather like a punishment or vengeance on
someone. A terrible emotional force, but a tragic force."

At a meeting of the Moscow Composers' Union in February 1938, one
critic complained that Shostakovich had failed in his symphony because of
the finale's sudden blast of hope. It "breaks in upon the symphony *from without,* like some terrible, shattering force." He was confused. The end was supposed to sound celebratory, but for some reason, it didn't. That bothered him.
"The general impression of this symphony's finale is not so much bright and
optimistic as it is severe and threatening."

The poet Pasternak, who had cautioned his friend Mandelstam for
speaking too openly, even in a whisper on the middle of a bridge, clearly
felt that the Fifth Symphony was about Stalin's purges and the Great Terror.
"Just think," he groused jealously. Shostakovich "went and said everything,
and no one did anything to him for it."

Many years later, when a young musicologist talked to Shostakovich about the finale, the composer supposedly said: "I think that it is clear to everyone what happens in the Fifth. The rejoicing is forced, created under threat. . . . It's as if someone were beating you with a stick and saying, 'Your business is rejoicing, your business is rejoicing,' and you rise, shaky, and go marching off, muttering, 'Our business is rejoicing, our business is rejoicing.' . . . You have to be a complete oaf not to hear that."

That seems very clear. This must be what he really meant.

But though the statement is very convincing, it is taken from a difficult source. In 1976, a young Soviet scholar, Solomon Volkov, emigrated to the West. He brought with him what he claimed were Shostakovich's memoirs. They were published under the name *Testimony: The Memoirs of Dmitri Shostakovich*. He claimed that he had interviewed Shostakovich, taken notes on everything that was said, and written it all out as a narrative. This new, bitter Shostakovich was very different from the one who appeared in Soviet newspapers.

The problem is, it is not clear that these are Shostakovich's memoirs at all. Solomon Volkov was never able to produce the notes from which he supposedly wrote down these stories. The most likely scenario is that Volkov just wrote things down largely from memory, trying to capture Shostakovich's style of speech and way of telling stories. That means that we never know if any particular detail from *Testimony* is accurate or not, if Shostakovich ever truly said it or not. So this passage, for example, about the finale of the Fifth: Is it Shostakovich? Or is it Solomon Volkov trying to make Shostakovich into a particular kind of hero? And even if these "memoirs" were totally accurate records of things the aging, dying composer said, can we understand them as the "true" Shostakovich? The composer at sixty was not the same as the composer at thirty. Would he tell the truth about himself? Or would he revise his own past?

Which Shostakovich do we believe? The early Shostakovich or the late Shostakovich?

We can trust no one. In a regime where words are watched, lies are rewarded, and silence is survival, there is no truth.

There is no way to write a biography of Shostakovich without relying on hearsay and relaying the memories of people who have many private reasons to fabricate, mislead, and revise.

So what about the finale of the Fifth Symphony? Optimistic or tragic?

No one would disagree that there is struggle in the last movement. At one point, the whole orchestral mechanism breaks down and shudders to a halt. The question instead is: Who wins that struggle? Does Shostakovich end by offering genuine hope?

Perhaps it became whatever the individual listener needed it to be. That's the miracle of music. For the Communist Party officials, it was the perfect Socialist Realist ending, ablaze in glory. But for those sitting there that night who had lost friends and family members and who still had been told that life was getting merrier — for those who had not been allowed to cry, because this, of course, was a time of victory — for them, the finale's brutal undertones were clearer. They heard the menacing growl: "Your business is rejoicing. Your business is rejoicing."

For them, this was the symphony's triumph, the reason they rose from their seats in captivated astonishment: Here, at last, was someone avowing this in public, shouting the thing they all had been wanting to say. And here he was, doing it in such a way that his tracks were covered. He was masked.

It meant different things to different people, but somehow it meant them all *intensely*. Shostakovich's words just confuse the issue. His symphony itself is what remains.

Listen to it.

It is your symphony to write with him.

Let us allow ourselves to be buoyed up by the hope some hear in the finale for a moment and allow Shostakovich to finish the 1930s in peace. Let's overlook the fact that the Great Terror still ground on. For the moment, let us say that Shostakovich seemed to be safe. Let's allow him some joy.

On May 10, 1938, Nina Shostakovich gave birth to their son, Maxim.

The couple loved their children desperately. Perhaps under the happy influence of family life, Shostakovich wrote a relaxed and youthful string quartet. He wrote to a friend, "I would call it 'spring-like.'" He started it the month Maxim was born — on Galina's second birthday.

He wrote a Sixth Symphony, which, though it began dark-hued and somber, ended in two fast, playful movements. Certainly, on the one hand, he found his plans for a new opera interrupted when the regime banned the libretto, the script. On the other hand, they granted him an award, the Red Banner of Labor, for his work in the movies.

In 1939, he was elected as a representative to the Leningrad City Council. Perhaps this was a way for him to give something back to the city of his birth. He was also teaching at the Leningrad Conservatory, where he had studied in the years following the Revolution. He had applied for a job there during his long silence after the suppression of the Fourth Symphony, explaining meekly that composing was "not working out."

He became a beloved teacher. Though his manner was distant and sometimes strange, he was kind and generous with his students. They were amazed at his prodigious memory. In the course of a class, he could sit down at a piano without any sheet music and play through not only, it seemed, 150 years' worth of works from the past, but also the music his students had recently written and showed him for critique. "No matter how many musicians approached him, whether they were from Central Asia or Russia or amateurs, he would always give them time and never criticized anyone," a student remembered. He may have been secretive about his criticisms, but those who knew him well could tell when he didn't like something: He would maintain "an eloquent silence" (as he had done during the "Mess Instead of Music" flap); he would blandly praise the high quality of the paper the student had written on; or he would disappear to smoke a cigarette. When he was able, he supported several of his students financially. Many of them became his lifelong friends.

Sometimes there were parties at his apartment. People would drink and jabber to one another while, in the background, Shostakovich banged out songs on the piano. Occasionally, they played drunk soccer in his living room.

Shostakovich still loved soccer. He thought about taking a course to become a referee. "He said the stadium was the only place you could express yourself openly. When a player scores, you can cheer, 'Hurray!' because you're happy, not because you're forced. You can't lie all the time!"

He bought season tickets and never missed a game. Once, when Nina was away, Shostakovich invited the whole Zenith team over to dinner. His friend Glikman came, too. They ate their grub, then they all sat around in Shostakovich's study. One of the players strummed a guitar while Shostakovich played the piano. According to Glikman, "When the last guest had departed, Shostakovich stretched out on the sofa with the air of a man who knows he has done a good day's work, and said: 'Well, now we've actually got to know some of our heroes. Up till now we've only been able to see them from far off at the top of the stands.'"

Shostakovich's family life was deeply important to him. He doted on his children. Galina now was a little girl with two blond braids, and tiny Maxim was a toddler. Their aunt Maria, Shostakovich's sister, had returned to Leningrad from exile in Central Asia. She now had a little boy, too. The effervescent Zoya had finally given up the arts altogether to become a veterinarian in distant Samarkand. Shostakovich would brag that he had a little sister who "could cure elephants."

The composer's daily schedule was extraordinarily regular. He got up at six in the morning and dressed in a suit. He liked formality of dress, though he and Nina didn't care much otherwise about clothing. (She often bought the same bolt of fabric for the whole family's outfits.) Dressed in his suit, Shostakovich would go into his study and begin to compose. He came out for meals at precisely nine a.m., two p.m., and seven p.m. His concentration was incredible. "If it isn't singing or shouting, noises don't affect him at all," Nina wrote. "The door of the room where he works is usually open, and often the children romp around in his room. Sometimes Galya [Galina]

Shostakovich with his children, Maxim and Galina

Shostakovich got up promptly at six each morning and dressed in a suit to compose.

The composer enjoying his favorite pastime: watching a soccer match. He was a fanatic, and once even signed up to train as a referee—a career path that unfortunately did not work out.

climbs onto his knees while he is composing, but in such cases she sits quietly." Young Galina knew not to touch her father's pens or add anything to his newly composed pieces.

When Shostakovich finished a piece, he would quietly pour himself a glass of rowanberry vodka and invite over a few colleagues. After the premieres of pieces, he would take everyone out to a restaurant.

As Maxim grew, it became clear that both he and his sister had a mischievous streak. They would stand under the window of one of their nation's other foremost composers, Sergei Prokofiev, and chant, "Sergei Sergeich, tra-tra-tra! Sergei Sergeich, tra-tra-tra!" until the master of Russian ballet started screaming, "I'll box your ears!" and hurled everything on his desk at them, including his paperweight.

Once, little Maxim thought it would be funny if he pretended he was dead. Galina hid in the bushes. When Maxim saw his parents coming along the road, he lay down on the tarmac next to his bicycle as if he had been hit by a car and killed.

The children could not understand why their parents were so angry.

Shostakovich loved his children, a friend said, "with a kind of abnormal, morbid love, and lived in constant fear that some misfortune would befall them."

The "Mess Instead of Music" crisis had left its mark on him. One of his dearest friends in later life, the soprano Galina Vishnevskaya, said, "The hatchet job done on him in that 1936 *Pravda* article had, like a public slap in the face, left an imprint on his whole life. He had reacted in an agonizing, physical way, as if his skin were searing from the brand that had been put on him."

Yet this time of trouble was in many ways the moment he reached his full maturity. Vishnevskaya claimed, "The Fifth Symphony was a turning point not only in his creative life but in his outlook as a Russian. He became the chronicler of our country; the history of Soviet Russia is nowhere better described than in his compositions."

In the descriptions that remain of him, he is often remembered for his kindness and generosity, for his gentleness, and for "the childlike, vulnerable smile." But perhaps he survived because there was another side to him.

When the writer Zoshchenko — a poker partner of the composer — was confronted by one of these descriptions, he responded sharply,

> It seemed to you that he is "frail, fragile, withdrawn, an infinitely direct, pure child." That is so. But if it were only so, then great art . . . would never be obtained. He is exactly what you say he is, plus something else — he is hard, acid, extremely intelligent, strong perhaps, despotic and not altogether good-natured (although cerebrally good-natured). . . .
>
> In him, there are great contradictions. In him, one quality obliterates the other. It is conflict in the highest degree. It is almost a catastrophe.

The Great Terror continued unabated. The loss is incalculable. Roughly eight million people had been arrested in the space of a few years. Around a million of them were shot; seven million more were sent to prison camps. Of those sent to the camps, about two million died in 1937 and 1938, the height of the Terror, from starvation, exposure, disease, and exhaustion. It was a full assault on the nation by its own government. It hit hardest many of the regions the Germans would attack a few years later.

Stalin's purges had begun in Leningrad. They were devastating. They were that city's first siege. Then, like an invasion, they had spread the length and width of the Soviet Union. They had hit the intelligentsia, the military, and the Communist Party itself particularly hard, just as the deaths and imprisonments during the Five-Year Plan of the early thirties had decimated the ranks of the peasantry.

How had Shostakovich avoided arrest? We don't know precisely, though it may have had something to do with his international celebrity. News of the Great Terror was leaked to the West, but Stalin made efforts to conceal its unimaginable scope. The disappearance of one of the USSR's most famous citizens would have made the global community suspicious. On the other hand, the NKVD was clearly collecting materials with an eye to building a case against the composer at some point. It may be that their attention was simply diverted by the onset of the Second World War in 1939.

Regardless, Shostakovich, like everyone who lived in the cities, felt the cold breath of the Great Terror daily for several years. As Nadezhda Mandelstam wrote, "Anybody who breathes the air of terror is doomed, even if nominally he manages to save his life. Everybody is a victim — not only those who die, but also all the killers, ideologists, accomplices and syco-phants who close their eyes or wash their hands — even if they are secretly consumed with remorse at night. Every section of the population has been through the terrible sickness caused by terror, and none has so far recovered, or become fit again for normal civic life." A whole society was traumatized and brutalized, trained up against compassion. Terror "is an illness that is passed on to the next generation, so that the sons pay for the sins of the fathers and perhaps only the grandchildren begin to get over it — or at least it takes on a different form with them."

To get away from it all in the spring of 1941, Dmitri and Nina Shostakovich went on vacation in the Crimea. Nina went hiking in the mountains. Her husband wandered around the volleyball courts, climbed up in the referee's chair, and began to score matches between the other guests.

Shostakovich was relaxed, or as relaxed as the twitchy man got. He had just received a Stalin Prize, First Class, for his new Piano Quintet.

Perhaps there, where the mountains met the sea, he actually felt joy.

It is a shame that, to the west, Hitler had turned his malevolent gaze on the Soviet Union. He believed the Russians were an inferior race, and more-over, he knew that their own leader had just spent six years systematically destroying their armed forces, their industry, and their economy.

And so, on a summer night when the sun never went down, Adolf Hitler launched a surprise attack on Russia, and the second siege of Leningrad began.

PART ★ TWO

Adolf Hitler surveys military plans in August 1941, shortly after his invasion of Russia.

FRIENDSHIP

For years, as Stalin rose and waged war upon his own citizens, to the west of him, in Germany, Adolf Hitler, also rising to power, watched him carefully, planning future invasion.

Hitler believed in the absolute biological superiority of the German people, the brightest and boldest descendants of the ancient Aryan race. In his writing and in the speeches he bellowed out to crowds of thousands, he demanded that the Germans seize their birthright back from "weaker" races such as the Jews and the Slavs. (Recent DNA tests suggest that he probably was not pure Aryan himself and likely had Jewish blood in his ancestry.) He made no secret of the fact that one day he planned to invade the Slavic nations — central and eastern Europe as well as Russia. These regions would be cleared of their supposedly subhuman peoples, after which the Germans could seize upon their fields and forests for *Lebensraum* — "room to live." Hitler declared: "We National Socialists [Nazis] must hold unflinchingly to our aim in foreign policy, namely, to secure for the German people the land and soil to which they are entitled on this earth."

Despite the fact that Hitler and Stalin both called themselves socialists, Hitler's Nazi Fascism and Stalin's Soviet Communism were, in many ways, natural political enemies. Communism was an extreme left-wing ideology; Fascism was an extreme right-wing ideology. In the late 1930s, as Stalin's secret police hunted down and murdered supposed Fascist spies for crimes they didn't commit, Hitler's secret police executed Communists he claimed were trying to overthrow his regime in Germany.

The citizens of the USSR were trained to hate the Nazis. During the show trials of the Great Terror, broken prisoners testified that monstrous conspiracies of German sympathizers were striving to undermine the Russian state. Soviet cartoons depicted Germans as brutes in horned helmets. As Nazi policy toward the Jews became ever more destructive, the Soviet intelligentsia looked toward Germany in growing horror.

There was one important exception, however: after Hitler secretly sent death squads to assassinate all his rivals in the Nazi Party — a bloodbath known as the Night of Long Knives — Stalin couldn't help but admire his enemy's ingenuity. "Did you hear what happened in Germany?" he gushed to an adviser. "Some fellow, that Hitler! Splendid! That's a deed of some skill!"

Despite their ideological differences, after all, Hitler and Stalin had one thing in common: despotic totalitarianism. As fellow dictator Benito Mussolini defined it, totalitarianism meant "Everything within the state, nothing outside the state, nothing against the state." This attitude was something these very different governments shared. In this way, Communism, moving to the left, and Fascism, on the other hand, moving to the right, met like fists behind the back and clutched each other there, where none could see.

In spite of Stalin's boyish enthusiasm for Hitler's gift at massacre, he was afraid of German imperial intentions. Hitler was on the move. The Soviets — like the western Europeans — watched with fear as Hitler calmly and ruthlessly seized Austria in 1938 and Czechoslovakia in early 1939. Stalin could not ignore the fact that Germany was eating away at the nations that lay between Hitler's new Reich and the Soviet Union. Soon, the two sworn enemies would stand face-to-face. There would be no fat to cushion the scraping of bone against bone.

In March of 1939, as the Great Terror began to grind to a halt, Stalin and his advisers started to ask how they would protect the USSR in the case of a German attack. They had decimated their own army. They had gutted their own economy.

They looked to western Europe. Cautiously, Stalin suggested to the French and the English that perhaps the three nations should form a triple alliance against Germany in case of further Nazi aggression. The English and French held back. Though few outside the USSR understood the full brutality of Stalin's regime, they did not trust him. He waited, exasperated, while weeks went by with no reply. When a reply did come, the English merely said that perhaps they would think about an alliance, in due time.

Behind closed doors, Stalin and his Politburo began to consider the unthinkable: making an alliance with Germany instead.

The Russian public was worried. Shostakovich's Leningrad neighbor Lyubov Shaporina wrote in her diary about her dread of "little Hitler striding across Europe like Gulliver over the Lilliputians." She wrote in awed horror,

> He doesn't even do battle, he just strides along, driven along by the sheer force of his iron will, before which everyone gives way. Like the waves of the Red Sea before Moses. What next? . . . If you follow it to its logical conclusion, the moment of the most monstrous treachery in the world is at hand.
>
> The stage is set.
>
> And how terrible that it has befallen our poor generation to bear witness to it all.

In the summer of 1939, Stalin met with representatives from both Germany and England to decide whom to support. His patience with England and

France was wearing thin. They had delayed giving him a firm answer for months. When England finally sent a representative to Moscow, they sent the man by ship rather than plane: they were clearly in no hurry to begin talks. As if to underline the fact that they did not take the meeting with Stalin seriously, they delivered a representative with no power to actually negotiate a treaty and no important role in the British government: an obscure military nobleman by the unpromising name of Admiral Sir Reginald Aylmer Ranfurly Plunkett-Ernle-Erle-Drax.[*]

Stalin, looking at the credentials of the English admiral and the French representative, General Joseph Doumenc, growled, "They're not being serious. These people can't have the proper authority. London and Paris are playing poker again."

Molotov, the minister of foreign affairs, cautioned him, "Still the talks should go ahead."

"Well, if they must, they must."

There was a frosty meeting between the murderous Politburo and the hapless Admiral Sir Reginald Aylmer Ranfurly Plunkett-Ernle-Erle-Drax. The admiral drawled through the list of his titles and honors. Though he had no power to negotiate, he was, he explained, a Knight of the Order of the Bath. The Russian translator, bewildered, reported that the Englishman had apparently just said he was of the Order of the Bathtub.

Marshal Kliment Voroshilov, who had sat by while Tukhachevsky was killed, interrupted. Incredulous, he said, "Bathtub?"

While the ice-eyed Communists stared him down, Admiral Plunkett gabbled a cute fairy tale about how in days of old, English knights had slain dragons and rescued maidens in distress and had then gone back to the royal palace for a soothing bath. This, he said, was the origin of the title.

It was not, perhaps, the right fable to impress a group of men who had

---

[*]Plunkett-Ernle-Erle-Drax was, incidentally, the younger brother of the early fantasy writer Lord Dunsany. Admiral Plunkett himself was an author as well. He had written a pamphlet called *Handbook on Solar Heating.*

ordered their own monarch and his family to be dragged into a basement and shot, stabbed, incinerated with acid, and thrown into a mine shaft.

The talks ended inconclusively.

About a week later, the Germans sent their own representative to woo Stalin. They did not send some obscure functionary but one of Hitler's right-hand men, Foreign Minister Joachim von Ribbentrop. He and his thirty-two assistants landed in two gleaming Fw 200 Condors. He strode from his plane in a leather coat, flanked by swastika banners while an orchestra played "Deutschland Über Alles" ("Germany Above All"). This was to be a very different visit.

Stalin probably did not believe that a treaty with Hitler would last for-ever. He believed, however, that if war did break out, he might be able to buy himself a few years to prepare his armies while Germany exhausted itself in battle with England, the Low Countries, Scandinavia, and France. While sitting at a banquet, he explained to his advisers, "Of course it's all a game to see who can fool whom. I know what Hitler's up to. He thinks he's outsmarted me but actually it's I who tricked him."

And so, astonishingly, a day after Ribbentrop landed in his silver plane, sworn enemies Nazi Germany and the USSR signed a nonaggression treaty known as the Molotov-Ribbentrop Pact, after the two foreign ministers who negotiated it.

In the portions of the treaty that they made public, the two governments agreed not to go to war with each other and to increase trade with each other. Germany would sell equipment to Russia, and Russia would sell Germany coal, oil, and grain.

As historians have pointed out, there was some irony to this agreement. Hitler wanted to attack and subdue Russia as well as Europe. He knew that Germany could not wage war on a global scale with its small reserves of raw materials such as oil, rubber, and grain. Hitler arranged for the Russians to furnish him with everything he would need to invade Russia. Stalin essen-tially agreed to supply the attack on his own country.

There was a secret portion of the Molotov-Ribbentrop Pact, too. In it, the two foreign ministers carved up Poland and the Baltic nations into two "spheres of influence." They each had the right to invade certain territories without the other interfering.

So, to the shock of the world, on August 23, 1939, Communism and Fascism shook hands. As one astonished English politician observed, "All the isms have become wasms."

Nine days later, free now to attack, Hitler invaded Poland.

This obliged Britain and France to take up arms in Poland's cause.

The Second World War had begun.

The citizens of the Soviet Union were shocked at the new alliance with Germany. Suddenly, the Soviet government, which had put citizens to death for collaboration with the Nazis, was warning people not to criticize the Nazis on pain of imprisonment.

To use one example from Shostakovich's own circle: The film director Sergei Eisenstein and the composer Sergei Prokofiev had just created their masterpiece *Alexander Nevsky*, a movie about a medieval Russian hero destroying an army of barbarian German knights in an epic battle on the ice of a frozen lake. It had been filmed at great expense the previous summer. Red Army soldiers had been hired as extras, dressed up in armor, and had assaulted one another in an icy wasteland that was in fact made of crumbled asphalt and white sand, sizzling with heat in the sun. Stalin had loved the movie when it came out in the last days of 1938 — applauding its pro-Russian, anti-German sentiments — and it quickly became a Soviet favorite. Schoolchildren sang its choruses.

That was 1938, however. In 1939, the Germans became allies — and the movie, with its invading hordes of horned Teutonic Knights, was withdrawn from circulation.

It would reappear later, and for good reason.

Over the next year, the world watched in horror as Hitler swept across Europe. Pleas for peace did nothing to stop the invasions, the slaughters, the destruction of cities. The German army struck so rapidly and mercilessly that its assault tactics came to be called *Blitzkrieg* ("Lightning War"). The republics that surrounded Germany were astonished at the combination of mechanized accuracy and homicidal fury. One by one, with terrible swiftness and at terrible cost, nations fell: Poland, Denmark, Holland, Norway, and Belgium.

In June of 1940, France collapsed. The Nazis paraded in victory through Paris. "The war machine rolled down the Champs Elysées: gleaming horses, tanks, machinery, guns and thousands upon thousands of soldiers," wrote an eyewitness. "The procession was immaculate, shining and seemingly endless . . . like a gigantic green snake that wound itself around the heart of the broken city, which waited pathetically to be swallowed up."

The news of France's fall hit the Russian leadership hard. Stalin had hoped that the French and the Germans would exhaust each other through years of warfare. Instead, France had fallen in little more than a month.

Statesman Nikita Khrushchev later recalled, "Stalin was in a great agitation, very nervous. I had seldom seen him in such a state. As a rule he seldom sat in a chair during meetings, usually he kept walking. On this occasion he was literally running around the room, swearing terribly. He cursed the French. . . . 'How come they allowed Hitler to thrash them?'"

But at the same time, Stalin, like an eager pupil, had used the Soviet-German nonaggression pact to invade several of his smaller neighbors — eastern Poland, Latvia, Estonia, Lithuania, and Finland — and enforce his will over them. The citizens of the USSR were apparently somewhat bewildered by this. On the streets, they were asking, "Are we at war; with whom and why?" "What has gone wrong with the neutrality pact signed with the express purpose of keeping us from war?" Of course, Stalin had a different idea of the pact.

Stalin justified his invasion of Finland with the claim that he needed to keep Leningrad safe. (Leningrad was just across the border from Finland.) This brief "Winter War" proved to be a disaster. Though the Russians technically won, the world watched as the Red Army suffered losses in the

Hitler tours his newest acquisition, the city of Paris, on June 23, 1940, the day after the invading Germans forced the French to sign a humiliating armistice. Exactly a year to the day after the French capitulated, Hitler would stage his massive invasion of the USSR.

Everyone appears to be relieved after the signing of the Molotov-Ribbentrop Pact. Flanked by German foreign minister Joachim von Ribbentrop on the far left and Soviet foreign minister Vyacheslav Molotov on the far right, Stalin stands, grinning, in the middle.

snowy woods at the hands of a few proud Finns on skis, their artillery pulled by reindeer. The incompetence of the Russian military was visible to everyone. They had, after all, lost most of their best officers in the Great Terror.

Hitler watched this episode with particular interest. He decided that it was time to start planning his invasion of Russia.

His plan for invasion was called Operation Barbarossa. It was named after a medieval German emperor, Frederick Barbarossa, who, according to legend, would rise from an aeon-long sleep beneath a mountain to reclaim his empire.

"The Führer estimates the operation will take four months," wrote Hitler's minister of propaganda, Joseph Goebbels. "I reckon fewer. Bolshevism will collapse like a pack of cards."

Invasions of Russia had failed in the past due to the harshness of the northern Russian winter. Hitler therefore decided that he would launch his attack in early summer 1941. By the winter months, he calculated, the USSR would have fallen. Moscow would be flooded and turned into a reservoir. Germans would settle Ukraine and farm there. The Slavs would be slaves.*

At dinners, he boasted about his future conquests over the Russian "subhumans." He spoke warmly of the way the United States government had exterminated so many of the Native Americans in the nineteenth century, seizing and settling their land. He hoped to do the same in Russia. He called the coming assault on the Soviet Union a *Vernichtungskrieg*—a war of total annihilation. Whole races of people (as he understood them) were about to be wiped out entirely. Nazi leader Heinrich Himmler told friends at a weekend party, "The purpose of the Russian campaign is to decimate the Slavic population by thirty millions." (In the end, they would not fall far short of this goal: the war would claim twenty-seven million Soviet lives.)

---

*Hitler frequently played on this pun in his dinner conversation: "The Slavs are a mass of born slaves," he'd say with a snort. In fact, the pun is no accident: the words are related, based on an ancient enslavement of southern Slavic peoples.

German newspapers began to run sections of Hitler's book, *Mein Kampf,* which talked about the country's need for *Lebensraum* in the Slavic lands to the east.

On New Year's Eve, 1940, Hitler sent a friendly holiday greeting to Stalin. He mentioned in passing that some funny rumors were circulating that Germany was going to invade the USSR. Of course, he said, these rumors were all started by the English, whose cities Hitler was bombing, and they were just designed to stir up trouble between Russia and Germany. "On the basis of information in my possession," he wrote, "I predict that as our invasion of the [British] Isles draws closer, the intensity of such rumors will increase and fabricated documents will perhaps be added to them." Thus he soothed Stalin and said the Russians should pay no attention to any of these misleading documents, these concocted rumors.

No need to worry at all.

Happy New Year.

Secret reports from pro-Soviet spies all over the globe began to pour into Moscow suggesting Hitler was preparing to break the truce and strike at the Soviet Union.

"Zeus" in Bulgaria warned of German motorized divisions gathering at the Soviet border. "Dora" in Zurich and "Extern" in Helsinki wrote to tell Stalin that invasion plans had been finalized. "ABC" in Bucharest predicted the attack would come in June. "Mars" in Budapest and "Ramzai" in Tokyo both pinned down the date of attack: June 15, 1941.

Stalin didn't believe any of them.

Ramzai wrote again from Tokyo to correct the date of the coming invasion: Operation Barbarossa would be launched on June 22. Stalin scoffed, "There's this bastard who's set up factories and brothels in Japan and even deigned to report the date of the German attack as 22 June. Are you suggesting I should believe him too?"

Ramzai's information — all of which was excellent — was stuffed into the "folder of dubious and misleading reports."

EUROPE ON THE EVE OF OPERATION BARBAROSSA, JUNE 1941

By the summer of 1941, Germany and its allies, known as the Axis powers, had conquered most of Europe. Further, as part of the nonaggression pact between Germany and the USSR, Poland had been divided between them—with western Poland swallowed by Germany and dubbed the General Government and eastern Poland broken up into several pieces and absorbed into the Soviet Union. The USSR had also annexed Estonia, Latvia, and Lithuania. Now nothing lay between the Soviets and Germany. At this point, Hitler turned his eyes to the east and prepared for invasion.

Stalin ignored the warnings; instead, eager to please Hitler, he stepped up the shipment of raw materials to Germany. Express trains rumbled across the Russian borders carrying record deliveries of copper, tin, rubber, oil, cotton, and grain to the Nazis.

Several loosely connected circles of spies in Germany — the so-called Red Orchestra — had infiltrated Nazi high command. They warned Moscow that the German air force was readying reconnaissance flights over the USSR. They sent concrete evidence that Hitler was ready to discard the Molotov-Ribbentrop Pact. Full plans had already been drawn up for the occupation of the USSR, complete with high-speed roads to link Berlin with fortified garrison cities and new German imperial palaces throughout the former Soviet republics.

People risked their lives to broadcast these reports to the Soviet government. In the end, most members of the Red Orchestra were caught and killed.

Stalin didn't believe a word of their reports. "This is not a 'source' but a disinformer," he wrote on one communiqué, and followed it up with a rude comment about what the spy could do to his own mother.

Winston Churchill, England's prime minister, sent more information on the German plan of attack. It was ignored. The Red Orchestra spies feared their messages were not getting through to Stalin. They got word of the coming invasion to the Americans, who passed it on to the Soviet ambassador in Washington, D.C. The Soviet ambassador immediately picked up the phone and called the Germans to warn them about the awful rumors the Americans were spreading about them.

German minister of propaganda Joseph Goebbels gloated in his diary, "Stalin and his people remain inactive, like a rabbit confronted with a snake."

Stalin feared Hitler, but unfortunately, he also admired him. He did not believe Hitler was going to break his word — or at least not yet. Historians have struggled to understand how Stalin could have been so easily duped. It is likely that he thought that Hitler, who was already engaged in the Battle of Britain to the west, would not open up another battle front to the east—a move that would bleed German strength in two directions. Furthermore, Stalin was entertaining the idea of his own attack on Germany, perhaps to be launched in 1943. He knew that the Red Army was not yet ready to engage the might of the German war machine, the Wehrmacht. After all, Stalin had just purged the military in the wake of the Tukhachevsky trial. As a result, 70 percent of the higher-ranking officers in the armed forces had been in command for less than two years. Stalin knew that they needed to learn and to prepare. In a sense, he *needed* to believe that he had bought Russia time.

But also, it appears that there was some peculiar rivalry, some obscure schoolboy bully mentality, that led Stalin to at once envy Hitler, and wish to impress him, and wish to defeat him, and yet believe in some brotherhood of dictatorship.

As the writer Alexander Solzhenitsyn observed, "Not to trust anybody was very typical of Josef Stalin. All the years of his life did he trust one man only, and that was Adolf Hitler"—the twentieth century's most notorious genocidal liar.

In May 1941, Shostakovich and his family went on vacation to a cottage on the Gulf of Finland. It got them out of the heat of Leningrad. It was a particularly sweltering summer. During the week, Shostakovich went back to their city apartment to wrap up the term at the Leningrad Conservatory. On the weekends, he took the train up to see Nina and the children.

Though he did not know it, German reconnaissance planes were flying daily over the borders into Soviet airspace and taking pictures of all the routes to Leningrad and the other major Russian cities. In May and early June, ninety-one Nazi planes buzzed over Russian territory.

When questioned, the Germans simply purred that these flights were designed to look for forgotten war graves from World War I. Russian military command didn't believe a word of this. The Soviet defense minister,

Semyon Timoshenko, and General Georgi Zhukov of the Red Army confronted Stalin. Timoshenko said, "Zhukov and I think we should start shooting the German planes down."

Stalin tried to calm them. Nothing was wrong, he said. "The German ambassador has explained that their air force has too many youngsters who are not well trained yet. Young pilots can easily lose their way. The ambassador has asked us to ignore the wandering planes."

Zhukov and Timoshenko pointed out that these bewildered young pilots were flying slowly over military bases.

Stalin replied that Hitler should be told immediately. "I am not sure he knows about that."

One of the Nazi planes had to perform an emergency landing while on a recon mission. The pilots were temporarily taken into custody. Red Army soldiers searched the aircraft and discovered high-power cameras. The film negatives showed images of bridges and railroads. The soldiers scrambled to get word to Soviet high command.

Moscow ordered the soldiers to let the Nazi pilots go free.

Reports were coming in from several locations that tanks and transports were gathering at the borders. Soldiers on guard duty heard the constant grinding of machinery in the woods.

Hitler reassured the Russian ambassador, "Please do not worry when you hear about the concentration of our troops in Poland. They are going there for massive training before major strikes in the West" against England.

On June 11, the NKVD discovered a hidden telephone cable snaking underneath a river at the border. Apparently, the Nazis had been listening in on Red Army phone conversations.

On June 13, Ramzai—the Soviet spy in Tokyo—tried again to warn Stalin of the coming attack. "I repeat: Nine armies with the strength of 150 divisions will begin an offensive at dawn on June 22."

At the same time, German ships began to disappear from Soviet ports.

Some turned around without even picking up their cargos. By June 16, there were no German ships left in Soviet waters.

On June 21, the secret police reported thirty-nine German reconnaissance flights over Soviet territory. The commander of the Soviet Third Army reported that the Germans were pulling out the barbed-wire fences on their side of the border. The officer he spoke to calmed his fears: "Believe me, Moscow knows the military and political situation and the state of our relations with Germany better than we do."

A vast army of Germans, Croats, Finns, Romanians, Hungarians, Italians, and Spaniards was assembling all along the thousand-mile western border of the USSR from the Gulf of Finland in the north to the Black Sea in the south. It included 146 army divisions, about four million Axis troops. Some 3,600 tanks and 2,700 airplanes prepared for assault.

That evening, a Nazi soldier defected and swam across a river at the border. He staggered into a Red Army border encampment and warned the troops there of the coming catastrophe.

Moscow ordered him put to death for his pains. He was killed as a "deserter-informant."

Stalin, pacing in the Kremlin, worried that Hitler was trying to provoke him somehow. Stalin refused to be drawn in. Lavrentii Beria, the fawning head of the secret police, reminded him of "your wise prophecy: Hitler will not attack us in 1941."

Stalin, hedging his bets, demanded that a confusing order be sent out: troops should be on the alert, but they should not allow the Germans to "provoke an incident."

What did that mean? Should troops return fire or not? No one knew. Commanders were perfectly aware of one thing, however: if they prepared for an attack when Stalin said there would be no attack, they could be tried for treason and shot; on the other hand, if there was a surprise attack and they weren't prepared, they could be tried for incompetence and shot.

Regardless, many did not even receive Stalin's bewildering command.

At midnight, German commandos had slipped across the border and snipped the telephone and telegraph wires hanging on gaunt poles throughout the western marches. Many troops, therefore, had no way to communicate with headquarters.

Meanwhile, Hitler sealed a letter to fellow Fascist dictator Benito Mussolini of Italy, informing "il Duce" of his motives in invading the USSR. Hitler wrote, "Since I struggled through to this decision, I again feel spiritually free. The partnership with the Soviet Union . . . was . . . often very irksome to me, for in some way or other it seemed to me to be a break with my whole origin, my concepts, and my former obligations. I am happy now to be relieved of these mental agonies."

Stalin's mental agonies were just beginning. In the early hours of June 22, the summer solstice, the longest day of the year, he nervously decided that no invasion was going to happen. He retired to his quarters.

General Zhukov and Defense Minister Timoshenko were not so certain. They decided to stay the night in Timoshenko's office at the People's Commissariat of Defense. They sat down and waited.

At three thirty in the morning, Stalin went to bed.

At about the same time, German border guards near Kolden called out to the Red Army soldiers on the other side of the Bug River and asked them to walk over so they could "discuss important matters."

As the Russian soldiers crossed the bridge, they were gunned down in cold blood.

Stalin may have slept fitfully; he may have lain awake, staring at the ceiling.

In either case, half an hour after he went to bed, out in the hot night, orders were shouted and Nazi soldiers waved tank armies across bridges and over fields. Swarms of planes sped eastward in formation.

In the dark of the morning of June 22, 1941, the largest invasion force ever assembled in European history poured across the border into the Soviet Union, and the unthinkable cataclysm began.

In the opening days of Operation Barbarossa, Stuka dive-bombers streak over Soviet territory, making their own grim music of invasion with screaming "Jericho horns" attached to their wings, designed to terrify victims below.

BARBAROSSA

In late June, the sun barely sets in Leningrad. This city of palaces, courtyards, and canals is so far to the north that midsummer is almost a continual day, while in midwinter, there is long, gloomy darkness, lit only by a few scant hours of light.

In the "White Nights"—these sunny summer evenings so bright that the skin burns even at eight—the city celebrates. There are concerts and shows. The bars are full and loud. People walk the boulevards and chase one another across the bridges. Couples stroll through the parks. They sit on the stone embankments and watch the unset sun linger over the Neva River.

In the midst of this festival atmosphere, Dmitri Shostakovich had clear plans for the day of June 22. He was scheduled to administer a few final exams at the Conservatory, and then he and his friend Isaak Glikman were going to a tasty soccer doubleheader (Dynamo and Zenith) followed by dinner.

Just after the quick slip of night, however, as the sky turned pink again, eighteen Ju 88 bombers with German crosses on their wings and swastikas on their tails buzzed into view above the Gulf of Finland. They were headed for the nearby naval base at the port town of Kronstadt.

Soviet antiaircraft gunners watched them approach. The planes were still over the water, however, when they began dropping their payloads: magnetic mines that would attach to ships' hulls and blow them apart. The mines splashed into the sea.

The Russian gunners did not know what to do. They were not officially at war. They held their fire. The German bombers wheeled and flew on.

Out in the bay, on a Russian pleasure ship, a band played and young men and women danced to greet the solstice sunrise.

At the same time, up and down the whole Soviet border, the German air force (the Luftwaffe) began to bomb cities and airfields. Kiev, Sevastopol, Rovno, Lvov, Zhitomir — all of them woke to blasts and detonations. The world was on fire.

The Kremlin was swamped with reports of sudden attacks. Outraged and unbelieving, Georgi Malenkov, one of the most senior Communist Party leaders, called Sevastopol's military headquarters and demanded to know what was going on. An admiral confirmed reports: "Yes, yes. We are being bombed." As he spoke, Malenkov heard a huge blast over the phone. The admiral blurted, "Just now a bomb exploded quite close to staff headquarters!" Planes streaked by above him.

The Luftwaffe was unopposed in the air. The Soviet air force didn't have time to scramble. Their planes were still lined up neatly on their airfields, uncamouflaged, parked wingtip to wingtip. Within a few short minutes of Operation Barbarossa's official launch, 738 Soviet aircraft had been destroyed without ever leaving the ground. Within a few hours, the Luftwaffe had blasted apart twelve hundred Soviet aircraft. By noon on the first day of Operation Barbarossa, the Germans had destroyed more planes than they did in a whole year of their air assault on Britain. The Russian air force had been neutralized almost without firing a shot. The Western Front's air force commander, staggered at the overwhelming futility of the loss, took out his gun and killed himself.

All over the country, Red Army units desperately tried to get in touch with General Headquarters. Many found their lines were cut. Others found HQ skeptical. "We are being fired on!" one unit announced.

The only reply they got was "You must be insane. And why isn't your signal in code?"

At the Kremlin, General Zhukov and Comrade Timoshenko were frantic with worry as reports of bombings flooded in from the south and west. They did not want to be held responsible for the wrong decision and executed. They forced their subordinates to put their reports in writing and sign them — so that if anyone was accused of treason later, there would be a clear trail of evidence. This paralyzing fear of action was one of the fruits of Stalin's Terror.

Nonetheless, someone had to inform the Man of Steel that his country was under attack. General Zhukov called Stalin's country house.

NKVD general Nikolai Vlasik answered the phone, his voice gruff with sleep. "Who's calling?"

"Zhukov. Chief of Staff. Please connect me to Comrade Stalin. It's urgent."

"What? Right now? Comrade Stalin's sleeping."

"Wake him immediately. The Germans are bombing our cities."

Vlasik put down the phone and stumped off to wake the Leader.

Zhukov hung on impatiently. Minutes passed.

There was a rattle. Stalin was on the line. Zhukov reported that Soviet cities all along the western border were under attack. He asked permission to return fire.

Silence on the line. Stalin did not speak. Zhukov could only hear heavy breathing.

"Did you understand what I said?" he insisted. "Comrade Stalin?"

There was no sound but shocked breath.

Zhukov waited.

At last, Stalin spoke: "Where is the People's Commissar of Defense?"

"Talking to the Kiev Military District. I am asking for your permission to open fire to respond."

Stalin snapped, "Permission not granted. This is a German provocation. Do not open fire or the situation will escalate. Come to the Kremlin and summon the Politburo."

At 5:45 a.m., they met at the Kremlin. Stalin still believed it might be possible to avert war. He was pale and seemed uncertain of the world into which he had woken up. Though he held his trademark pipe in his hand, it was empty of tobacco.

Stalin insisted that the bombing raids might well be some turncoat German attempting to start a war with Russia without Hitler knowing. He was very clear on this point: Hitler must not have been informed about the attacks.

Timoshenko replied, "The Germans are bombing our cities in Ukraine, Belorussia, and the Baltics. This doesn't look like a provocation."

Stalin ordered, "Call the German Embassy immediately."

When Foreign Minister Molotov called the embassy, he discovered that the German ambassador was expecting his call and had an important announcement to deliver in person.

They met at Molotov's office. The German ambassador recently had provided assurances that nothing was wrong.

Now the ambassador announced that Germany and the USSR were officially in a state of war.

Comrade Molotov, representative of one of the most brutal regimes in history, could do nothing but stare at him, shocked, and then whine, "But what have we done to deserve this?"

In Leningrad, the day was blue and bright. Shostakovich was on the way to his Dynamo-Zenith doubleheader. It promised to be a fine afternoon.

Then the city's loudspeakers crackled to life. There was going to be an announcement by Comrade Molotov, commissar of foreign affairs.

"Men and women, citizens of the Soviet Union!" The commissar spoke

PLAN OF OPERATION BARBAROSSA

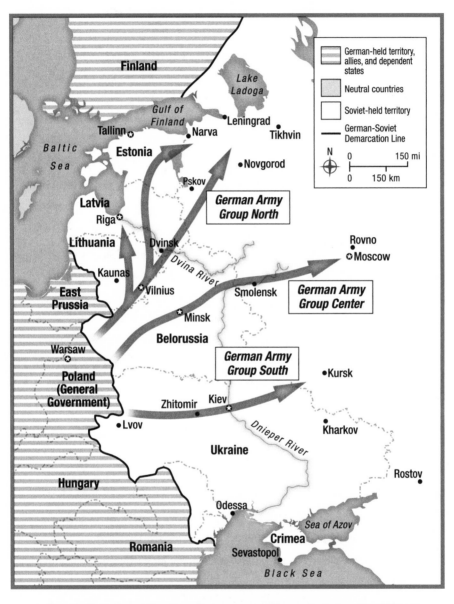

In Operation Barbarossa, Hitler planned to sweep across the new territories of the USSR and into the Soviet heartland. German Army Group South would seize the fertile, resource-rich lands of Ukraine. Army Group North would push for Leningrad. Army Group Center would drive straight for Moscow, the capital. On June 22, 1941, Operation Barbarossa was launched, and the largest invasion force ever assembled in Europe burst across the Soviet border.

anxiously, with a barely controlled stutter, as if he were out of breath. "At four a.m., and without declaration of war and without any claims being made on the Soviet Union, German troops have attacked our country, attacked our frontier in many places and bombed from the air Zhitomir, Kiev, Sevastopol, Kaunas and other cities." People around Leningrad listened, aghast, knowing that this same announcement was being heard throughout the nation. "The government calls upon you, men and women, citizens of the Soviet Union, to rally even more closely around the glorious Bolshevik Party, around the Soviet Government and our great leader, Comrade Stalin." He finished, "Our cause is just. The enemy will be crushed. Victory will be ours."

The announcement was over.

Chaos broke out in the streets. People charged out of their offices and homes. They called out news to one another. Soon the stores were mobbed with citizens buying emergency food. The avenues were full of hubbub.

Leningraders were so intent on responding to the Nazi threat that on that first day of the assault, a hundred thousand of them volunteered to take up arms. The city government was bewildered, at first, by what to do with this wave of spontaneous response.

Shostakovich immediately decided that he, too, would sign up for military service. He wanted to be useful somehow, in a real and concrete way. "Until now I have known only peaceful work," he wrote. "Now I am ready to take up arms. Only by fighting can we save humanity from destruction." He and one of his students, Venjamin Fleishman, set off to enlist together.

Why would Shostakovich sign up voluntarily to serve Stalin's regime? Why did so many Leningraders sign up? Why did the Soviet people in general fight so long and so hard to protect a government that many of them hated?

Stalin himself had clearly thought about this question and gave his frank answer to a Western diplomat: "The population would not fight for us communists, but it will fight for Mother Russia."

A writer who volunteered at the time remembered, "Very few families

People stop on the streets to listen to Foreign Minister Molotov's declaration of war against the Germans on June 22, 1941.

Volunteers crowd around to sign up for military service at the Sverdlov machine-tool plant.

Leningrad soldiers walk with their families to their departure points for the front.

had not suffered under Stalin. And we students never believed in those fabricated trials [of the Great Terror]. But you have to understand. . . . We thought that it was just Stalin overdoing things in eliminating his opponents, that all these reshuffles at the top would soon be over. And everyone understood that Stalin was one thing and the country was another."

As people all over Leningrad—all over the Soviet republics—responded to the call for help, they were doing so to protect their cities, their towns, their families. They knew their very existence was under threat. For many, it was also an opportunity to be part of something larger. This did not mean that there weren't those who, even on this first day of war, expressed the secret hope that the Nazis would overthrow the Communist regime. One Leningrad diarist, for example, wrote that the day after the launch of Operation Barbarossa, her landlady was in the courtyard, "sitting on a tall trunk and smiling sarcastically. She made no attempt to hide her hatred for the Soviet government and saw in this war and the eventual victory of the Germans the only possible salvation. In many respects, I share her views; but that smile irritates me."

There were as many different responses to the patriotic call as there were citizens. But for most, they wanted to protect their homeland. This meant, at least for the short term, that they had to fight for Stalin's regime.

Shostakovich and his pupil Fleishman made their way through the chaotic streets. In the *gastronomi*, or grocery stores, people were buying sacks of nonperishable foods, grabbing canned goods, and lugging boxes of them home. The lines stretched out into the streets.

The branches of the State Savings Bank were also mobbed by people clamoring to withdraw all their cash. By three o'clock, the banks were out of money—they had to close. Police detachments ushered out angry patrons shouting for service.

When Shostakovich and Fleishman got to one of the military recruitment centers, they must have found it mobbed. The lines trailed through the hallways, through the doors, and out onto the streets. It took hours, and for some, even days, to get to the desks at the front. "People were writing out applications as they stood in the corridors, on the staircases, by the windows, resting their papers on the sills."

When they got up to the front of the line, Fleishman was accepted. He had written most of an opera (*Rothschild's Violin*) under Shostakovich's tutelage. In the first days of July, he and thirty-one thousand other militia volunteers were called up as part of a new quasi-military force called the People's Volunteers. He put his opera aside unfinished, left his family, and went off to the front. He would never return.

Shostakovich was turned down by the People's Volunteers. An official told him, "You will be called when required." His poor eyesight may have been the reason they gave. It is likely, however, that his application was rejected because of his celebrity. The government wanted to make sure he remained safe.

There was a use for composers in wartime. The Communist regime believed deeply in the power of music—particularly singing—to stir people up and to raise morale. Song inspires bravery almost as well as vodka (which the government was also liberal in handing out). As one composer said, a song is "a mighty weapon which could strike the enemy."

On the first day of Operation Barbarossa, shortly after Molotov's announcement, some of the leading members of the Composers' Union were sitting in their Moscow headquarters, discussing what to do. They wanted to contribute somehow to the war effort—even those who were far too old to fight. They decided they would begin to write mass songs. They needed words, however. So they filed out of their club and headed for the Writers' Union.

If we are to believe the story, halfway there, in the middle of the street, they met the writers heading in the opposite direction. The members of the Writers' Union had been pondering lyrics and were looking for someone to set them to music. They had just been marching over to talk to the composers.

Thus began a national campaign to create rousing songs for the fighting masses (and to filter out the less successful songs, as hundreds were being written). Shostakovich would quickly become involved with this effort.

In this war — the Great Patriotic War, as the Russians still call it — everything and everyone, from farmers to watchmakers to cobblers to composers, would have to contribute to the life-or-death fight against the Nazi invader. As the slogan ran, *"Vse dlya fronta, vse dlya pobedi."*

"Everything for the front, everything for victory."

Red Army soldiers fight to defend their homeland.

THE APPROACH

In those first days of the invasion, the German army advanced on three fronts. Army Group South roared toward Ukraine, a fertile southern state where a lot of the USSR's natural resources were extracted. Army Group Center rolled directly east, toward Minsk, Smolensk, and — their final destination — Moscow itself. Army Group North was headed for Leningrad.

The Russian defensive forces scattered before them. The Soviets were simply not prepared. It didn't matter how valiantly Red Army soldiers stood up against the invaders: many infantrymen had been issued antique rifles from the First World War, and quite a lot of them hadn't been issued any ammunition. Many, therefore, had absolutely no way to return Nazi fire.

The Russian fighter planes and bombers that hadn't been destroyed sitting on their airfields in the first few hours of the war were generally terrible in battle. They were slow. They were easy targets. Most of the planes didn't have two-way radios, so they couldn't communicate with one another to coordinate attack, reconnaissance, or even just to stay in formation. Pilots could receive messages — through a crackling thicket of static — but they couldn't relay messages. This made recon difficult: in order to deliver a report, a plane had to fly all the way back to base. In any case, there was rarely enough fuel to keep them as active as they needed to be.

The Red Army's tanks were in no better situation. The Soviets had one excellent tank model: the T-34, which was strong, sturdy, and simply built. They didn't have many T-34s, however, and most of the rest of their tank fleet was antiquated. (They had about fourteen thousand tanks in all, but only about two thousand of them were modern and up-to-date.) They, like the planes, were perpetually short of fuel and ammunition. Moreover, as Tukhachevsky had complained, the Red Army's understanding of tank strategy was poor. Stalin and his ex-cavalry marshals did not trust tanks. Within the first few weeks of the war, the Red Army suffered the loss of roughly 90 percent of their tank strength.

The first days of this Great Patriotic War were a massacre. Cities were in flame. German bombers arrived in waves, releasing clutches of explosives and incendiaries. Terrified citizens waited for the Soviet air force to arrive, but no one came. People fled their homes forever. Tens of thousands of refugees clogged the roads. German fighters strafed them with machine-gun fire.

The whole of the Soviet Tenth Army simply disappeared somewhere near Bialystok. No one could reach them or find any trace.

German Army Group North was making sickening progress. On June 25, they took Kaunas, the capital of Lithuania (which had become a satellite state of the USSR only a year before). The Nazi SS arrived to "cleanse" the city. They ordered all the Jews to be rounded up. People were arrested in broad daylight. On June 26, a thousand Jews were beaten to death in a garage. The SS arranged for locals to perform the massacre. They thought it might look distasteful if they carried it out themselves.

Since the deed was performed by conscripted citizens of Kaunas, the Nazis could report it neatly as a "spontaneous self-cleansing action."

Even German Wehrmacht officers were appalled. The war machine, however, could not be stopped.

Their Panzer divisions were already a hundred miles deeper in Soviet territory, rumbling swiftly along the Kaunas-Leningrad highway. To proceed, they had to cross the Dvina River. For this, they had to capture the bridges at the town of Dvinsk. As the tanks approached Dvinsk, they slowed, and out of their midst drove four Soviet trucks. They had been captured and were now being driven by Russian-speaking Germans.

The trucks pulled ahead of the tank column. It was their job to make sure that the bridges in town were not blown up by the Russians as the tanks approached.

The four decoy trucks approached the Soviet checkpoints. The sentries gabbed with them: "Where are the Germans?"

"Oh—a long way back!"

The sentries waved the Nazi impostors through.

The trucks accelerated toward the Dvinsk Bridge. Soldiers ran out to stop them. The Germans in the trucks were ready and mowed them down. Within a few minutes, the impostors controlled the bridges.

Out beyond the sentry stations, the tank division heaved into view.

The Nazis had taken Dvinsk. Their Fourth Panzer Group rolled on past, over the rushing river Dvina, and headed toward Leningrad.

The ease with which they defeated Soviet forces initially gave the Germans a false sense of superiority. In a letter, a tank gunner crowed, "The war against these subhuman beings is almost over. . . . We really let them have it! They are scoundrels, the mere scum of the earth — and they are no match for the German soldier." He was to find that the war was hardly begun — and that the Slavs were made of sterner stuff.

Hitler issued an order that his soldiers did not need to worry about the usual rules of civilized warfare when fighting the Russian "subhumans": "The troops must be aware that in this battle, mercy or considerations of international law with regard to [the Slavs] are false. They are a danger to our own safety and to the rapid pacification of the conquered territories." His excuse was that the USSR had never ratified the Geneva Convention

Operation Barbarossa: A German soldier approaches a burning Soviet BT-7 light tank.

Soviet I-16 fighter planes soar in formation. By the beginning of the Second World War, they were technologically somewhat obsolete and were quickly destroyed in battle by the German Messerschmitts, which could fly over a hundred miles per hour faster.

Soviet I-16 fighters, destroyed on the ground in the first hours of the German invasion without even taking off.

articles. The troops were allowed to treat prisoners of war and enemy combatants however they pleased.

As the Fourth Panzer Group made its way northeast, the commander explained to his men:

> This war with Russia is a vital part of the German people's fight for existence. It is the old fight of German against Slav, the defense of European culture . . . and the repulse of Jewish Bolshevism. This war must have as its goal the destruction of today's Russia — and for that reason it must be conducted *with unheard-of harshness.* Every clash, from its conception to its execution, must be guided by an iron determination to annihilate the enemy completely and utterly. There is to be no mercy for the carriers of the current Russian-Bolshevik system.

They roared on toward Leningrad.

As the chaos bled east, Shostakovich, strangely, found himself spending several days wrapping up the school semester as he always did. He graded exams and made the arrangements for Conservatory students to graduate.

On June 27, Leningrad's city council announced that all able-bodied men and women had to contribute to the defense of the city. Factories, schools, and businesses had to register their workers and their students. Those with full-time jobs reported for three hours' civil defense work after hours. Others were sent out into the field for whole days, digging trenches and erecting barriers.

Shostakovich and his Conservatory colleagues were no exception. They did not make particularly effective ditchdiggers, Shostakovich remembered in his putative memoirs:

> I thought of Tukhachevsky when I dug trenches outside Leningrad in July '41. They sent us beyond the Forelli Hospital, divided

us into groups, and handed each of us a shovel. We were the Conservatory group. The musicians looked pathetic and worked, I might add, very badly. It was a hot July. One pianist came in a new suit. He delicately rolled up his trousers to his knees, revealing his spindly legs, which were soon covered with mud to the thigh. Another one—a highly respected music historian—kept setting aside his shovel every minute. He had arrived with a briefcase stuffed with books. Heading for a shady bush, he would pull out a thick volume from his briefcase.

Of course, everyone tried hard. So did I. But what kind of ditchdiggers were we? All this should have been done before. Much earlier and more professionally. It would have had more effect. The little that had been done earlier in terms of defense had been done under Tukhachevsky.

When Tukhachevsky insisted on increasing the number of planes and tanks, Stalin called him a harebrained schemer. But during the war, after the first crushing defeats, Stalin caught on. It was the same with rockets. Tukhachevsky began rocketry while in Leningrad. Stalin later had all the Leningrad rocketry experts shot, and then [during the war] they had to start from scratch.

When Shostakovich was not knee-deep in mud, hacking out a defensive fosse with a grim-faced task force of Chopin scholars, he was performing lighter war work: the creation of music for the troops. He wrote simple arrangements of songs and Classical pieces that could be performed by one of the small ensembles that drove between platoons, raising morale. He directed the music for satirical skits put on by the People's Volunteers and even wrote them a march tune, "The Fearless Regiments Are on the Move." Another song he wrote, the "Oath to the People's Commissar," became one of the most popular tunes of the war.

These musical efforts were important. The Soviets were fighting an enemy who considered Slavic culture to be inferior, even subhuman. The Nazis taunted the Russians by specifically defacing cultural monuments as if the nation's great thinkers, poets, and musicians had never mattered. They ransacked the house of writer Anton Chekhov and used Leo Tolstoy's manuscripts to light fires. They looted museums. When the Nazis captured the town where the great Russian composer Tchaikovsky had lived, they turned his house into a motorbike garage.

Shostakovich wrote in anger: "The Nazi barbarians seek to destroy the whole of Slavonic culture," but, he said defiantly, "Russian culture is immortal and never will the Nazis succeed in destroying it."

One of the purposes of the music troupes that played for the Red Army soldiers, the navy, the air force, and the Home Guard was to remind them of the power and legitimacy of their own culture, so slandered by the invading horde. In pursuit of this goal, Leningrad's musical corps staged an average of 160 concerts per month for citizens and soldiers.

Shostakovich did not just *write* music for these ensembles. On a couple of occasions, he went out to perform for the troops and raise morale himself. "I visited front-line units on two occasions and witnessed numerous instances of the courage that is typical of our people. Simple people, men you meet every day, turned out to be real heroes."

Elsewhere, however, those heroes, despite their sacrifices, were suffering terrible defeat.

On June 28, the Kremlin received word that Minsk, the capital of the western USSR, had fallen to the Germans. The Luftwaffe had bombed it from the air the first morning of Barbarossa. They had returned to bomb it again. Eighty percent of the buildings in the city had been reduced to rubble. By the time a Soviet relief force arrived, Minsk was an inferno. The air was thick with smoke, and, as one historian writes, "Even the parks were in flames."

For a few days, the Red Army held up against the city's invaders. The Nazis offered them generous terms for surrender, as long as the Soviet officers would murder the Communist Party members and Jews —

Stalin sits beneath a portrait of Karl Marx, the nineteenth-century political economist whose *Communist Manifesto*, urging the working class to rise up in the face of injustice, was one of the inspirations for the Russian Revolution.

the "commissars and kikes"—in their ranks themselves before they raised the white flag.

The Red Army stood strong for a few days. Eventually, they were overrun. The Nazis took four hundred thousand prisoners. They now controlled the capital of Belorussia, the westernmost of the Soviet states.

Stalin and his Politburo received this news heavily. Stalin looked hunted and angry at the same time. He demanded a solution from General Zhukov.

Zhukov proposed that the Red Army concentrate its forces in two concentric arcs in the middle of the country—to protect Moscow regardless of what happened. The only problem with the plan was that it would pull troops away from the north and south. Leningrad would be exposed.

Stalin was desperate. He agreed. Then, for the first time, he demanded the truth from his generals: How was the defense going overall?

They told him the truth at risk to their lives. His armies were hiding out in the woods. Teeming herds of refugees wandered the roads. Already, after only a few days of war, the German army had penetrated 350 miles into Soviet territory in the north, 150 miles in the south. Twenty million Soviet citizens were living in occupied territory, at the mercy of the Nazi Wehrmacht and the SS. This might be a war Stalin could not win. Finally, he understood that he had led his country into disaster.

Slowly, he walked out of the conference room. He left the building and went to his car. As he got in, he looked bleakly at the fortress towers of the Kremlin and muttered, "Everything's lost. I give up. Lenin founded our state and we crapped all over it."

He closed the door, and his driver pulled out.

It was at this point in the Great Patriotic War that Stalin disappeared. He would not answer the phone. He hid at his house and did not respond to questions.

The Soviet Union had no leader. No one knew what to do. And the Nazi terror drove onward.

Young snipers on a Leningrad rooftop keep watch over the Troitsky Bridge.

THE FIRST MOVEMENT

At about the time that Stalin retreated to his country house in despair, Shostakovich decided that he needed to take a more active part in the defense of the city. On July 2, he went again to try to enlist in the People's Volunteers. Once again, he was turned down.

His ditchdigging lasted for about a week; then he was reassigned to the Conservatory's rooftop fire-fighting squad. His family was still off at a cottage in the country, so Shostakovich moved into a barracks in the Conservatory so that he wouldn't have to cross the city each day to carry out his duties.

The Leningrad City Council had created about ten thousand special firefighting units posted on the roofs of apartments, factories, office buildings, warehouses, and theaters. Shostakovich's job as a rooftop firefighter was to watch for incendiary bombs during Luftwaffe air raids and to extinguish any that landed on the Conservatory before the blazing thermite could set the building on fire. He would have had to dive into the black smoke, drench the searing fragments with water, shovel sand furiously onto the bomb — or, if possible, lift the bomb with his spade and dump it into a tub of sand, which would boil with the heat.

As it happened, however, there were no Luftwaffe air raids during the month of July. Unlike cities to the south, Leningrad was not yet under attack from the sky. The Germans had destroyed all the Soviet runways to the west on the first day of the war. Now they had to pause and fix them so that they themselves could use them to launch attacks further into the Russian interior.

There were already air-raid drills, however, during which sirens would wail and a recorded voice would scream through the streets and the antiaircraft guns would begin their test-firing. Occasionally, a German plane flew over — but these were merely reconnaissance missions. Antiaircraft guns would blaze for a minute, and the enemy would disappear into the distance.

The rest of the time, Shostakovich stood on the hot metal roof, looking out at the trees of the parks, the dome of Saint Isaac's, the great gray arms of columned Kazan Cathedral, the spire of the Admiralty, and the blue onion-turrets of the Church of Saint Nicholas. From this height, the city must have looked serene.

In the streets, however, feverish preparation was taking place. At the foot of Kazan Cathedral, teens were employed digging bomb shelters. On break, they made a mud Hitler and hit him with shovels. Street signs were covered up, painted over, or taken down, to disorient Germans in case of invasion. Trolley-car drivers no longer announced the names of stops, and anyone foreign asking for directions was watched carefully.

The city's famed statues were heaped with sandbags to protect them in the case of bombing. In apartments all over the city, people crossed each individual pane of their windows with an X of tape to reduce shattering in the case of nearby blasts.

The military set up checkpoints throughout the streets and on the city's perimeter to control all entrance and egress. They laid out huge tangled asterisks of metal in the squares to stop the onrush of invading tanks and hid antiaircraft guns in remote quarters of the city's slums.

At the Hermitage Museum, once part of the palace of the tsars, hundreds worked to remove all the artwork so it could be shipped farther east, into the Ural Mountains, for safekeeping. Old Master paintings depicting half-remembered wars and nude nymphs bathing at the dawn of the world were taken out of their frames and rolled up in crates. Trains full of priceless paintings and Scythian gold headed off into the hills. In remote Sverdlovsk, the tsar's treasures were stowed in the same basement where he and his family had been murdered. What remained back at the Hermitage was a strange, haunting scene: marble corridors and galleries where empty frames hung on the walls, an exhibition of blankness, vacancy.

Out in the palace gardens, groundskeepers buried statues in the dirt. As *Justice* and *Peace* were entombed together, a workman wrote on one flank, "We'll come back for you." The grave was covered with leaves to conceal it.

Shostakovich wrote,

> It is with a feeling of admiration and pride that I watch the heroic deeds of Leningrad's people. Despite frequent air-raid alarms, everyone goes about his work with precision and efficiency. People are calm and life continues normally. Factories and offices successfully cope with the rush orders. Theaters are as active as ever and give the people that spiritual encouragement which helps them in their work at the front or rear. Everyone shares the common cause and strives for a common aim. . . . Even children are doing their bit to help strengthen Leningrad's defenses.

As the days went by, and Shostakovich stood watch on the roof, change in the city became more obvious from above. The golden spires now were painted a camouflage-gray. (The dazzling peak of the Admiralty had been climbed and then blotted out by a music teacher and Alpine mountaineering hobbyist named Olga Fersova.) Leningrad Communist Party Headquarters was swathed in camouflage netting and encircled with machine-gun nests and antiaircraft guns. Tarpaulins were draped over domes.

Workers rush to bury one of Leningrad's most famous monuments: Falconet's famous statue of Tsar Peter the Great, founder of the city, mounted on a horse, trampling the serpent of treachery. This landmark, a defining feature of the city center and the subject of one of Russia's most famous poems (Pushkin's "The Bronze Horseman"), could not be removed from its giant boulder base (the legendary Thunder Stone). Instead, the boulder was swamped in dirt. The horse and rider were packed in sandbags and surrounded by a wooden shell of planks. The statue made it through the bombardment and stands to this day, confronting the Neva River.

Antiaircraft guns fire in a park near Saint Isaac's Cathedral.

Then, like grazing beasts, barrage balloons (great lozenges and blimps) drifted up and took their places in the summer sky. Their hides glowed with sunset after the city below had fallen into twilight. As the breeze blew, they all turned slowly as if the herd regarded the approach of strangers.

Their cables were designed to catch the wings of bombers and hack them off or hurl the planes out of the air.

Shostakovich watched Leningrad prepare for an assault. No one knew, however, where the Germans were or when they would attack. There was no reliable word from Moscow.

For two days after Stalin retreated to his country house, the government stalled. No one would sign anything for fear of being blamed and executed when the Friend of the People returned from his hibernation.

At four in the afternoon on the second day of Stalin's absence, five of the most powerful men in the administration were gathered in the office of Foreign Minister Vyacheslav Molotov. They were panicked.

In low tones, they discussed how they were going to convince Stalin to return to the Kremlin. They were not sure that he would be ready. One of the men turned to Molotov and, probably without thinking, said, "Then you lead us, Vyacheslav! We will follow."

Five anxious minds turned over exactly what this meant. There were two ways it could be heard.

Was he just urging them all to get in their cars and go out to the suburbs to speak to the Chief?

Or was he suggesting that Molotov should rule? That Stalin should be toppled? Had he blurted out treason?

They waited to see who would speak next and what that person would say.

History might have taken a very different direction if someone had taken up the second meaning.

The head of the NKVD, however, the monstrous Lavrentii Beria, was one of the five in the room. He knew that if Stalin were discarded, he himself

Barrage balloons being carried past Saint Isaac's Cathedral in the heart of Leningrad (above) and down fashionable Nevsky Prospect (below)

would last only a few days before he was hunted down and killed, either legally or illegally. He chose to hear the comment as an invitation to go talk things over with the Leader.

He conducted them to their cars; they drove out to Stalin's house.

They found Stalin in his dining room, slumped in an armchair. He looked thin and weak. Molotov stepped forward. The others followed. Stalin asked the five, "Why have you come?" He looked fearful.

He seems to have expected an announcement of his arrest.

Molotov explained that they wanted to create a State Committee for Defense and put Stalin at the head of it.

Stalin seemed surprised. "Can I lead the country to final victory?"

Marshal Voroshilov said gallantly, "There is none more worthy."

Stalin agreed.

He returned to the Kremlin. He took up the reins of dictatorship again. A few days later, he accepted the title of supreme commander. Now he ruled with a sense that he had been called back from the brink.

That strange suburban afternoon was perhaps the closest Stalin ever came to being overthrown.

Now that he had returned, Stalin finally addressed the whole of his people on the radio. Previously, he had remained silent because he did not want to connect himself with defeat. Now he wanted to inspire victory. At six thirty in the morning, he spoke through loudspeakers throughout the nation:

> Comrades! Citizens!
> Brothers and sisters!
> Fighters in our army and navy!
> It is to you I appeal, my friends.

He had never before called his people his family. Now he listed all the nationalities that made up the USSR, calling on every one of them—from the deserts to the tundra—to take part. He warned that "whiners, cowards, deserters, and panic-mongers" would receive stiff punishment. Despite the fact that his Georgian accent made him somewhat difficult to understand on the radio — and despite the fact that he kept slugging back water in the middle of the speech and the gurgling also echoed nationwide — people were genuinely moved. He warned his citizens that this was not an ordinary war — but an eternal fight between Soviet freedom and German slavery.

"All the strength of the people must be used to smash the enemy! Onward to victory!"

The same day, Hitler announced that he would be holding a triumphal parade through the squares of Moscow by August.

It could not have been long into July when Shostakovich realized that his wife and children were in danger. Nina, Galina, and Maxim were up in their cottage near the new border of Finland. The Finnish army was on the move, trying to take back land they had recently lost during Stalin's "Winter War."

Wary of the risk, Shostakovich fetched his family. As Dmitri and Nina loaded suitcases into the car, Maxim and Galina watched them solemnly. Little Galina clutched a giant doll she'd just been given, certain that some-how it would be taken from her or left behind. She did not know what was happening, but she knew something was wrong.

They all drove back to the apartment in Leningrad. The summer was hot, however, and the city was sticky, which made the children miserable. The Shostakoviches may also have worried that Leningrad would soon be attacked by air, as the Luftwaffe had attacked so many other cities. It didn't seem safe. After a few days, the composer and his wife took the kids south to the town of Vyritsa. Shostakovich settled the family there for a few weeks and returned to the barracks in the Conservatory.

In hindsight, this doesn't seem like a wise decision. A German Panzer division had just taken the old medieval city of Pskov and was set to roll straight up the highway toward Leningrad. It would pass right by Vyritsa, which, as a town with a railway connection into Leningrad, would be an

Stalin at his country home: In this domestic scene, the Man of Steel works in the background with documents spread out on the table before him, while his daughter, Svetlana, snuggles on the lap of mass murderer Lavrentii Beria, later Stalin's head of the secret police.

obvious target. Shostakovich had placed his children directly in the path of the invasion force.

The Shostakoviches, however, almost certainly did not know the strategic lay of the land. All news of the fighting had to pass through the new Soviet Information Bureau (Sovinform), which often provided misinformation to Soviet citizens. Newspapers and radio announcements frequently didn't mention the names of towns or cities that were under attack. They didn't admit that the country was losing the war. When they did mention specific battles, there was often a delay of several days, so the information was stale. This made it almost impossible to tell where the front lines actually were.

For example, the Germans took Pskov on July 8. The Red Army blew up the town's bridge and retreated. On July 12, four days after it had fallen, Sovinform finally announced to the nation that Pskov was under attack. Twelve days later, on July 24, the news still referred to it as a "battleground," as if the Red Army hadn't abandoned the town sixteen days earlier.

Then, ominously, they stopped mentioning Pskov altogether.

As the grim joke ran, the headlines were always the same: "We're winning, but the Germans are gaining ground."

Back in Leningrad, the city government was starting to demand that children be evacuated, as the very young had been evacuated from London when the city was attacked by the Luftwaffe the year before. Thousands of children were put on trains; many were sent to precisely the area where Nina, Galina, and Maxim were staying.

On July 18, city officials passed out ration cards, and citizens were required to present them in order to buy staples such as bread and butter. The stores, however, still had displays of rich foods. No one was worried, yet, about starvation. Official newspapers reassured Leningraders that there would be no food shortages and that the Germans would never reach the city itself.

It appears these lies fooled even the city government. When the Soviet

trade minister sent a massive convoy of food staples to Leningrad for use
in case of siege, Marshal Voroshilov and Leningrad Party boss Andrei
Zhdanov decided it would look bad if the city government accepted the
food. They didn't want to appear desperate. They waved the shipment away,
saying there was "insufficient warehouse space." This was just one of the
ways that Marshal Voroshilov doomed Leningrad to a year of desperate
starvation.

With his family safely (or so he believed) settled in the countryside,
Shostakovich began to think again about a large-scale work. He may have
had scraps of ideas for a new symphonic piece floating around in his head
for a while. He often mulled over music for a period of months, perfecting it,
before writing it down. In particular, he seems to have thought of a cheerful
march tune many months before—an irritating little tune. Cute. So chipper
it was detestable. Some would later say that it sounded like "the patter of iron
rats dancing to the tune of a rat catcher." Shostakovich started to plan out
repetitions and variations of this tune. When he played it to friends over the
next few months, it sounded to them like the distant approach of a triumphant but wicked army.

As he heard this march getting louder and louder, more and more fearsome, he realized that it was part of something bigger. In the barracks,
he began to write. On July 19, as the Germans struggled toward the city,
Shostakovich set down the beginning of his Seventh Symphony—which
would eventually be called the *Leningrad* Symphony.

Vyritsa, the town where Nina and the children were staying, was about halfway between Leningrad and a growing line of defensive antitank ditches
hastily designed to protect the city from the German approach. The Leningrad
city government was daily shipping trainloads of teenagers and older women
out into the countryside to dig a system of gorges and trenches stretching
from the town of Luga up to Narva, near the Gulf of Finland (see map,
page 205). Many of the teenagers had volunteered, thrilled to be of service.
Others had been conscripted, pulled off the streets of Leningrad and sent

summarily down to the Luga Line. They hadn't been allowed to go home and change, so they still wore sundresses or bathing suits. They dug under difficult conditions. They were underfed and slept on the ground. Stuka dive-bombers blasted at them as they worked.

Incredibly, this huge team of amateur conscripts and volunteers managed to dig three rings of defense around Leningrad — 340 miles of antitank trenches — in a few weeks. They laid out four hundred miles of barbed-wire fencing before the Germans arrived. It was a stunning achievement.

And it was there, at the Luga Line, that, for the first time, the Russians managed to stall the German advance toward Leningrad. Accompanied by Red Army divisions, the newly formed People's Volunteers were thrown against the German Eighth Panzer Division on July 13. The volunteers were terribly armed (supposedly just three rifles for every four volunteers) and hastily trained. They stumbled out of cattle cars into scenes of frenzied attack: villages burning, horses screaming, cows lowing, peasants fleeing, and clouds of choking black smoke clotting the air. They were urged forward into combat by commanding officers who, in the grand tradition of Russian armies, saw the lives of their infantry as expendable, and therefore favored blunt, frontal assaults. The casualties were overwhelming. Incredibly, however, this volunteer militia, manning earthworks dug by amateurs, slowed German Army Group North for almost a month. In just the first few days of fighting, the Eighth Panzer Division lost almost half its tanks. The delay from early July until roughly August 8 gave Leningrad vital time to prepare and probably saved the city from absolute destruction.

Military resistance along the Luga Line wasn't the only thing slowing the German advance now. Heavy summer rains made the terrain hopelessly muddy. Even when the treads of tanks could churn through the muck, the trucks that supplied the tanks couldn't move. The whole German armored column, stretched out for miles, sat motionless in the downpours. They had to wait until the sun came out for a day and dried the mud before they could proceed on their grinding race toward Leningrad.

* * *

A volunteer force of women dig a defensive trench outside Leningrad. As the Germans approached from the west, work troops like this dug 340 miles of antitank trenches, most famously those along the Luga Line.

Women litter a field with concrete "dragon's teeth" designed to stop the advance of tanks.

As the Germans crawled closer—not only from the south but from the west as well, closer to the shore—rumors of their advance reached Leningrad. The real news of the front arrived not through the loudspeakers or the pages of *Pravda*, but across kitchen tables and in alleys behind factories. People had to be careful as they whispered their updates; there was a new law announcing that "defeatists" who spread "false rumors provoking unrest among the population" could be arrested and tried by a military tribunal. But it was clear to the people of Leningrad that things did not look good.

German reconnaissance flights over the city became more frequent. Everyone by this point had heard that the Luftwaffe was bombing Moscow. The Russian air force responded but could not stop the attacks on the capital. It seemed like Leningrad would be next.

The city government was obviously planning for a siege. Not only were children being evacuated—so were whole factories. Assembly-line machinery was dismantled and packed into crates. Factories traveled by train or long convoys of trucks, all covered with birch branches to camouflage them from above. An observer wrote, "One can judge the time these trains spend on their way by the freshness of the branches. The trucks carry fly wheels, cog wheels, lathes, small machine parts, all kept separate, carefully greased and wrapped in parchment. Behind come the vans that carry the workers' families; these vans are heated by stoves, and in one carriage there are children on hard plank beds. . . . The children, huddled together, look out of the window. There isn't a smile amongst them."

The workers had little reason to smile. Often, when they reached their new factory sites far to the east, they had to live in holes dug in the ground while they built their factories from scratch. This is how Stalin managed to keep industrial production out of German hands. It was an incredible effort: in just a few months, ninety-two defense-related factories were relocated. But the gargantuan effort had a real cost for hundreds of thousands of people transplanted into the wilderness.

Even more ominous than the evacuations was the return of evacuees. Hundreds of children had been sent to summer camps in the Luga

Before the freeze set in, the Germans struggled with the Russian mud. Here, lines of soldiers haul a car through a rut.

Factory machinery is disassembled for transportation out of Leningrad to the east. In remote sites far behind the lines of battle, the equipment would be reassembled and put to use even before the new factories had walls or the workers had huts to live in.

region, just south of where Nina and the children were hidden away. Those children now reappeared in the city. Their camps were no longer safe. The Luga Line was under attack. People muttered that it wouldn't be long until the Germans swarmed across it.

It was time for Nina, Galina, and Maxim to return from the countryside. They rejoined Shostakovich at the apartment. The composer and his wife debated: Should the family leave the city entirely? Nina, apparently, thought they should take the children and flee.

But it was a point of pride for Shostakovich to stay in his native city for as long as possible. He seems to have insisted that he wanted to work on his symphony there, rather than risk being disrupted by a move. Nina later remembered, "For a long time my husband could not reconcile himself in thought to the necessity of leaving Leningrad." Shostakovich was not alone: there were many who refused to abandon their homes. A Communist Party official later remembered, with some anger, that local governments "viewed citizens' refusal to evacuate as a patriotic act and were proud of it, thus involuntarily encouraging people to remain." This meant that millions of people were needlessly trapped when the Nazis arrived.

Every day, new evacuations were announced. Several times, Shostakovich was invited to join groups that were packing up and leaving for Central Asia: the Composers' Union, the Conservatory, the Leningrad Philharmonic. He refused.

On August 10, the city government announced mandatory evacuation for all children under the age of fourteen. They were to be sent east without their parents, with their names and destinations written on their hands. This seemed too awful to many parents, and they resisted. Shostakovich and Nina were among those hundreds of thousands who ignored the order.

Shostakovich kept working on the new symphony — sometimes even taking it up onto the roof of the Conservatory so he could keep writing while performing his duties as a fireman. When friends came to his house to say good-bye before they headed off on one of the few train lines that hadn't been cut off by the Germans, Shostakovich played his sketches for them on the piano. His friend Isaak Glikman remembered:

> It was a steel-gray, depressing sort of day. Famine had not yet gripped Leningrad in its deadly embrace; even so, Shostakovich looked as if he had lost weight. Hunger, I was surprised to see, had made him seem taller; it had stretched out his form and given him an air of fragility. His face was unsmiling, frowning, thoughtful. He told me the reason he had wanted to see me was to show me the first pages of a new work that he was planning; one, however, that might be of no use to anybody now that this war of unprecedented savagery was raging.

Shostakovich played the piece through, as it existed at that point. When he got to the plucky, ghastly little march that grew and grew, Glikman heard in it "the Fascist invasion."

This may have been Shostakovich's intention: the tune was very similar to an aria from a chintzy German operetta, Franz Lehár's *Merry Widow* — one of Hitler's favorite pieces of music, written by one of Hitler's favorite composers. Late in the summer of 1941, at about the same time Shostakovich was writing his march, the German propaganda ministry even released a movie about Lehár, celebrating his work. We don't know, however, if Shostakovich knew of Hitler's enthusiasm for the operetta composer. The tune may also have had more personal associations for Shostakovich. In Russian, it was sung to the words "I'll go see Maxim," so Shostakovich may have used it to tease his little son. Eventually, Maxim and Galina thought of that march as their own special tune. "They often beg their father to play [it] for them," said Nina, "and they climb onto the lid of the grand piano and sit as quiet as mice, all ears."

Glikman heard this plucky tune become huge, terrifying, pounded out furiously on the keyboard. "We were both extremely agitated; it was a rare event for Shostakovich to play a new work with such manifest emotion. [Afterwards] we sat on, plunged in silence, broken at last by Shostakovich with these words (I have them written down): 'I don't know what the fate of this piece will be.'" The composer was worried people might compare this repeated march with another popular piece, Maurice Ravel's *Bolero*. "Well, let them," he said. "That is how I hear war." Glikman later mused, "I believe that on that memorable August day Shostakovich was still quite unaware of the titanic scale of his symphony, for which a fate unique in the history of music was already in preparation. Parting, we embraced and kissed, not suspecting that before us lay a prolonged separation."

As the Germans cut off the train lines to the west and to the south, as the Finns cut off the train lines to the north, it became harder for Leningrad to feed itself. By late August, the quest for food took up a lot of the day. One diarist described: "By chance, you might accidentally overhear that in the Petrograd section of town they are distributing something or other. So you run there. After that, to Narvsky Gate. And then on to Vasilevski Island. You buy up everything you can lay your hands on. But there isn't anything substantial or nourishing. The stores are all but empty. Everywhere there are enormous lines. And the crowds grow whenever sugar or butter appears in the commercial stores."

Still, Shostakovich and his family stayed on.

Evacuation itself was becoming more and more dangerous. The German advance had swallowed up most of the train lines. (It had engulfed Vyritsa, for example, the town where Nina had been staying just a few weeks before.) The direct Moscow-Leningrad route was blocked, and trains had to be rerouted to the east at a station called Mga.

Still, trains and truck convoys full of child evacuees made their way along the few routes left. With the speed of the German advance, however, this finally led to disaster.

"Now we realize that we were travelling towards the Germans," a

THE BLOCKADE OF LENINGRAD, SEPTEMBER 1941

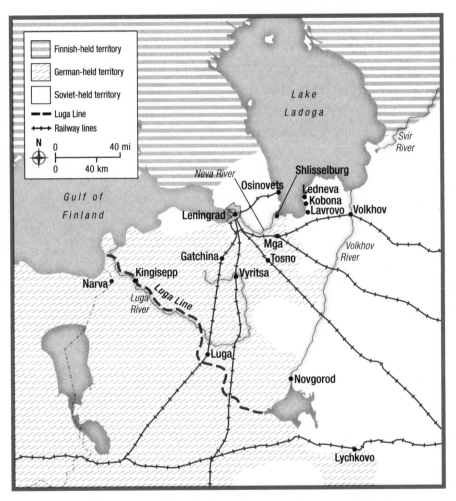

The Luga Line, a system of Soviet trenches and antitank defenses, was hastily created in July 1941. It played a major role in slowing down the terrible advance of German Army Group North for almost a month. By the beginning of September, however, the Germans had pushed past it and were at the gates of Leningrad, trapping millions in the city.

survivor remembers, "but at the time nobody knew that. Why should we have? It was a good area, a remote area."

On a late August day, children were being settled at collective farms far to the south of Leningrad. The kids had arrived at their destination, and their chaperones were trying to coordinate their placement. "We worked out where everybody was going to stay—and there were several thousand to accommodate. But then an urgent order came through. We had to move the children on. Then we realized that the Germans were moving fast towards us." At one collective farm, where the children were receiving welcoming cups of tea, someone ran up and yelled, "There are Nazi paratroopers ahead!"

The adult chaperones scrambled the children back to their trucks and rushed them to the Lychkovo train station. The station was now mobbed with thousands of kids. Adults tried to keep order in the midst of panic. "Just imagine! We had a lot of nursery-school children. They were all hungry and exhausted."

"The children had started to board the train. . . . Then German planes appeared. They circled and came back towards us. It was dreadful."

A survivor of this scene—Ivan Fedulov, just a boy at the time, standing on the train platform, helping with the younger kids' luggage—remembered, "Suddenly, I heard a terrible cry. Someone was shouting, 'Bombers! Bombers!' A plane flew right over us—and along the length of the train—dropping bomb after bomb, with terrifying, methodical precision. There was a huge explosion, and when the smoke cleared carriages were scattered everywhere, as if they had been knocked off the tracks by a giant hand."

A woman on the train recalled: "The nursery school teacher was sitting there, with the children around her. Goodness, how many of them there were! And each time a bomb exploded they all cried: 'Mummy! Mummy! Mummy!' It was dreadful! For the first time in my life I lied to a child. 'Don't be afraid,' I said. 'Nothing to be afraid of! They're our planes!' As for myself, I went out onto the porch, and, you know, he was flying so low, he'd take a look, press a button—and a bomb would immediately explode."

An antiaircraft gun on the banks of the Neva. Even before the first air raids on Leningrad, German planes occasionally flew over the city, prompting sirens to wail, citizens to flee into their basements, and antiaircraft gunners to scramble into their positions, firing at the sky.

She remembered with fury that later on, the Germans claimed they hadn't known that they were massacring children. "What rubbish! They knew very well, and, of course, they could *see* everything perfectly well. The fact was that the children from the Dzerzhinsky district were already boarding the train then, and they bombed the kids at the station. It was very fine weather. The children were dressed in their best, bright clothes. He could see very well what he was bombing."

The boy Ivan Fedulov and some of the kids around him sprinted toward a potato field and tried to hide there. Others followed, scampering through the weeds. "A plane circled, and came back. Then it began machine-gunning the fleeing children. It was flying so low that I could clearly see the pilot's face — totally impassive."

A mother remembered: "When they began shelling the coaches, there were immediately dead and wounded. We put the children under the seats with mattresses on top of them for protection and flung ourselves on top of the mattresses. . . . A bomb fell on the engine. . . . All the same, we managed, when things quietened down a bit, to get out of the coach. It was already getting dark. The station was on fire. We couldn't find anybody. It was absolutely dreadful! The chief of the evacuation train was sitting on a stump, clasping his head in his hands. . . . Every time we heard some kind of noise or the sound of shooting, we would get down into a ditch, the children like this, flat on the ground, and we would lie on top of them. And I would throw blankets over them."

Eventually, trains filled with Red Army soldiers came limping along the tracks, headed back to Leningrad. Either by catching a ride on these troop trains or by walking through the countryside for days, people found themselves back in the city, speaking out boldly not just against the Germans but also against the incompetence of the city officials who'd sent children into harm's way. "When I got back to Leningrad I was told I had dreamed it all," said one survivor. "More than two thousand children had died at Lychkovo, and others were wandering around the countryside, distraught and lost, but the official version was that this had never happened."

The massacre at Lychkovo threw the parents of Leningrad into a frenzy. People were desperate to get out of the city, but at the same time, they worried about which routes were still safe.

Time was running out to escape Leningrad before the German noose pulled tight.

Shostakovich's friend Ivan Sollertinsky came to say good-bye. He was fleeing to Central Asia and was shortly going to catch a train. Shostakovich played him the new piece, now almost finished, or so he thought. Sollertinsky was a professor at the Conservatory and a brilliant man. As they talked it through, Shostakovich realized that the piece needed to be part of something larger. He had a glimpse of a grander design.

He said good-bye to Sollertinsky. They did not know it, these two friends who'd spent their youth cackling together, but they would never see each other again.

When Sollertinsky left, Shostakovich told Nina that this new piece, the Seventh Symphony, was going to be much longer than he had planned. He was reluctant to leave the city, which might disrupt his work.

Nina was furious. She said sternly that the children's safety had to come first. They had to get out while they still could.

Somewhat gloomily, Shostakovich agreed. The next morning he called the authorities and informed them that he and his family were going to evacuate with Lenfilm Studios (who had made most of the movies for which he'd written music).

He wrote to Sollertinsky, "Dear Ivan . . . We'll be leaving for Alma-Ata in about two days." His sister Maria had been exiled to Alma-Ata, in Kazakhstan, a few years before. Now she was back in Leningrad, and Shostakovich was headed there.

He and Nina made preparations for their evacuation.

They did not know it, however, but it was already too late. They had lost the chance to flee.

* * *

On August 25, Mga—the last rail link with the rest of Russia—came under attack. An evacuation train filled with children had left Leningrad in the morning. They were supposed to stop at Mga, the transfer station, to pick up some more evacuees before heading east.

As they drew close to Mga, the train braked and slowed.

A little boy pointed out the windows at the sky and shouted happily, "Look at the balloons! Look, so many!"

People craned their necks and looked up. They saw that it was not balloons that were drifting slowly down around them. It was German paratroopers. They were landing in a nearby field.

Antiaircraft guns fired. The German soldiers struggled free of their parachutes and got into formation.

The train's conductor did not stop at the station. He accelerated. The evacuation train roared through Mga and kept going.

This was the last train to make it out of Leningrad.

About 636,000 people in all had been evacuated; that left 2.5 million civilians in the city.

After heavy fighting, Mga finally fell on August 31. At that point, the Germans had advanced all the way to the far bank of the river Neva, southeast of the city. Within a few short days, they had taken the town of Shlisselburg, on the shores of Lake Ladoga.

"Leningrad is surrounded," wrote a woman in her diary. "We are caught in a mousetrap."

The nine-hundred-day Siege of Leningrad—the longest siege in recorded history—had begun.

The Shostakovich family—along with two and a half million others—were trapped.

German soldiers storm
through a suburb out-
side Leningrad.

THE SECOND MOVEMENT

I wrote my Seventh Symphony, the *Leningrad,* quickly,"
Shostakovich remembered. "I couldn't not write it. War was all around. I had
to be together with the people, I wanted to create the image of our embattled
country, to engrave it in music."

War was quite literally all around him. To the north of the city was the
Finnish army. To the west was the Gulf of Finland, its fatal waters seeded
with floating mines. To the east was Lake Ladoga, which Germans bombed
from the southern shore. To the south were the German lines themselves.

The three prongs of Operation Barbarossa stuck deep in Russia's flesh
like the tines of a devil's pitchfork. German Army Group North surrounded
Leningrad. Army Group South had surrounded Kiev, in fertile Ukraine,
trapping four Soviet armies; the city would shortly fall to them, yielding up
some of the USSR's richest agricultural land to Nazi occupiers. Army Group
Central was now only two hundred miles from Moscow, the capital itself,
where Stalin and the State Committee for Defense watched its approach
with dread.

Shostakovich, toiling away at his symphony, finished a new draft of the first movement on September 3. He may have wanted to start immediately on the next movement—but the next day, for the first time, German shells tore into the city.

That morning, the avenues were filled with a delicate mist. Soviet snipers took up positions on rooftops south of the city so they could fire if the Germans continued their advance. The sky and streets were gray and shrouded.

At around eleven in the morning, artillery shells blasted into the streets; the city echoed with detonations. At Communist Party Headquarters, the desperate news spread quickly: the Germans were close enough to fire their long-range 240-millimeter siege artillery directly into Leningrad. Though the Soviets did not know it yet, the largest guns in Europe, devised by the famous firms of Krupp, Skoda, and Schneider, were gathered in the city's suburbs, blasting away according to detailed maps that marked hospitals, museums, and Communist Party Headquarters as targeted "firing points."

The shells hit freight yards and factories and collapsed Hydroelectric Dam No. 5. The bombardment lasted until six in the evening. It was terrifying, and yet would soon become routine.

On September 6, the people of Leningrad heard a low hum that they had not heard before. This was not the sound of shelling.

People looked up; their windowpanes were rattling.

A small force of German planes soared over the city. They were bombers. People ran for shelter as sirens blared. Antiaircraft guns blasted away in the suburbs. The sky over the avenues was laced with tracer fire. The planes roared by and released their deadly payloads. Incendiary bombs rained down over the city, flaring up on roofs. Home Guard volunteers blew whistles and bounded over copper sheathing to shovel sand on the dazzling thermite.

People looking out their apartment windows saw planes dipping low—

saw bombs streaking down the length of the wide, fashionable avenues. Walls catapulted into the street. Homes burned.

This was the first air raid on the city. As diarist Elena Skrjabina wrote, "It has made quite an impression. In the first place, our faith in Leningrad's being well protected has been shaken. . . . There are crowds around destroyed houses."

An even more devastating Luftwaffe assault force was to arrive two days later; it would damn the city to a winter of famine.

On September 8, Shostakovich began work on the second movement of the symphony. It is a careful, wary dance movement, supposedly written to recall happier times in Leningrad. He considered calling it "Reminiscences" or "The Dream." The day before, the city had suffered heavy shelling, but there is no hint of that horror in the elegant opening measures of this pleasant intermezzo, sketched out while a huge, coordinated assault force of Luftwaffe bombers banked toward Leningrad. Shostakovich, unaware, bent over his desk, quietly drawing note heads and stems.

Once again, throughout the city, windows began rattling. The water in the canals quivered. Factory sirens wailed and the loudspeakers screamed warnings. People rushed to their air-raid shelters — basements, vaults, dark warrens beneath munitions plants.

"I looked out the window," one diarist wrote.

> We heard the ack-ack guns firing with particular force and fury. Looking at the sky I noticed an unusual thing — instead of individual planes looking like little dots high in the sky, so tiny you could scarcely see them, there came a great mass of planes, flying in a definite, clearly planned, complicated formation. They were massed in such a way that their movement seemed menacing. And they really were menacing. Shells burst around them, we could see bursts of fire from the ack-ack guns. But the planes

moved steadily on: there was no looping, none of the complicated aerobatics we had seen in August. Even when one of them fell, wreathed in clouds of smoke, the others carried steadily on. It was obvious that this was no casual raid but a massive onslaught.

Twenty-seven German Ju 88 bombers sprayed more than six thousand incendiary bombs down on the parks and courtyards. "They flew at low altitude," a rooftop fireman recalled. "You could clearly see their engines, the shining disks of their spinning propellers, and the details of their tails. The aircraft dropped their bomb loads on the southern side of the city, and then proceeded north without changing direction, as if on parade. Where the bombs fell, a wall of smoke and dust appeared, rising higher and higher."

Shostakovich's friends Gavriil Popov and Lyubov Shaporina were whiling away the afternoon playing the piano when the air raid started. The nervous Popov ran to the window. They watched an enormous, apocalyptic cloud rising up above the city. "High in the sky there were white balls of explosions—the desperate efforts of the anti-aircraft guns. Suddenly, from behind the roofs a white cloud started to grow; it expanded quickly and other clouds piled on this one. They were all dyed amber in the setting sun. They filled up the entire sky; then the clouds turned bronze, while from below a black stripe started moving upwards. It was so unlike smoke that for a long time I could not comprehend that it was fire."

The smoke rose in a black bulb and hung motionless in the sky.

What was it? people wondered.

The news spread quickly: The Leningrad city bosses had decided in their wisdom to store all of the city's emergency food supplies in one place—a compound of thirty-eight old, wooden warehouses in the city's southwest quadrant—the Bedayev warehouses. The Germans, having figured this out, had aimed their incendiary bombs right for them. The warehouses were close together, filled with drums of oils and lard, filled with flammable grain, filled with the city's supply of meat. The whole sector burst into flame. Two and a half thousand tons of molten sugar swamped burning alleys.

Lavrentii Beria, the head of the NKVD, ingeniously homicidal himself, was outraged at the incompetence of storing all the food in one place. Years later, he hotly told his son, "[Leningrad Party bosses] Voroshilov and Zhdanov had been instructed to disperse Leningrad's food reserve and build new storage sheds in different parts of the city. The army and NKVD had pressed for this to be done urgently. Through sheer incompetence, the work was delayed, and the wooden storehouses were burnt down by the Germans, dooming the city to famine."

As the bulb of black cloud, lit by both sun and flame, hovered above the storehouses, the people of Leningrad looked on in choked awe. "It was an immense spectacle of stunning beauty," wrote Lyubov Shaporina.

The air smelled sweet as tons of sugar burned.

Somehow, in the midst of all of this fire and fury, Shostakovich managed to begin the first draft of the lightly tripping dance movement of his symphony. Halfway through that movement, it becomes a shrieking, sneering parody of itself. The screaming outburst in the middle isn't what he would have been writing as the bombs fell on September 8, however. He would have just been setting out the theme of the "Reminiscences." This suggests how complicated the relationship is between a composer's experience and the music they write. This was gentle music to be composing in the midst of hell.

The raid was not over. At around ten thirty that evening, another wave of bombers appeared. This time they were not carrying incendiaries but large high-explosive bombs ranging from five hundred to more than a thousand pounds each. Once again, the sirens wailed, the foghorns groaned, and urgent voices on the loudspeakers called for people to take cover.

"Whole new squadrons flew over us," one Leningrader said, "bombs fell endlessly, and the antiaircraft artillery blasted at full power. Sheer hell."

Another remembered: "We were all deafened by the roar of engines. We heard bombs exploding somewhere near by. The air, everything around, was crackling, booming. Our house was shaking, through and through. The earth, too, seemed to be seized with convulsions, as in an earthquake. My teeth were chattering from fear, my knees were shaking. I squashed myself into a corner, and pressed the children to me. They were crying with fear." The woman's hair started to go white in the space of a few hours.

In the air-raid shelters, the scene was equally chaotic. Diarist Elena Skrjabina wrote: "Down there were many people, especially children. They cry loudly, pressing closely to their panic-stricken mothers. With each new explosion, the women, many of whom are Communists, compulsively cross themselves and whisper prayers. In such moments, antireligious propaganda is forgotten."

Poet Olga Berggolts described the sensation of hearing the bombs falling above while crouched in a basement: "Everyone thinks, 'This one's for me,' and dies in advance. You die, and it passes, but a minute later it comes again, whistles again, and you die, are resurrected, sigh with relief, only to die again over and over. How long will this last? . . . Kill me at once, not bit by bit, several times a day!"

The next day, the people of Leningrad crept out of their cellars to find the city had changed.

"A few scenes have etched themselves into my memory," wrote Skrjabina, "probably until I die: a house demolished almost to its foundations, but one wall remained, still papered in the favorite cornflower design. There is even a picture hanging on it, as straight as ever. Above a heap of bricks, cement, and beams, a whole corner of an upper apartment of another house was preserved. In the corner, an icon; on the floor, toys, scattered everywhere as if the children had just finished playing. Further down was a room half buried in debris, but against the wall, a bed with fluffy pillows, and a lamp."

Another lone wall stood with its house entirely sheared away, leaving a quiltwork of pretty wallpapers; a large clock on a wall ticked away, telling time as if nothing had happened.

Weaponized listening: In the years before the widespread Soviet use of radar, the best way to detect oncoming air raids was the listening horn, seen here on the walls of the Peter and Paul Fortress. These sensitive devices allowed sentries with earphones to hear the distant roar of engines and even pinpoint the direction of the coming attack so the air-raid sirens could be sounded.

Smoke from the burning of the Bedayev warehouses—an act that doomed Leningrad to starvation

The streets were filled with a deadening mist. It smelled of ham and butter.

The same day that the Bedayev warehouses were destroyed, Hitler's high command called in a nutritionist, Ernst Ziegelmeyer, to discuss the food situation in Leningrad. Ziegelmeyer made a studied assessment of the rationing that would probably go into effect in the city. He calculated that the population would starve to death quite soon. His recommendation to the Führer, therefore, was that the German army should not invade the city at all but simply wait in a choking noose around it. "It is not worth risking the lives of our troops. The Leningraders will die anyway. It is essential not to let a single person through our front line. The more of them that stay there, the sooner they will die, and then we will enter the city without trouble, without losing a single German soldier."

The nutritionist supplied an exacting projected schedule for the mass death of the 2.5 million people still trapped in the city. Everyone was impressed with his clarity and insight. Hitler's propaganda minister, Joseph Goebbels, wrote in his diary, "We shall not trouble ourselves with demands for Leningrad's capitulation. It must be destroyed by a virtually scientific method."

Hitler's commanders on the Leningrad Front, however, foresaw a glitch in the scientific precision of this solution: when starvation reached a certain peak, there were likely to be attempts, perhaps even mass attempts, by women and children trying to make a break for German lines to submit themselves as prisoners in exchange for food. This was inconvenient; Field Marshal Wilhelm Ritter von Leeb, in charge of the northern invasion force, worried that young German soldiers, not yet hardened to atrocities, if confronted by starving women and children, wouldn't shoot. He wanted "to spare the troops having to fire at close range on civilians."

After a lot of thought, he eventually hit upon the happy idea of creating a deeper ring of land mines around the city. In addition, he ordered the long-range guns to focus on anyone trying to cross over this no-man's-land. "It is the task of the artillery to deal with such a situation, and as far away from our own lines as possible—preferably by opening fire on the civilians at an early stage [of their scramble out of the city] so that the infantry is spared the task of having to shoot the civilians themselves." The field marshal was relieved. "Even then a large part of the civilian population will perish, but at least not in front of our eyes."

With this delicate problem solved, the Germans sat back on their haunches and waited.

Food rationing had started in the summer; now it got much tighter. The city government instituted a strict hierarchy to the rationing very similar to the program in the prison work camps, the gulag. Soldiers and industrial workers got the most, office workers got about three-fourths as much, and "dependents"—children, the wounded, and the elderly—got about half as much.

By mid-September, after the destruction of the food warehouses, industrial workers got about 500 grams of bread per day; children and white-collar workers got about 300 grams; other dependents got 250. This was not enough for the elderly, in particular, to sustain life.

The Shostakoviches were lucky that their dependents, Galina and Maxim, were so young (five and three years old). The size of a child's ration allotment was the same whether the child was one year old or eleven. This was fine for the very young, but meant that a lot of ten-, eleven-, and twelve-year-old kids went hungry. Shostakovich was doubtless also worried about his mother, Sofia; his sister Maria (who had returned from internal exile just in time for the war to break out); and Maria's young son, Dmitri, Shostakovich's nephew, all of whom would have been on minimum rations.

There were families much worse off than the Shostakoviches; there were also families in power, families able to call in favors, who were much better off. One of the bitter experiences of the starving citizens during the Siege of

People taped crosses of paper across their windows to minimize the shattering of glass.

A Leningrad street littered with bodies from a blast. The militia prepares to cart them away.

A Leningrad facade blown apart by one of the daily German artillery barrages

The ruins of a life: In the background, like a stage set, a tasseled lamp hangs above a window and a samovar sits on an elegantly set table.

Leningrad was glimpsing the children of a few well-connected Communist Party members eating ham sandwiches or leaving juicy rinds of fat on their plates. Corruption, unfortunately, was rife.

In mid-September, many people were hungry but still struggling along. The ration levels kept dropping throughout the fall, however. Soon, many dependents were not getting enough food to allow them to retain weight. They were wasting away. Their ration cards were death sentences — people grimly called them *smertniks*, from the Russian word for death, *smert*.

Writer Lidiya Ginzburg described the astonishment with which civilized Leningraders first greeted starvation. They "didn't believe that the inhabitants of a large city could die of hunger. . . . On hearing of the first cases of death amongst their acquaintances, people still thought, Is this the one I know [dying]? In broad daylight? In Leningrad? With a master's degree? From starvation?"

The lines for food were even longer than usual, stretching around blocks. It was not easy to stand for hours, waiting for rations. The Nazis shelled the city every day — a routine observed with deadly German efficiency. Shelling began at eight in the morning and continued until nine, from eleven to twelve, from five to six, and from eight in the evening until ten. "This way," a German prisoner of war explained, "the shelling would kill as many people as possible . . . and most importantly, attempt to destroy the morale of the Leningraders."

People standing in the food lines had to decide whether to head for shelter and lose their places or stand firm and risk their lives as shells rained down on the city around them.

The shelling was regular and daily, but the Luftwaffe air raids were surprises. Every few days, they would fly over in waves, almost unopposed since the Russian air force had been all but obliterated on the first day of the invasion.

The German bombers had worked out a new routine: the first squadron dropped explosives, which blew buildings apart; the second squadron would drop the incendiaries, which would light the wreckage on fire. People on rooftops could see flames all over the city. The suburbs, too, were on fire.

Shostakovich generally did not allow the Luftwaffe to disturb him. Nina remembered, "Even during air raids, he seldom stopped working. If things began getting too hot, he calmly finished the bar he was writing, waited until the page dried, neatly arranged what he had written, and took it down with him into the bomb-shelter. Whenever he was away from home during an air-raid alarm, he always phoned me asking me not to forget to take his manuscripts down into the shelter."

When Shostakovich got up from his desk because the sirens and Klaxons were wailing, he wrote *v.t.* on the manuscript of his symphony. It stands for *vozdushnaya trevoga*, "air-raid alarm." We can see where he was interrupted. He returned some hours later and picked up where he left off, without a change in direction or mood.

One evening, the Shostakoviches' apartment shook. A house across the street had been hit by an incendiary bomb.

All night the building burned and cast its shadows on their walls.

Tenants vacate a newly bombed apartment block.

THE THIRD MOVEMENT

Stalin wanted some answers. He was irate.

How had the Germans encircled Leningrad so completely? What had happened to the food supply? How could it be that the second-most important city in his empire was starving to death?

When one of his most competent generals, Georgi Zhukov, flew out to Leningrad to investigate, it became clear that the military situation there was a mess. The Red Army was losing territory daily. The soldiers were demoralized and underequipped.

Zhukov looked through the maps and diagrams of the city and its surrounds and threw them angrily onto the floor. He pointed at a situation map on the wall and demanded, "What are our tanks doing in this area? There's something wrong here."

Timidly, the local commander admitted, "Those are actually tank mock-ups, Comrade . . . wooden dummies."

Zhukov was stunned. Unlikely as it might seem, most of the Leningrad tank force was made up of motionless decoys, nailed together by

Shostakovich's colleagues in the set-design team at the Mariinsky Theater. The local commander could at least report favorably that the fake theatrical tanks had been bombed twice. It was one of the most unusual contributions of the arts to the war effort.

Zhukov, recovering, snapped, "Get another hundred of them tonight, and tomorrow morning put them in these two places near Srednyaya Rogatka—here and here."

The local commander apologized that the set designers couldn't build a hundred fake tanks in one night.

"If you don't do it, you'll be court-martialed," rapped out General Zhukov. "I'll check up on you tomorrow myself."

It was clear to Zhukov that the city's strategic approach had to change. The man in charge of Leningrad's defense, the rather dim Marshal Voroshilov, was recalled to Moscow for a stern talk with Stalin. Tukhachevsky's foe Voroshilov had overseen the purging of the army after the marshal's execution. Now, in a sense, he was on trial for failing at Tukhachevsky's job.

Stalin was already responding to the military's failures with his favorite managerial maneuver: blaming people and having them killed. As early as July, he had ordered four of the commanding officers for the Western Front shot. Marshal Voroshilov must have been anxious that he would be next.

He met with Stalin at a dinner at Stalin's country house. Other members of the Politburo were dining with them (including Nikita Khrushchev, who wrote down the conversation years later). For a while, they ate and talked things over politely—but finally, Stalin could not contain himself. He leaped to his feet and started accusing Voroshilov of disastrous incompetence.

Voroshilov, bravely if foolishly, pushed back his chair, rose, and began shouting right back at Stalin. "You have yourself to blame for all this! You're the one who annihilated the Old Guard of the army; you had our best generals killed!"

It became a screaming match.

Voroshilov picked up the platter of roast suckling pig and slammed it down on the table.

Everyone was stunned. Probably Voroshilov as much as anyone else.

He was lucky he was not executed. It was still dangerous to disagree with Stalin. This fact was disastrous for the war effort. His generals were terrified of telling him bad news; it was safer to lie. For the first several months of the Great Patriotic War, therefore, he often didn't know the real strategic situation. Even worse, military experts couldn't question his amateur civilian judgment without fear of death.

At one point, for example, Stalin held a meeting with the Politburo to talk about the failures of the Soviet air force. He questioned the commander sharply about why so many planes and so many pilots were lost.

The air force commander at the time, Major General Pavel Rychagov, was young and hot-headed. He was furious at the low quality of Russian fighter planes and bombers. (In the course of the war, the USSR lost 80,300 planes; only about half this number were actually destroyed by the enemy.) When Stalin needled Rychagov, the young airman barked back defiantly that the death rate among pilots was so high "because you're making us fly in coffins!"

The room fell silent. No one in the Politburo dared to speak. Stalin often held meetings while strolling around his office, puffing his pipe. Now he paced behind their backs. He murmured softly, "You shouldn't have said that."

He slowly walked around the table.

He repeated, "You shouldn't have said that."

Rychagov was deprived of his command and shot.

This fatal pressure only made commanders more deceptive, hesitant, and incompetent.

At the same time, a peremptory brutality trickled down through the ranks.

Up on the Leningrad Front, General Zhukov was reorganizing the city's defenses. One of the first things he did in mid-September 1941 was to create new "blocking units," which would be posted behind Red Army detachments — and which would shoot any soldier who tried to run from the Germans. Their families would also be shot.

This protocol, originally issued in Leningrad, became general to the whole of the Red Army. By the end of the war, about three hundred thousand soldiers had been killed by their own army for attempted flight or desertion.

This was simply an extension of Order No. 270, issued by Stalin back in August, which mercilessly proclaimed that any soldier who allowed the Germans to take him prisoner was a "traitor to the Motherland." The families of those who surrendered or were captured would have their ration cards taken away from them (and so would starve to death) or would be arrested and imprisoned in the work camps.

With his "blocking units" in place to stop his soldiers from retreating, General Zhukov attempted to break through the iron ring the Germans had forged around Leningrad.

He threw Red Army units against the Germans at several key points along the Neva River. This stopped the Germans from advancing any farther but did so at a huge loss of Russian lives.

As the Red Army troops formed up in their ranks for another hopeless sally, German loudspeakers mocked them: "It's time to assemble at your extermination points again — we shall bury you on the banks of the Neva." Then the German guns would start roaring, and so many projectiles would hit the river that the water would start to boil.

At the time, Zhukov was praised for halting the German onslaught. He had, in fact, reorganized the city's defense well in many ways. What the Russians did not know, however, was that the Nazis were no longer interested in subduing Leningrad. They did not want to *defeat* it anymore — they only wanted to encircle it and starve it to death — so they no longer needed a full invasion force. Many of their tanks were recalled and trundled off to the south to join the assault on Moscow.

Hitler released Secret Directive No. 1a 1601/41, codifying what everyone in German command had been saying about Leningrad for months.

It was called "The Future of the City of St. Petersburg." (He used the old, pre-Soviet name for the city, as if the last twenty-five years of history had not happened.) The memo ran:

1. The Führer has decided to erase the city of St. Petersburg from the face of the earth. I have no interest in the further existence of this large population point after the defeat of Soviet Russia.

2. The previous demands by the fleet concerning the maintenance of [St. Petersburg's] dockyards, harbors, and similar important naval facilities are well known to [German high command]; however, the satisfaction of these does not seem possible in view of the general line of conduct with regard to St. Petersburg.

3. We propose to closely blockade the city and erase it from the earth by means of artillery fire of all caliber and continuous bombardment from the air. . . . If a request of surrender is announced, it will be rejected.

And so the Red Army, squeezed between two of the most brutal dictators in human history, fought on.

Someone in power had discovered that Shostakovich was writing a new symphony. Word came down that, to boost morale, he should talk about it on the radio.

On the morning of September 17, he put down his pen and set off for the radio committee headquarters. He walked through a surreal landscape.

The air in the city smelled of "pulverized brick and melting iron." Huge holes were blasted in the roads. There was no one to fix them. Much of the city no longer had any electricity. Wires sagged uselessly over the streets. Apartment buildings stood without walls.

With houses sheared in half, Lidiya Ginzburg wrote, communal life was exposed in a devastated cutaway cross section:

> You begin to realize with astonishment that as you sit at home in your room you are suspended in space, with other people similarly suspended above your head and beneath your feet. You know about this of course, you've heard furniture being moved about upstairs, even wood being chopped. But all that is abstract, unpicturable, like the way we are borne along through space on a ball rotating about its axis. . . . Now the truth had been revealed in a dizzyingly graphic fashion. There were skeletal houses with preserved facades, shot through with darkness and depth.

Collapsed roofs "hung at an angle and looked as if they were still sliding down, perpetually falling, like a waterfall." Leningrad now literally resembled one of the fractured Cubist landscapes of the 1920s avantgarde — or, as Ginzburg remarked, one of Vsevolod Meyerhold's stage sets.

Just a few minutes before leaving for his radio engagement, Shostakovich had put the finishing touches on his final draft of the dancing second movement of the symphony. Perhaps, as he walked, he thought about what he would do in the third movement. Perhaps he thought about what he would soon say on air, though it may already have been written for him by someone else. He made his way past the massive revetments of the Peter and Paul Fortress and crossed the Neva. The bridge was studded with antiaircraft guns.

At some point along his route to Radio House, an air raid struck the city. The whistles blew; loudspeakers called out warnings. The Luftwaffe was on its way.

Shostakovich took shelter. As the planes snarled overhead and bombs detonated distantly, he was anxious: time was passing, and he did not like being late. He often would scold people for even a tardy minute.

While the air raid continued, the radio simply broadcast the ticking of a metronome. This maddening, steady, even ticktock became the musical voice of the city under siege. It echoed through the streets whenever there was no programming—a heartbeat to mark the passing of the seconds.

Then the all-clear sounded. Shostakovich came out of hiding and continued to make his way to the Leningrad Radio House. He arrived just in time.

The building was in some disarray. Staff members had already started sleeping there instead of going home at night. Eventually, the whole staff would take up residence on the seventh floor, building crude cubicles to sleep in, sharing their food, their clothes, everything, to make sure that the official station was always broadcasting. Down on the fourth floor, exhausted journalists worked on programming.

Shostakovich's acquaintance Olga Berggolts was living there by that time. She officially was still living at the city's block of writers' apartments, a building called the "Tears of Socialism," but she rarely went home. (It was not all selfless: she was having an affair with a coworker.) Though she had suffered greatly at the hands of the regime, she now turned her poetry to supporting the efforts of the city to remain strong in the face of the enemy. In her poems, she described and broadcast what people experienced all over the city—and so her poetry became, in many ways, the voice of the people. Many were expecting Shostakovich's Seventh Symphony to perform a similar role. Whatever his intentions for the piece might have been originally, this was the direction people were pushing him in: to understand the growing work as a testimony of Leningrad's struggles and strength.

He settled himself in front of the microphone. He was on air. He began to speak: "An hour ago I finished scoring the second movement of my latest large orchestral composition." His voice was rough.

> If I manage to write well, if I manage to finish the third and fourth movements, the work may be called my Seventh Symphony. . . .

Olga Berggolts broadcast her poems regularly from Radio House.

Shostakovich walks past an image of Joseph Stalin in military garb.

Why am I telling you this? I'm telling you this so that the people of Leningrad listening to me will know that life goes on in our city. All of us now are standing militant watch. As a native of Leningrad who has never abandoned the city of my birth, I feel all the tension of this situation most keenly. My life and work are completely bound up with Leningrad.

He spoke rapturously and warmly of the city of his birth. He described it not as he had just seen it — with buildings mounded in sandbags, with empty windows gaping to the sky, with streets filled with rubble, with hillocks of debris. Instead, he recalled the city as those who lived there and loved it recalled it: as a city of wide avenues and gracious parks. Of course, he did not describe the city precisely as he had known it, shaken by revolution and hounded by terror. He described it, perhaps, as it had never quite been in his memory but had often been in his dreams.

He closed by promising the people of his city, "In a little while I shall have finished my Seventh Symphony. At the moment the work is going quickly and easily. My ideas are clear and constructive. The composition is nearing completion. Then I shall come on the air again with my new work and wait anxiously for a fair and kindly appraisal of my efforts."

With that modest flourish, he signed off.

As the radio committee had hoped, the story boosted morale around the city. "I am moved by the thought that while the bombs rain down on this besieged city Shostakovich is writing a symphony," one woman wrote in her diary after the news had been picked up by the local Communist Party newspaper. "*Leningrad Pravda's* report on it is tucked away between communiqués from the southern front and reports of petrol bombs. And so, in all this horror, art is still alive. It shines and warms the heart."

The night of the broadcast, Shostakovich and his family celebrated his progress with a small gathering at the apartment. A group of friends came by, and Shostakovich played them the two completed movements of the Seventh Symphony on the piano.

He played them the march that inexorably repeated like the scuttling of "iron rats," eventually growing to towering, ghastly dimensions. He played them the mischievous, strange little dance that followed.

A composer who was there wrote in his diary, "[Shostakovich] told us of the over-all plan. The impression we all had was tremendous." He was stunned at Shostakovich's ability to take "surrounding experiences" and transmute them into "a complex and large form."

Outside, the air-raid alarms sounded: foghorns, factory whistles, loudspeakers.

No one moved.

Someone asked him to play the whole thing again.

Shostakovich apologized and said that he had to take Nina and the children to the shelter in the basement. He excused himself.

When he came back up, despite the air raid, he played his half a symphony again.

The evening was a huge success. His friends were overwhelmed by his new work. It spoke somehow to what they all were feeling, trapped in that city.

When they left, Shostakovich couldn't calm himself down. He had ideas for the third movement—a slow Adagio he would eventually say described Russia's "Native Expanses."

There was no electricity. He lit a candle and sat down.

In the dark of night, he began to write again.

Propaganda displays hang on the columns of Kazan Cathedral in Leningrad.

FABLES, STORIES

Sometime in the 1950s, if we are to believe the story, a great Russian composer approached a neurosurgeon. Some might say the composer was named Dmitri Shostakovich. This composer explained to the neurosurgeon "that he had a piece of metal embedded in his head and wondered whether it should be removed."

The composer — once again, let us say it was Dmitri Shostakovich — explained that during the Siege of Leningrad, a shell had exploded in the street, and that shrapnel had lodged in his brain.

The neurosurgeon, somewhat surprised by this revelation, took some X-rays and then sat the composer in front of a fluoroscope. He could clearly see the metal fragment "in the temporal horn of the left ventricle (a cavity within the brain filled with cerebrospinal fluid)." He told the composer "it was probably advisable" to remove a large chunk of metal from his skull.

The composer looked uneasy. Suddenly he wasn't sure he wanted the neurosurgeon to extract it. When he was pressed, he admitted sheepishly that "since the fragment had been there, . . . each time he leaned his head to one side he could hear music. His head was filled with melodies — different each time — which he then made use of when composing." Conveniently enough, he could switch it off: "Moving his head back level immediately stopped the music."

The composer admitted he did not want to lose his metallic muse.

The neurosurgeon referred the problem to the surgeon-general of the armed forces. The surgeon-general shrugged and said to leave the shrapnel there. "After all, a German shell will have done some good if it helps produce more music."

This bizarre story sounds like something written by one of Shostakovich's writer friends, Daniil Kharms or Mikhail Zoshchenko. But is it true?

It would be very surprising if it were. First of all, we have this story only thirdhand. The neurosurgeon (who remains nameless) supposedly told the story years after the fact to a Chinese neurologist, who published an article about it many years after that, in 1983. In his record of the encounter, he depicts the neurosurgeon being somewhat cagey about the name of the composer in question, for reasons that are unclear.

The most damning argument against a shrapnel-based understanding of Shostakovich's art is his schedule during the siege. Given what we know about his activities, he simply did not have time to be hospitalized with a serious head wound and to convalesce.

No one at the time talked about a head wound. When she spoke later about the period, his daughter, Galina, old enough at the time to recall, did not mention her father being injured.

The Soviet press made the most of everything Shostakovich did as he composed his Seventh Symphony. They never said a thing about shrapnel. If Shostakovich had been hit in the siege and bravely gone on penning his intermezzo, it would have been a tremendously useful piece of propaganda. The Sovinform Bureau flooded the airwaves and newspapers with morale-boosting tales of freak heroism: a soldier who was buried alive when a Panzer rolled over him but whose distinctive boots stuck out of the soil, so his friends could find him and save him; a plucky Russian nurse who escaped a Nazi death camp through song. The writer Vasily Grossman snidely called news items like this "Ivan Pupkin killed five Germans with a spoon" stories. They filled the airwaves when the real news was too grim to report. The Shostakovich shrapnel story, if true, would have been milked for all it was worth.

The moment Shostakovich spoke over the radio, the story of the Seventh Symphony started to sparkle and to effervesce into myth. It became a public story used by others for their own ends. This does not mean that people lied — but people blurred details; they tugged; they nudged.

Take, for example, Shostakovich's stints on the roof of the Leningrad Conservatory, watching for incendiary bombs. A photo of him dressed in a firefighter's uniform became one of the most enduring images of the Great Patriotic War. It is quite likely that this photo was staged, however, and it's not even certain he typically wore this uniform, in which he stands with the stiffness of a paper doll clipped into a new outfit.

Though Shostakovich claimed that he had to stand guard every day, he also pointed out, "No firebombs fell on my sector and I never got a chance to put one out." A Conservatory official, Aron Ostrovsky, later admitted to Shostakovich that he had arranged the schedule to make sure that the composer was not on the roof during times of real danger. We cannot really tell, given the swirl of contradictory accounts, whether Shostakovich was still standing guard regularly in September, when the bombing started, or whether he primarily was employed as a fireman in July and August, when he simply would have been watching the horizon for raids that hadn't yet arrived.

Shostakovich hated the way propaganda amplified his life and sought to make it heroic. It galled him. He was naturally shy. Fame was deadly in Stalin's Russia. It marked you out for destruction.

Shostakovich had a hard life during the war — because everyone did. His life was often in danger, but no more so than that of any other civilian. He

Shostakovich as a firefighter on the roof of the Leningrad Conservatory in July 1941

knew that there were people suffering far worse than him. "The war became a terrible tragedy for everyone," he later said. "I saw and lived through a great deal, but the war was probably the hardest trial. Not for me personally, but for the people. For composers and, say, poets, perhaps, it wasn't so hard. But the people suffered. Think how many perished. Millions."

His own dislike of publicity and discomfort at fame, however, did not stop people from enlarging his story. Once his Seventh Symphony became famous, everyone tried to associate themselves with him. Stories about him multiplied. There are, for example, several versions of the events surrounding the fireman photograph. One of his soccer buddies claimed he went by one day with a photographer from the newspaper and they found Shostakovich training on the roof. They supposedly shot the pictures then. One composer even claimed that Shostakovich had never even acted as a lookout—he just stuck the fireman's hat on his head for a photo op. (This tale seems to be a cynic's rumor circulated by those who wanted to be "in the know.") Everyone wanted to be able to tell a story about Shostakovich. Uneasily, he felt himself being transmuted into legend.

In reality, phantom shrapnel in his head was the least of his problems.

Why would a symphony become so important to a country? How could sounds quivering in the air make any difference when the skies were full of solid metal shards and chemical explosives?

The answer is morale. "Morale is the big thing in war," explained British general Bernard Montgomery. "We must raise the morale of our soldiers to the highest pitch. They must be made enthusiastic."

Hope and belief seem insubstantial. Unlike shrapnel, they leave no trace when they lodge in our heads.

Yet ask athletes the secrets of their successes, and they will tell you of the importance of their mental state. Rage, pride, a taunt, or cheering on the sidelines can make the difference between success and failure.

Hope, belief, and despair are not simply moods. They change our physical performance. They alter how quickly we react, how hard we fight, how quick we are to give up.

Music can make a huge difference in how people see themselves and their struggle. We read, for example, of a Leningrad air raid. People crouched in a dark basement, terrified. Suddenly, an old man started to play upon his violin. "He is a really courageous person, and now I don't feel frightened either," a diarist wrote. "There are explosions all around us, and he is playing the violin as if he is leading us to safety. . . . The terror was somehow less powerful—it had lost its grip on us. It was outside us now; and inside we had our music, and everyone felt its power. There was a most extraordinary sense of belonging."

Moods and attitudes increasingly made a difference in Leningrad, even as concrete splintered and wood collapsed. The mental toughness of Leningraders made them capable of an endurance that should have been biologically impossible.

All the nations involved in the war used what we might call propaganda to change their citizens' moods. What is the line between art and propaganda? Art is, after all, supposed to affect our mood, is supposed to win us over to some understanding. And "propaganda" is often just what we call another nation's pride of country.

The Nazis, cold and clinical as their theorists might have been, believed entirely in the importance of emotion, mood, and propaganda. Feelings made a tremendous difference in the world of flesh and metal. Hitler put it in his own inimitable way: "Any violence which does not spring from a firm spiritual base will be wavering and uncertain. It lacks the stability which can only rest in a fanatical outlook."

The Nazis set out to make sure that their fanatical outlook was feared throughout the world. As Heinrich Himmler, the leader of the deadly SS, explained: "The reputation for horror and terror which preceded us we want never to allow to diminish. The world may call us what it will."

He got his wish: to this day, the Nazis are still used as the benchmark of human cruelty.

It is not clear if this "reputation for horror and terror" always worked in their favor as they swept across the USSR, however. In many of the Soviet satellite states and provinces, the Nazis were greeted at first with joy by the local population, who assumed they were being freed from Stalin's despotism. Some Latvians, Estonians, and Chechens even took up arms to fight against their local Soviet governments to ensure that the German invasion would go smoothly.

Ukrainians and Cossacks came out of their villages to welcome the Fascists with traditional gifts of bread and salt. They believed that the long horror of Soviet rule was over. Their churches, which the Communists had closed or turned into movie theaters or museums of atheism, would soon be opened again for worship. Peasants thought that the Nazis would dismantle the collective farms and drop the heavy government grain quotas that forced farmers to starve.

If the Nazis had simply been invaders, no more genocidal than any other conquering force, they probably could have held on to a lot of their captured territory without much trouble.

They believed, however, that they were dealing with subhumans. No sooner had they moved in than they began to slaughter the inhabitants and ship hundreds of thousands off to Germany as industrial slave labor. They did not dissolve the collective farms. Instead, they brutally demanded even more grain out of the peasantry. People starved. Himmler's SS tortured and shot their way through eastern Europe and Ukraine. In no time at all, the locals hated their new German overlords with a passion. They began an insistent, ceaseless guerrilla war, running through the woods and hiding in holes in the ground to harry the Wehrmacht.

If Germany had not worked so hard to make itself hated, it could perhaps have conquered whole Soviet territories without a fight.

This suggests the power of narratives and of philosophies.

* * *

"'Kill a German!' begs your elderly mother. 'Kill a German!' pleads a baby. 'Kill a German!' screams your Motherland. Avenge!"

Ukrainian prisoners of war march at the command of their German captors. Much of Ukraine — the USSR's fertile breadbasket — was quickly conquered by the Wehrmacht, supplying slave labor and resources for the Nazi war effort.

Shostakovich's symphony was born amid this struggle of ideas and hopes and fears. Hearing about it, people around Shostakovich buzzed with stories about him, some true, some reasonably true, and some far, far less true; to make things more complicated, Shostakovich himself occasionally also liked a good story. For this reason, who knows whether we can trust any given detail?

In later years, Shostakovich often told this story about the siege:

He was walking down one of the shell-pitted streets of the city. There was a funeral procession in front of him. (This was when there still were funerals for the dead, because death was still unusual in Leningrad. A few weeks later, no one would have bothered to bid the dead good-bye.) A band played Chopin's famous funeral march while a flatbed truck bumped along the road with the open coffin in the back. The mourners paced along behind.

Then came the shock: the corpse sat up.

People shrieked and fainted away.

"Can you imagine," Shostakovich said, "it wasn't a corpse they were going to bury, but someone who was in a state of lethargic sleep." The deceased was just fine.

The band, apparently more alert than the rest of the family, stopped playing the funeral march and swung into a lively rendition of the "Internationale," the Communist national anthem. The procession rejoiced, like some kind of Bolshevik New Orleans funeral party.

"Yes," Shostakovich claimed, "I saw this with my very own eyes."

One of his best friends, the cellist Mstislav Rostropovich, recorded this story. He said Shostakovich often told it. But Rostropovich didn't believe a word of it.

In the latter part of September, Shostakovich worked on the third move-ment—the Adagio—of his new symphony. During breaks, he'd go out into the streets for fresh air and inspiration. "Sometimes I'd wander off quite a distance from home, forgetting that I was in a city under siege that was regularly fired at and bombed.

"I looked at my beloved city with pain and pride. It stood singed in fires and tempered in battles. It had suffered the deepest anguish of the war and it was even more glorious now in its stern grandeur."

The bombings and shellings continued. On September 19, the Luftwaffe launched one of the most devastating air raids of the whole siege. Six waves of bombers, 264 aircraft in all, blasted at the city for more than seven hours. They dropped 528 high-explosive bombs and almost fifteen hundred incendiaries. Between air assaults, the German guns fired a hundred artillery shells into the belly of the city. Iconic buildings had holes smashed right through them: Gostiny Dvor, the old marketplace; the Engineers' Castle; the Russian Museum; and the Church of the Spilled Blood, with its gaudy onion spires. When the bombs were not actually falling, people in the city could hear a dull roar as crippled buildings collapsed. Gostiny Dvor burned quietly for more than a week.

The death toll was huge.

The Germans dropped leaflets over the city. They said, "We're giving you a respite until the 21st. If you do not surrender, we will grind you to a pulp." As one woman commented sharply, "It's unclear whom they were addressing. We common people are [insignificant]. As for Stalin, he has been grinding us to a pulp for the past twenty years."

What did Shostakovich write while the Germans battered the city in those late September days?

The third movement of the Seventh Symphony is slow, a long meditation or outcry punctuated with repetitions and transformations of a stark fanfare. He originally called it "Native Expanses," and perhaps that is what it depicts: pride in Russia's vastness, the dark taiga woodlands of Siberia, the lonely birch forests, the lapping shores of Lake Ladoga, the rich fields of Ukraine; to the north the tundra, to the east the desert, and to the south the grassy hills of Turkmenistan. It is filled with longing. It is suffused with a terrible tenderness.

His earlier symphonies—such as the suppressed Fourth—had been masterpieces of experiment and brittle irony. Now he allowed his music to sound painfully direct and vulnerable.

Shostakovich eventually removed the titles of his movements. When the piece was first performed and published, this third movement was no longer called "Native Expanses." What would it sound like if we didn't know that early title? Would it sound the same? Would we still hear evocations of gorgeous landscapes and beloved Russian wilderness? Or would we instead hear mourning and remembrance? Is the melody lyrical or tragic? Is it about love or loss? At one point, a savage march even stomps through the exquisite soliloquy. In some ways, this Adagio sounds more like a requiem for the dead than passages in the first movement that Shostakovich specifically described as a requiem. So how should we understand his own title — and how should we read its deletion? Every conductor, every listener, can ask themselves what the balance is between pride, tenderness, and loss, between love and lamentation.

Some love is so powerful, after all, that it must always include sadness, because encrypted within it is the knowledge that someday it will come to an end.

This is the music Shostakovich wrote as hundreds of bombers filled Leningrad with smoke, dust, and the cries of the dying.

On September 25, Dmitri Shostakovich turned thirty-five. For most of the day, he worked on his Adagio. In the evening, his family had a quiet little celebration. They had almost no food to eat. Some friends, however, "unearthed" a bottle of vodka. Another friend brought some crusts of black bread. The Shostakoviches were lucky enough to still have a store of potatoes. They broke bread with their friends. Perhaps Shostakovich's mother, Sofia, was there. Perhaps the children were allowed to stay up late. His sister Maria and her son, Dmitri, probably came. Outside the apartment was the blackened hulk of the building that had burned a few weeks before, a reminder of destruction, a memento mori.

Shostakovich had been born thirty-five years earlier in St. Petersburg.

He had seen revolution in the same city, then called Petrograd. Now he faced the possible destruction of Leningrad.

Was this still the city he was born in? Or had he in some sense gone into exile while only moving a few blocks away?

"I kept working day and night. There were times when the anti-aircraft guns were in action and bombs were falling, but I kept working."

He was done with the third movement, the Adagio, on September 29.

According to one story, he arranged for the three movements he had already written to be flown out of the city to safety that day.

If we are to believe this story, the poet Anna Akhmatova was being evacuated by plane to Tashkent. She had met Shostakovich at parties when he was only a boy in a sailor suit. During the years of the Great Terror, she had written a heartrending series of poems about the arrest of her son. They were too dangerous to be written down. She had circulated them by word of mouth: friends met to whisper them to each other, committing them to memory. (Similarly, Shostakovich later would write works that could not be performed in public, but only in secret, in apartments, when it was confirmed that no one present would snitch. And both of them learned to write things that could contain many meanings, as Akhmatova said: "I confess that I used / Invisible ink . . . / I write in mirror writing, / There's no other road open to me.")

Anna Akhmatova later claimed she had carried a manuscript of the Shostakovich Seventh on her lap when she was flown out of Leningrad to the east. We know he kept the full score, written out for full orchestra, with him; perhaps it was the piano version that she took.

Is this simply one of the stories people told about Shostakovich's Seventh, or did Akhmatova actually clutch the scribbled score on her knees as she soared out of the city? We don't know.

Later, when writing about that flight from the besieged city, she removed the part of the poem ("Poem Without a Hero") about the Seventh. She replaced it with a description of what she saw as she lifted above the broken horizon amid the bombardment of antiaircraft fire and soared off to safety.

It was unusual for the phone to ring in those days. Most of the phones in the city did not work. In mid-September, people all over the city had gotten calls from perky operators announcing, "This telephone is disconnected until the end of the war."

(Some were not disconnected fast enough. One day a blacksmith at the Kirov Tank Works picked up a ringing phone at the factory. The speaker on the other end spoke Russian with a heavy German accent. "Leningrad?" the voice quacked. "Very good! We will come tomorrow to visit the Winter Palace and the Hermitage." A menacing prank call: those were two of the great tourist attractions at the center of the city.)

Shostakovich must have been startled when his phone rang at eleven o'clock at night.

It was a call from a woman named Comrade Kalinnikova. She was phoning from Communist Party Headquarters. Shostakovich may have been worried, at least for a moment. The NKVD, even in the midst of war, arrested people in the middle of the night for spreading "defeatism."

But Comrade Kalinnikova was calling with good news. Shostakovich and his family needed to pack. They were going to be evacuated from Leningrad the next day. They would be flown to Moscow.

His whole family? No, only Nina and the children could come with him.

That meant that his mother, Sofia; his sister Maria; and his nephew, Dmitri, would be left behind.

Shostakovich made the arrangements for his family's flight. He was relieved that Galina and Maxim would no longer be in the besieged city. Surprisingly, he was still not ready to leave the city himself. He even asked if he could be flown back to Leningrad once the children were safe, so he could continue to work there.

He was leaving his "beloved home town"—but he hoped that they were all being flown to freedom.

Soviet soldiers man an anti-aircraft gun on the roof of the hotel in Moscow where Shostakovich and his family fled for safety. As the composer quickly discovered, no place was truly safe.

FLIGHT

On the afternoon of October 1, Shostakovich and his family loaded into his long black Emka automobile to go to the airport. The Germans were shelling the city. The guns were firing on the Pulkova Heights. As little Maxim got into the car, he asked his father what would happen if the Germans crashed into them.

Shostakovich was startled: it was the first time young Maxim had ever pronounced his *r*'s correctly.

They arrived at the airfield. Shostakovich apparently asked about the fate of his mother, his sister, and his nephew. He received assurances that they would be airlifted out soon.

It is unclear whether the Party just lost track of this promise or whether they were lying to the composer to get him on the plane. Regardless, Sofia, Maria, and her son remained trapped in Leningrad, as did Nina's family. The city officials had countless other things to worry about.

Dmitri, Nina, Maxim, and Galina were led out onto the airfield. They were taken to a transport plane. It was a small aircraft, and the

Shostakoviches were the only passengers. Inside the hold, there were no seats, just crates of cargo; they were not allowed to sit on the crates. The family settled themselves on top of their luggage. The plane had a glass turret, and a pilot positioned himself there to keep watch. He warned the family that if he gave a signal, they all had to flatten themselves on the wooden floor.

We do not know what time they took off, but we do know that there was a Luftwaffe air raid that evening. The pilots must have waited until the bombs stopped falling.

Finally, they taxied and lifted off over the city. The streets and buildings would have been dark beneath them. There was a blackout in effect to confuse German bombers.

They flew over the Wehrmacht's lines: first, the forward entrenchments — ditches where soldiers crouched — then, farther back, the German troops' bunkers and living quarters. Beyond that lay a flattened, devastated countryside with a new system of roads and ammunition depots created to supply armaments and food to the Wehrmacht on the front.

Maxim, craning his neck to look out the window, saw bright flashes popping in the darkness beneath them. He asked a pilot what the lights were.

"Someone explained to me that the Germans had opened fire on our aeroplane."

They were not hit. They flew over the ghostly landscape of occupied territory.

Early in the morning, they landed at a remote field in the forests near Moscow. The family clambered out of the plane with their luggage. They were taken to a nearby hut where they bedded down.

Behind them, the pilots dragged tree limbs out of the woods to hide the plane.

The next morning, they were driven into Moscow. It must have been a relief to be out of the line of fire.

Unfortunately, they had unwittingly left one theater of war for another. By terrible coincidence, Hitler, in the midst of a squabble with his generals, was turning his attention from Leningrad to Moscow. He launched a major attack on the Russian capital on the very day the Shostakoviches, tired and disoriented, arrived.

The Wehrmacht called its assault on Moscow Operation Typhoon. Colonel General Heinz Guderian and the Second Panzer Group had swerved north a few days earlier, and, on October 2, they began a steady, deadly crawl toward Moscow. Though Shostakovich probably did not know it, the Germans were closing in from both the west and the south.

The Shostakoviches were put up at the Moskva Hotel. They were promised an apartment sometime soon.

At first, the Shostakoviches found life much easier in Moscow than in Leningrad. They even took Maxim and Galina to a toy store so they'd have something to play with at the hotel.

Food, however, was still hard to come by. The shelves of grocery stores were empty of almost everything that hadn't been jarred and pickled. Milk was ten times as expensive as usual. Butter was even worse. There was no meat whatsoever.

Air raids on Moscow were frequent and devastating. The Soviet air force struggled to stop the waves of aerial assault, but they had lost too many planes to be effective. To confuse bombers, the medieval walls of the Kremlin were draped in huge canvases painted with rows of fake houses.

At first, the NKVD had discouraged evacuation from the city. Now it was letting people leave with signed permission. Certain government departments were being evacuated east to the city of Kuibyshev, modern-day Samara. They took all their files and records with them. Perhaps the most striking evacuee was the corpse of Vladimir Lenin. His preserved body was loaded into a specially built refrigerated freight car and taken off to Siberia over the Ural Mountains. The corpse of the grand statesman would be safer than most living Muscovites.

When the air-raid alarms sounded, Shostakovich and his family retreated to the basement of their hotel. It was cold and damp. The noise

A lookout surveys the Moscow skies.

A German flare lights up the Kremlin during a bombing raid on Moscow.

and violence of attack was every bit as bad as in Leningrad. During one bombardment, a conductor stumbled upon Shostakovich and his family there. The composer was pacing back and forth nervously, muttering to himself, "Oh, Wright brothers, Wright brothers . . . What have you wrought?"

On October 5, a Soviet Pe-2 light bomber flying a routine reconnaissance route spied a column of German tanks twelve miles long rolling up the Moscow-Warsaw highway unopposed and unnoticed. The German force was only eighty miles from the capital.

When the pilot returned to base and reported what he'd seen, no one believed him. In time-honored Soviet tradition, he was arrested for "provocation."

Soon enough, it became clear that he had not been lying: By five thirty the next morning, the German Tenth Panzer Division had captured Yukhnov. At the same time, the Seventeenth Panzer Division, rolling up from the south, took Bryansk. The Soviet general in the area did not know the region was under attack until the Panzers actually began firing at his headquarters.

On tactical maps, the German approach looked like clean arrows driving in from the south and west. On the ground, however, nothing was clean, and every inch of those abstract lines signified an unmeasurable gulf of suffering. Villages and fields were in flames. When Russians heard of the German approach, they were under orders to set their own property on fire before they fled. When they did not hear of the German approach in advance, they were often slaughtered and their towns torched in the assault. Millions lost their homes and everything they owned.

After the Germans took the city of Orel on October 3, journalist Vasily Grossman wrote about the chaos of mass evacuation:

> I thought I'd seen retreat, but I've never seen anything like what
> I'm seeing now. . . . Exodus! Biblical exodus! Vehicles are moving
> in eight columns, there's the violent roaring of dozens of trucks

trying simultaneously to tear their wheels out of the mud. Huge herds of sheep and cows are driven through the fields. They are followed by trains of horse-drawn carts, there are thousands of wagons covered with colored sackcloth, veneer, tin. . . . There are also crowds of pedestrians with sacks, bundles, suitcases. This isn't a flood, this isn't a river, it's the slow movement of a flowing ocean . . . hundreds of meters wide.

Stalin was bewildered by the German successes. Since the launch of Operation Barbarossa, the Soviets had lost twenty thousand tanks and some three million soldiers. The Red Army had started with five million men; now only 2.3 million were left. That was a loss of about forty-four thousand per day.

Ninety million Soviets — 45 percent of Russia's prewar population — were now living in occupied German territory. It seemed clear to the regime that within a few days, Moscow itself would be taken.

It is no wonder that in a vulnerable, stunned moment, Stalin croaked to his commanders, "Comrade Stalin is not a traitor. Comrade Stalin is an honest person. Comrade Stalin will do everything to correct the situation that has been created."

He spoke of himself in the third person, as if acknowledging that Comrade Stalin was at this point something larger than his own human self, something more akin to the godlike, mustached heads that stared out of banners and posters all over the nation.

Dismally planning for defeat, Stalin began to make arrangements for the utter destruction of Moscow in the case of a successful Nazi invasion.

Recently, his secret plans have come to light. He arranged for twelve hundred buildings to be rigged with explosives: prominent hotels, famous churches, and the Kremlin itself. Large country houses surrounding Moscow were booby-trapped, too, with the exception of his own. (He was worried that someone would detonate his house with him in it.) The capital's

As the Germans advanced, Russian peasants burned their own villages and fields and fled to the east. These "burnt earth" tactics deprived the Germans of food and bases for occupation as they swept across Soviet territory.

A German attack has left nothing but chimney stacks where a town once stood.

water and electrical supplies would be destroyed. A resistance network of 269 Muscovites with code names like Clamps and Whistler were prepared to take as many Germans down with them as they could.

Stalin calculated that if the Germans managed to take the city, there would be a grand gala celebration at the Bolshoi Theater, where Shostakovich's *Lady Macbeth of Mtsensk District* had once played. Stalin decided to turn the Germans' victory celebration into a massacre. The orchestra pit would be lined with explosives. Ballerinas and circus acrobats were trained to dance onstage with hand grenades.

Shostakovich's colleague composer Lev Knipper was given the job of assassinating Hitler. (Knipper was a secret agent, and his sister Olga was one of Hitler's favorite actresses.)

The city would have welcomed its new masters by erupting into a dazzling fountain of mass destruction. It was a desperate plan — the flattening of a city that had been a symbol of Russian national pride since the Middle Ages.

The ruinous self-destruction that was planned shows how close Stalin felt he was to defeat.

On October 11, Shostakovich went into the offices of *Sovetskoe iskusstvo* (*Soviet Art*) to play his piano score of the new, uncompleted symphony. He performed it in the editorial boardroom. He and his audience were unaware that their Leader was, at the time, considering blowing up the city in which they sat.

The piece, even in its unfinished state, made a huge impression. In particular, the people who heard it that day were struck by the first movement, in which "Shostakovich takes a monotonous Prussian march, sets it in the style of the most banal music-hall tune, then relentlessly and ingeniously turns it into a grotesque parody that implicitly, and with enormous force, stigmatizes the nonentity of German Nazism."

They heard in it the approach of the Panzers outside the city gates, the growing danger of invasion.

* * *

Two weeks after the Shostakoviches arrived in Moscow, they were finally granted the use of an apartment. They moved out of the Moskva Hotel immediately.

They slept only one night in their new home.

By the next morning, the military situation was so dire that the city was in an uproar. Even the Sovinform Bureau loudspeakers admitted, "The situation around Moscow has deteriorated." Ack-ack guns blasted away at the sky. There were rumors the Germans had reached the gates of Moscow — rumors that they would take the capital the next day.

Shostakovich and his family were told they were being evacuated immediately. They were going to be put on a train with other cultural workers and taken east — somewhere east — no one knew exactly where.

They rushed to the station. No buses or trolleys were even running. The streets were mobbed with refugees. People had been struggling to get into the city; now everyone was trying to flee. It has since been called *bolshoi drap*, "the Big Skedaddle." Confusion and flight were everywhere.

The main eastern routes of the city were jammed with trucks and cars while people fled on foot. Factory workers were outraged to discover that their bosses had requisitioned trucks to flee to safety with all their furniture — fancy beds, hall mirrors, "their rubber plants and chests of drawers" — leaving their workers behind. People blocked exits so the Party elite couldn't leave and even yanked their bosses out of cars mired in traffic. There were riots on the Highway of the Enthusiasts.

People were smashing the windows of food stores and looting. Gangs robbed people's empty houses or grabbed things from refugees on the streets. The police were nowhere to be found. Government officials were destroying incriminating paperwork as quickly as they could, burning all the records of their war arrangements and their homicidal pasts. The smoke and ashes of decades of Soviet bureaucracy filled the sky.

"Black snow flew," one man remembered. "It was a scene out of the Apocalypse."

* * *

Things at the train station were just as chaotic as out on the streets. The square in front of Kazan Station was packed with people. Shostakovich and his family made their way through the crowds.

An artist and friend of Shostakovich's, Nikolai Sokolov, was being herded onto the same train. He remembered the departure:

> Inside the station writers, painters, musicians and artists from the Bolshoi and Vakhtangov Theatres were huddled beside their belongings, trying to make themselves comfortable. The loud-speakers continuously blared announcements. At last we were informed that the train was ready to board. People put on their rucksacks, picked up their bundles and suitcases, and made for the platform, which was enveloped in terrible darkness. Underfoot the snow was wet and squelchy. Everyone pushed and shoved at each other with their belongings. We had a single ticket for a whole group of artists, which got torn in half in the crush. We had been designated carriage no. 7; a queue had formed out-side it. Somebody stood guarding the door, blocking the entrance, shouting, "This carriage is only for the Bolshoi Theatre."

Shostakovich had never been particularly good at fending for himself. In this bustling mob, he was at a loss. The nephew of a friend spotted him on the train platform. "He looked completely bereft. He was holding a sewing machine in one hand and a children's potty in the other, while his wife Nina Vasilyevna stood beside the children and a mountain of stuff. I helped them load their things on to the train. Later, when I made my way home from the station, I was struck by the number of howling dogs roaming the snowy streets, having been abandoned by their owners."

Despite his generous offer of aid, the young man evidently didn't do a great job helping the Shostakovich family with their belongings; they were soon to find that most of their luggage was missing, either stolen or left on the platform.

Shostakovich was paralyzed in the midst of the crowd. Another composer came to his aid. "Allow Shostakovich and his children to pass!" he bellowed.

Dmitri, Nina, Galina, and Maxim squeezed their way onto Railway Car No. 7. Other composers jammed themselves through the door behind them. It was a car meant for forty-two passengers. It was holding more than one hundred.

The precious manuscript of the Seventh Symphony had been wrapped in a blanket and, apparently, removed from the luggage for safekeeping. As the family struggled onto the train, the unthinkable happened: the score of the Seventh, scribbled down between bombing raids, symbol of the city's endurance, the main reason Shostakovich had delayed his family's escape from the city — this bundle of papers had disappeared.

At the time, the composer didn't even notice. Everyone was crammed in too tightly.

At ten at night, the train set off.

Moscow was blacked out to confuse enemy bombers. The locomotive crawled through the darkened city. "It travelled very slowly," the artist Sokolov remembered. "Near Ryazan it picked up speed; the town was being bombed by the Fascists. Some of us were on our feet throughout the night. As morning dawned we started to scrutinize each other in the light. Some people gave up their seats to those who had been standing. In other words, people started to soften and show kindness."

The train headed to the east.

A many-fingered Shostakovich using his music as a weapon — it sticks out of his rifle like a bayonet and is strapped around his chest like a bandolier. The caricature is by the Kukryniksy cartoonists, one of whom traveled with the composer on Railway Car No. 7.

RAILWAY CAR NO. 7

Railway Car No. 7, with its cargo of ballerinas, poets, painters, and symphonists, rumbled slowly across the frozen plains.

There was not enough room for everyone to sleep at once. At night, the women would lie down and sleep. During the day, the men slept.

The artist Sokolov remembered, "A wet snow, almost rain, was falling. By morning, it had frozen. People got out of the train and wandered by the carriages. They looked to each other for reassurance." Everyone was dazed.

Nikolai Sokolov had worked with Shostakovich before. He was one of a group of three cartoonists who had smashed their names together (Kupriyanov, Krylov, and Sokolov) and called themselves the Kukryniksy. They signed their work in common. Together they had created the grotesque sets for the first act of Meyerhold and Mayakovsky's *Bedbug*, the part of the play set in the 1920s.

Sokolov wasn't the only person the Shostakoviches knew in Railway Car No. 7. Many of the nation's most famous composers were also crammed into the seats and swaying in the aisles.

Two of Shostakovich's suitcases had disappeared. One had his clothes in it, and the other had Maxim's and Galina's things. He looked desperately for his luggage but couldn't find it anywhere. Even worse, he now discovered that the score to his Seventh Symphony had disappeared. Presumably, he had kept it out of his luggage precisely because he wanted to keep it safe by his side, but it was gone. Oddly, another composer, a friend of his named Vissarion Shebalin, had also lost a symphony. Shebalin pushed his way through the car, asking people if they'd seen his work. Shostakovich, however, simply sat numbly, without moving, and stared.

"I saw Shostakovich getting out at the stations to fetch boiling water," said Sokolov. "He washed his crockery with snow at the side of the carriage. He was traveling in an old worn suit, and his legs got soaked through."

Sokolov offered him some dry socks. Someone else, seeing that he didn't have a change of clothes, lent him a shirt. "He took these things very shyly and thanked everybody in a state of great agitation."

Dmitri and Nina worked out a system: When the train stopped at a station, one of them would run and buy food. The other would get hot water from the stationmaster to wash the children's clothes.

On the platforms around them loomed huge machines shrouded under tarpaulins—armaments and assembly-line mechanisms ready for shipment east or west.

Railway Car No. 7 traveled for days. The passengers were heading for cities all over the eastern Soviet republics: Alma-Ata, where Shostakovich's sister Maria had been exiled a few years earlier; Tashkent, where the poet Anna Akhmatova had flown; Kuibyshev, where the government was relocating in case Moscow fell. It appears that initially the Shostakoviches were considering Tashkent, perhaps because the Leningrad Philharmonic had already fled there a few months earlier. As it turned out, they would not make it that far.

The train did not move quickly. Often, it would be diverted onto railway sidings and would sit motionless for hours. While it idled, other trains rushed past in the opposite direction, carrying troops, tanks, and artillery toward Moscow's battlefields. Hospital trains barreled off to the east, carrying the wounded away from the front. Long rail caravans headed for distant republics carried dismantled steel mills and agricultural machinery chained down to flatbed cars. Refugees from collective farms rode in the freight cars with their tractors and plows, peering out at the forests flashing past. As one eyewitness described it, "There was almost unbelievable misery among the refugees. There were hunger and disease. There was everything except a spirit of defeatism."

In Moscow, now almost encircled by the Wehrmacht, the State Committee for Defense also struggled to avoid a spirit of defeatism. Stalin toyed with the idea of evacuating east himself and taking up residence in Kuibyshev, but he decided to risk staying in the capital.

The trains Shostakovich saw swaying past delivered fresh troops from Siberia, the south, and the east to the Moscow region. They were immediately put into the field, ready or not, and made valiant stands against the onslaught of Army Group Center and its Panzer divisions. Despite their efforts, the Germans fought their way to a town only twenty miles from Moscow.

At this point, Stalin no longer worked from the Kremlin. He and his staff had set up barracks and offices deep beneath the city, in the subway tunnels. The Moscow Metro system was famous for its splendor, the marble colonnades and gleaming arches that welcomed commuters. Now many of the war department's staff slept in subway cars on unused tracks. Stalin assembled a temporary office in Mayakovsky Station—named after the ill-fated Futurist suicide—and from there, he directed his generals and received his communiqués.

He had not been a military man at the beginning of the war, but he was learning quickly.

Meanwhile, up above on the streets, the populace was uneasy. "People are saying things out loud that three days ago would have brought them before a military tribunal," a journalist wrote in his diary.

The hysteria at the top has transmitted itself to the masses. People are beginning to remember and to count up all the humiliations, the oppression, the injustices, the clampdowns, the bureaucratic arrogance of the officials, the conceit and the self-confidence of the party bureaucrats, the draconian decrees, the shortages, the systematic deception of the masses, the lying and flattery of the toadies in the newspapers. . . . People are speaking from their hearts. Will it be possible to defend a city where such moods prevail?

On the fourth day of the clattering voyage east, there was finally some good news for Dmitri Shostakovich: his brilliant new symphony was found, wrapped in a blanket, on the bathroom floor.

It was sitting in a puddle, swamped with dirty water and urine. Nina could barely stand to touch the bundle, even to save a masterpiece.

When the Shostakoviches gingerly unwrapped it, they discovered that the score was almost entirely unstained.

The lesson here: a true masterpiece can marinate in filth and still come out clean.

The journey went on for a week. Maxim and Galina were bored and going stir-crazy. Shostakovich spent his time reading plays or chatting with his fellow composers.

One of the composers who had escaped on Railway Car No. 7 was a young man named Tikhon Khrennikov. He had idolized Shostakovich when he was a student. Now he became one of Shostakovich's poker partners. In a few years, he would denounce Shostakovich in front of the whole nation.

For the moment, they all talked about music and wished they could hear some. They also bickered about where they thought Shostakovich should get off the train. Everyone had advice, and he was too timid to tell them to stop pestering him. He sat miserably while they all discussed his fate and badgered him about where he and his family should stop off: Kuibyshev or

Tashkent. Kuibyshev, one claimed, was where everyone from the government was fleeing; it would be crowded and there would be no food left. "Why not continue to Tashkent?"

"No!" bellowed another. "Why drag the children on another eight days' journey to Tashkent?"

"In Tashkent he won't go hungry, but what awaits him in Kuibyshev?"

As the group debated what his family should do, Shostakovich murmured things like, "Yes . . . yes . . ." or "Possibly, possibly . . ."

"But Dmitri Dmitriyevich, how about . . . ?"

The argument showed no signs of flagging. Shostakovich wandered away without listening, stepping over luggage and packages to return to his wife and children.

On the morning of October 22, the train reached the great Volga River. Relatives of his close friend Sollertinsky wrote:

> The impression when the train began to cross the bridge was a little unnerving. Those who had been in Leningrad under constant fire, hearing the explosions of bombs nearby, and those who had flown by night over the enemy positions to escape, should of course have feared nothing here, but still, involuntarily, they held their breath while the train moved — for an eternity, it seemed — over the Volga; only the steel struts of the bridge moved outside the windows, and they could see leaden ripples and menacing little flecks of foam far below.

The train had reached Kuibyshev, seat of the government in exile.

It was there that the Shostakoviches decided to get off the evacuation train and seek shelter and safety.

Soviet tanks on parade in Kuibyshev Square, November 1941

KUIBYSHEV AND LENINGRAD

Kuibyshev was overrun with refugees. The old storefronts and apartment buildings were occupied by ministries and commissariats that had fled Moscow when the Germans launched Operation Typhoon. The lampposts were plastered with desperate notes from lost, fleeing family members looking for one another.

The city of Kuibyshev must have seemed like the middle of nowhere to the Muscovites who now roamed its unpaved, dirt streets. There were few cars; most people used horse-carts or camels. Every morning, workers were loaded onto squeaking, antique trams and taken to work in a nearby industrial suburb called Nameless. Now rapid construction prepared drab Kuibyshev to become Russia's most important city, if necessary. In the crammed factories of Nameless, workers assembled planes for the front. An underground headquarters was being built for Comrade Stalin. (As it turned out, he never used it.)

Shostakovich and other refugees from Railway Car No. 7 were shuttled to a school building already occupied by dancers from the Bolshoi Theater.

They divided themselves up, eighteen to a classroom. This was their temporary home. Everyone slept on the floor, pressed close together. No one had a mattress. Outside the door was a mound of muddy overshoes.

Still, the situation was better than it had been on the train. Shostakovich found that the rations for his family were much better than they'd had in a while — including not only butter and sweets but also salami.

Nikolai Sokolov fondly remembered the high artistic bar set by the whistling in the boys' bathroom. The nation's most famous opera singers and musicians hummed arias while they bathed and shaved.

It appears that after a few days, the Shostakoviches were put in a smaller room with just one other couple, a set designer and an actress. They clipped up some cotton curtains to try to get some privacy.

There was no question of Shostakovich working on his symphony. There was too much confusion, too much fear, too much sorrow. One day, Sokolov asked him how work on the fourth and final movement was coming along.

Shostakovich said miserably, "You know, as soon as I got on that train, something snapped inside me. . . . I can't compose just now, knowing how many people are losing their lives."

He did not write a note for a month and a half.

He thought of his native city.

Leningrad in November 1941 had begun to sink into darkness. The days were short. The winter had set in. By the middle of the month, the temperature dropped below zero. This was not unusual, but this year, people did not have fuel. Their furnaces were empty. There were no more deliveries of coal. Even if trains had been able to get through, the coal mines of the south and west were now in German hands. There were no reserves of firewood: the city had been surrounded before the usual winter deliveries had been made. People were freezing.

Many of their windows had been blown out by nearby explosions. The

cold air drifted in. People blocked up the empty window frames with anything they could find: boards, furniture, rags, plywood, a handmade Turkish
carpet. Most people had no electricity, so the blocked windows meant that
they sat in the dark. It was hard to get candles or lamp oil. The population
passed their days in cavelike apartments, listening for the air-raid sirens.

"The temperature is really dropping now," a Leningrad soldier noted
in his diary, "and hunger is a constant presence among us. The food we
are issued is very poor. Today I saw some civilians crying by the road-
side—they were so desperately hungry. They told me their babies are
dying from malnutrition." The city government still passed out ration cards,
but almost nothing on the cards was actually available. The bread ration
shrank, it seemed, week by week.

The man hired to make announcements about rationing, Ivan
Andreyenko, later spoke angrily about the fact that more people hadn't been
evacuated before the Germans arrived. In particular, he cursed the propaganda that had convinced people like Shostakovich that they should stay in
their native city rather than abandon it. "From one point of view, you see, it
was good, but from another it was bad, because we shouldn't have evacuated
636,000 but many more than that, twice as many, even three times." As it
was, about two and a half million people remained in Leningrad, desperately
hungry, miserably cold, some without shelter.

Among them were Shostakovich's mother, Sofia; his sister Maria; and
his nephew, Dmitri. It had become very clear that the government had no
real intention of flying them out.

They were stuck in the city as it starved to death.

The Leningrad authorities were running out of flour to make the rationed
bread. They started to use substitutes. In September, white flour was mixed
with horse fodder. In October, a supply of grain that had been sunk on
barges in Lake Ladoga during a German air attack was dredged up and used
to bake loaves that stank of mold. In November, the government bakeries

resorted to "edible" cellulose made from pine sawdust and floor sweepings. By November 20, the bread ration had been reduced to the point where factory workers got 250 grams a day; Sofia, Maria, young Dmitri, and most of the rest of the population would have gotten 125 grams a day. Officially, this was about a quarter of what an adult needs to retain normal body weight. Unofficially, there was so much filler in the bread that was not food that the real nutritional value of it was much, much lower.

A Leningrad mother later remembered, "In those days when you took [the bread] in your hand water oozed from it and it was like clay. Imagine bread like that for children! True, my children weren't in the habit of asking for things, but you could see it in their eyes. You should have seen those eyes!"

Meanwhile, the Germans dropped leaflets that taunted, "Finish your bread; you'll soon be dead!"

"There have been cases of increasingly weak workers falling unconscious in the workplace," the German intelligence service reported with delight. "The first starvation deaths have also been recorded. It can be concluded that in the coming weeks we will see further significant deterioration in the food situation of the civilian population of Petersburg." They were thrilled.

The people of Leningrad stood in the bread lines day after day as the temperature dropped and dropped. They did not only have to worry about the Luftwaffe bombing them from above; men also lay in wait near the ends of lines to grab bread out of people's weakened hands and cram it into their own mouths. On the wrong day, that small theft could mean the difference between life and death.

Families found that hunger drove them to creative solutions. They stripped wallpaper off the walls and ate the paste. Some had read adventure novels in which starving explorers ate leather. They boiled belts and animal pelts. Unfortunately, treated leather, unlike rawhide, was saturated with polish and tanning chemicals. It took a long process of trial and error to learn how to cook a belt. They scraped the joiner's glue from furniture.

The writer Aleksandr Fadeyev recalled the recipe for "Leningrad blockade jelly": "As everybody knows, carpenter's glue is got from bones. Here was the reverse process: you cooked the glue, removed all the bone scum—or rather, the scum of what had once been bone—and added gelatin to the rest. Then you let it cool." Some people garnished it with bay leaves. They smeared it with mustard to hide the flavor.

People fought over cakes of cattle feed made of pressed seed husks. Men and women ate lipstick or used it as cooking grease to make pancakes of face powder. Factory workers discovered that industrial casein, used to make paint, was barely edible. It made them sick, but it was better than death.

A mother, desperate to feed her family, boiled the pages of books. Their father fed them felt.

An NKVD agent reported: "I witnessed a scene in the street where a cab driver's horse collapsed from exhaustion. People ran up to it with hatchets and knives. They hacked off pieces of the horse and carried them home. This was horrible. They looked like executioners."

One man rapturously remembered the day that a woman on an armament assembly line invited him over for several handfuls of tank lubricant. They were so hungry that it tasted delicious.

One diarist wrote: "Protein—meat—we hardly see at all. Recently Professor Z. told me, 'Yesterday my daughter spent all day in the attic searching for the cat.' I was prepared to be deeply touched by such love for animals, but Z. added: 'We eat them.'"

People were ashamed by what they were doing, by the scrounging, by the theft, by the bickering, but they were starving. They were no longer themselves. Or as one woman wrote, perhaps they were even more themselves: "Before the war, people adorned themselves with bravery, fidelity to principles, honesty—whatever they liked. The hurricane of war has torn off those rags: now everyone has become what he was in fact, and not what he wanted to seem."

In the months that followed, this question of what people were really made of and what the human animal really was would become a desperately important one.

Many died of cold or hunger.

"The city is literally flooded with corpses," wrote diarist Elena Skrjabina toward the end of November. "Relatives or friends take them to be buried, tied on by twos and threes to small sleds. Sometimes you come across larger sleighs on which the corpses are piled high like firewood and covered over by a canvas. Bare, blue legs protrude from beneath the canvas. You can be certain this is not firewood."

And around the same time, she noted that people had begun whispering that meat had begun reappearing at the markets — and that it was made of the flesh of the dead.

In Kuibyshev, Shostakovich found some relief from his anxiety. The city was far from the front. The composer and his family had finally been moved into their own room. It had beds in it. The Commissar of the Council of the Arts had even found him a piano. It was expected he would soon get back to work.

Artist Nikolai Sokolov dropped by one day to talk to him. Shostakovich drummed his fingers on the table. He was anxiously pondering how little or how much people needed to be happy.

> You know, Nikolai [he said], when I got into that dark carriage with the children in Moscow I felt that I was in paradise! But by the seventh day of the journey I felt that I was in hell. When we were settled in the classroom of the school, and what's more given a carpet and surrounded by suitcases, I again felt myself to be in paradise; but after three days I was fed up; in these circumstances you can't get undressed, being surrounded by a mass of strangers. I again perceived this as hell. And then we were allocated this room to ourselves, with decent conditions. . . . And what do you think? Shortly, I felt that I must have a piano. I was given a piano.

A precious bread ration card

A man suffering from dystrophy clutches his ration.

When horses died, they quickly became food for the people around them.

Everything seemed just fine, and I thought to myself again, "This is paradise." But now I notice how inconvenient it is to work in a single room; the children are rowdy and disturb me. Yet they have every right to be noisy, they are only children, but unfortunately I can't work.

At the beginning of December, their living arrangements improved even more: they got an apartment with two rooms. One became Shostakovich's study, with the piano and a desk. They slept in the other one. A young woman from upstairs, Flora Litvinova, a daughter-in-law of the Soviet ambassador to the United States, had some children's clothes that didn't fit her son. She gave them to Nina for the kids. Flora Litvinova also took Nina shopping, and they bought bowls, glasses, and mugs, though even the department store for the bureaucratic elite was running out of goods.

Their apartment was now outfitted.

Still, Shostakovich couldn't finish his symphony.

Flora Litvinova, listening through the apartment floor, heard him try for a few minutes and give up. "Today (2 December) I heard the piano and some obviously Shostakovich-like sounds. I got terribly excited. I stood next to the radiator so that I could hear better." The music, however, quickly stopped. Instead, Galina and Maxim started bawling out a song: "Three soldiers in a tank, three jolly friends!"

Knowing what he did about the plight of Leningrad and the precarious situation of the country as a whole, Shostakovich couldn't work on his piece.

Who could have?

Who cared?

A parade of tanks makes a show of strength in Moscow, November 1941. Displays such as this were important to calm the fears of the populace.

AN OPTIMISTIC SHOSTAKOVICH

Early in December 1941, two things changed the direction of the war entirely.

The first was that the Red Army began to win their desperate, grappling battle against the Germans near Moscow. The German troops were exhausted. Their generals had planned for an easy victory before the winter set in. Everyone knew that invading Russia in winter was futile, disastrous. Napoleon, leading his Grande Armée, had made it to Moscow more than a century earlier, but even he, one of the most famous generals in the history of Europe, found that the Russian winter sapped his army's strength, trapped his forces without food and ammunition, and killed hundreds of thousands of his soldiers.

Operation Barbarossa, Hitler's invasion of Russia, had been launched on the anniversary of Napoleon's invasion. To Hitler's generals, that detail now seemed gloomily prophetic.

The winter had closed in. The snow was deep. As the Germans prepared to snap their iron ring shut around Moscow, the temperatures ranged between zero and forty below. It was so cold that when a man spat, it hit the ground frozen. Yet the Wehrmacht troops did not have winter gear or heavy coats. Their uniforms had been issued for a July invasion. There was a rumor that Hitler did not send them to the front with adequate coats because he wanted to force them to win the war by autumn. This is not true, we know now; German supply lines were simply stretched too thin. Winter clothing had been issued, but it was stuck in depots back in Poland.

The cold caused machinery to freeze. Tanks, finally freed by the first frosts from the autumn mud-wallows, now seized up and would not start at all. Planes couldn't fly in the harsh conditions. The supply lines were so tenuous that the Germans often couldn't get oil or ammo.

As one Panzer officer complained, "We have blundered, mistakenly, into an alien landscape with which we can never be properly acquainted. Everything is cold, hostile, and working against us."

Once Stalin had made a firm decision not to abandon Moscow, he stubbornly would not let anyone else flee, either. The troops that had passed the Shostakoviches on the railways were now arriving at the front. Stalin and his generals immediately sent them into the field against the Wehrmacht. Their losses were huge, but Stalin would not let them retreat. Russian frontline soldiers were overwhelmed and bewildered by the relentless casualties. As one machine-gunner put it: "The frontal attacks puzzled me. Why advance straight into German machine-gun fire? Why not make flank attacks?" These suicidal charges worked occasionally only because Stalin did not care how many of his own soldiers died.

When the Germans were within seven miles of General Zhukov's headquarters, one of Stalin's men in the field called the Leader to pass on a request from the men there to abandon their command center and move headquarters east of Moscow, where they would be farther from the fighting.

Stalin listened to the request over the phone. He considered. Finally, he said, "Comrade Stepanov, ask them whether they have any spades."

"I'll find out straight away." Stepanov turned and talked to the members of the military staff. He returned to the phone. "What sort of spades, Comrade Stalin? Entrenching tools or some other kind?"

"It doesn't matter what sort."

"I'll find out straight away." There was a pause. "Yes, there are spades, Comrade Stalin. What should they do with them?"

"Comrade Stepanov, tell your comrades to take their spades and dig themselves some graves. The [high command is] not leaving Moscow. I'm not leaving Moscow. And they're not going anywhere."

Slowly, painfully, with the loss of more than a third of the troops in the area, the Red Army pushed back the Germans. The tide turned in the second week of December 1941. The Soviets repelled all three of the German armor divisions around Moscow, destroying almost five hundred tanks, and they scattered almost all of German Army Group Center.

For the first time in World War II, one of Hitler's land armies had been stopped.

It was huge news. Still, the Sovinform Bureau did not report the victories for days. They needed to be sure, apparently. On December 13, they finally allowed the headline to break: "The Collapse of the German Plan to Surround and Capture Moscow—Defeat of German Forces."

It was this news, supposedly, that led Shostakovich to think he could perhaps resume work and write a triumphant finale to his symphony.

There was, however, another military event at around the same time that would change the course of the war. On December 7, 1941, the Japanese launched a surprise attack on the American naval base at Pearl Harbor. Eight battleships were sunk to the bottom of the harbor or left in flames. During a devastating air raid that resembled the Germans' on the first day of Operation Barbarossa, 188 American planes were destroyed, most of them never even leaving the ground. Two-thirds of the American military aircraft in the Pacific were wiped out in the space of a few minutes.

Red Army soldiers crouch in defensive positions in the countryside outside Moscow.

The Red Army, dressed in winter gear, struggles to defend Moscow from attack.

German Panzers advance on Istra, to the west of Moscow. Roughly a thousand German tanks took part in Operation Typhoon. Almost half of them were destroyed in the bitter winter fighting.

Unprepared for the ferocity of the Soviet counterattack and the brutality of the Russian winter, German Army Group Center suffered heavy casualties during its failed attempt to capture Moscow. Twenty-four thousand Wehrmacht soldiers were killed; five thousand more went missing in action.

The Japanese bombing of the American naval base at Pearl Harbor delivered a powerful surprise blow and brought the United States into the war at the close of 1941.

Stalin (on the left) and his unlikely collaborators in the Grand Alliance: American president Franklin D. Roosevelt (center) and British prime minister Winston Churchill (right) in a 1943 meeting

The United States formally declared war against Japan. This activated a series of interlocking treaties and agreements. Now Great Britain, the USSR, and the United States found themselves officially united against the Axis powers (Japan, Germany, and Italy)—alliances that would have seemed bizarre and impossible just a few months earlier.

This gave the Russians hope, however. Perhaps now the western Allies would open up a "Second Front" in Europe, trying to take back France, and the Germans' troops and attention would be distracted from their savage assault on the Soviet Union.

Things seemed to be looking up.

Nikolai Sokolov remembered, "As soon as the news came through that the Fascists had been smashed outside Moscow, [Shostakovich] sat down to compose in a burst of energy and excitement."

At the same time, the composer spent a lot of time writing to various government offices in Kuibyshev, trying to get them to evacuate his mother, sister, and nephew from Leningrad. "He was very distraught," a neighbor remembered. "At the Leningrad airfield they had promised to put his mother [Sofia] on the next plane out, but they hadn't. Now he was obsessed with the idea of chartering a plane to go and fetch her." This didn't come to anything, but he kept on trying.

He intervened for friends and colleagues, too. Shostakovich didn't have a problem using his celebrity status to help other people. He had a nervous horror, however, of asking for things for himself. Friends were surprised that he didn't request a car in Kuibyshev. "He never asked for anything for himself," Isaak Glikman said. "It was so much against his nature that he was actually incapable of doing so." The composer almost fell to pieces with gratitude when he received an extra half a can of jam for his family.

Once people knew he was in town, he found himself constantly approached by strangers asking for favors. He couldn't even cross the courtyard to get the family's buckets of hot water in the morning without running into ballerinas and playwrights asking him to put in a good word for them.

Nina was useful in these situations. She was always calm and firm. She said no for him because he was incapable of saying it himself. She made sure he got time to work.

While he wrote the fourth and final movement of the symphony, an artist who lived in the apartment above him started sculpting a bust of him. Shostakovich sat uneasily while he was being sculpted. He couldn't sit still. His fingers kept tapping as he played scales and chords on his cheeks. He slumped over with his head between his knees, covering his head with his hands.

Galina and Maxim secretly collected the clay that fell on the floor and played with it. "We took pencils from our father's table," Galina recalled, "and stuck the small bits of clay on the ends of them so that they looked like little sausages or rather chicken legs. In fact that's what we called them, 'chicken legs.' And the next thing we did was to throw them at the wall and try to make them stick there."

When the sculptor was done with the bust, he submitted it to the chairman of the Committee for the Arts. The chairman was not impressed. The statue did not serve the correct propagandistic purposes. He explained to the artist, "What we need is an optimistic Shostakovich."

Shostakovich himself was delighted with this response. "What we need is an optimistic Shostakovich," he would often repeat, in miserable glee. "An optimistic Shostakovich!"

For a brief time, the world actually got an optimistic Shostakovich: he was putting the finishing touches on the last movement of the symphony, originally entitled "Victory." "In the finale," he wrote in *Soviet Art*, "I want to describe a beautiful future time when the enemy will have been defeated." He now could imagine what triumph might seem like.

On December 27, 1941, the Shostakoviches had a party. They often invited their upstairs neighbors, the Litvinovs and Slonims, down for a drink by tapping out greetings on the water pipes. This party, however, was a larger affair. By the time Flora Litvinova got her son, Pavel, to bed and made it downstairs, guests were already swigging vodka. Shostakovich convinced her to try some. (He was fond of saying, "There is only good vodka or very good vodka. There is no such thing as bad vodka.") They were eating some sausages that someone, somehow, had discovered. Shostakovich and another composer banged out trashy songs on the piano while people danced in the corridor. He grabbed Nina and joyfully spun her in a dance.

In the midst of the mayhem, Shostakovich mentioned quietly to Flora Litvinova, "And, d'you know, today I finally finished my Seventh." Even more astonishingly, he had written the final bars as the guests showed up. Nina made small talk while he finished his masterpiece.

It was not long before he played it on his piano for a crowd of musicians and composers. They were particularly struck by the repeated march in the first movement. Litvinova recalled: "Everybody spoke at once about this theme, Fascism, the war and victory. Someone immediately dubbed the theme 'rat-like.' [The conductor] Samosud declared that the Symphony was destined to have a great success."

When all the guests from the listening party had gone home and the apartment was quiet, Flora Litvinova sat with Nina and Dmitri, sipping tea. They talked about the new work and whether it was truly about the Germans. "Of course — Fascism," said Shostakovich. "But music, real music, can never be literally tied to a theme. [Nazism] is not the only form of Fascism; this music is about all forms of terror, slavery, the bondage of the spirit."

Soon after this, a rumor started that the rat-like "invasion" theme of the Seventh Symphony was not about invasion at all. Ex-students whispered that Shostakovich had played this theme and its increasingly crazed variations long before the Germans had ever invaded. In fact, this argument runs, the theme encodes the rise of Stalin.

This interpretation became popular many decades later, after the publication of Solomon Volkov's supposed memoirs of Shostakovich, *Testimony*. In that book, Volkov has Shostakovich say,

> The Seventh Symphony had been planned before the war and consequently it simply cannot be seen as a reaction to Hitler's attack. The "invasion theme" has nothing to do with the attack. I was thinking of other enemies of humanity when I composed the theme. . . . Hitler is a criminal, that's clear, but so is Stalin. . . . Actually, I have nothing against calling the Seventh the Leningrad Symphony, but it's not about Leningrad under siege, it's about the Leningrad that Stalin destroyed and that Hitler merely finished off.

This seems very clear. Certain musicologists use it as proof that the whole piece is an encoded attack on Stalin. After all, the irritating little march starts cheerful and small. The Germans, on the other hand, attacked suddenly, fortissimo, with fury. Isn't the theme more like Stalin, then, with its clumsy, kitschy charm, its twinkle in the eye, before it rises up and unleashes its full psychopathic rage?

There are several problems with this passage in the Volkov memoir, though. For one thing, only one page earlier, Volkov has Shostakovich say the opposite: "I wrote my Seventh Symphony, the 'Leningrad,' very quickly. I couldn't not write it. War was all around. . . . I wanted to write about our time, about my contemporaries who spared neither strength nor life in the name of Victory Over the Enemy." He absolutely contradicts what he says on the very next page.

Years later, Shostakovich, like most others, referred to the theme as "the 'invasion' episode." That also, of course, means little, as it appeared in a magazine, and he often didn't write his own articles.

So what is the truth? Is it a picture of Hitler or Stalin?

Perhaps the most likely explanation is given by one of Shostakovich's colleagues, Lev Lebedinsky, who claimed that Shostakovich called the famous march the "Stalin theme" before the war—but then incorporated it into the symphony, at which point its meaning seems to have changed for the composer. He began calling it the "anti-Hitler" theme—and then, even more generally, the "'theme of evil,' which was absolutely true, since the theme was just as much anti-Hitler as it was anti-Stalin, even though the world music community fixed on only the first of the two definitions."

A symphony is built not just by the composer, the conductor, and the musicians, but by the audience. The wartime audience heard the approach of the German Wehrmacht. A more recent post-Soviet audience wants to hear the cruel antics of Stalin and believe that Shostakovich was speaking in code.

But Shostakovich himself does not seem to have restricted the meaning of the piece—hearing in it instead an abstract depiction of "the bondage of the spirit," all those petty, ugly things that grow disastrously within us and lead us all in a dance of destruction.

The government news outlets were not in doubt about the piece's meaning; they were anxious to have a musical rallying point to convince the masses of eventual victory.

A first performance, under the baton of Samuil Samosud, was scheduled for early March. It would have to happen in Kuibyshev. Rehearsals started right after the New Year.

Shostakovich announced that the piece was dedicated to Leningrad itself. "All that I wrote into it, all that I expressed in it is tied up with that beloved native city of mine, is connected with the historic days of its defense against fascist oppressors."

Shostakovich was finally done with his symphony, written in the midst of air raids and evacuation. His sense of triumph did not last, however. He wrote to his friend Glikman:

Things are not good with me. Day and night, I think of my family and loved ones, whom I had to leave behind in Leningrad. I seldom get news of them. There are no more cats and dogs left. Not only that but my mother is short of money, because she cannot rely on what I regularly send her; it often gets delayed or misrouted on the way. [Nina's father] Vasily Varzar is ill with malnutrition and Nina's niece Allochka has the same problem. . . . Every day I try to do something about getting my loved ones away from Leningrad, and until I manage to do this I am not going to leave Kuybïshev, because from here I can sometimes manage to get things sent to them from Moscow, even occasionally directly from here.

One day he got a smudged, rumpled letter from Maria. It said that they had eaten the family dog.

Things had improved for Dmitri Shostakovich. The world was awaiting the premiere of the Seventh, which they now called the *Leningrad* Symphony.

But things in Leningrad itself were only getting worse.

By midwinter, the people of Leningrad had grown used to the sight of the dead lying in the streets and simply walked around them.

THE CITY OF THE DEAD

The city was quiet and empty, wrote a Leningrad girl after taking her mother to be buried. "I couldn't even describe to you what the city was like. Somehow it always seemed to us like a city at the bottom of the sea, for everything was covered with hoar frost. . . . The trams stood immobile, frozen. It was like a frozen realm of some sea king."

St. Petersburg had once been a town of fantasy operas about undersea palaces and invisible cities. Now, in midwinter, when the sun set by three, leaving everything in darkness, Leningrad looked like a set from some tale of a nightmare kingdom.

In February 1942, a soldier on the Leningrad Front trudged home to the city to see his family. "The city of death greeted me and took leave of me with corpses, darkness, dirt, and silence, sinister silence." He discovered that his daughter was dead and his son was swollen with starvation. He took his daughter's body to be buried in a common grave. "In 4 or 5 days I'll describe everything, but now I'm in a state of such severe depression that I haven't the strength to write." When he did try to write about the city, he just repeated lists of words: "dirt, snowdrifts, snow, cold, darkness, starvation, death."

Survivors of the siege today describe the conditions in a similar, singsong phrase: *"Kholod, golod, snaryady, pozhary"* ("cold, hunger, artillery shells, fires"). It is as if there is no syntax, no grammar, that can contain their suffering. Only a list of things perceived.

The "sinister silence" fell over the city because the Luftwaffe had stopped its almost daily air raids. It was too cold for planes to fly. More important, there was no reason for the Nazis to bomb the population. They were dying by themselves, in silence. "At present our nights are indescribably quiet," wrote diarist Vera Inber. "Not a klaxon, nor the sound of a tram, nor the bark of a dog, nor the mew of a cat. There is no radio. The city falls asleep in dark icy flats, many never wake up." That far north, the nights were eighteen hours long. In those many hours of obscurity, people passed away without a sound.

Just within the limits of besieged Leningrad, there where days when more than ten thousand people died. Over the course of January and February alone, there were roughly two hundred thousand deaths. We cannot know the numbers exactly. All authority in the city had broken down. No one recorded deaths anymore. No one removed the bodies from the streets.

In December, it had not been uncommon to see people dragging the wrapped dead on sleds. Now bodies often lay wherever the dying fell. Their relatives were too weak with starvation to pull them to mass graves. A woman on the street would feel dizzy and sit; a few minutes later, she would be a corpse freezing to a wall. No one would move her. Nobody had the energy. Perhaps after a few days, her coat would be gone, or her shoes. Gradually, corpses were stripped.

In black, sooty apartments, no warmer than the frozen streets outside, dead friends and relatives lay on beds while families sat at their tables, dining. Descriptions like the following were common:

> We are all ill. . . . From room to room [in a communal apartment]
> there are dead people, a corpse for every family. It has been
> almost a month since Anna Yakovlevna Zveinek died from star-
> vation. She's still lying there in her freezing, dirty room — black,
> dried-up, teeth bared. Nobody is in any hurry to clean her up
> and bury her; everyone is too weak to care. Two rooms away lies
> another corpse — her daughter Asya Zveinek, who also died of
> starvation, outliving her mother by twelve days. Asya died two
> steps from my bed, and Vsevolod and I dragged her away because
> it was too warm in our room for a dead body.

The temperatures that winter were often down to twenty below zero, and so
the corpses did not decompose. Bodies were usually stacked in apartment
courtyards or cellars.

Beyond fatigue, there was another good reason to delay taking the
dead out of an apartment: until the death was declared, the family could still
collect rations in the name of the deceased.

One woman, Klavdia Dubrovina, described sleeping in an apartment
with her friend and with a dead family who were stacked, frozen, around
the room. The windows had all been blown out, "and the frost, the cold, were
frightful." One day Dubrovina came home and discovered her friend had
died, too, during the day. "Yes. I came home and she was lying there dead.
Somehow this was also a matter of indifference to me. People were dying
all around. I'd simply get into that burrow [in the bed] — I'd take my coat
and boots off — and I'd get into it, for the cold was frightful, and I'd put
on an old scarf, too. When I rose in the morning that scarf was frozen to
my skin all around my neck. I'd tear it off, get up, put on my coat and go
to work."

Death had lost its dignity. As one man, Dmitri Likhachev, was dragging his father's corpse to the cemetery, he was passed by a procession of
gravediggers' trucks.

After wood became a precious commodity for heating, people stopped using coffins for their family members. Instead, the corpse "was wrapped in a white shroud, and the knees were clearly discernible, the sheet being tightly bound. A biblical, ancient Egyptian burial. The shape of a human form was clear enough, but one couldn't tell if it was a man or a woman."

Many who collapsed on the street were simply left where they had fallen.

I recall one truck that was loaded with bodies frozen into fantastic positions. They had been petrified, it seemed, in mid-speech, mid-shout, mid-grimace, mid-leap. Hands were raised, eyes open. I remember the body of a woman: naked, brown, thin, upright. . . . The truck was going at speed, leaving her hair streaming in the wind . . . as they went over the potholes in the road. It looked as if she was making a speech — calling out to them, waving her arms — a ghastly, defiled corpse with open, glassy eyes.

A woman who found employment loading those trucks described how she stopped feeling anything at the sight of the dead. "[At first] I was afraid of dead bodies, but I had to load those corpses. We used to sit right there on the trucks with the corpses, and off we'd go. And your heart would seem to switch off. Because we knew that today we were taking them, and tomorrow it would be our turn, perhaps." Many people similarly described this emotional emptiness, the heart "switching off."

At the entrance to one cemetery, some comic gravedigger had propped up a frozen corpse with a cigarette in its mouth, pointing the way to the burial pits. Citizens, wrapped head to foot in their winter coats and hats, dragged their mummy-wrapped loved ones past through the brown snow. The ground was frozen, so mass graves had to be excavated with explosives.

Gradually, like the immigration of an insidious, phantom population, Leningrad belonged more to the dead than to the living. The dead watched over streets and sat in snow-swamped buses. Whole apartment buildings were tenanted by them, where in broken rooms, dead families sat waiting at tables. Their dominion spread room by room, like lights going out in evening.

The elderly and the very young tended to succumb to starvation first. Statistically, gender also played a role: "Within a single family . . . the order in which its members typically died was grandfather and infants first, grandmother and father (if not at the front) second, mother and older children last."

In the case of the family Shostakovich left behind—his mother, Sofia Shostakovich; his sister Maria Frederiks; and his nephew, Dmitri Frederiks—there were no men left. Maria's husband, the physicist Vsevolod Frederiks, had been off in a prison camp for years. (He would die of starvation there in 1944.) Sofia, apparently, was hardest hit by hunger. She was skeletal.

Shostakovich sent her money. It was often delayed, or disappeared entirely. (Letters were regularly opened and searched by the NKVD.) In any case, paper money was almost valueless in Leningrad by this point. People bartered. They exchanged a gilt clock from some tsarist salon for a few meat patties; an inlaid wood dresser, in the family for generations, for a little cooking oil.

Among the living population, families and coworkers watched one another gradually manifest the symptoms of dystrophy, the malfunctioning of the body as it succumbs to hunger. "Hunger changes the appearance of all," wrote the diarist Elena Skrjabina. "Everyone now is blue-black, bloodless, swollen." Leningraders came to call this discoloration of the skin a "hunger tan." As the weeks went by, "People were discovering bone after bone" jutting just under the skin, another diarist wrote. The gums of the starving receded. It looked as if their teeth grew with hunger, as if the need to devour dominated their faces, kind or cruel. Eventually, their teeth began to fall out.

Their movements became slow and mechanical. Their speech slurred as their vocal cords atrophied. It became difficult to move at all. A survivor recalled, "It was roughly the feeling that your foot wouldn't leave the ground. Can you understand? The feeling that when you had to put your foot on a step, it just refused to obey. It was like it is in dreams sometimes. It seems you're just about to run, but your legs won't work. Or you want to shout out, and you've no voice."

Even though factory employees received more substantial rations than any other group except soldiers, work was grinding to a stop as people on the assembly lines slowed. They moved like broken automatons. At the

Leningraders draw water out of a hole in the Neva River ice and struggle to bring it back to their apartments.

An old woman drags a young man on a sled because he is too weak from starvation to walk.

Izhora Factory, a diarist wrote, "Everybody is now walking very slowly, and some can barely lift their legs. It is hard to imagine such debilitation. We are just sitting here starving."

The Soviet utopians of the 1920s had fantasized about a mechanized future where people were part of a vast machine. The Cubo-Futurists had painted visions of human cogs and gears, and composers had written clangorous works depicting the vitality of industry.

Now humans were winding down beside their machines. Empty streets echoed with the slow ticking of the metronome through iced loudspeakers. The city, like a giant clockwork mechanism unwound, froze slowly to a stop.

Perhaps the most heartbreaking collapse in this mass starvation was not physical, however, but moral. People were forced to confront nightmare decisions about who they should allow to live or die. As the soldier who returned from the front to find his daughter dead wrote, "There is much that is revolting. But that's life: a mother of four children takes the baby from her breast in order not to die herself. The baby will die. But then three others will live, who otherwise, without their mother, would die. Was the mother's decision justified? No doubt about it, it was. When Maria [his daughter] bought a stolen bread ration card, she did right, yes, she saved the lives of three children."

These ghastly decisions were made in a welter of starvation, which sharpened the senses but confused thought. "The brain is devoured by the stomach," said one sufferer. Tempers flared irrationally. Children subsided into dementia, sitting at the table and tearing up paper into smaller and smaller pieces or wailing without cease. Deterioration caused some people to go insane. Brothers killed brothers for ration coupons. Parents murdered their own children.

As a foreman at the Kirov Tank Works said, "Human beings showed what they were like in those days. I don't suppose people had ever before witnessed such a revelation of greatness of soul on the one hand and of moral degradation on the other."

There were those who banded together to find strength and connection.

Then there were those who looked out only for themselves and who hunted alone.

There are two words for cannibalism in Russian: *trupoyedstvo* ("corpse-eating") and *lyudoyedstvo* ("person-eating").

Corpse-eating was far more common. Mourners would descend to their apartment building's shed or well house, where their relatives' bodies were being stored, only to discover that the thighs or buttocks had been hacked off in the night. Militia searching buildings for survivors came across the bodies of the neglected dead with limbs missing. One man found several heads in a snowdrift; a little girl's still had its blond hair in long Russian braids. The NKVD files are unspeakably macabre. One family (a father, a mother, and a thirteen-year-old boy) were arrested for stealing bodies from a hospital morgue, presumably for resale as food. A nurse was arrested for purloining amputated limbs from the surgery room floor. A mother shared the body of her eleven-year-old son with two fellow workers from the Lenin Plant.

The criminal profile of corpse-eaters was surprising. Only 2 percent had a previous criminal record. They were primarily women, uneducated females with no employment and no local Leningrad address. They were, in other words, often refugees who had fled to the city and who therefore did not have ration books at all. They had to make a choice between eating those already dead or dying themselves.

A Leningrad woman named Elena Taranukhina, who lived with her mother and her baby daughter, was disgusted to find that several of the corpses in the courtyard of her apartment complex had been hacked up for food. This was not the worst of it, however. One morning as she stood in one of the endless bread lines, waiting for rations, she "felt that something was horribly wrong," and left her place in the queue to rush home.

When she got there, the scene was like one out of the worst Grimm's fairy tale: The baby was in the aluminum bathtub over a flame, but without water. The grandmother, pushed over the edge into insanity by hunger and cold, was cooking her granddaughter, muttering, "What a fatty child, what a fatty child, what a fatty child."

Taranukhina restrained the frantic old woman and saved her daughter. Two days later, the grandmother died of hunger.

This was the line between "corpse-eating" and "person-eating": killing someone for food.

Most of those who were caught and tried for person-eating acted alone. It was, after all, the ultimate expression of individualism: the absolute belief that one's own life matters more than another's. One woman, a girl at the time, described being chased down a dark corridor by a cannibal who no longer looked human to her. As he scrambled after her through the dark, he "looked like a beast." He had an ax. She was saved by some passing soldiers.

A woman named Vera Lyudyno recorded the disappearance, one by one, of children in her apartment building. Finally their clothing was found in the apartment of a nearby violinist, along with the clothing of his own five-year-old son.

In another part of the city, a mother whose child disappeared went to the police. They directed her into a room filled with crates of clothing marked by number. They told her to search for her child's clothes. When she found the clothing, she could report the number on the crate to the police and they would tell her the district where her child was eaten.

Rumors whispered at the time that there were organized bands of cannibals hunting in the streets and alleys. A young couple, for example, went to the Haymarket to search for a pair of felt boots. As currency, they clutched 600 grams of bread they had carefully hoarded for weeks. The Haymarket was located in the crooked quarter of the city described by the great Dostoyevsky in his novel *Crime and Punishment* and was a place fraught with pickpockets and con men in the best of times. The couple searched the stalls and could only find stiff, old, ill-fitting military shoes — until they spied a tall man in a nice sheepskin coat, serenely holding a single boot and searching the crowd for buyers.

They approached him and asked about the boot; he said that yes, he had two, but he had left the other one back at his apartment for safekeeping. He would give them the pair for two pounds of bread. The young couple haggled with him. Finally, they got his price down to 600 grams and showed him their loaf. He agreed to take the young man back to his apartment to fetch the other boot.

The young man followed the gentleman in sheepskin through the maze of streets to an apartment building. Walking up the stairs, he felt a strange chill. He couldn't help but notice how well-fed the man looked. They walked up floor after floor. The man seemed to have a spring in his step.

When they got to the top of the staircase, the man in the sheepskin coat said, "Wait for me here." He knocked on a door.

"Who is it?" said a male voice from inside.

"It's me," said the man in the sheepskin coat. "With a live one."

The door opened a crack, and the young man spied a hairy red hand, and, in the background, lit by bobbing candlelight, "a glimpse of several great hunks of white meat, swinging from hooks on the ceiling. From one hunk he saw dangling a human hand with long fingers and blue veins."

He bolted toward the stairs as the two cannibals made a rush for him. Though he was weaker than the two sleek, well-fed person-eaters, fear and alarm gave him speed. He tumbled out into the street. Farther up the lane, a truck of soldiers was headed out of the city for duty on Lake Ladoga. The young man shouted, "Cannibals!" and the truck pulled to a halt; the soldiers came running.

He saw them dive into the building. A few seconds later, shots rang out.

When the soldiers came out of the building, they were carrying the cannibal's coat, complaining about the bullet hole that had ruined it. They told the young man that they'd found the remains of five bodies in the apartment, and handed him a hunk of bread — his, as it turned out — that they'd reclaimed from the murderers. With that, they climbed back in their truck and headed off to the east.

Horror stories like this — and the issue of Leningrad cannibalism as a whole — could not be talked about openly during the Soviet period. Such an admission of the breakdown of society was considered demoralizing. Only in 2002 were NKVD files opened so academics could discover the gruesome statistical realities of person-eating.

It appears that especially in late January and in February, when order utterly broke down in some districts of the city, there really were a few organized cannibal bands that hunted down lonely military couriers for food or lured people from bread lines and clubbed them over the head. By and large, the far greater danger was those lone individuals who lost contact with others and were driven crazy by animal hunger.

There were nine arrests for cannibalism in the first ten days of December 1941. Two months later, this number had jumped to 311. A year later, the final figure, which includes arrests for both corpse-eating and person-eating, was 2,015. Those who ate the dead usually got off reasonably lightly; those who murdered and then ate their victims were shot.

What does this mean about us as an animal? Was this creature that loped down sooty corridors, hunting others, what we all are at heart?

There were many who came to think so. An anonymous eyewitness who was eleven years old in 1941 later wrote:

> After the blockade I visualized the world in the shape of a beast of prey lying in wait. . . . I grew to be suspicious, hard, and as unjust to people as they had become to me. As I looked at them I would be thinking, "Oh yes, you're pretending at the moment to be kind and honest. Yet, take away your bread and warmth and light and you'll all turn into two-legged wild beasts." And it was during the first few years after the blockade that I did a few abominable things which to this day lie heavily on my conscience. It took almost a decade for me to become rehabilitated. Up till about the age of twenty I felt that something inside me had grown irreversibly old and I looked upon the world with the gaze of a broken and all-too-experienced person. It was only in my student years that youth came into its own and the fervent desire to become

involved in work beneficial to mankind enabled me to shake off
my morbid depression.

And as all of this happened, informants passed on updates about Leningrad's
deteriorating morale and morality to the Germans. The Nazis asked carefully about when precisely people stopped helping one another in the streets,
about how many people were being arrested for cannibalism. As one diarist wrote in December, "Countless tragedies are taking place every day,
dissolving into the silence of the city. . . . Meanwhile, the Germans look at
Leningrad with cold curiosity."

Brutal self-interest was not the only way to survive in Leningrad, however.
There was another way. "A kind of polarization seemed to be taking place
among people," said a historian who spent the war trapped in the city, burning classical encyclopedias for warmth. Some people had chosen to "survive in any way possible at the expense of a relative, a friend — anybody."
But there were many others who "acted honestly, according to their conscience, whatever the circumstances. . . . Human feelings and qualities, love,
marriage, family ties, parental feelings — were subjected to a stiff test."

If we are a predatory animal (canines bared), we are also an animal that
has survived and flourished through cooperative action. This proved true in
the besieged city, too.

People moved in with friends and relatives. This kept rooms warmer
through breath and body heat. Also, tasks could be shared and divided.
Able-bodied adults could go out and collect rations if someone was too sick
or too weak to move. Kids made forays out to bombed buildings for wood to
burn. Many apartments now had small makeshift stoves called *burzhuiki*
with stovepipes leading out the windows.* Friends and neighbors found furniture to feed the fire. Others had to go out to the frozen canals and the Neva

---

*The name *burzhuika* most probably comes from the word *bourgeois*, or middle class, and
may reflect the fact that the stoves were potbellied, like little fat capitalists.

River to dredge up water. This was an overwhelming task for those weakened by dystrophy, and there were always corpses frozen near the watering holes. At times, however, people formed huge cooperative bucket brigades. All of these tasks made it almost impossible to survive alone. Only by creating sanctuaries where many came together to share the work, the food, and the warmth could people carry on. "We moved into one room and lived as a family, playing chess, reading Pushkin out loud in the evenings," one man remembered. "It was vital to keep helping others."

A young nurse named Marina Yerukhmanova, for example, worked at the Grand Europe Hotel, which had been turned into a hospital. As a hospital, it had gradually deteriorated. There was no running water. The toilets had frozen and exploded. The patients — many of them ex-convicts from the Soviet Sixteenth Punishment Battalion — had taken over a lot of the ex-hotel, strolling about in bedsheets draped piratically like capes, robes, and turbans. They lay in wait in the dark and mugged the orderlies.

Yerukhmanova, her sister, and several other nurses ended up forming a sort of "ark" in one of the upstairs rooms. They all camped there together. They uncovered a bottle of medical alcohol in the pharmacy and sold it for a *burzhuika* stove. They protected one another and checked one another for lice. At night, they would sit feeding their tiny stove with broken furniture and the hotel's pre-Revolutionary account books, reading old letters from bellboys, butlers, and pastry chefs before tossing them into the flames.

Many people found refuge at their places of work. By banding together, they survived, pooling their resources, creating communal laundries, baths, and child-care centers. Brigades of factory workers went out to check on missing employees. They took food to the dying and helped families deal with the sick and the dead. A group of schoolteachers took it upon themselves to search empty buildings for children whose parents had died; so did the Communist Youth League.

As one survivor said, "Everyone had a savior." Another claimed, "Helping others was crucial to survival. . . . Sharing became our way of life, and helping others, keeping busy, working, taking responsibility, gave strength to people."

The Leningrad Public Library remained open throughout the siege and became a place for people to congregate. "People came to the library to read, even when weak from cold and exhaustion," one of the librarians explained. "Some died in their places, with a book propped in front of them. We would carry the bodies outside, hoping that the trucks would take them away, but increasingly they were simply left in the snow."

The building itself had been seriously damaged during air raids—though fortunately, the shell that fell on the interlibrary loan department didn't explode. In the course of the war, the librarians greatly expanded the collection, purchasing books from the starving, who were desperate to sell anything for food. Some of the city's librarians scoured bombed ruins for volumes, scrabbling over the piles of brick with their backpacks full of salvaged books.

The heat in the library gave out early, and the plumbing eventually froze and burst. In late January, the building finally lost its electricity. The librarians still searched the shadowed stacks with lanterns, and, when they ran out of oil, with burning pieces of wood. They still served patrons and sought out the answers to practical questions posed by the city government: alternative methods of making matches or candles, forgotten sources of edible yeast. As the building grew colder and more battle-scarred, they closed the reading rooms one by one. Finally, patrons and librarians all huddled in the director's office, where there was still a kerosene lamp and a *burzhuika* stove.

Reading novels and writing diaries and poetry were surprisingly popular during the siege, especially when the circumstances grew particularly grim. Activities like these reminded people of another life and prodded them to remember the codes and routines of civilization in the midst of chaos. It allowed them escape when they were entrapped. As it happens, many famous Russian novels are quite long. This was a perfect time, some soldiers and civilians found, to read Dostoyevsky's *Crime and Punishment* or Tolstoy's *War and Peace*. There were other benefits to fiction: a Red Army lieutenant reading an early sci-fi novel, Jules Verne's *The Mysterious Island*, got an idea for how to use the hydrogen in the city's barrage balloons to self-propel them when they were being lowered and relocated.

Of course, many found a more direct use for books — as fuel. "We warm ourselves by burning memoirs and floorboards. Prose, it turns out, provides more heat than poetry. History boils the kettle to make our tea."

In the vaults and crypts beneath the Hermitage Museum, research still went on. In Bomb Shelter No. 3, hundreds of scholars hunkered down by candle stubs, barely alive, slowly scratching out monographs on the art of the Netherlands or Sumerian philology. Their rations were minimal; a few of them died each night. The rest were kept alive by frying a few small, frozen potatoes in the linseed oil used to prepare artists' canvases. During the day, some of them walked the nearly ten miles of galleries and corridors in the abandoned Hermitage Museum and Winter Palace, clearing debris, shutting off rooms where the windows had been shattered by bombs, carrying bodies to their makeshift morgue. For a while, they even managed to arrange for a fluctuating flow of electricity by snaking wires across the granite embankment and hooking them up to the generator on the tsar's private yacht, the *Polar Star*, which stood frozen in the ice of the Neva River. Altogether, about two thousand lives were saved in Bomb Shelter No. 3 in the stone arcades beneath the empty museum.

An old Russian proverb runs, "When the guns speak, the Muses fall silent." Shostakovich famously retorted that in Leningrad, the Muses were not silent: "Here, the Muses speak together with the guns." This was true — and it made a huge difference in morale and people's ability to go on from day to day.

Surprisingly, Leningrad's Musical Comedy Theater remained open, though the performances grew more feeble as the weeks passed. An actress recalled the conditions for a performance of *The Three Musketeers*, for example: The theater was well below freezing. She had to thaw out her

A bombed facade on Nevsky Prospect, Leningrad. In the background, the windows of the famous "House of Books," a bookstore still open today, are covered in plywood. Except for a few months in the middle of the winter in 1941, the store remained open throughout the siege.

A hole blown in the wall of the Hermitage by German shelling. A force of about thirty or forty volunteers, mostly women over fifty-five, spent their days patrolling the museum's roughly ten miles of empty corridors, clearing out debris like this from more than a thousand rooms.

makeup over a lamp. Her costume was skimpy, so she muffled herself with a heavy coat until she went onstage. (Sometimes, people from the audience would shout out to her to cover up.) Halfway through the performance, she saw that one of the Musketeers had died of hunger. He lay on the floor with a shattered cup in his hand. The show, quite incredibly, went on. An announcement was made. The actress went out onstage to speak her lines and could not talk for grief. Everyone waited, knowing what she was going through. Somehow, she found the strength to carry on. They finished the play with only two Musketeers.

Leningrad's radio station also kept broadcasting. No one had much strength, so for many hours of the day, they broadcast only the ticking of the metronome. The poet Olga Berggolts, now yellow with jaundice and swollen with edema, spoke to the city of the dead about "human brotherhood." "Through the hallucinations of hunger, [Berggolts's] compassion and love broke through to people," two soldiers on the front remembered. "These came from a woman who was undergoing the same agonies, was also starving, who understood everything, felt everything herself."

One night, faint with hunger, Berggolts set out from Radio House to see a friend, who told her she'd found a bottle of cod-liver oil they could feast on. It was only a walk of two blocks, but Berggolts felt overwhelmed by the mounds of snow, the ruts of ice. She doddered like an old woman — tripped over something, and fell. As she lay there, she realized she had stumbled on a dead body, frozen into the slush in front of Philharmonic Hall. She did not think she could get up. The night, the darkness, the snow, the cold, the silence covered her, and it seemed as if she should just lie still and give up.

At that point, all around her, disembodied, she heard her own voice, speaking softly to her of hope. She could no longer understand what was happening. She wondered whether the corpse she'd tripped over was her own, whether she already was dead.

Then the voice in the air stopped reciting her poetry, and an announcer for Radio Leningrad came on. She had been hearing her own program, broadcast from a loudspeaker on the corner of the Hotel Europa.

Shaken, she slowly climbed to her feet and continued the walk to her friend's apartment. Her poetry had saved many others in moments of despair; now, strangely, it had saved her own life, too. Many people compare the role of her poetry to that of Shostakovich's music.

His music was being discussed in the city. There was a push to get music played on the radio again. The only orchestra left in the city, in fact, was the Radio Orchestra. They had stopped playing a few months before. Leningrad's Communist Party boss, Andrei Zhdanov, was irritated by the radio's political speeches and the ticking of the metronome: "Why spread such doom and despondency? Could we have at any rate some music?"

Late in the winter of 1942, Radio House decided to try to reassemble its orchestra and play favorite classics, such as Beethoven and Tchaikovsky. At a meeting of the Radio House staff with a propagandist visiting from Moscow, a pale young journalist urged, "Is it possible to get the score of Shostakovich's Seventh Symphony?" Party Secretary Zhdanov agreed that a performance of the piece in Shostakovich's own city was vital for morale. An order from him survives in the Radio House vault: "By any means, get a score of the Seventh from Moscow. Transport it to Leningrad as soon as possible."

They presented the idea of performing the Seventh to Karl Eliasberg, the conductor of the Leningrad Radio Orchestra. He was excited by the idea but said it was not yet possible. Shostakovich's symphony called for a huge orchestra. Eliasberg estimated that half his musicians were dead. As someone told Olga Berggolts, "The first violin is dying, the drummer died on the way to work, the French horn is near death."

A performance of Shostakovich's new symphony in Leningrad would have to wait for many months.

Artistic flourishes like this may have seemed like a waste of energy, but they were central to the survival of the city and the pride of its inhabitants. As one woman boasted, "Just think! The Germans are outside the city, and here we sit and talk about everything, about our whole life, the whole of our history, and we sing songs and have been ready to spit at the Germans.

They'll all rot in the earth, as hundreds of thousands and millions of them have already rotted in the earth, and our city will stand and we shall still live in it and work and write poetry and sing our Russian songs."

Strangely enough, doctors and nurses noted that activity actually prolonged life, when it should have shortened it. Those who lay down and tried to conserve energy often were the ones who trailed off and died first.

One medical student got angry at his mother, who kept telling him to get up, move around, and go to classes. "But Mother, when you're lying down you use less energy so you need less food."

She snapped back, "It's paradoxical, but it's true—those who move about will work and live. So move about!"

Astounded, people in hospitals, factories, and communal apartments saw that this was true. The survivors were the people who committed themselves to washing, to eating off plates, to going to work through snow and sleet. "Not counting the old people, the sick or those constitutionally in poor health, the first to die among those in normally good condition were people of weak character, those who gave in morally, who lost the will to work and thought too much about their stomachs. I noticed that when someone gave up washing his neck and ears, stopped going to work and ate his ration of bread right away and then lay down and covered himself with a blanket—he wasn't long for this world."

A district nurse concluded: "I found in my work that it was not only nutrition that was conducive to survival, but morale." A doctor studying "life at the limit" found that he could not explain by simple scientific means how some of his patients were still alive. He concluded, "Something else is coming into play, something that we don't understand." Attitude became the difference between life and death. It made a profound physiological difference.

"What saved us all (well, I don't know about all) was hope and love," one woman wrote. "Well, I loved my husband, my husband loved his family, his daughter. He was serving in the army nearby. When we sat down to eat something, his photograph was there before us, and we were expecting him to come back. And it was only because of that love, because of that hope that we were able to keep going. It was really difficult. Now I can't imagine how we survived."

Characteristically, Nazi SS commander Heinrich Himmler did not emphasize "love" when discussing the miraculous survival of the city. "The hatred felt by the population was an important motivating mechanism for defense."

He was not wrong, either. The Nazi propaganda of fear had only strengthened opposition to the Germans. As a boss at the Kirov Tank Works said, "If anyone were to ask me what sort of feeling was most vividly at work among the Kirov workers I should without hesitation reply: the desire for vengeance. . . . Their feeling towards [the Germans] is one of hatred, of insistent, personal, mortal hatred. Sometimes it seems to take an almost exaggerated form, as if they seek vengeance in the labor of their hands."

On the artillery shells produced in Leningrad, workers stenciled messages to the Germans: "For the blood of our workers," "For our children's anguish," and "For our murdered friends."

These curses were fired from the mouths of guns, and their words killed thousands.

Love and hate made a tactical and strategic difference.

One day, many years after the siege was lifted and the war was over, two nutritionists met by chance. They introduced themselves. One, Alexei Bezzubov, had worked at Leningrad's Vitamin Institute, seeking out new sources of protein for the hungry. The other, as it turned out, was Ernst Ziegelmeyer, deputy quartermaster of Hitler's army, the man who'd been assigned to calculate how quickly Leningrad would fall without food deliveries. Now these two men met in peace: the one who had tried to starve a city, and the other who had tried to feed it.

Ziegelmeyer pressed Bezzubov incredulously: "However did you hold out? How could you? It's quite impossible! I wrote a deposition that it was physically impossible to live on such a ration." Bezzubov could not provide a scientific, purely nutritive answer. There was none. Instead, he "talked of faith in victory, of the spiritual reserves of Leningraders, which had not been accounted for in the German professor's 'research.'"

And so the city of the dead carried on its life at the limits, dark for all but a few hours of the day, silent, frigid — and yet filled with small cells of light. Some chose to respond to the crisis by giving in to their hungriest, most brutal selves; others fought to work together, to recall the trappings of a civilization that lay in heaps around them.

Every night, unmarked and unmourned, thousands of them died.

Shostakovich, in distant Kuibyshev, no longer starved and no longer had to fear falling bombs and fire from the sky. He could not have known everything that was going on in Leningrad, his native home. (The radio and newspapers would not allow any talk of it.) But he knew that even the silence from the city meant the situation was dire.

In a letter to a friend, he wrote, "Our life here carries on without too many problems, in peace and quiet." But then, without transition, he continued, "Sometimes at nights I don't sleep, and I weep. The tears flow thick and fast, and bitter. Nina and the children sleep in the other room, so there is nothing to prevent me from giving way to my tears."

МЫ ЗЛОМУ ВРАГУ ВСЕ ОТРЕЖЕМ ПУТИ,
ИЗ ПЕТЛИ, ИЗ ЭТОЙ ЕМУ НЕ УЙТИ!

In a political cartoon by the Kukryniksy, Adolf Hitler is being strangled by the Grand Alliance (Great Britain, the USSR, and the United States) coming at him from three sides. Allied propaganda tried to smooth over the differences between these new comrades-in-arms.

MY MUSIC IS MY WEAPON

It took the orchestra in Kuibyshev forty rehearsals, supposedly, to master Shostakovich's *Leningrad* Symphony. It required a huge orchestra—more than a hundred musicians. A legend circulated (and still persists) that Shostakovich wrote for such a large orchestra because he knew that all "the musicians performing the piece got a quadruple norm of food, and he knew that while they were rehearsing they would be fed better." He was ensuring their employment by writing parts for them.

Once, Shostakovich brought his kids to a rehearsal. Nina recalled: "There they sat in the director's box, and when Professor Samosud, the conductor, asked them: 'What have you come to listen to?' they replied: 'Our symphony.' But in the middle of the first movement Maxim suddenly started 'conducting' with such desperate energy that he had to be taken home."

Maxim Shostakovich would later become a conductor himself.

The Soviet government had started to realize that Shostakovich's new symphony had an important role to play on the world stage. Conductors from the

Allied countries were beginning to clamor for the rights of first performance. The Soviet ambassador to the United States, Maxim Litvinov — whose relatives were camped out in the apartment above Shostakovich's — was fielding requests from American conductors all the way from New York to California. The USSR's cultural propaganda wing, the All-Union Society for Cultural Relations with Foreign Countries (VOKS), quickly realized that this was a chance to solidify relations with an important ally, now that the Americans had entered the war.

Why was it so important to send a symphony to the United States?

For years, the Russians and the Americans had eyed each other with suspicion. The average citizens of neither country knew much about the other. Though few Americans understood the full tragic price of the Five-Year Plan and the Great Terror, most knew enough to feel a deep distrust of Stalin and his Communist Party. The Russians, on their side, were disdainful of America's capitalist excesses. Humorists Ilf and Petrov explained, "The word 'America' has well-developed grandiose associations for a Soviet person, for whom it refers to a country of skyscrapers, where day and night one hears the unceasing thunder of surface and underground trains, the hellish roar of automobile horns, and the continuous despairing screams of stockbrokers rushing through the skyscrapers waving their ever-falling shares." After having rambled through the country in the midst of the Great Depression, Ilf and Petrov wrote that for them, the United States represented "the most advanced technology in the world and a horrifyingly oppressive, stupefying social order."

Relations with the Americans were not helped by the fact that, until only a few months before, Russia had openly allied itself with Nazi Germany. Now, suddenly, Stalin and his ministers were demanding aid against Hitler.

They were asking the Allies for two things: First was a "Second Front," an assault on Germany from the west via France, which would force the Wehrmacht to turn its ferocious attentions away from Russia. The second thing the Soviet ambassador requested was free aid in the form of planes, tanks, weapons, radios, jeeps, food, and medical supplies.

The United States could not immediately grant the first request. They were already fighting and losing a war in the Pacific against the Japanese. They did not have the strength to launch a frontal attack on Nazi-held France at the same time.

But American president Franklin Delano Roosevelt immediately agreed to send the Soviets aid shipments. He even agreed, over the angry protests of many, not to ask for anything in return for the military matériel and food-stuffs he supposedly "lent" them or "leased" them. From his point of view, the important thing was to strengthen the Soviets so they could hold off the Germans and would not capitulate. The Allies had to stand together or they would soon fall together.

Many disagreed with his generosity. Several American generals believed that the USSR was about to collapse. It seemed to them that any weaponry shipped to the Russians would soon be in German hands, helping the German cause. Congressmen were angry that the secretive Russians refused to provide any details of how they used the goods they were sent. Many were outraged that the Russians should be given so much for free. The American ambassador to Russia scolded President Roosevelt: "Stop acting like a Santa Claus, Chief! And let's get something from Stalin in return."

To make things worse, an intense cultural difference soured negotiations over the aid packages: the Americans expected profuse thanks and shows of gratitude from the Russians; the Russians were much more hardheaded and practical, knowing that they were taking the brunt of the Germans' military might. This led to anger on both sides.

The American secretary of agriculture, for example, complained about the way the Soviet bureaucrats made their demands. "They simply walked in, all of them sober-faced, never cracked a smile. . . . They said, 'Here is what we want.' And they'd just sit there. There wasn't much negotiation to it." British prime minister Winston Churchill later wrote, "Surly, snarly and grasping, the Soviet Government had the impression that they were conferring a great favour on us by fighting in their own country for their own lives."

This Soviet impression was not necessarily mistaken. They eventually suffered 95 percent of the military casualties inflicted on the three major Allied powers (the U.S., the U.K., and the USSR)—and 90 percent of Germans killed in combat died fighting them. This was a considerable battlefield contribution made through a very considerable sacrifice. A Soviet writer argued, "God knows we paid [the West] back in full—in Russian lives." As a Soviet official commented sarcastically, "We've lost millions of people, and they want us to crawl on our knees because they send us Spam."

It was a serious diplomatic problem. President Roosevelt knew the strategic importance of substantial aid to the Soviets, but he also knew the kind of opposition he faced given the poor relations between the two powers.

What the Russians needed was some way to convince the Americans that they were not the rude, cold Communists of capitalist nightmare. Somehow, the Russians had to stir up American sympathies, to remind them of the shared battle, to persuade Americans, in the gung ho words of *Life* magazine, that Russians are "one hell of a people" who "look like Americans, dress like Americans, and think like Americans." Or at least that their sorrows and triumphs for the next few years would also be American sorrows and triumphs.

So the Soviet government turned its attention to Shostakovich's symphony. Here was a piece apparently about the war, depicting the life of Soviet citizens, the horrors of German invasion, and the triumphant victory to come. It was by one of Russia's only international celebrities. It would remind the West that Russians were not Bolshevik barbarians. They were writing symphonies even in the midst of siege.

As a flow of American tanks, planes, and canned meats headed toward Russia over waters thick with U-boats and through skies patrolled by the Luftwaffe, Russian diplomats began to make arrangements for the symphony to be shipped to the West.

* * *

The world premiere of Shostakovich's *Leningrad* Symphony took place in Kuibyshev on March 5, 1942, with Samuil Samosud conducting the Bolshoi Theater Orchestra.

Shostakovich was a nervous wreck that day. "He was in and out of our apartment all day," wrote the sculptor Ilya Slonim, "never staying longer than ten minutes, looking even paler than usual and, almost stammering, imploring us not to go to the concert, hoping all his friends would stay away, and the next moment calling up the theater and begging for 'just one more ticket,' for a girl in the post-office who had asked him to get her in."

As he rushed past Flora Litvinova, clenching his fists, Nina explained to her, "He's always like this on the day of a first performance. . . . He is frightened it'll be a flop."

He was even more anxious at the theater, right before the concert. "He seemed to suffer agonies," recalled Ilya Slonim. "The audience insisted on seeing him before it began, and he stood up on the platform, rigid and unsmiling."

He spoke both to the audience in front of him and the radio audience listening to the broadcast. What he said was presumably similar to the statement he released later: "My music is my weapon," he declared. "We are struggling for the highest human ideals in history. We are battling for our culture, for science, for art, for everything we have created and built. . . . I dedicate my Seventh Symphony to our struggle with fascism, to our coming victory over the enemy, and to my native city, Leningrad."

Then Samuil Samosud raised his baton — and for the first time, the world heard Shostakovich's symphony.

The opening strides forth confidently. If it is a portrait of a city, it is a city animated with purpose and pride. Then a second melody follows — this one gentle and tender, quiet. But it is at this point that the symphony itself is "invaded."

Very softly, with the rattle of drums, Shostakovich's irritating little march starts — plucky, even twee. It does not seem menacing yet. But it is repeated again and again. It is as infuriatingly memorable as a propaganda slogan drilled into the ears over months. It grows in volume until its empty repetitions have forced everything else out of memory. The symphony's previous themes are gone. There is only this one untiring, repeated statement.

Once again, people in the audience thought of this theme as the approach of the Germans, of "War and Hitlerism": "One, two, left, right — machines as intelligent as men and men as soulless as machines approached our frontiers," wrote journalist Yevgeni Petrov. People thought of the news bulletins announcing city after city falling prey to armored tank divisions. The stupid melody grew; it blared. "It shakes the hall," Petrov wrote. "Some iron machine runs over human bones and you hear them crack. You clench your fists. You want to shoot at this monster with a zinc snout that is marching down upon you."

No longer does the march sound cute. Its full brutality has been revealed, and then it comes to a climax in a gesture Shostakovich used often: a brief intake of breath followed by huge, held, ghastly chords, tremulous with hatred — a vision of evil unveiled.

Little Maxim Shostakovich, attending his first concert, could not stop thinking about the menace in that theme later in the evening, once he had been taken home. "I kept on hearing this music even when I was asleep at night. The drums starting from afar, then getting louder and louder. . . ." He awoke in a panic, jumped out of bed, and ran to the old woman who took care of him and Galina. She soothed him by making the sign of the cross over his head and whispering an illegal prayer.

The rise of this march in the first movement, the so-called invasion theme, is what most people remembered about the symphony as it was heard all over the world in the year to follow.

The first movement ends with a quiet return of the original peacetime melodies. Shostakovich once described their transformation and repetition as a "requiem," though perhaps they sound more exhausted than sorrowful. Just when they seem to have come to rest, we hear a distant echo of the ugly march, with a trumpet playing an echo of the hideous, perky tune offstage.

Shostakovich attends a rehearsal of the Seventh Symphony in Kuibyshev.

The *Leningrad* Symphony had its world premiere in Kuibyshev on March 5, 1942.

War is not over. It is simply distant for the moment.

The orchestra was deeply committed to the piece as they played. Samosud wrote, "Never in my thirty-three years as conductor have I ever seen professional musicians perform a work in a state of agitation verging on tears."

Shostakovich's Seventh Symphony is more than seventy minutes long. After the oddly lilting second movement, the stark, lonely fanfares of the third, the watchfulness and brave struggle of the fourth — the piece ends in final triumph. Suddenly, in the midst of euphoria, the confident melody that started the whole symphony strides forward again, now potent and in control.

With that, the massive piece comes to a spectacular close.

As before, with the Fifth Symphony, the audience was overwhelmed. Shostakovich had told their story in music. He was forced up onto the stage. As his neighbor Tatyana Litvinova described it, "Nobody who saw him taking his bows on the platform after his music had been performed could forget his crooked figure, his grimace of misery and the fingers that never stopped drumming on his cheek. It was torture just to watch him! He minced his steps and bowed like a circus pony. There was something robot-like in his movements."

He didn't need to be nervous. The symphony was immediately a huge success. The authorities were thrilled with it; the intelligentsia was moved by it. Conductors all over the world clamored to perform it.

Perhaps more important to Shostakovich was some good news he had just heard: the government was going to try to help his mother, his sister, and his nephew escape from Leningrad — across the ice of frozen Lake Ladoga.

A convoy of horse-drawn sleds crosses Lake Ladoga on the Road of Life.

Lake Ladoga hemmed Leningrad in from the east. It was part of the noose around the city. Now that it had frozen completely and solidly, however, it was the only escape route.

It had frozen in November, blocking the last attempts to ship food to the encircled city by water. Only a few days later, scouts were sent out across the ice with long poles, tapping to find out how much weight the expanse could support. Roped together and wearing white camouflage, they struggled against the wind. One of them fell through but was quickly pulled out before he died of hypothermia or drowned. They reported back to Leningrad Party Headquarters: there was still an area that was not frozen, but it would not be long before the lake would support heavy shipments.

By late November, the ice was thick enough for horse-drawn sleighs to bring food to the city. Soon, the city sent out huge, arrow-shaped plows to forge what was essentially a six-lane highway from the port of Osinovets to the town of Kobona. Trucks began running the route, taking supplies toward Leningrad and carrying refugees toward the eastern shore, away from the city of the dead. This route was called the Road of Life. Thousands were fleeing across it each day. At the beginning of March, Dmitri and Nina Shostakovich's families got word that they had spots reserved.

Once the Road of Life became fully active, it saved countless lives. Almost a million people escaped across Lake Ladoga in 1942, and 270,900 tons of food made it to the city over the ice that winter.

It was not an easy crossing, however. Tens of thousands died in the attempt. Some cynics called it the Road of Death.

The road started at Finland Station, in Leningrad, where refugees caught the train to Osinovets, on the shores of Ladoga. A woman who lived near the station described the scene: "Having dragged sleds to the station, piled with their possessions tied up in bundles, people would settle down in small packs in the cold, shabby, unheated little station, or on the platform out in the open, if there wasn't a shelling going on. They would sit down and wait. . . . They waited for a long time, sometimes for several days, and sometimes they never even managed to leave."

Shostakovich's relatives had dysentery. They would have had to conceal this from guards at the station. Security forces wouldn't allow the sick to travel.

Though the distance from Finland Station to the shore was not great — only thirty miles — it often took the trains several days. The rinky-dink, small-gauge track was not made for much traffic. There were constant delays.

Once the train reached the processing centers at Osinovets, refugees swarmed out of the carriages and started fighting for places on trucks that would cross the ice. When the route was first established, Osinovets was full of screaming mobs. People had to bribe drivers even to get the spot they had already reserved. Circulating through the crowds were bandits who stole the few possessions the weak still clutched and, if anyone resisted, killed them and plunged them under the ice. By the time the Shostakoviches' relatives were evacuated, the system had become more streamlined, and the port was less chaotic.

The most deadly part of the journey still lay ahead: the crossing itself.

* * *

The Germans held the southern shore of the lake. They had a clear view and a clear shot to the Road of Life. The trucks made easy targets. German guns blasted at the convoys day and night. Occasionally, Luftwaffe planes flew over and dropped bombs, opening up huge wounds in the surface of the ice.

Red Army soldiers skated back and forth on fan-propelled sleds, patrolling in case the Germans launched an infantry attack on the food deliveries, fuel tankers, and refugees that were trundling past.

Hundreds of thousands risked their lives on what one survivor described as "this worn-out, bombed, tormented road which knows no peace, day or night." She said, "Its snow is turned to sand. Wrecked machines and spare parts are lying everywhere — in ruts, pot-holes, ditches, in bomb craters, there are wrecked vehicles."

The crossing took hours, sometimes a full night, and was long, loud, frigid, and deadly.

Though a few buses were heated, most of the trucks carrying refugees were not. People squatted on flatbeds or cowered under canvas tarps as a night wind whipped across the snowy plain, bringing temperatures down to −40°F. Some nights, blizzards raged. The refugees were encrusted in snow and ice. Many died of exposure on the route to safety.

The trucks usually chose to drive with their lights on. Even though the lights attracted German fire, the hazards of driving in the dark were greater. Gouges and fissures in the ice loomed out of the night, and drivers had to be quick to swerve. Some were not quick enough. They shot into the water, their headlights glowing eerily as they sank into the darkness.

The trucks behind them did not stop to help; they careened around the holes in the ice and sped up. Stopping was too dangerous. If an engine cooled, the truck would often not start again, and no one wanted to be a sitting target for the Germans.

At first, especially, drivers made the trip with their doors wedged open so they could jump out if the truck was hit or went into a hole in the ice. Those sitting in the canvas-hooded seats in back had to decide whether they

THE BLOCKADE OF LENINGRAD, LATE 1941

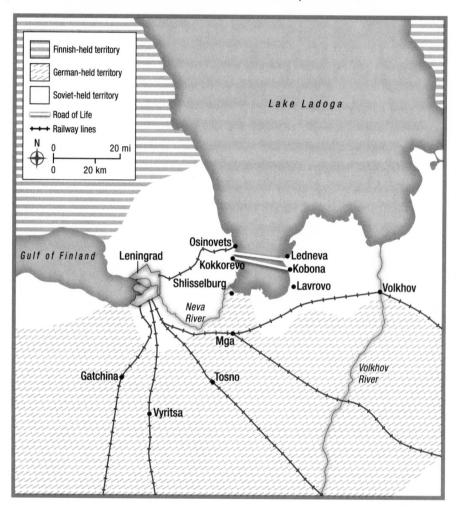

In the winter of 1941–1942, the treacherous Road of Life across the ice of Lake Ladoga was the only route around the German blockade of Leningrad.

Lake Ladoga was patrolled by aerosleds on skis, blown across the surface by propellers.

The Road of Life transported supplies in one direction and refugees in the other. By January 1942, two thousand tons of food were being delivered daily.

would huddle closer to the cabin, where it was warmer, or toward the back, where it was dangerously cold but closer to a quick escape route.

Lone figures, swaddled in fur hats and winter camouflage capes, stood out on the ice, waving poppy-red flags to direct traffic away from holes and wrecks.

Drivers on the Road of Life liked to boast about how many trips they could make in one shift. Typically, they only made one. It became a contest, though. Soon drivers were bragging that they were two-trip men, three-trip men, four-trip men. This hectic speed meant more people could escape the city and more food could make it into the city. It also meant that the trip got more and more rough for weak evacuees, as the wind knifed over them and they were jolted and juddered mercilessly.

The Road of Life brought together privileged Party members and citizens who had suffered enormous deprivations. One woman remembered having to bite her tongue on the long ride across the lake as a high-ranking couple brayed about all the food they'd secured since the siege had started. "During the blockade we ate better than before the war. We had everything," the man said.

His girlfriend piped up: "We ate whole boxes of butter and chocolate. Of course, I didn't see any of that before the war."

They were speaking to a truckful of people with eyes wide from hunger and dystrophy, families who had watched children die or who had made decisions to leave beloved grandmothers and great-aunts behind to starve so that their own children would have a chance of escaping alive.

The boyfriend drawled that he was leaving Leningrad because it was getting so boring there. No one, he complained, went out dancing anymore.

On the far side of Lake Ladoga, at Kobona, all the refugees who had survived the trip so far were given rations to revive them.

Even this had its dangers. Some of the evacuees could not stop themselves from devouring everything they were given at once. Their stomachs were no longer used to solid food. There was a rash of deaths before a doctor realized that the rations given out had to be decreased so people wouldn't gorge and die.

From Kobona, the refugees were driven in convoys a few final miles to railway stations. From there, they were shipped out east or south to other destinations, to find new lives.

Many, weakened by the voyage, succumbed to death on the far shore. At each station, corpses were unloaded from trains. This was also the point at which many passengers developed dysentery and other stomach ailments and spent much of their journey shivering by the cargo doors to the freight cars they rode in, ready to slide open the doors and squat in the wind when the need overtook them.

Sofia, Maria, and little Dmitri got off a train at Cherepovets. From there, Sofia sent a telegram to Shostakovich: "Got away safely from Leningrad longing to see you soon love to all Grandma."

Shostakovich was overjoyed. Incredibly, his family had made it. He was nervous, too, however. "How will they be?" he kept repeating. "I wonder what state they'll be in."

On March 19, 1942, the three finally arrived in Kuibyshev. They were sick and emaciated. Shostakovich wrote to his friend Glikman that Maria and young Dmitri were all right but that Sofia was "nothing but skin and bone."

Shostakovich brought the three of them back to his apartment. He was living in a slightly larger place now, which was good: only a few days later, in Moscow, he picked up Nina's father and mother, who would also be living with them in Kuibyshev. After he met the Varzars, Nina's parents, at the station, he wrote to his friend Glikman, "Vasily Vasilyyevich [Nina's father] looked absolutely terrible and his wits seemed to be wandering. . . . I now face a big problem which is seriously worrying me: how to feed and care for all the members of my family who have come to be with me." There were now nine people in the Shostakoviches' apartment. Soon, there were thirteen: Nina's sister, brother-in-law, niece, and old nurse arrived.

Still, it was a triumph: they were all together again. The conversations around the cramped dinner table, however, were not easy. As their neighbor Flora Litvinova described it, Shostakovich "was churned up by their stories of the cold and the hunger, deaths of their friends and near and dear ones. He nervously drummed his fingers against the table." In secret, Maria divulged: "You know, once we ate a cat. Of course, I didn't tell Mother or little Mitya."

The news from the city was not good. A quarter of Shostakovich's colleagues in the Leningrad Composers' Union had already died. One of the dead was his student Venjamin Fleishman, whom he had gone with to sign up for military service right after the announcement of Operation Barbarossa. Fleishman died in combat on September 14, 1941, valiantly blowing up a tank and himself with a string of grenades. Shostakovich was deeply moved by Fleishman's death. The young man had almost finished an opera, and Shostakovich felt he was very promising. Shostakovich mourned, "He went into the People's Volunteer Guard. They were all candidates for corpsehood. They were barely trained and poorly armed, and thrown into the most dangerous areas. A soldier could still entertain hopes of survival, but a volunteer guardsman, no."

Later, Shostakovich would finish his dead student's opera, called *Rothschild's Violin,* for him, and would see it staged.

The house was full, but it was good to have everyone out of danger. Shostakovich later wrote to his friend Glikman: "Everybody in my family is well, and spends the whole time talking in a loud voice about things to eat. As a result of these conversations I have forgotten a large part of my vocabulary, but I have excellent retention of the following: bread, butter, half a kilo, vodka, two hundred grams, ration card, confectionary department, and several other words."

There was another mouth to feed now, too. Maxim and Galina had adopted a shaggy street dog. "We hadn't the heart to shoo him away," Shostakovich explained, "so now he lives with us. The children call him Ginger (*Ryzhik*). He seems to like his name." Galina remembered Ginger fondly. "He was lively and undemanding—a typical mongrel."

They did not record the story of their previous dog, eaten in the Siege of Leningrad.

Now that his family was safely with him, Shostakovich could turn his attention to another feat of transportation: the international efforts to get copies of his Seventh Symphony. "It seems to have become a very fashionable piece just now," he told his friend Glikman. "Couriers arrive from all over the place, asking me to help them get a copy of the score. . . . Couriers, couriers, couriers. Nothing but couriers, thirty-five thousand of them!"

Shostakovich didn't know how to help all the people requesting the music. Copies were difficult to come by. Paper was scarce. (At this point, Shostakovich was out of paper himself and wrote his letters on small white pieces of old cardboard.) The initial printing of three hundred copies of the score had already expanded to seven hundred.

The government was intent on three special performances of the piece, which they wanted to stage for propagandistic purposes: a performance in London, a performance in the United States, and, last, a performance in the besieged city of Leningrad itself. Shostakovich was particularly insistent about wanting the piece to be played back in his home city "in the not-too-distant future."

State copyists were writing out the parts of the piece as quickly as they could. (The score includes the music for the whole orchestra stacked up so a conductor can see how the whole piece is supposed to work; the parts include just the music each individual instrumentalist needs.) The parts were done hastily and were full of errors.

The government took the score and all the orchestral parts and photographed them. The photographs were reduced and put on single strips of microfilm—2,750 pages on one hundred feet of film. The rolls of microfilm were stowed in small wooden boxes. These were to be sent to the West.

The copy for North America was supposed to travel to the United States on a flight chartered by the American ambassador. We don't know what happened; somewhere in the Soviet bureaucracy, the microfilm got rerouted and disappeared. It was never handed over to the plane's pilot. It was to take a much more surprising route across the oceans.

Meanwhile, Shostakovich wanted the piece to be sent to the orchestra of his alma mater, the Leningrad Conservatory. They were now hiding out in Tashkent. The faculty of the Conservatory had huddled around a shabby radio and heard the piece broadcast from Kuibyshev. They knew they wanted to have it performed. Shostakovich soon sent a telegram inviting his friend Isaak Glikman to travel by train to Kuibyshev and pick up a copy.

Sending someone on a train journey during wartime was difficult. Special permission had to be granted for train voyages, and somehow, food had to be found for the courier to eat on his travels. To this end, the faculty of the Leningrad Conservatory had a meeting to determine how many pies to give Glikman for his voyage. One faction argued that it was a ten-day journey and that he should therefore receive ten pies. Another faction demanded twenty. The train might get stuck somewhere, "in which case [Glikman] would be reduced to gnawing the wood of [his] sleeping berth." The twenty-pie faction won.

Glikman set off on the train for Kuibyshev on April 5. When he woke on the first morning of the journey, he pulled out the first of his pies. It was stale and had to be knocked around to break it open. He was disgusted to find that "Horror of horrors! It was alive with little Tashkent ants, like poppy-seeds."

Glikman stared at his twenty ant-infested pies with growing despair. They were all he had to eat for the next week and a half.

A doctor was in the seat next to him. The doctor coolly picked up a chunk of the pie, ants and all, and popped it in his mouth. He clicked his tongue and pronounced: "Speaking as a doctor, I can assure you this pie is perfectly edible."

"The two of us dined together for the ten days of the journey," Glikman remembered, "demolishing all of the twenty pies and becoming connoisseurs, for the first and I hope the last time, of the singular taste of the Central Asian ant."

Shostakovich met Glikman at the Kuibyshev train station. The composer looked thin and nervously smoked his cheap, cardboard-filtered cigarettes. He told Glikman they would have to walk back to his apartment: a typhoid epidemic was sweeping through the refugee community, and he didn't want to ride on public transportation for fear of catching it. Though he could have gotten a car from the government, he refused to request one. He didn't want to be indebted to anyone. They walked through the crowded streets of Kuibyshev together. (Shostakovich, like many of the refugees, eventually did catch typhoid and spent several months in a sanatorium, feverishly writing his Second Piano Sonata.)

Glikman stayed with the Shostakoviches for a month, sleeping on a sofa in the composer's study amid the hubbub of the composer's extended family. By the middle of May, a score and parts were ready for Glikman to take back to Tashkent. He flew back, and Shostakovich's music was reunited with the orchestra of his own beloved school where he had studied and taught. It was given a triumphant performance there. Glikman wrote defiantly, "No material hardship could stifle the voice of the muses, nor could the guns. The fire of the spirit burned as fiercely as ever, there was no lessening of passion for music in general and for Shostakovich's new symphony in particular. Everywhere there was a burning desire to hear this work performed."

Meanwhile, the Soviet Embassy in Washington, D.C., had noticed that the microfilm score of the symphony had never arrived in America. It had gone missing entirely.

On May 23, an anxious Soviet diplomat appeared at the U.S. Department of State, begging to know where the Shostakovich microfilm had disappeared to. It had supposedly left Moscow on an American plane on April 9.

The Department of State made inquiries. They discovered that the pilot had never received any microfilm box and had no idea that he was supposed to be transporting the cargo to the United States.

An eager public awaited "the greatest musical event of the year — and perhaps the generation"—and American conductors argued ferociously about who would get to play the piece first—but the score seemed simply to have vanished.

We're used to thinking of information as something that drifts through the air invisibly all around us. But in an age before satellite telecommunications, complex information could not simply shoot across the globe through the ether. Information was earthbound and had a solid, physical form (paper, film, photos). So geography mattered.

The score of the Shostakovich Seventh Symphony had to go either east or west to get to the United States. In either direction, it would have to pass through dangerous territory patrolled by Axis ships and planes—the Japanese to the east and the Germans to the west. In the cold, icy seas of the north, American shipping convoys fell prey to battleships. Airplanes found it hard to refuel when they could not touch down safely almost anywhere in Europe.

This may explain the symphony's somewhat eccentric route. We know now that the box of microfilm took an epic and surprising journey.

It was stowed in a diplomatic pouch and flown to the Middle East. It landed in Tehran, capital of Iran, a hub of Soviet shipments from the west. (The Soviets and the British had in fact ousted the lawful shah of Iran just to make sure the country could continue to serve as a transportation corridor for oil and war matériel.) In Tehran, the diplomatic pouch was probably handed over to a courier who drove it in a truck across the desert into British territory. It went over the mountains and into Iraq. The roads were terrible, and the drivers were constantly jolted and thrown around. Tires that lasted eighty thousand miles on America's highways were worn through after only four thousand miles of this rugged terrain.

Passing along the same roads in the other direction was the early trickle of British and American Lend-Lease aid to Russia. The three Allied nations were working together desperately to try to find a reliable route for the delivery of armaments and food that wouldn't be threatened by German U-boats or the Luftwaffe.

As the aid flowed east from America to Russia, the symphony, a gesture of thanks and friendship for that aid, was driven east to west along the same route.

The microfilm reached Cairo, Egypt. In the Libyan deserts nearby, massive Fascist tank armies were engaged in heavy fighting amid the sands. Cairo acted as British headquarters. The city's streets were full of soldiers and spies. At tony clubs like the Kit Kat, afloat on the Nile, drunk English officers swapped stories while dancing girls and water boys listened in, taking notes for the Germans.

Here, the Shostakovich microfilm was probably handed over to an American pilot. The *Leningrad* Symphony, composed in the frigid north, was flown out over the pyramids and across North Africa.

It probably touched down once more in Africa — perhaps in Casablanca, perhaps in Accra — and then set off across the Atlantic. Flying the other way were B-52 and A-20 bombers being delivered to the Russians for their struggle against the Luftwaffe.

The microfilm landed in Recife, Brazil, at a landing field that was, at that point, only a few metal Quonset huts. From there, a U.S. Navy plane flew the diplomatic pouch north to Florida, and from there, to Washington, D.C.

Shostakovich's symphony had crossed the majority of the earth's continents.

On May 30, the diplomatic pouch was delivered to the U.S. State Department. Someone there unsealed it and discovered the wooden box with the microfilm inside; it was passed along to the Soviet Embassy.

On June 2, 1942, it was handed over to an agent from the Am-Rus Music Corporation. Am-Rus had been hired by the Soviet government to promote the work of Russian composers. They were responsible for getting Shostakovich's score into the hands of American conductors.

The agent from Am-Rus left the Soviet Embassy with the microfilm and went to lunch. It was there that he left the box on his tray. After a journey of almost twenty thousand miles — flown out of besieged Leningrad, taken by train across the width of Russia, flown again to Tehran, driven through the Middle East, bounced across the Atlantic—the priceless score almost ended up in the trash.

The music agent took it to New York City the next day. The Am-Rus Music Corporation—three people in an office over the Russian Tea Room on West 57th Street—now had to make hundreds of copies very quickly.

This was not as easy in 1942 as it would be now. They worked day and night. The individual pages had to be blown up from the photographic negatives. The original images were weak and hard to read. The parts were riddled with errors. All of these had to be corrected. Given the wartime shortage of paper, the only thing they could find to print on was glossy and shone under the theater lights while musicians squinted at it, trying to make out the notes.

The Am-Rus Music Corporation finally anointed conductor Arturo Toscanini—a noted anti-Fascist—for the piece's American premiere. He would perform the Seventh Symphony over the air with the NBC Radio Orchestra. But it was summer, and all the musicians were on vacation. They had to be called back to New York. The clarinetist discovered that Russian clarinets had an extra hole. He had to bore his own. The head of the NBC music department was exhausted by the whole process: "I wouldn't care if I never heard another word about Shostakovich's Seventh. It has been one vast headache."

Toscanini and the NBC Radio Orchestra had only four rehearsals to prepare the huge piece. Nonetheless, they were deeply moved by the symphony. It was "the most thrilling experience of my musical career!" exclaimed one musician.

Prompted by the tales of Leningrad under siege and the microfilm trip across several continents, Americans went Shostakovich crazy. According to Eugene Weintraub, the Am-Rus agent in charge of promotion, he barely had to lift a finger to get New York wild about "this hot baby of a Seventh symphony." Before the public even heard the symphony, they saw the photos of the composer in his firefighting gear. A painting of Shostakovich appeared on the front of *Time* magazine—the first composer ever to make it onto the cover. He stands in defiant profile, dreaming up a tune while defending burning Leningrad.

The *Time* article acquainted Americans with the myth of Shostakovich. He was not some neurotic Bolshevik artiste or some Communist Party stooge, the article suggested, but just a regular guy. During the Russian Revolution he had been "a pale, slight, impressionable little bourgeois boy who clung to a servant's hand in the battle-littered streets of Petrograd." In propaganda for the Soviets, the last thing Shostakovich would have wanted said about him was that he had ever been "bourgeois" in the age of Lenin. That was enough to get you shot. Now, however, for an American audience, it was important to come from a middle-class family, to have had servants.

And it was also important to prefer sports to music: "The climax of joy," the composer is quoted as saying, "is not when you're through a new symphony, but when you are hoarse from shouting, with your hands stinging from clapping, your lips parched, and you sip your second glass of beer after you've fought for it with 90,000 other spectators to celebrate the victory of your favorite team." Everything in the article is designed to suggest that Shostakovich is really just like an American dad reading *Time*, sprawled on his sofa.

The first performance of the *Leningrad* Symphony in the Western Hemisphere took place in England, at the studios of the BBC (the British Broadcasting Company). The London Philharmonic Orchestra had received its own copy of the microfilm, sent on a similar route through Cairo. Now, under the baton of Henry Wood, they performed the piece on June 22, 1942—a year to the day after the Germans had launched Operation Barbarossa.

And then, finally, came the much-anticipated American premiere of the piece. On July 19, 1942, Arturo Toscanini conducted what turned out to be one of the most famous concerts of the twentieth century, broadcasting the Seventh Symphony on NBC. Sent out on the airwaves, the music reached millions of homes, though somewhat garbled, supposedly, by heavy clouds.

Shostakovich, dressed as a firefighter in the blazing ruins of Leningrad, became the first composer ever to appear on the cover of *Time* magazine. After *Time* and other magazines printed photos of Shostakovich on the roof of the Leningrad Conservatory, the United States went Shostakovich crazy. "People who had no interest in music, people who still stutter over Tchaikovsky's name could pronounce the name of Shostakovich," said his American agent, Eugene Weintraub.

Americans in their living rooms, worried about fathers, sons, and husbands who had already been sent into battle overseas, leaned in close to hear the new war symphony. It was a phenomenon, the most anticipated piece of music in the world that night.

The recording that remains of that performance is brittle, loud, and tinny. Many critics were unimpressed with the piece. The American public, however, was powerfully moved. Through their radios, the symphony spoke to each of them.

But what did it say? No one seems to have thought that it was about Stalin, about that first assault on Leningrad during the 1930s. No one, at least, wrote that down. People heard it according to their circumstances and thought it was about the German advance. And they heard their own lives in this music: The symphony, a biographer wrote in 1942,

> tells the man who hears it, not the story of a stranger, but his own
> story. It makes him the hero of it; it cries out his own sorrows and
> celebrates his own victories. . . . Shostakovich states that at the
> beginning of the Seventh he depicts the peaceful life before the
> war in the quiet homes of Leningrad. But to a listener in Iowa it
> could mean the meadows and the rolling hills around his home.
> After the fantastic theme of war, Shostakovich has put into his
> music a lament for the dead — and the tears of a Russian mother
> and of an American mother are the same.

All this talk about the similarity of the Russian citizen and the American patriot was often accompanied by pleas for aid. An organization named Russian War Relief held charity benefits where they played the music of Shostakovich and emphasized the new friendship between the heartlands of capitalism and communism. American propaganda spoke rousingly of the common fight against Fascist horror.

Conductors all over the Americas scheduled performances of the *Leningrad* Symphony. In the United States alone, it was played sixty-two

A telegram from Shostakovich to conductor Arturo Toscanini, via the Russian Embassy and agent Eugene Weintraub: "Dear friend, I'm happy to know you'll conduct my Seventh Symphony. I'm confident that with your consummate, inherent talent and superlative skill you'll convey to [the] public of democratic America [the] concepts which I've endeavored [to] embody in this work."

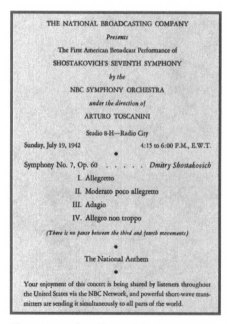

The program from Toscanini's American premiere of the Seventh Symphony, broadcast from the NBC studios

Right: Two posters urge Americans to donate to Russian War Relief, Inc., by emphasizing the strategic connection between the U.S. and Soviet causes.

times in different cities before the end of the year. It was performed by an orchestra out in the California desert for an audience of twenty thousand tank soldiers about to be shipped off to North Africa. ("It was universal war music," the *Los Angeles Times* wrote, "the language of a warrior over-leaping race and language and boundaries.") It was broadcast on almost two thousand radio stations all across the country, from the mountains to the prairies, often played by a local symphony orchestra. In Ohio, for example, the Cleveland Orchestra tromped through this epic piece depicting Soviet blood and struggle on Sammy Kaye's *Sunday Serenade* and *The Pause That Refreshes on the Air,* sponsored by Coca-Cola. It was a strange fate for a Communist war symphony.

Meanwhile, an exotic dancer wrote to the Am-Rus Music Corporation to ask if she could do a striptease to the "invasion" theme. "What a movement that would have been," agent Weintraub quipped.

Hollywood clamored to produce movies about the symphony and its creator. Leopold Stokowski, who had conducted the music for Disney's *Fantasia,* proposed a film in which Shostakovich's music would accompany scenes of the composer in besieged Leningrad. Director Howard Hawks, best known at that point for screwball comedies in which wealthy dingbats fell in love and moved to Connecticut, bought the film rights to the symphony and its story. He hired American author William Faulkner (*As I Lay Dying, The Sound and the Fury*) to write the script. The movie, *Battle Cry,* was supposed to be a propaganda piece combining heroic stories from all the Allied nations. The Russian segment would have told the story of Shostakovich's Seventh interwound with a fictional romance between two Soviet fighter pilots, a man and a woman. The story was not subtle. It was typical Hollywood: for example, the female aeronaut gives birth to their child in the cockpit of her plane while evading German flak fire during the Battle of Stalingrad.

Later, she writes to her son about Shostakovich's symphony: "You will hear that music one day, my son—the whole of the world will hear it—but not as we heard it . . . with guns blasting, shells screaming—buildings pulverized!" She takes a break in her letter writing for a brief bombardment. When she returns, she writes, "It was our music—he wrote it for us! He wrote it with hands singed from the fires of Nazi bombs—he wrote it with cold eating at his fingers, my son!"

Hollywood hype here meets with wartime propaganda. Shostakovich was extremely uncomfortable with these Tinseltown exaggerations. He did not want to be a hero, and his hands had never been singed by Nazi bombs. He wrote to the Am-Rus Music Corporation saying that he didn't want the project to go forward. Am-Rus agent Weintraub agreed: "We were inclined to respect his wisdom when the film people suggested gilding the lily by filming the composer with one arm in a sling, the other penning his music."

Shostakovich later remembered, supposedly, "At first it seemed that a wider celebrity might help me, but then I remembered Meyerhold and Tukhachevsky. They were much more famous than I, and it didn't help them one bit. On the contrary." The composer knew being too high-profile in Stalin's Russia was often fatal.

"I was just uneasy," he said. "The Allies enjoyed my music," but they didn't seem to be opening up the European Second Front against the Nazis that Stalin wanted so much. "They shouldn't have made such a fuss over my symphonies, but the Allies fussed, and fussed deliberately. They were creating a diversion, at least that's how it was interpreted here in Russia. The ballyhoo kept growing, which must have irritated Stalin."

So, how successful was Shostakovich's symphony in America? Obviously, it was a success in that it was one of the most talked-about musical events of the twentieth century.

It clearly worked to popularize the Russian cause. As *Life* magazine reported, "By now it is almost unpatriotic not to like Dmitri Shostakovich's Seventh Symphony. . . . This work has become a symbol of the Russians' heroic resistance. People who temper their praise of the Seventh or express dislike of it are looked on as musical fifth columnists who are running down our brave Russian allies."

But did it actually work to increase aid?

It did not produce the Second Front that Stalin hoped for so desperately. In the summer of 1942, the Allies were stretched too thin to think of attacking the Germans on European soil. Stalin was furious, but the British and American forces would delay the Second Front until 1944.

On the other hand, American aid to Russia in the form of airplanes, tanks, ammunition, medicine, and food rapidly increased. It played a vital role in the Allied war effort, supporting the USSR in its battle against the invaders. President Roosevelt believed deeply in the strategic importance of this aid. Shostakovich's symphony was the most visible element of a wider program to convince the public that assisting Russia at that desperate point in the war was essential. By January 1943, polls showed that 90 percent of Americans believed that food aid to Russia should be increased, even at the expense of domestic food supplies. Just a year and a half before, the Soviet Union had been viewed as an enemy.

Now goods flowed copiously back to Russia over the path that the symphony had taken to America. U.S. donations to the Russian war effort had almost quadrupled in one year. As it turned out, the American bombers and tanks sent initially were not as useful as they might have been. (They were somewhat obsolete models and easily overcome by superior German technology.) What made a really substantial difference in the Russian war effort was radio equipment, food, industrial machinery, and the American jeep. The jeep became a favorite vehicle of Soviet troops for bouncing over rugged terrain, as did American-built motorcycles and the Studebaker automobile. In terms of food supplies, American aid provided the equivalent of "one pound of concentrated ration per day for 6 million soldiers, virtually the whole [Red] Army." Aid on this scale was extremely important to the Soviet war effort and to eventual Allied success. During the negotiations over aid in the summer of 1942, Shostakovich's symphony played a small but appreciable role in convincing Americans that aid like this was justified.

The piece was used even more directly by Russian War Relief, which held benefit concerts of the Seventh and other Shostakovich works to gather funds for the Russian Red Cross and Red Crescent. In 1942, Russian War

Relief donated about ten million dollars to support the Soviet people (a huge sum at the time), and furthermore shipped them about seven million dollars' worth of clothes, medication, and even seeds to replant ravaged fields. They used Shostakovich's music to alert Americans to the unbelievable suffering and strength of the Soviet people.

The microfilm transfer of the symphony around the globe and its use to provoke donations of weaponry and foodstuffs remains one of the most striking stories of World War II. But there still was one story left to play out that was even more bizarre and astounding. There was one place that the *Leningrad* Symphony had not yet been performed: in the city of Leningrad itself.

It was there, played by an army of starving, emaciated musicians, that Shostakovich's Seventh was to receive its last—and most important—premiere.

Leningrad's Volkovo Cemetery
in the midst of a thaw

SYMPHONY FOR THE CITY OF THE DEAD

There was no one left in Leningrad to play the *Leningrad Symphony*. It had always been a city of music, but it had fallen silent. Its best-known orchestras had fled before the Germans ringed the city. Only the Leningrad Radio Orchestra remained, and it had shut down in mid-winter. Their last live broadcast had been on New Year's Day, 1942. They'd played excerpts from an opera called *The Snow Maiden*. Later that night, the opera's tenor had died of hunger.

The final note in the orchestral logbook reads: "Rehearsal did not take place. Srabian is dead. Petrov is sick. Borishev is dead. Orchestra not working."

It went into hibernation as the city starved.

In March, the Leningrad Party bosses decided music was needed to improve morale in the dying city. Posters appeared around town: "All Leningrad musicians please report to the Radio Committee."

The acting conductor of the Radio Orchestra, Karl Eliasberg, a thin man with peering spectacles, went from door to door, trying to find out which of his musicians still remained alive. He found them lying in dark apartments, emaciated. He himself was suffering from starvation.

An oboe player named Ksenia Matus heeded the call. She had not played with the Radio Orchestra before, but according to her, she had dated most of its members. She prepared to go to the first rehearsal. "I grabbed my instrument and when I opened the case [the oboe] also turned out to have dystrophy. All the pads had turned green, the valves had turned green. The oboe wouldn't play, but I took it as it was." Eventually, she brought it to a repairman, who said he would fix it for dog meat. Matus told him it was being fixed for the Shostakovich piece, and he smiled with delight. He even agreed to accept cash.

All the musicians who could stir themselves from their burrows showed up for the first rehearsal on March 30, 1942. There were only fifteen of them. They were dying of hunger, blackened with soot. The radio studio was freezing cold, like a cave of ice.

Eliasberg, the conductor, shuffled to the front of the room. He addressed the few musicians sitting in front of him. "Dear friends, we are weak but we must force ourselves to start work." He raised his arms for the downbeat. No one moved. The musicians sat shivering with cold and weakness.

Once again, Eliasberg raised his gaunt arms. "He lifted his hands and they were trembling," oboist Matus remembered. "To my imagination, he was a wounded bird, whose wings are hurt, and is about to fall. But he didn't fall."

Creakily, the remains of the orchestra began to play. They were awful. The wind players could barely blow. The pianist had to warm bricks and put them on either side of the keyboard to keep his fingers moving.

When it came time for a trumpet solo, there was silence. Eliasberg looked over at the first trumpet. He was on his knees. "It's your solo," Eliasberg said. "Why don't you play?"

The trumpeter replied, "I'm sorry, sir. I haven't the strength in my lungs."

There was, an eyewitness remembered, "a terrible pause." Eliasberg collected himself. Then he insisted softly, "I think you do have the strength."

That moment of belief was enough. The trumpeter raised the instrument to his lips and began to play.

"Everybody did their best, but we played badly," oboist Matus remembered. "It was hopeless."

The first rehearsal was scheduled to last for three hours.

They broke up after fifteen minutes.

The score for the Seventh was flown into Leningrad on a transport plane delivering medicine to the besieged city. Eliasberg finally got his hands on the precious piece, but there was little sense of victory. He despaired. "When I saw the symphony, I thought, 'We'll never play this.' It was four thick volumes of music."

It called for a huge orchestra of more than a hundred players. He had only fifteen, and they were near death. He crept down the length of Nevsky Prospect to Communist Party Headquarters and informed the authorities that he needed more musicians if he was ever going to perform the Shostakovich. General Leonid Govorov, commander in chief of the Leningrad Front, agreed to pull wind players from the Red Army regiments surrounding the city.

The Radio Orchestra could not immediately tackle the Seventh Symphony. In the meantime, they played pieces they already knew. Their concerts were broadcast on the radio, to break up the awful silence that came when none of the pundits had anything left to say and all that was heard was the deadening tick of the metronome. The orchestra's first concert was on April 5. The hall was below freezing. The orchestra played some light waltzes.

"When we finished the first piece the audience started to applaud, but there was no sound because everyone was wearing mittens," Ksenia Matus remembered. "Looking out at the crowd, you couldn't tell who was a man and who was a woman—the women were all wrapped up, and the men were wearing scarves and shawls, or even women's fur coats. Afterwards we were all so inspired, because we knew that we had done our job and that our work would continue."

Eliasberg was elated they had played at all. He noted other triumphs: "On May 1, under heavy shelling, we played the Sixth Symphony of Tchaikovsky."

Trombonist Viktor Orlovsky was astonished by the audiences. "Listening to music gave the city's inhabitants a form of escape, and an opportunity to rise above hardship and suffering. Even when the bread ration had been reduced to 125 grams, some would exchange their daily meal for a ticket to a classical concert."

The rehearsals ran every day from ten in the morning until one in the afternoon. Eliasberg, too weak to walk to the rehearsal hall, had to be dragged on a sled like a corpse. He and his wife were staying on the seventh floor of the Astoria Hotel. Once one of the city's most exclusive and expensive spots, it was now a hospital for the starving. Its former glamour was gone: "The hotel is dead," wrote one journalist who was convalescing there. "Like the whole city there is neither water nor light. In the dark corridors rarely appears a figure, lighting his way with a hand-generator flashlight or a simple match. The rooms are cold, the temperatures not rising above 40 degrees." Adolf Hitler, predicting that he would take Leningrad in a few short months, boasted that he would be celebrating with champagne in the ballroom of the Astoria Hotel on August 9. Rumors said that the invitations were already printed.

It is from this building that Eliasberg daily was dragged.

The musicians got food for their efforts — "not really soup," recalled Matus, "more water with a few beans in it, and a teaspoon of wheat germ." This kept them from death, but during the rehearsals they still found it hard to concentrate. Eliasberg had to explain each point slowly two or three times before the musicians could understand. Sometimes, weakened by hunger, players simply toppled over and passed out.

The recruits from military bands still had their frontline duties as well as their rehearsals. Captain Mikhail Parfionov, a trombonist from the Red Army's Forty-Fifth Division wind band, recalled: "Rehearsals in the morning, then straight to the front for concerts, then our military duties. One day we went from rehearsal to Piskayorsky cemetery to bury piles of corpses in mass graves. . . . We were back to rehearse the music next day."

Leningrad was thawing. The ice on the Neva was starting to groan and crack. (Trucks on the Road of Life now splattered through water that was axle-deep. Soon, they had to stop trips entirely until the routes could be undertaken by boat.)

Tens of thousands of people came out of their chilly apartments and appeared on the streets and squares to start a citywide cleanup. They carted away debris. They cleared avenues. They had to move quickly: as the snow melted, piles of filth — corpses and manure — started to fester.

"You should have seen it, what it was like," remarked a survivor. "None of the people believed it could ever be tidied up. But as soon as the sun began to have a bit of warmth in it everybody turned out, just like a single person. There wasn't anybody who didn't come out on the streets. There were housewives and school children and educated folk — professors, doctors, musicians, old men and old women. . . . Some of them hardly had the strength to drag their legs."

They came together to plant vegetable gardens in public parks and odd strips of dirt. Outside Eliasberg's windows at the Astoria Hotel, the grounds of Saint Isaac's Cathedral were sown with cabbages.

Even before the vegetable seeds were in the ground, people had started to devour any green thing that grew. "Grass, grass, grass," wrote a diarist. "The whole city is eating different kinds of grass. At the garden fences children are calling out to each other, hauling grass through the rails, eating it as if they were rabbits." City employees pasted lists of edible wild plants on walls and kiosks. People devoured dandelions and boiled nettles. In the nearby forest, small boys perched on tree limbs, eating new leaves like flocks of sparrows.

As people came together to clean up the city and prepare for the next phase of the siege, many felt hope for the first time in months. "As they

As soon as the growing season started, people planted gardens all over the city. Here, the lawns near Saint Isaac's Cathedral are devoted to growing cabbages.

After the hard winter of 1942, citizens of Leningrad emerged to clean the streets of the besieged city.

worked, people passed on their strength to each other," a resident recalled. "And through this strength came an affirmation of our common cause. We would defy Hitler's cruel order that our city should be erased from the earth. It would stay habitable. We were proud to be called Leningraders."

The musicians of the Radio Orchestra were not all so hopeful. Clarinetist Viktor Koslov drearily mocked the excitement of the populace. "'Look, here comes spring!' But what did it bring? Decomposing, dismembered corpses in the streets that had been hidden under the ice. Severed legs with meat chopped off them. Bits of bodies in the bins. Women's bodies with breasts cut off, which people had taken to eat. They had been buried all winter but there they were for all the city to see how it had remained alive."

This was what the Leningrad Radio Orchestra struggled with as they set about to prove the importance of humankind's better nature. In the face of Nazi scorn for Slavic "subhumans," the Russians wanted to show that they were making art even as the Germans made war. They were resolutely remaining human—but what did that mean? What was the human animal in the midst of the siege? An herbivore that crawled on all fours, browsing on dirty grasses. A predator that hunted alone or in packs. A social animal that spoke of noble art and wound violin strings from the guts of dead sheep and pigs. A creature with canine teeth for tearing, but with a tongue for speaking, too. A mouth that could devour or sing.

The rehearsals for the Seventh started in earnest in July. Many of the musicians had to copy out their own parts by hand. A few of these copies remain. In the margins, they have doodled Red Army soldiers on the march and grim little Nazis goose-stepping.

In contrast to the stories of rehearsals for the piece in New York and Kuibyshev, the Leningrad musicians did not feel deeply moved by the music as they practiced it. "To be honest," said Captain Parfionov, the trombonist, "no one was very enthusiastic." The piece was so long they never once played it all the way through until the dress rehearsal, three days before the performance. Clarinetist Viktor Koslov admitted, "It was a very complex piece of work, and we were only rehearsing piecemeal. Most of us felt daunted by it. We would start rehearsing, and get dizzy with our heads spinning when we blew. The symphony was too big. People were falling over at the rehearsals. We might talk to the person next to us, but the topic of conversation was hunger and food — not music."

Eliasberg tried to maintain the ensemble's discipline. When musicians insisted, "It's no good, I can't play it," he snapped, "Go on. No complaining!" One man explained that he had arrived late because he had been burying his wife. Eliasberg was furious. "This must not happen again. If your wife or husband dies, you must be at the rehearsal."

Three of the orchestral players died before they ever got to play the piece in full.

The orchestra may have been too exhausted to appreciate what they were doing, but among the city's population, excitement for the piece mounted. Diarists recorded their anticipation. "The event was unmissable," one later declared. She tried to forget the Germans crouching a few miles away as she purchased her ticket. "This music had been dedicated to us, and to our city. Can you imagine the power of that?"

The Leningrad premiere of Shostakovich's Seventh Symphony took place on August 9, 1942. The day was chosen as a deliberate gesture of defiance: it was the date Hitler had boasted that he would be celebrating with a feast in the Hotel Astoria's ballroom.

The premiere did not merely require musical coordination. It also involved military action. General Govorov of the Red Army had spent the month of July fighting fiercely to repel another German assault and to ensure that Hitler's triumphal meal never happened. Now the 9th had come, and Govorov realized that the Grand Philharmonia Hall would be an obvious target for bombing — lit up in the midst of a blackout. To ensure the performance would not be interrupted, he launched a diversionary attack on German lines on the opposite side of the city. He called the action Operation Squall.

That evening, as the orchestral players tuned up and the audience filed into the auditorium, the Red Army pounded the enemy with three thousand high-caliber shells to draw fire away from the concert hall. Artillery officer Vasily Gordeev remembered, "First we hit the enemy's batteries, next their observation points, their communication centers. . . . Later we shifted attention to their headquarters and kept them under continuous fire for two hours and thirty minutes. . . . The results? The results were that not a single shell exploded on the streets of Leningrad. An artillery squall across the whole front. And in this way the performance of the Seventh was made possible." Later, when General Govorov met Karl Eliasberg, he wryly told the conductor, "We played our instrument in the symphony, too, you know." Eliasberg had no idea what he was talking about. The public wouldn't hear about Operation Squall for another twenty years.

Meanwhile, the musicians finally were getting excited. Clarinetist Koslov remembered, "I awoke that morning a different man." Ksenia Matus recalled walking to the hall with oboe in hand, "feeling strangely happy for the first time since the blockade."

The lights burned brilliantly in Philharmonia Hall. This in itself was surprising. "I'll never forget that," said Koslov. The lights had never been on during the rehearsals or previous concerts. "I'd forgotten what electric light was like."

The audience poured in: not just the city's artistic circles, not just the Communist Party elite, but hundreds of others who had gone without food to hear the piece played. Many soldiers came straight from the front in their uniforms; a few still carried their automatic weapons.

In the audience was an eleven-year-old boy named Yuri Ahronovitch, who had been on an evacuation train caught in one of the railway bombardments of the previous August. He had spent two months wandering by foot that fall trying to make it back to the city. He had managed to live through the winter. Now he came to hear what Shostakovich had written about Leningrad. He would later become a well-known conductor and would lead the Seventh Symphony himself.

Captain Parfionov of the trombone section looked out at the crowd. "It had been an everyday job until now. But we were stunned by the number of people, that there could be so many people starving for food but also starving for music. Some had come in suits, some from the front. Most were thin and dystrophic. Some I recognised from fishing before the war. That was the moment we decided to play as best we could."

Though it was summer, the orchestra was bundled up for the performance. "We were dressed like cabbages, with so many layers of clothes on," said oboist Matus. The musicians' bodies, racked with starvation, could not regulate heat. "It was too cold to play without gloves. We wore them like mittens with the fingers cut off; even then it was hard to move the keys on my instrument."

When Eliasberg shambled out onstage to conduct, his tailcoat and trousers swamped his emaciated frame.

Now, as it had been heard in so many cities around the world, Shostakovich's Seventh was finally heard in Leningrad itself. The confident first theme strode forth.

It was heard not merely inside the hall that night. Loudspeakers broadcast it through the streets of the city, over the canals, past the sandbagged palaces. The army had set up speakers to blare it across no-man's-land at the enemy lines, where German soldiers huddled in their trenches and gun emplacements.

The whole of Leningrad heard the music that evening. A soldier in the Red Army wrote in his journal, "On the night of 9 August 1942, my artillery squadron and the people of the great frontline city were listening to the Shostakovich symphony with closed eyes. It seemed that the cloudless sky had suddenly become a storm bursting with music as the city listened to the symphony of heroes and forgot about the war, but not the meaning of war."

A woman in the hall remembered, "It was so meaningful for all of us. We realized that this concert might be the last thing we'd do in our lives."

"One cannot speak of an impression made by the symphony," wrote a composer in the audience. "It was not an impression, but a staggering experience. This was felt not only by the listeners but also by the performers who read the music sheets as if they were reading a living chronicle about themselves."

It was not only the Russians who reacted. The Germans listened, too, as the music rose up through the leafy streets and above the gilt barrage balloons. It barked out of the radios in the Wehrmacht barracks. Years later, a German soldier told Eliasberg, "It had a slow but powerful effect on us. The realization began to dawn that we would never take Leningrad." That was enough in itself. "But something else started to happen. We began to see that there was something stronger than starvation, fear and death — the will to stay human."

The symphony meant many things to many people. To many Americans, it forged strong ties of kinship and friendship. To many Russians, it sang of the hope of victory. It may have shamed some Germans into realizing that they could no longer despise the Slavs as subhumans. But for the people of Leningrad, it meant something else entirely: it gave them an identity. "We listened with such emotion, because we had lived for this moment, to come and hear this music," remembered a woman who was in the hall that night. "This was a real symphony which we lived. This was our symphony. Leningrad's."

Like the spring cleanup that brought people together in the streets, the symphony showed them that they *belonged*. It gave them a story to tell about themselves in which they were heroes and in which their hideous trials were a mark of pride. It transformed them from victims into the pride of Russia.

This suggests some of the power of stories.

Not long ago, English journalist Ed Vulliamy sought out the musicians who remained from that orchestra, and in a series of deeply moving interviews, recorded their memories of that night. He found clarinetist Viktor Koslov watching and rewatching videos of Leningrad's tragedy, as if still trying to make sense of it — or as if it were the only thing that made sense of anything else.

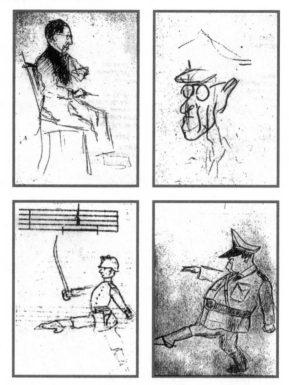

Doodles on the orchestral parts of Shostakovich's Seventh Symphony. Musicians sketched conductor Karl Eliasberg, goose-stepping Fascists, and one another.

Karl Eliasberg and the Leningrad Radio Orchestra rehearsing. Even though they are starving to death, many still dress in coat and tie.

A soldier buys a ticket to the Leningrad premiere of Shostakovich's Seventh Symphony.

Karl Eliasberg leads the battered, starving Leningrad Radio Orchestra in the city's premiere of the *Leningrad* Symphony.

Koslov gestured to the suffering on the screen (the corpses on sleds, the shattered buildings). "It's what we lived with every day! It's what we walked past on the way to rehearsals. Ah, but the concert itself—it was our answer to the suffering. I have seen it in my sleep many times, and still hear the thunder of applause from the audience. That will be the last image before my eyes when I die."

As the brass blared out the finale, bringing back with triumph the striding theme that had begun the whole work, Captain Parfionov began to wobble with exhaustion. "It was so loud and powerful that I thought I'd collapse."

He saw the audience rising in their seats, however, "willing [the orchestra] to keep going."

With a mighty blast, the *Leningrad* Symphony was over.

There was silence. And then, of course, the wild applause. "It felt like a victory," remembered trombonist Viktor Orlovsky. "At the end, our conductor, Eliasberg, received one bouquet of flowers from a teenage girl." This was remarkable because no one in the city grew flowers when they could grow vegetables. The girl turned to the orchestra and explained, "My family did this because life has to go on as normal—whatever happens around us." The players could not restrain themselves any longer. They turned and embraced one another. They kissed. It was like they had been through a battle.

Sitting in the audience, diarist Vera Inber had little doubt the symphony was about the city. "The rumbling approach of German tanks—there they were." But she pointed out that part of the piece was just fantasy: "The shining conclusion is still to come."

For many, however, that night seemed to mark a turning point.

Eliasberg stooped in his oversize tailcoat. "When we had finished, everyone was satisfied. Me? I was shattered, that's all."

Leningrad Communist Party boss Andrei Zhdanov invited the whole orchestra—or those who didn't have to return immediately to the front—to a huge gala reception. He greeted the musicians personally and told them how proud he was of them. Ksenia Matus was delighted with the spread. "On the table there was beefsteak and — oh, everything delicious was there! It was the first we had eaten since the beginning of the siege." Unfortunately, they weren't used to rich food, and after gobbling it all down, they vomited it all up.

It didn't matter much, said Matus. "No one could feed us, but music inspired us and brought us back to life. In this way, this day was our feast." More important, the Germans were not singing the Horst Wessel Song at Leningrad's Astoria Hotel. "They never had their party," said Matus. "Instead, we played our symphony, and [later] Leningrad was saved."

Eliasberg remembered that night for the rest of his life. (It was to be the high point of his career.) "People just stood and cried. They knew that this was not a passing episode but the beginning of something. We heard it in the music. The concert hall, the people in their apartments, the soldiers on the front — the whole city had found its humanity. And in that moment, we triumphed over the soulless Nazi war machine."

In 1992, on the fiftieth anniversary of the Leningrad performance, the same orchestra was called together in the same hall to play the piece again. By that time, only fourteen of them remained alive. Their reunion recalled that first rehearsal in 1942, except that age had now seized those whom siege had not.

Trombonist Mikhail Parfionov met again with oboist Ksenia Matus. "Dear Edith," he said, "when we first performed this together we were young and beautiful."

She replied tartly, "And now?"

Gallantly, he answered, "Now, dear Edith, you, at least, are more beautiful than ever."

Ksenia Matus mused to Vulliamy, "So many years have passed since that day and memory is a funny thing, like drying paint. It changes color as it dries. But that symphony has stayed with me the way it was that night. Afterwards, it was still a city under siege, but I knew it would live. Music is life, after all. What is life without music? This was the music that proved our city had come back to life after death."

PART ★ THREE

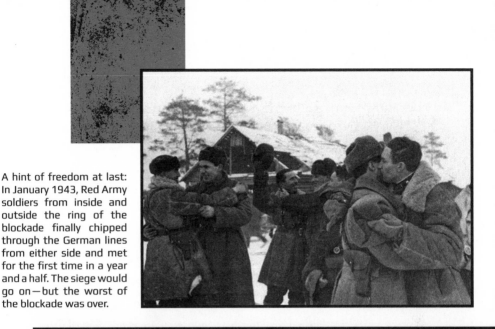

A hint of freedom at last: In January 1943, Red Army soldiers from inside and outside the ring of the blockade finally chipped through the German lines from either side and met for the first time in a year and a half. The siege would go on—but the worst of the blockade was over.

COLD WAR AND THAW

The story should end there, but of course it does not. History does not allow for perfect cadences.

The performance of the Seventh Symphony in besieged Leningrad is remembered now as a turning point in the assault, but only because it changed the way people saw themselves and the war effort. It shaped memory. In fact, the siege went on for another year and a half—but people recognized that the worst was over. Step by step, Leningraders reclaimed their city.

Already, things were changing. A flotilla of warships, freighters, and barges carried hundreds of tons of supplies to the city across Lake Ladoga. At the end of the summer, pipes were laid under the lake so Leningrad would not be as short of fuel when the winter came. The NKVD, in one of its secret dispatches, reported more good news to the Kremlin: "In connection with the improvement of the food situation in June, the death rate went down by a third. . . . The number of incidents of use of human flesh in food supply decreased. Whereas 236 people were arrested for this crime in May, in June it was just 56." As autumn arrived, the city laid in supplies for the winter and increasingly shipped out noncombatants, who fled to their families elsewhere.

In December 1942, General Govorov planned a major offensive against the Germans in another attempt to break the iron ring around the captive city. He gathered forty-five hundred powerful guns and mortars on either side of the Wehrmacht blockade and prepared to push from both sides. "By the beginning of January," said Govorov, comparing his assault to a Shostakovich symphony, "all the musicians in our artillery orchestra knew their scores, and we were ready to launch our own offensive."

Operation Spark, as it was called, began on January 12, 1943. A bombardment of German positions lasted hours. Fleets of mighty Katyusha rocket launchers blasted away at Nazi gun emplacements. Soviet planes streaked through the sky. A surprise infantry force on skis crossed the snows of frozen Lake Ladoga to retake Shlisselburg, looking much like the knights in Eisenstein's movie *Alexander Nevsky* fighting the Germans six hundred years earlier. For days, the Red Army kept up a fierce attack.

By January 18, they had broken through the German encirclement of the city. At eleven o'clock that night, radio announcer Yuri Levitan declared over the airwaves, "Troops of the Leningrad and Volkhov fronts have joined together and at the same time have broken the blockade of Leningrad." Soldiers from inside the city and outside the blockade ring swarmed together and embraced in joy.

The siege would go on — but the blockade was over. "This snowy moonlit night of January 18–19 will never vanish from the memory of those who experienced it," writer Vera Inber told the people of the city over the radio. "All of us will experience happiness and grief in our lives. But this happiness, the happiness of liberated Leningrad, we will never forget."

Poet Olga Berggolts raved, "The cursed circle is broken."

Quickly, the Soviets built a makeshift railroad running through the corridor of recaptured territory. One of the construction workers remembers,

"We were determined to get foodstuffs into the city as quickly as possible. The Nazis kept the whole route under constant surveillance. Our trains and trucks could only travel at night, and even then there was constant artillery shelling. But when things got bad, we thought of the women and children we were trying to reach." In just three weeks, food and other supplies were being brought to the city by train. It was not an easy journey. In contrast to Lake Ladoga's Road of Life, train engineers spoke of this new railway as the Corridor of Death. The Germans still shelled the tracks regularly. (Crews had to repair the tracks twelve hundred times in 1943.) But by February, supplies were pouring into Leningrad.

Dmitri Shostakovich spent several months that winter in a sanatorium recovering from typhoid fever. After that, he went to work in Moscow. Soon, out in the countryside, staying in a henhouse he'd been granted by the government, he was writing his Eighth Symphony. It is a powerfully distressed piece, unremitting in its depiction of war.

The Eighth, being gloomier, did not get quite the reception the Seventh did, but that hardly mattered. The Seventh had brought him the gratitude of his whole nation. "The Seventh Symphony of Shostakovich is significant beyond the bounds of a merely musical event," wrote one Soviet commentator. "It has become a cultural entity of our people, a fact of political and social significance, and an impulse to struggle and victory." Stalin's regime could not have been happier with the composer. When propagandist Aleksandr Fadeyev announced the government's wishes for creative artists of all kinds, Shostakovich was held up as the great example: "Let us try to create now, during the war, works that are real, serious, big, but ones that can be used right now as weapons, not set aside for later. . . . Make it, for now, like the Seventh Symphony."

In Moscow, Shostakovich found himself writing music for the NKVD's song-and-dance troupe. It may seem strange that he agreed to this. Many of his friends had been hounded or killed by the NKVD. Why would he agree to provide light entertainment for the men who had tortured and executed

Meyerhold? (Though at the time, he could not have known Meyerhold's fate for sure.)

This was the way Dmitri Shostakovich survived. He was a mixture of defiance and compliance. "He was only a man," conductor Kurt Sanderling said. "He was a coward when it concerned his own affairs, but he was very courageous when it concerned others." When the NKVD approached him and told him to start dreaming up dance numbers, he was, supposedly, "too scared to refuse." It is easy to blame him when we ourselves are safe, when we do not have a family watched by agents willing to kill, when we do not have imprisoned relatives whose survival depends on our good behavior.

For the NKVD, Shostakovich wrote a suite of nostalgic, light music called "Native Leningrad," remembering his hometown. He wrote a song called "Burn, Burn, Burn." It was about torches used during the blackouts. It became a national hit.

He sat sullenly in the meetings as the NKVD officers talked about what entertainments they preferred. He perked up once: when they requested music for a dance number about soccer. "May I compose the music for 'Soccer,' if you have nothing against it?" he asked. A colleague mused, "I don't know why he was so keen on writing soccer music. He was a funny man. . . ."

The NKVD's enthusiasm for soccer was as intense as Shostakovich's, however. At the time, NKVD head Lavrentii Beria and Stalin's son Vasily were engaged in a cruel game of fan favoritism, arresting, releasing, and kidnapping again the Dynamo team's manager, Nikolai Starostin. Beria wanted Dynamo to lose, so he had Starostin seized and sent to a labor camp. Vasily Stalin wanted the man to head up the air force soccer team, so he sent his own plane to airlift Starostin out of exile. The hideous tussle went back and forth, a game played with Starostin's life. Even the entertainments of the NKVD could carelessly destroy people.

Shostakovich did use his new connections with authority to help composers who were destitute, in exile, or on the front. One day when he was in Moscow, for example, he received the score of a symphony from a young composer named Mieczysław Weinberg. Weinberg, a Polish Jew, had been living in Warsaw with his mother, father, and sister when the Nazis invaded in 1939. The Polish government announced that Jewish men should flee the city before the German SS arrived. Young Weinberg took his little sister and ran. Unfortunately, his sister complained that day that her shoes chafed. She wanted to go back to their parents. He let her return and kept moving east.

She was with her parents in Warsaw, therefore, when the Nazis arrived and shipped them all to a concentration camp in Trawniki, where they were massacred. Weinberg knew none of this. He fled through the countryside, making his way across fields and farms, through scenes of ghastly carnage, until he reached the border of Russia. He was lucky to be let through. He had to keep running, however, when the Nazis launched Operation Barbarossa.

By the time he wrote to Shostakovich, he was in the city of Tashkent, married to Natalya Mikhoels, the daughter of a prominent Russian Jew. He was unknown, just a composition student, but he deeply loved Shostakovich's music.

The older composer looked at Weinberg's First Symphony and was impressed by its energy and ingenuity. He arranged for Weinberg to be brought to Moscow and supported as a composer. Weinberg became one of his closest friends. Shostakovich needed real friends.

For the first several months Shostakovich was in Moscow, his family was still in Kuibyshev. Shostakovich spent his lonely nights playing cards with other composers. One of them, a young, burly writer of light operas, Tikhon Khrennikov, had been in Railway Car No. 7 with Shostakovich when they fled Moscow. As they watched each other carefully, playing poker, neither could have known that in a few years, Khrennikov would denounce Shostakovich publicly in front of the Composers' Union and would bring about his downfall.

They played their cards carefully.

The tide had turned. The Russian war effort now won its victories, the names of which are enshrined in military history: the apocalyptic fight for

Stalingrad; the struggle for Kharkov; the liberation of Kiev; the colossal tank battle of Kursk, an epic clash of three thousand armored vehicles (from a tiny tank only two feet high to massive giants designed by Porsche) all rumbling through fields of sunflowers; and Operation Bagration, a Soviet counteroffensive launched on the third anniversary of Hitler's invasion. Russian industry was back on its feet. Transplanted factories were producing thousands of tanks and planes monthly, many of the new models (like the Yak-9 fighter plane) even better than the older Western prototypes they were based on.

On January 14, 1944, the last vestige of German Army Group North was finally forced away from Leningrad. The citizens who were left in the city (not many — only 575,000, down from 2.5 million at the beginning of the siege) climbed up onto their rooftops to watch the final shelling. On January 27, General Govorov declared, "The city of Leningrad has been entirely liberated." The siege had lasted 872 days. It is the longest siege in recorded history.

"Suddenly Leningrad emerged from the gloom before our gaze," wrote Olga Berggolts. "To the last crack in its walls, the city was revealed to us — shell-pitted, bullet-riddled, scarred Leningrad, with its plywood windowpanes. And we saw that despite all the cruel slashes and blows, Leningrad retained its proud beauty. In the bluish, roseate, green and white of the lights, the city appeared to us so austere and touching we could not feast our eyes enough on it."

Now that they were on the offensive, the Red Army pounded the Germans backward at an astonishing rate of fifty miles a day. In Moscow, where the Shostakovich family finally reunited and decided to settle, there was an air of excitement, even celebration. Concerts were no longer interrupted by air-raid sirens and detonations; they were interrupted by the firing of cannons announcing new victories: rivers crossed, cities taken.

Red Army soldiers marching through Germany saw that the tables had been turned. One wrote: "Estates, villages and towns were burning. Columns of carts, with dazed German men and women who had failed to flee, crawled across the landscape. Shapeless fragments of tanks and self-propelled guns lay everywhere, as well as hundreds of corpses. I recalled such sights from the first days of the war"—from the days, in other words, just after Hitler had launched Operation Barbarossa and swept into the USSR.

As the Red Army drove deep into German territory, its troops began to come across the death camps. The full dimensions of Nazi atrocities became clear.

At the same time, the soldiers' years of suffering and loss, their utter disgust at the cruelty of the enemy, led them to commit atrocities of their own. Civilian populations from the Baltic nations to the Balkans succumbed to mass executions and individual brutalities. Witnessing the savagery of the Red Army, a Hungarian wrote: "They were simple and cruel like children. With millions of people destroyed by Lenin, Trotsky, Stalin or in the war, death to them had become an everyday affair. They killed without hatred and let themselves be killed without resisting."

One of the cruelest ironies of the Red Army's westward push was their treatment of Russian prisoners of war liberated from Nazi camps. These people were lucky to have survived. (Of the 5.8 million Soviet soldiers captured by the Nazis, roughly three million died.) Now, according to Stalin's Order No. 270, which had forbidden surrender, they were considered traitors. Hundreds of thousands had survived the hell of German prison camps only to be shot or exiled to camps in Siberia.

In April 1945, three Soviet army groups surrounded Berlin, capital of Nazi Germany. They numbered two and a half million men, with six thousand armed vehicles and more than seven thousand bombers and fighter planes. The Germans confronted them with armies of old men and young boys — the only males left who had not already died.

On April 12, the German Philharmonic Orchestra held its last concert in Berlin — a counterpart to the performance of the Seventh Symphony in

Leningrad. But the music they played was the end of a piece by Wagner depicting the twilight of the old German gods, and their sacred stronghold, Valhalla, burning.

It was clear that the remaining Wehrmacht forces could not protect the city. Still, Hitler would not surrender, though at this point, there was no question he would lose. The Red Army attacked. The city burned.

Hidden deep in an underground bunker like an overlord of hell, Hitler despaired. On April 29, in a ceremony held beneath the earth, the dictator and his lover, Eva Braun, were married. The next day, when the sky was full of Soviet flame, the newlyweds celebrated their union by committing suicide together. She took cyanide; he shot himself.

Now Berlin was the city of the dead. "A ghost town of cave dwellers was all that was left of this world metropolis," remembered a Red Cross worker. "The imperial palace, the splendid castles, the Royal Library . . . hardly anything was left." The survivors lived, as another woman wrote, "without electric light or gas, without water. . . . We are living like ghosts in a field of ruins . . . a city where nothing works apart from the telephones that sometimes ring, glumly and pointlessly, beneath piles of fallen masonry."

On May 8, 1945, the Germans surrendered, and the war in Europe was over.

In Moscow and Leningrad, the rejoicing began. The army fired blank tracer bullets into the night skies. People shouted hysterical slogans in the streets. Soldiers embraced.

In Moscow's Red Square, there was a grand parade to celebrate the victory. Representatives of all the armed forces marched in tight formations beneath the approving wave of Comrade Stalin. There were thunderous displays of unity and symmetry. The medieval walls of the Kremlin echoed with shouts of triumph. Captured battle standards from all of Germany's defeated armies were hurled in a heap at Stalin's feet, beside the black tomb of Comrade Lenin.

Victory: The skies over Leningrad are bright not with tracer-fire and incendiary bombs, but with celebratory fireworks.

Russian soldiers rally at the Brandenburg Gate, Berlin, 1945.

People were overwhelmed by their joy. It rained that day, but no one cared: the Great Patriotic War was over.

Poet Olga Berggolts wandered in the burned ruins of the Peterhof Palace, to the west of Leningrad. Before the war, it had been famous for its formal gardens; its terraced fountains had glittered with gold and spray.

The Nazis left nothing but a blasted shell. They had stolen the statuary, blasted through the floors, delighted in desecrating Russia's proud history.

Berggolts, walking there after the war, felt a strange sense of hope.

> Again from the black dust, from the place
> Of death and ashes, will arise the garden as before.
> So it will be. I firmly believe in miracles.
> You gave me that belief, my Leningrad.

The Soviet sense of triumph at the end of the war was so great because their sacrifices had been unimaginable. Historians now estimate that about 27 million Soviet citizens died during the conflict — more, in other words, than the dead of all other nations combined. (The total dead in World War II numbered roughly fifty million.) About 13.6 percent of the Soviet population had died.

The Siege of Leningrad alone cost approximately one and a half million Russian lives — more than the combined World War II casualties of both the Americans and the British — a higher death toll, in fact, than the number of all Americans killed in battle in all wars fought since the United States' first founding. As historian Max Hastings wrote, "Both Hitler and Stalin displayed obsessive stubbornness about Leningrad. That of Stalin was finally rewarded, amid a mountain of corpses. A people who could endure such things displayed qualities the Western Allies lacked, which were indispensable to the destruction of Nazism. In the auction of cruelty and sacrifice, the Soviet dictator proved the higher bidder."

The USSR was devastated by the conflict. Seventy thousand villages had been destroyed. Forty-one thousand electric power stations no longer operated; thirty-two thousand factories were in ruins. Forty thousand miles of railroad track would have to be repaired and relaid. The epic battles had destroyed forty thousand hospitals, eighty-four thousand schools, forty-three thousand libraries. The war's wounds would take generations to heal.

How were the Russians able to withstand this onslaught? It is one of the sick ironies of the war that they probably would not have been able to if they had not learned to absorb loss in the nightmare of Stalin's purges. Peasants and workers, soldiers and the intelligentsia — all were used to clinging fiercely to life even when everything seemed lost. Stalin could demand things of his people few other regimes could imagine: he could plant NKVD gunners behind his soldiers and tell them to shoot if anyone showed signs of cowardice. He could send battalions of prisoners into battle, marching toward almost certain death. He could relocate millions of factory workers by command in the space of a few weeks. He could rely on the slave labor of millions in the gulag. As Sir Alan Brooke has written, "It was the Russians who provided the oceans of blood necessary to defeat Germany."

But how effective, truly, are dictatorships in times of war? Is ruthlessness a sound strategy? The truth is complicated. "The real reason why Hitler lost the Second World War," wrote historian Andrew Roberts, "was exactly the same one that had caused him to unleash it in the first place: he was a Nazi." His fanaticism worked well for him early in the war, surprising and shocking the world as he conquered nation after nation. The same delusional self-confidence, however, encouraged him to overextend his Wehrmacht forces, picking a fight on his Eastern Front, in Russia, while he still was fighting the British in the west. His military leaders warned him of the stupidity and risk of this move, but increasingly, he did not listen. Drunk on the idiotic belief in racial superiority, he couldn't accurately assess the Russian threat or recognize that he would hold power more easily in lands liberated from the Soviet Union if he didn't turn welcoming villages into burning charnel-houses.

If Hitler lost the war for the same reason he had started it, Stalin won for the same reason he had initially lost so much so quickly — the delusional self-confidence he shared with the German Führer. They did not necessarily recognize the realities of the world around them. Stalin purged the military of dissenters and, at first, listened only to those who agreed with him. He ignored the intelligence of spies. He disdained the warnings of the capitalist Allies. The cost for the people of the Soviet Union was unimaginable.

Yet, after he recovered from the shock of almost complete defeat, his ability to treat his own citizens like fodder, to ignore their sufferings when it was convenient, often led to victories, however costly. Could a western democracy have fared as well? It is unclear, though historian Robert Service is not alone when he contends, "The ultra-authoritarian features of the Soviet regime caused harm to its war effort." Self-delusion and fanaticism allowed Hitler and Stalin to accomplish things no one would have thought possible — but just as often caused them to stumble and fall at the most obvious hurdles. Both caused inconceivable suffering to their own populations because of their shortsighted, almost delirious, egotism.

At the end of the war, the Soviet Union and the other Allies turned on each other. Historians still argue about who was responsible. Regardless, Stalin's attitude toward the West hardened. He wanted to make sure the Soviet Union's western border would forever be protected. As the countries of eastern Europe flailed in chaos, reduced to civic ruins, Stalin devoured them. Diplomatic relations between the USSR and the other Allies fell apart. The Iron Curtain slammed down, severing Europe in two. Stalin looked with both greed and anxiety at the Americans' new invention, the atomic bomb. The United States and the USSR sized each other up with renewed suspicion. Remarkably swiftly, brothers-in-arms united by Germany's attack became locked in a fifty-year-long stranglehold called the Cold War.

Within the Soviet Union, anything that reminded the regime of the West was now dangerous. For the last years of the war, the NKVD had made it a crime to praise American technology. Now western movies, western novels, and western music were all forbidden again. Russian nationalism was on the rise. French bread was renamed "city bread." The government began speaking out against "rootless cosmopolitans" with ties to other countries—by which, it became clear, they usually meant the Jews.

Shostakovich had been eulogized in the West. He had appeared on the cover of *Time* magazine. Their article had celebrated the fact he was "bourgeois." As Leningrad writers once again came under attack, the composer must have realized that his efforts on behalf of the war would not keep him safe.

Another assault was coming.

In February of 1948, Leningrad Communist Party boss Andrei Zhdanov called together prominent musicians, composers, and musicologists to discuss Soviet music and present them with a decree. He condemned "formalism" in modern music; he complained that the music of "anti-people" composers such as Shostakovich and Prokofiev sounded like "a piercing road drill, or a musical gas-chamber."

It was a return to the attacks of 1936 and "A Mess Instead of Music."

Zhdanov had already denounced Leningrad's most famous writers, Anna Akhmatova and Mikhail Zoshchenko, both of them friends of Shostakovich's. (Shostakovich supported Zoshchenko by slipping him money after the denunciation.) Stalin still resented the fame of the Leningrad elite and wanted to illustrate their powerlessness. He was quietly removing the heroes of Leningrad's siege from office so they didn't attract too much national celebrity. He had the director of the Museum of the Defense of Leningrad arrested for accumulating weaponry—that is to say, the exhibits of guns and tanks at the museum—and shot as if he were a traitor. Though Shostakovich now lived in Moscow, he still bore the stink of a Leningrad intellectual.

The success of the Seventh Symphony did not protect him. People were eager to show that they were in total agreement with the Party's new attack on him. They pointed out that Shostakovich's music was catnip to the bourgeois, decadent West. Even worse, they pointed out that when Russia was losing the war, he wrote his triumphant Seventh, whereas when the tide of war shifted and Russia began to win, he wrote his gloomy, despairing Eighth.

Their dangerous implication was clear: perhaps he didn't want the Soviet government to be the victor.

The composers gathered at this February meeting looked to Shostakovich to reply to Comrade Zhdanov's historic decree on musical formalism. Shostakovich gave nothing away. He merely said, "A close study of this remarkable document ought to be of great help to us in our work." His comment seemed to be a kind of doublespeak. The word *remarkable* could mean many things.

On his way home from the meeting, Shostakovich stopped at the apartment of Mieczysław Weinberg (the young composer who had escaped from Warsaw) and his wife, Natalya Mikhoels. Natalya's father, a famous Jewish actor and activist, had been murdered the night before, perhaps on Stalin's orders. He had been lured to a friend's house for a drink, injected with poison to stun him, and then run over by a truck to make it look like an accident.

When Shostakovich heard about the death, he whispered, "I envy him."

A friend of Mikhoels and Weinberg's who had a relative in the Politburo came by to talk to the couple. She led them into the bathroom. She turned on the water so no one could hear. She whispered to them that her uncle in the Politburo sent his greetings, "and he told me to tell you never to ask anyone about anything."

That was all the help they got.

Around the same time as this murder and Zhdanov's historic decree on musical formalism, composer Sergei Prokofiev's ex-wife, Lena Prokofiev, was called downstairs to pick up a package, grabbed by a bunch of men, and thrown into a black car. She was tortured and disappeared. She would not reappear for fifteen years. Her sons turned to Shostakovich for help. They knew he would be of more use than their father.

Shostakovich wrote letters to the authorities, but he was in no position to help anyone. Galina wrote, "My father is pacing from room to room in our apartment, chain smoking. Both Mother and he hardly say a word. Maxim and I are also quiet: it is not the right moment to be asking questions."

Zhdanov's historic decree had been published. Newspapers that had praised Shostakovich for his Seventh Symphony now ran trumped-up letters from workers about how his music was incomprehensible. "I do not understand Shostakovich's music," wrote a naval artillery engineer. "It tires me out. It is an empty collection of sounds."

The Shostakoviches pulled Maxim out of the music school he attended. His class was going to be studying the historic decree on formalism. On tests and reports, he would have to denounce his own father. His sister, Galina, was jealous that he suddenly didn't have to go to school.

At the First Congress of the Composers' Union in April, Shostakovich's friend and poker partner Tikhon Khrennikov was appointed general secretary. If Shostakovich expected any help from him, he was sorely disappointed. Instead, Khrennikov stood up in front of the crowd and agreed with everything in Zhdanov's historic decree. He attacked Shostakovich personally as a formalist whose symphonies were "a peculiar writing in code," which "often reflected images and emotions alien to Soviet realistic art," such as "tenseness, neuroticism, escape into a region of abnormal, repulsive, and pathological phenomena." Shostakovich's music was too modernistic, said Khrennikov. It was unintelligible to the people.

In 1936, Shostakovich had avoided responding publicly to criticism — except in the form of his Fifth Symphony. At the Congress of the Composers' Union, he was not allowed to remain silent. He could not avoid responding. He had to make a public confession.

His name was called, and he got up to walk to the front of the room. He did not know what he was going to say when he got there. He thought, *Well, I'll muddle through somehow.* As he ascended the steps to the podium, a Party official handed him a statement, hissing, "Take this, please."

Shostakovich looked at him in confusion.

"It is all written down here, Dmitri Dmitrievich. Just read it out."

"And I got up on the tribune," he later remembered, "and started to read out aloud this idiotic, disgusting nonsense concocted by some nobody."

He read out hearty thanks to those who had criticized him. He found himself admitting that he was wrong. "I know that the Party is right. . . . I know that the Party is showing concern for Soviet art and for me, a Soviet composer," he found himself saying. "I shall work on the musical depiction of the heroic Soviet peoples, from the correct ideological standpoint. Equipped with the guidance of the Central Committee, I shall renew my efforts to create really good songs for collective singing."

He later told a friend, "I read like the most paltry wretch, a parasite, a puppet, a cut-out paper doll on a string!" Then he shrieked the last phrase again and again "like a frenzied maniac": "A paper doll on a string! A paper doll on a string!"

In a recent interview with Tikhon Khrennikov, shortly before his death, a reporter asked him how he could have denounced his friend Shostakovich. Khrennikov replied, "What else could I have done? If I had refused, it could have been curtains . . . death. They made me do it." In his defense, he also claimed that he shielded many other composers from arrest and execution. There is still a great deal of bitter argument about his role in Russia's musical life, whether he was a champion or a traitor. "My word was law," he remembered. "People knew I was appointed personally by Stalin and they were afraid of that. . . . I would go and tell Stalin about them. I was Stalin's Commissar." He shouted at his interviewer, "When I said No!, it meant No."

He pooh-poohed Shostakovich's anxieties. "They say Shostakovich lived in fear. You know what? I think all of this has been terribly exaggerated. Shostakovich was such a cheerful man."

In 1948, Shostakovich's music was banned. That fall, he was fired from his teaching positions at the Moscow and Leningrad Conservatories. He ran low on funds. He made money by composing film scores for movies in praise of Stalin.

Next to his family's cottage, there was a rest home for retired secret police officers. The ex-officers threw their garbage over Shostakovich's fence and yelled obscenities at him. They broke one of his windows. They called him a formalist, a traitor, and an American spy.

Maxim sat up in a tree and defended his father's honor by pelting rocks at them with a slingshot.

It seemed as if Stalin was preparing for another purge, this time centered on the Jews. Composer Mieczysław Weinberg was arrested. Shostakovich and Nina wrote up the paperwork to act as guardians for Weinberg and Mikhoels's daughter in case her parents were liquidated. Shostakovich wrote several works on Jewish themes, which he consigned "to the desk drawer." They were only performed in secret, for friends.

He also, in his silent fury, wrote a piece called *Anti-Formalist Vaudeville*, a crass parody of the historic Zhdanov decree. Idiots named Numbers One through Three—clearly based on Stalin and a few Party pawns—get up and babble about how formalist music is written by formalists, while Realist music is written by Realists. Zhdanov's decree had demanded that Shostakovich use folk material, and he does in *Anti-Formalist Vaudeville:* a particularly moronic passage is set to Stalin's favorite tune ("Suliko"), and the whole piece ends with a kick-line in traditional style.

The words at that point are a chorus of gleeful paranoia and denunciation:

> Look over here!
> Look over there!
> The enemy is everywhere!
> Look over there!
> Look over here!
> And let the enemy feel fear!

Early in the morning of March 1, 1953, General Secretary of the Communist Party Joseph Stalin collapsed in his bedroom from a stroke. He lay there alone, semiconscious, drenched in stale urine, for almost a full day. He had ordered his guards never to disturb him, and they were too frightened to take a risk and knock. When members of the Politburo arrived, none of them wanted to call a doctor, since Stalin had recently accused several prominent doctors of murder. (His own doctor was being tortured at the time.)

Comrade Stalin never regained full consciousness. He died on March 5.

Lavrentii Beria, the psychopathic head of Stalin's secret police, was killed soon after. He was dragged out of a meeting of the Presidium and executed; he died, perhaps fittingly, shot point-blank through the forehead, with a towel shoved in his mouth to stifle any screams for mercy.

In prison, Shostakovich's friend Weinberg noticed that the guards suddenly got a lot more polite. Soon, he was given papers to sign and sent on his way.

There was to be no new purge.

After Stalin's death, the labor camps began quietly to release their prisoners. About eight million of their twelve million prisoners went free and found themselves wandering through their home cities in the old, stained clothes they had been wearing years before when they were torn from their families. Poet Anna Akhmatova looked forward to the reckoning that was to come: "Now those who have been arrested will return, and two Russias will look each other in the eye — the Russia that sent people to the camps, and the Russia that was sent to the camps."

Shostakovich worked hard for the rehabilitation and release of his friends, family, and colleagues. Maxim remembered, "Our home was sometimes like a small hotel for people who came back."

Shostakovich's friend Galina Vishnevskaya sarcastically recalled the bravery of the Soviets once Comrade Stalin was dead: "Bonfires blazed all over the country, burning any and all pictures of Stalin. Heads were hacked off sculptures of the Leader and Teacher of All Times and All Peoples — this took quite a bit of time, since there was not a single factory, school, theater, university, street, square, or park in the country that was not adorned by a likeness of the General Secretary of the Communist Party. And now, in a marvelous display of boldness and heroism, the whole nation could tie a rope to his feet, pull him down from his pedestal, and execute him, pounding the mute, dead mass to their heart's desire."

For his part, Shostakovich wrote his Tenth Symphony, which contains his musical monogram — the letters DSCH — played secretly, yet defiantly, as notes in a tune. At first, he calls out his own name with anxiety, until, late in the symphony, it returns in triumph, as if he is finally able to shout, "I AM DMITRI SHOSTAKOVICH! I AM DMITRI SHOSTAKOVICH!"

In 1956, Nikita Khrushchev, the new first secretary of the Communist Party, called for a closed meeting of Party delegates. No one knew what to expect. Once the doors were shut, he astounded them all, railing about the brutal excesses of Stalin for four hours as audience members left the room to vomit. The whole nation, he said, had been caught up in a "cult of personality" that had done incredible harm to the interests of the country and the Party. He did not, of course, mention his own role in Stalin's purges. But suddenly it was legal to speak of what had happened, legal to discuss all the years of silence and torment.

This speech, "The Cult of Personality and Its Consequences," was informally called "the Secret Speech," but it could not remain a secret for long. Within days, copies of it circulated all over the Soviet Union, and people felt that the lengthy winter of Stalinism finally had yielded to thaw. Shortly after, Shostakovich, together with many others, was rehabilitated — there was no longer a ban on his work. For the first time, the world heard his grotesque and furious Fourth Symphony, withdrawn back in 1936.

Of course, the Soviet Union was still a police state. When Shostakovich went abroad, the authorities still made sure that members of his family remained behind so he could not defect. That did not stop New Yorkers from trying to convince him to flee his handlers and stay in America when he visited. They held up signs reading, SHOSTAKOVICH! JUMP OUT THE WINDOW!

Still, occasionally, his works were censured or suppressed. In 1960, he was forced to join the Communist Party. He broke down sobbing.

Was he brave or was he a coward? Or, as the sensationalist tagline of a Shostakovich biography asks: "Loyal Stalinist or Scornful Dissident?" The answer is neither. He kept himself alive.

On the one hand, he always tried to use his position and influence to help friends. He wrote so many letters to the government that eventually the bureaucrats stopped paying much attention to him. His acts of generosity, however, were often discussed in the musical world. He secretly paid for the son of an executed "Enemy of the People" to be given a conservatory education. When he could, he gave money to friends (like the writer Zoshchenko) who had run afoul of the government. He did everything he could to clear the names of innocents imprisoned or killed during the Great Terror.

Shostakovich's compassion in the midst of a traumatized society was unusual. "Kindness is not, after all, an inborn quality," Nadezhda Mandelstam wrote. "It has to be cultivated, and this only happens when it is in demand. For our generation, kindness was an old-fashioned, vanished quality, and its exponents were as extinct as the mammoth." Shostakovich had the courage to hold on to his compassion, even when he was suffering blows from all sides.

On the other hand, as he got older and sicker (he had spent his life smoking cheap Soviet cigarettes), he did not put up much of a fight when he was asked to sign defamatory articles written for him by Party hacks. "I showed lack of courage, was faint-hearted," he admitted. "I'd sign anything even if they hand it to me upside down. All I want is to be left alone." He was ashamed when he saw some of the things he signed in print.

Sometimes he tried to avoid the "pestering officials" sent to get his approval for articles or pronouncements. Once, for example, giving a courier the slip, the composer and his wife rushed off and hid in a movie theater. They spent the day watching old films, one after another. "But their efforts were in vain; shortly after their return home late at night, the door-bell rang and the unwelcome official appeared with the document ready for signature."

A new generation was growing up who barely remembered what it was like during Stalin's Great Terror. They felt things were getting easier in the

Soviet Union, and they wanted to agitate for change. They did not understand why Shostakovich was so careful, so jumpy — why he would croak bitterly, "Just be thankful that you're still allowed to breathe."

For his son, Maxim, he wrote a joyous, mischievous piano concerto, full of the boy's glittering wit and energy. Maxim eventually became a famous pianist and conductor. Galina, inheriting the scientific brilliance of her mother's side of the family, studied biology and went on to do heart research. Shostakovich loved them both to a fault.

Over the last years of Shostakovich's life, his new symphonies (he wrote fifteen in all) still moved people to tears with their compassion and their defiance. At the same time, he was writing his series of string quartets, a "diary" that, according to his wife, spelled out "the story of his soul." As he grew older, the story told in the quartets grew stranger and more remote. When asked how to play his slow, death-haunted Fifteenth String Quartet (his last), he replied, "Play it so that flies drop dead in mid-air, and the audience start leaving the hall from sheer boredom." His late quartets do, in fact, seem to be made of small, lonely things like the wings of dead flies, pieces of string, and bits of shell left in drawers.

The power of his compositional voice was undiminished up until the time of his death. His work was played and respected around the globe — and not simply on the planet's surface. A piece by Shostakovich was the first human song sung in outer space. Cosmonaut Yuri Gagarin, catching sight of the earth beneath him as he headed home from orbit, was so moved that he burst out into Shostakovich's song "The Motherland Hears." By that point, few remembered that the song was written by Shostakovich. But a song sung in space was a fitting tribute to a man who had been friend of the Futurists in his youth.

He kept composing even when hospitalized and very sick. The rest of the time, he watched soccer on television.

His final work was a sonata for viola and piano. Its last movement is haunted by the urgent peal of bells he had written into his "Suite for Two Pianos" when he was fifteen, more than fifty years earlier. Then, he had

Shostakovich eventually wrote fifteen symphonies and fifteen string quartets. "The quartets are messages to all his friends," said conductor Kurt Sanderling. "The symphonies are messages to mankind."

Soprano Galina Vishnevskaya wrote, "Shostakovich's music is the soul of the twentieth-century Russian people."

been mourning the death of his father; now, softly, spectrally, he tolls the bells for himself. Their melody grows hazier, weaker, perhaps gentler, and finally fades into an incomprehensible horizon.

Shostakovich died on August 9, 1975, on the anniversary of the night the Seventh Symphony was played in besieged Leningrad.

"The majority of my symphonies are tombstones," Shostakovich is supposed to have said shortly before his death. "Too many of our people died and were buried in places unknown to anyone, not even their relatives. It happened to many of my friends. Where do you put the tombstones for Meyerhold or Tukhachevsky? Only music can do that for them.

"Looking back, I see nothing but ruins, only mountains of corpses. . . . I'm not exaggerating, I mean mountains. . . . I'm sad, I'm grieving all the time."

The philosopher Walter Benjamin (who died tragically while fleeing the Nazis) once famously described a figure he called the Angel of History in terms that recall Shostakovich, chronicler of his people, looking back over his shoulder:

> His face is turned to the past. Where we see a chain of events reaching backward, he sees only a single, great catastrophe which heaps wreckage upon ruin, hurling it all at his feet. He would like to pause, to linger, to awaken the dead and repair all that has been broken. But a storm is blowing from Paradise, and it tears at his wings so fiercely that the angel cannot close them anymore. The winds blast him toward the future, to which his back is turned, while the heaped wreckage mounts up toward the sky. This storm is the thing we call "progress."

But for millions of listeners, Shostakovich's music is not simply a record of death. Conductor Gennady Rozhdestvensky proclaimed, "His work is the chronicle of his life. Of the life of his entire people, of his country."

There are few composers whose music and whose own lives reflect so exactly the trials and triumphs of a nation. The music of his youth was electric with the boldness and experimentation of Leningrad's explosive revolutions. With his music of the '30s, he came to know the grotesque brutality of the Terror. As Stalin closed his fist around Leningrad and the arrests and disappearances began, Shostakovich was in the middle of it. His Fifth Symphony, composed in a time of mute fear, was an answer to the authorities — but, at the same time, it spoke other truths, out of the side of its mouth, to all who had suffered loss and could not speak, could not cry. He gave a voice to the silenced. He showed them that they were not alone.

When the war came and there was another assault upon Leningrad, Shostakovich gave them an epic piece they could read as a portrait of themselves not simply in battle but in the coming victory.

His music was at once clear and clever; obvious and obscure; public and private; sorrowful, but full of a fierce joy in living; marked with codes and messages, but famous for its direct and earnest communication. As musicologist Richard Taruskin has said, "What made Shostakovich's music the secret diary of a nation was not only what he put into it, but what it allowed listeners to draw out."

Contemporary composer Sofia Gubaidulina has written, "I believe that Shostakovich's music reaches such a wide audience because he was able to transform the pain that he so keenly experienced into something exalted and full of light, which transcends all worldly suffering. . . . We listened to Shostakovich's new works in a kind of exaltation."

And Anna Akhmatova, Leningrad poet who suffered through everything with him, wrote about his music:

> It creates miracles. . . .
> It alone talks with me
> when others are afraid to come near,
> when the last friend has turned his eyes away.

It was with me in my grave

and sang like the first storm,

or as though all the flowers had burst into speech.

Leningrad is now called St. Petersburg again. Once more, it is one of the most beautiful cities in the world.

The parks are cool and green in summer. Couples walk by the canals and sit side by side on the banks of the wide Neva. In fashionable restaurants, people laugh and talk with a freedom Shostakovich could only imagine. The spires and domes glimmer again in the evening.

The artists and writers who gather there now depict a new Russia with new challenges.

A few miles to the north of the city, through Soviet-era suburbs of massive, weather-beaten apartment blocks and cracked car parks, lies Piskarevsky Cemetery, where many of the dead of besieged Leningrad were buried anonymously in ditches.

It is serene there now. At the entrance, an eternal flame burns. Almost half a million bodies lie under long communal mounds. These mounds were once trenches, blown open with dynamite to crack the frozen earth, then crammed with hundreds of corpses. The mounds lie in orderly, peaceful rows. Each is marked only with a single year carved in stone; no names. In the summer, grass grows over them. In the winter, the bodies sleep under deep snow.

Above the dead stands a statue of Mother Russia raising her garlanded arms in mourning. Trees whisper in the breeze. Loudspeakers play soft music. It is not Shostakovich's Seventh Symphony, but rather music of decorous Baroque sorrow: Purcell, Albinoni, Bach. Inscribed in granite is a poem by Olga Berggolts, which defiantly declares:

Let no one forget.

Let nothing be forgotten.

At Piskarevsky Cemetery, Mother Russia bears a funeral garland in memory of all those who died during the siege of Leningrad.

Each mound, filled with hundreds of the war dead, is marked with the year they were interred.

A sacred memorial flame burns in the cemetery day and night.

Old women in head-scarves walk between the mounds. The mounds are soft, even, equal, green.

History is not simply the great tumults and tragedies but the accumulation of tiny moments and gestures.

It is after the war is over. Shostakovich and his family have returned to the same cottage on the coast of the Gulf of Finland where they were staying on that bright summer day the Germans first invaded.

Shostakovich and his daughter are riding their bikes in the forest. Shostakovich is teaching Galina the Highway Code. As they glide through the woodland, he demonstrates how to indicate left and right turns, "although in the empty and twisting forest paths it looked excessively cautious." The man and the girl act out regulations. He extends a slim pianist's hand, signaling to no one, preparing his daughter to navigate on her own when they have left the woods.

They ride down the dirt roads, making their mute signs.

That far north, in the summer, it seems as if the sun will never go down, as if the night will never fall, as if the forest will never grow dark.

Even the basic facts of Dmitri Shostakovich's life are often contested, as a glance through the end notes of this book attests. How do we reconstruct the story of someone who lived in a period in which everyone had an excuse to lie, evade, accuse, or keep silent?

The standard biography of the composer is Laurel Fay's meticulous *Shostakovich: A Life*. Her work is colorfully supported by Elizabeth Wilson's English-language collection of memoirs and oral histories, *Shostakovich: A Life Remembered*.

The most problematic source is *Testimony: The Memoirs of Dmitri Shostakovich*, edited (or perhaps written) by Solomon Volkov. As described on page 140, there is a great deal of disagreement about how trustworthy this source really is. When it came out, it revolutionized the way that people saw Shostakovich in the West. It appeared to put to rest any lingering suspicion that he was an enthusiastic, lock-step Soviet citizen, joyfully writing agit-prop poster symphonies about Lenin — if, indeed, anyone had ever believed such a thing. In the years that followed, it became the focus of an increasingly ugly academic debate about the meaning of Shostakovich's music and the shape of his life. People argued not only about whether *Testimony* was actually Shostakovich's own memoirs, dictated word for word to young Solomon Volkov, but also about whether the book's bitter musings were an accurate or useful picture of the composer in any case. As musicologist Richard Taruskin mused, "*Testimony* may be authentic and true, or inauthentic and false, or authentic but false, or even inauthentic but true."

As the years have gone by, the debate has mellowed. One of the main disputants committed suicide. The arguments about the literal authenticity of *Testimony* seem less important now that more documents and statements have swum to the surface supporting its general depiction of Shostakovich: letters to his friends Isaak Glikman and Ivan Sollertinsky, for example, or the score of his snide, defiant *Anti-Formalist Vaudeville*, which shows that he did not just sit back and take Party criticism lightly. More and more, we have found individual anecdotes and stories from *Testimony* hinted at in other sources, recalled by colleagues, or even endorsed by Maxim Shostakovich as things his father genuinely thought and said. In the light of recent scholarship, Shostakovich's anti-Stalinism no longer seems surprising or controversial, and was not unusual for the intelligentsia of Moscow and (in particular) Leningrad.

In writing this book, I have approached *Testimony* cautiously, as if it were an oral history, a possible record of Solomon Volkov's memories of things told him by Shostakovich. As one Shostakovich biographer put it, "*Testimony* is a realistic picture of Dmitri Shostakovich. It just isn't a genuine one." In my opinion, the book has much the same status as many of the memoirs in Elizabeth Wilson's *Shostakovich: A Life Remembered,* in which friends, relations, and colleagues of the composer tell stories and remember dialogue many decades after the fact, after the composer's death, which therefore may contain any combination of truth, accuracy, error, imaginative expansion, and strategic falsehood. I have used it as a source when what it describes seems noncontroversial.

All of this speculation is fitting in assessing the life of a composer whose music seems to demand interpretation but resists it, a man who learned to live behind a mask, a father who realized that, in order to keep his children safe, he had to create speech that was silent, and silence that spoke.

Speaking of language, I am hugely indebted to Alina Ryabovolova, who acted as a translator and research assistant for this project, chasing down obscure sources in the archives of Moscow. I'm also grateful to novelist Ellen Litman for additional translation help. For aid and encouragement in the complicated maze of Shostakovich scholarship, thanks particularly to David Fanning, Ludmila Stern, and Christopher Gibbs, all of whom pointed me toward useful sources. Any blunders that may have followed are, of course, my own. Thanks to Jim Nolte and Taylor Davis-Van Atta of the Vermont College of Fine Arts Library, who fetched material, English and Russian, for me from across the globe. A particular thanks is also due to Timothy Nenninger, chief of modern military records at the United States National Archives and Records Administration. Thanks to Olga Prutt of the Museum "The Muses Were Not Silent" in St. Petersburg and Tatiana Shavlyuk, who kindly acted as interpreter there; thanks also to Lidia Ader of the Rimsky-Korsakov Apartment and Museum.

Thanks to all the people at Candlewick Press whose enthusiasm and hard work made this project possible — in particular my editor, Liz Bicknell; designer Sherry Fatla; associate editor Carter Hasegawa; and copyeditor Hannah Mahoney. Your efforts were, as the Soviets would say, Stakhanovite.

I'm grateful to the many people who talked to me about this book through the years, but particularly to N. Griffin, as well as letters T., D., and L. — all of whom had to hear me whistling the "invasion" theme from Dmitri Shostakovich's *Leningrad* Symphony, op. 60, for four years solid.

PROLOGUE

p. 1: An American agent . . . : Anderson.

p. 2: First the American agent stopped for lunch . . . : It seems likely this agent of the Am-Rus Music Corporation was David Grunes, but the records are insufficient to confirm this.

p. 4: More than a million . . . : Inber, 5.

p. 4: "The Führer has decided . . . defeat of Soviet Russia": Amery and Curran, 197.

p. 4: Men inspected it with magnifying glasses: Anderson.

p. 5: "Dedicated to the city of Leningrad": Volkov, *Shostakovich*, 179.

p. 5: The day of his radio broadcast . . . : Sollertinskys, 101.

p. 5: "This is the local defense headquarters! . . . Air raid!": Simmons and Perlina, 144.

p. 5: "An hour ago I finished scoring . . . orchestral composition": Sollertinskys, 101.

pp. 5–6: "In spite of the war and the danger . . . enrich the fruits of culture": Ibid.

p. 6: We still have the piece of paper . . . : Salisbury, 284.

p. 7: "the Leningrad that Stalin . . . finished off": Volkov, *Testimony*, 156.

p. 7: For much of the war . . . : From the reminiscences of Arnold Ferkelman, Wilson, 105.

PART ONE

THE DEATH OF YESTERDAY

p. 11: "the Window on the West": This oft-repeated phrase is originally from Pushkin's poem "The Bronze Horseman." Alexander Pushkin, *Collected Narrative and Lyrical Poetry*, ed. and trans. Walter Arndt (Woodstock and New York: Ardis, 2002), 426.

p. 13: "In Russia there is no elective government . . . can never obtain justice": Lenin, 2.

p. 13: In 1905, the year before Dimitri Shostakovich's birth . . . : Shostakovich's aunt Nadejda Galli-Shohat made the claim that Dmitri Shostakovich Sr. was present at the march on "Bloody Sunday" (Seroff, 34). As noted, her garrulousness both provides us with much of our information about Shostakovich's childhood and calls into question the veracity of her revelations.

p. 14: When it was over, the bodies of hundreds lay bloodied in the snow: Accounts range from an official estimate of just over a hundred dead to accusations of thousands. Modern historians estimate the death toll to have been in the region of 800 to 1,000 (e.g., Shukman, 105).

p. 14: Shostakovich's mother, Sofia, sheltered Jews . . . : Wilson, 6.

p. 14: One night the tsar's secret police . . . : Seroff, 35.

p. 14: As Shostakovich's father told the little boy . . . : Volkov, *Testimony*, 8; Seroff, 77.

p. 16: The builder had mistaken the measurements . . . : According to Zoya Shostakovich, in Wilson, 5.

p. 16: "He never seemed to take anything seriously . . . on the floor around him": Seroff, 56.

p. 16: "I think you would say . . . the one to eat them": Selby, 13.

p: 16: "The nine-year-old boy . . . his inner hearing": Wilson, 12.

p. 16: "He was somewhat absent-minded": Ibid., 5.

p. 16: "Yet he was a wonderfully kind . . . the fun out of him": Ibid.

p. 17: The young composer preferred blocks: Fay, *Life*, 8–9.

p. 17: The next day . . . : Seroff, 59; Blokker and Dearling, 17.

pp. 17–18: In the first year and a half . . . : Gleason, 270.

p. 18: In February 1917: By the Old Style calendar. According to the modern calendar, this uprising took place in March.

p. 18: On the morning of February 27, 1917: Old Style date.

p. 18: Sofia Shostakovich was eating breakfast . . . : The details about the Shostakovich family and their reaction to the February Revolution are taken from Seroff, 68 and following, except where noted.

p. 19: The Cossack horsemen rode along . . . : Viktor Shklovsky, *A Sentimental Journey: Memoirs, 1917–1922*, trans. Richard Sheldon (Ithaca: Cornell University Press, 1984), 10; *Russian Diary of an Englishman*, 101, 105; Houghteling, 66n.

p. 19: Soldiers told to take up arms . . . guns to the Revolutionaries: Service, *History*, 32; Houghteling, 64.

p. 19: "Let's denounce the old world . . . Forward!": The so-called "Workers' Marseillaise," or, in Russian, "Rabochaya Marselyeza." Lyrics by Pyotr Lavrov. http://self.gutenberg.org/articles/worker's_marseillaise. Eyewitnesses testify to the ubiquity of this anthem in the early days of the Revolution. It was eventually replaced by the Communist "Internationale."

p. 20: "Children — Freedom!": As quoted by Zoya Shostakovich, in Wilson, 6.

p. 20: On March 2, 1917, Nicholas II . . . : Though Nicholas II abdicated on March 2 (Old Style), officially the dynasty did not end until the third, when the tsar's brother Grand Duke Mikhail turned down the offer of the succession (White, 80–81). For a timeline of the February Revolution, see Shukman, 124.

p. 20: The tsar and his family were exiled . . . : For the story of the tsar and his family, see Candace Fleming's *The Family Romanov: Murder, Rebellion, and the Fall of Imperial Russia* (New York: Schwartz & Wade, 2014).

p. 20: The red flag of the Revolution was hoisted . . . : *Russian Diary of an Englishman*, 116, 121.

p. 21: "Arise, arise, working people! Forward! Forward!": Ibid., 137–138.

p. 21: His older sister, Maria, and her classmates . . . : The first conductor of Shostakovich's Second Symphony (*To October*) claimed that Dmitri's memory of the boy slain for the apple was represented in one section of that piece by a fiddle jig that leads the listener by the hand into a shrieking fugue. Shostakovich's supposed memoir, *Testimony*, recalls the story without mention of an apple (Volkov, *Testimony*, 7). For details and a debate about the credibility of this episode, see Wilson, 18–20.

p. 21: "filled with soldiers . . . in those days": Volkov, *Testimony*, 7.

p. 21: "You fell victims in the fatal struggle . . . great, mighty, and free": https://www.marxists.org/history/ussr/sounds/lyrics/vy-zhertvoiu.htm.

p. 21: The Shostakovich children climbed . . . : Seroff, 72–73.

p. 21: "a concluding chord in the symphony": Trotsky, *History I*, 17.

pp. 21, 23: We are told that when young Mitya . . . : Seroff, 73.

p. 22: "The funeral procession . . . symphony of the [February Revolution]": Trotsky, *History* 1, 17.

p. 23: He would use them in symphonies . . . : Shostakovich's Eleventh Symphony (*The Year 1905*) and Twelfth (*The Year 1917*) both rely heavily on Revolutionary tunes to tell their stories. The tune "You Fell Victims in the Fatal Struggle" and fragments of his own "Funeral March for the Victims of the Revolution" are used in the second movement of the Eleventh Symphony, lamenting the dead killed at the Winter Palace, and in the second movement of the Twelfth Symphony, which supposedly depicts Lenin brooding about the past and the future in the summer of 1917. Critics still argue about whether these two symphonies are tinny propaganda, sincere Leninism, or secret critiques of Soviet power (which is not impossible, particularly in the case of the Eleventh — see Wilson, 320; Volkov, *Stalin*, 40, 42; and Bartlett, 5). Whichever one believes, the West's impatient dismissal of these works as empty exercises is unfair: these Revolutionary experiences were very real and visceral in Shostakovich's personal memory and in the history of his family. He cannot be blamed for finding in them an emotional charge that Western audiences may not understand or share.

p. 23: One diarist talks about the surprise . . . : Houghteling, 77.

p. 24: Cars also rattled down the street . . . : Ibid., 82; Seroff, 75.

p. 24: Mitya Shostakovich and his friends . . . : Sollertinskys, 9.

pp. 24–25: "The only way to put an end . . . all the workers": Lenin, 2.

p. 25: "The world-wide Socialist revolution . . . socialist revolution": Ronald W. Clark, *Lenin: The Man Behind the Mask* (London: Faber and Faber, 1989), 210–211.

p. 25: they had nothing to lose but their chains: Karl Marx and Friedrich Engels, *Manifesto of the Communist Party*, http://www.gutenberg.org/cache/epub/61/pg61.html.

pp. 25–26: "The spectacle of a billowing sea . . . symphonic canvases": Sollertinskys, 9.

p. 26: Shostakovich's biographers write that Lenin's . . . : Wilson, 6. His son, Maxim, also claims to have heard the story (MacDonald, 16).

p. 26: "They say that the major event . . . I don't remember a thing": Volkov, *Testimony*, 7.

p. 26: Or was this story of him viewing . . . : See Fay, *Life*, 12–13.

p. 26: Moreover, Shostakovich's parents . . . : They were supposedly Narodniks (Volkov, *Testimony*, 7–8; MacDonald, 19n) — a leftist group that had radical ties in the nineteenth century but that, by 1917, had reassembled as a much more moderate party, voting against the Bolshevik takeover.

p. 26: Many of the details of Shostakovich's youth . . . : Shostakovich was furious with Galli-Shohat for publishing material from private letters (Khentova, *Voynï*, 171).

p. 27: "one of those wonderfully frank . . . into the subway": Selby, 13.

p. 27: In the summer of the Revolutionary year 1917 . . . : E.g., Wilson, 16.

p. 27: On October 25, 1917, Lenin and the Bolsheviks . . . : Old Style date. For the events of the October Revolution, see, for example, White, chapter 8.

pp. 27–28: Bolshevik forces attacked the palace . . . : Trotsky, *History III*, 45.

p. 28: Still, when elections for the nation's legislative body . . . : White, 174–176.

p. 28: "not popular": "The masses . . . bewilderment": Conquest, 4–5.

p. 30: Immediately after the Bolsheviks . . . : Shukman, 28–29; White, 189–191.

p. 30: Bolshevik thugs killed two of the previous members . . . : Andrei Shingarev and Fyodor Kokoshkin were killed by Baltic sailors in concert with Lenin's Red Guard. Orlando Figes, *A People's Tragedy: The Russian Revolution, 1891–1924* (New York: Penguin, 1988), 536n.

p. 30: Dmitri Shostakovich was asked to play . . . : Wilson, 12; Fay, *Life*, 12.

THE BIRTH OF TOMORROW

p. 31: "Despite all the difficulties . . . warm feeling": Fay, *Life*, 8. He's speaking here of his years in the Petrograd Conservatory.

p. 31: Workers and peasants would walk the streets . . . : Fitzpatrick, 18.

p. 32: "Man in Socialist societies . . . lay down rules for oceans": Gleason, 271.

p. 32: "We invited up to thirty people" and "There was nothing much . . . miss out on the dancing either": Wilson, 7–8.

pp. 32–33: "It was wonderful to be among the guests" and "when the bony boy . . . her wordless son": Sollertinskys, 12.

p. 33: The classrooms were freezing . . . : Ibid., 18.

p. 34: One of Shostakovich's friends, Leo Arnshtam . . . : Film director Leo Arnshtam's wonderful memoir of Conservatory life in that period is in Wilson, 20–23.

p. 34: "The Conservatoire of my youth . . . it breathed inspiration!": Ibid., 21.

p. 34: "hungry, but nevertheless happy" and "This thin and apparently fragile . . . point of numbness": Ibid., 23.

p. 35: "An excellent musician . . . development is remarkable": Sollertinskys, 20.

p. 35: "Music triumphed . . . the music of the revolution": Wilson, 22.

p. 35: "Art belongs to the people . . . education and culture": Schwarz, 3.

p. 36: "The streets are our brushes . . . Drag the pianos out onto the streets": Mayakovsky in his "Orders to the Army of the Arts" (1918), quoted in Wilson, 22.

p. 36: Lenin needed word of Communism . . . : Fueloep-Miller, 138–139.

p. 36: On the anniversary of the October Revolution . . . : Barron and Tuchman, 68.

p. 36: The Futurist Mayakovsky created bizarre propaganda . . . : Haas, 185; cf. Jangfeldt, 157–158. This play was directed by Vsevolod Meyerhold (discussed later) and had sets by the great Suprematist painter Kazimir Malevich (Gleason, 289).

p. 36: "The thunder of the October cannons . . . mildew of the past": Kovtun, 11 (translation modified for clarity).

pp. 36–37: "Blow up, destroy . . . the new man not dream of this": Volkov, *Stalin*, 54.

p. 37: "Inside us we had youth and joy . . . times of hope and fantasy": Maria Siniakova, quoted in Barron and Tuchman, 73.

p. 37: They talked about achieving weightlessness . . . : Kovtun, 23.

p. 37: They wanted to leave the earth behind . . . : Barron and Tuchman, 212.

p. 37: Constructivist Vladimir Tatlin designed a flying machine . . . : Kovtun, 193.

p.37: Vasily Kamensky's career as a painter . . . : Barron and Tuchman, 160.

p. 37: Composers, too, wanted to celebrate Russia's new modernity . . . : E.g., the work of composers such as Alexander Mosolov, Nikolai Roslavets, Samuil Feinberg, Sergei Protopopov, and, finally, Arthur Lourié, who was not only important in the arts administration of Leningrad, but also the poet Anna Akhmatova's lover.

p. 39: The names of these pieces suggest their brutal, mechanical energy . . . : This trend of machine-related music was popular all over the globe in the 1920s and included pieces such as Honegger's *Pacific 231;* Milhaud's *Agricultural Machinery;* Antheil's *Ballet Mécanique,* "Airplane" Sonata, and "Death of the Machines"; and Szpilman's "The Life of the Machines." What we might think of as Soviet-style pieces in praise of factory work were also joyfully produced in a consumer capitalist context, most notably Frederick Converse's "Flivver Ten Million," a light epic ode in praise of the "birth of a hero": the ten millionth midprice Ford auto to roll off the assembly line.

p. 39: Prokofiev's *Leap of Steel* . . . and Ornstein's *Suicide in an Airplane:* Both Leo Ornstein and Sergei Prokofiev had studied at the St. Petersburg Conservatory like Shostakovich, though both of them, by this time, were living abroad.

p. 39: "The orchestra must become like a factory": Tassie, 105.

p. 39: In the city of Baku . . . : Fueloep-Miller, 183–184.

p. 39: Industrial output in 1921 was only a fifth . . . : Service, *History,* 109.

p. 40: "Spit on rhymes and arias . . . Give us new forms!": "Order No. 2 to the Army of the Arts," Mayakovsky, 147, 149.

p. 40: Now he stood before young Mitya . . . : Ibid., 18.

p. 40: "No gray hairs streak my soul . . . might of my voice!": Ibid.

p. 40: He did not imagine he would soon be working . . . : These descriptions of
Mayakovsky are from Marina Tsvetaeva's poem "To Mayakovsky." Marina Tsvetaeva,
Selected Poems, trans. Elaine Feinstein (New York: Penguin, 1993).

p. 40: "The state is an instrument of coercion . . . the interests of our workers": *Pravda,*
November 22, 1917, quoted in Shukman, 182.

pp. 40–42: In the cities, workers discovered that they did not . . . : While one of the
first things Lenin did when he came into power was decree that factories belonged to
their workers, he quickly reversed this policy and replaced workers' boards with state
managers. See Shukman, 28–29.

p. 42: The bodies of Orthodox Christian saints . . . : Fueloep-Miller, 186.

p. 42: "It makes me want to say kind things . . . beat them without mercy": Patrick
Lloyd Hatcher, *North Atlantic Civilization at War: The World War II Battles of Sky,
Sand, Snow, Sea, and Shore* (Armonk, NY: M. E. Sharpe, 1998), 67. Cf. the more brutal
translation in Fueloep-Miller, 176.

p. 42: The teenage Shostakovich did not take politics very seriously: He seems, in this
period, to have been, like many of the intelligentsia, a casual Marxist, though not
necessarily a Party supporter. See Fay, *Life,* 36.

p. 42: "to explain the difference . . . work of Chopin and Liszt": Ibid.

p. 44: "We are living now on our grand piano . . . old watch": Seroff, 82.

p. 44: In the winter, these trains could be frigid . . . : This version of his death is recorded
by Boris Lossky (Wilson, 30). Shostakovich's aunt claimed that Dmitri senior died of a
heart ailment (Seroff, 84–85). Scholarship tends toward the pneumonia explanation (for
example, Fay, *Life,* 20).

p. 44: six monks came to sing the coffin on its way . . . : Wilson, 31.

p. 44: "Mitya and Zoya stood a little off to one side . . . go to him with condolences":
Elena Trusova, quoted in Sollertinskys, 26–27.

p. 45: "Now I feel like a stone": Wilson, 31.

p. 45: He and Maria played it for salons of musicians: Fay, *Life,* 21.

p. 45: Mitya offered to drop his studies . . . : Seroff, 120, 125–126.

p. 45: a man followed her home from work . . . : Wilson, 27.

p. 46: The family rented out four of their apartment's seven rooms: Seroff, 87, 99;
Khentova, *Mire,* 49–50.

p. 46: Writers of those years often describe the tense unpleasantness . . . : This was a
specialty, for example, of the satirist Mikhail Zoshchenko, who later became a friend
of Shostakovich's.

p. 47: "My character . . . What haven't I studied": Seroff, 113.

p. 47: Her mother told her that if the ceiling of the apartment fell in . . . : Ibid., 174.

p. 47: "They spoke of it . . . long-wanted rest": Ibid., 129.

p. 47: His mother, determined to make his birthday a happy one . . . : This anecdote is from two accounts in Wilson, 31–32. Wilson herself suggests that the two witnesses are describing the same party, which seems very likely, given the time frame.

p. 48: They sold a piano so he could be treated: Wilson, 29.

p. 48: "You . . . love your own family": Seroff, 91–92.

p. 49: Mitya was studying hard . . . : Sollertinskys, 29.

p. 49: In the summer of 1923 . . . : Ibid., 30. It should also be mentioned that Glazunov, from the Conservatory, found money for Shostakovich to convalesce—a characteristic act of generosity.

p. 49: he was getting soppy over some popular girl . . . : Fay, *Life*, 22.

p. 49: "small, slim . . . a round, pretty face": Sollertinskys, 31.

p. 50: "How could anybody not have . . . end of his life": Ibid., 32.

p. 50: Shostakovich was not fond of his job . . . : Wilson, 60–61; Fay, *Life*, 29.

p. 52: He did sometimes use his job . . . : Sollertinskys, 33–34.

p. 52: His trio is undoubtedly music by a boy in love . . . : This is his First Piano Trio, Op. 8. His Second Piano Trio, Op. 67, was written decades later and if it is drunk at all, is a bitter drunk, drunk on death.

p. 52: Shostakovich pointed out . . . : Wilson, 61.

p. 52: "He asked me . . . But I held my own" and Shostakovich sued the owner . . . : Volkov, *Testimony*, 11. The chronology of Shostakovich's work in this period has been simplified slightly. The only biography to have clarified the precise chronology of these years is Fay, *Life*, 22–32, which corrects various other anecdotal accounts.

p. 52: "Now I'm writing a symphony . . . have done with the Conservatory": Fay, *Life*, 25.

p. 53: "No, I want her to stay here. It helps me": Wilson, 87.

p. 53: "was the center of life . . . his mother's influence": Ibid., 88.

p. 53: "The main thing in life is good cheer . . . Everywhere there is joy": Fay, *World*, 13.

p. 54: "St. Leninburg": Fay, *Life*, 36.

p. 54: "second birth": Wilson, 47.

p. 54: "in a state of such indescribable excitement . . . displaying his agitation": Ibid., 49n.

p. 54: "Mrs. Shostakovich outwardly reserved . . . was still anxious for her brother": Sollertinskys, 35.

p. 56: "By nine o'clock the hall was completely packed . . . very hard to bear": Wilson, 50–51.

p. 56: "Everything went off brilliantly . . . long and tumultuous ovation": Ibid., 51.

p. 57: Shostakovich waded into the ultramodernism of Leningrad: During his time at the Conservatory, he steered a path between the conservative and experimental elements of the faculty. See Haas, passim.

p. 57: If music without words can have "characters" . . . : His first four symphonies, for example, are full of the same quirky, even grotesque soliloquies one finds in writers like Yuri Olesha and Andrei Platonov. The formlessness of pieces like his Second and Third Symphonies, in which one section grows out of another, never to look back, is very similar to an absurdist work like Mikhail Bulgakov's weird dream-novella *Diaboliad*. In general, the violent absurdism of much of his work echoes that of experimental writers of his acquaintance such as Daniil Kharms, who combined brash nonsense with formalistic play. (For examples of the experimentalists, see Ostashevsky's anthology *Oberiu*.) Shostakovich knew many of these writers personally and later thought about collaborating with several of them on opera projects.

p. 57: Shostakovich's Second and Third Symphonies . . . : This excellent observation was made by musicologist Marina Sabinina and is discussed at length in Haas, 185–194.

p. 57: "Proletarians of the World, Unite!": MacDonald, 46.

p. 57: It supposedly even depicts the death of that boy . . . : Wilson, 63; but also see Fay, *Life*, 40.

pp. 57–58: "Nobody will ever deprive us . . . October, the Commune, and Lenin": Translation by Decca in the program booklet for *Shostakovich: The Symphonies*, conducted by Bernard Haitink (Decca 475 7413).

p. 58: "quite disgusting": Wilson, 61. The first conductor of the piece admitted, "Bezymensky's words were bad. Shostakovich did not like them and simply laughed at them" (Fairclough and Fanning, 157).

p. 58: Shostakovich tested the score . . . : Fay, *Life*, 44.

p. 58: "We should forbid the performance . . . in the revolutionary republic": *Zhizn iskusstva*, September 8, 1923, quoted in Barron and Tuchman, 72.

p. 58: Audiences loved his "Tahiti Trot": This was actually an orchestration of a piece from a musical by Vincent Youmans. Shostakovich used it in the ballet *The Age of Gold*, and his version became a standard in Russia. See Fairclough and Fanning, 201.

p. 58: He even wrote a ballet about soccer . . . : There is an enticing description of this ballet in Fairclough and Fanning, 198–203.

p. 59: Shostakovich loved the brutal Russian form of soccer . . . : MacDonald, 142.

p. 59: He and his friends screamed at the field . . . : Fay, *Life*, 110.

p. 59: It was very profitable to bet against Dmitri Shostakovich: Sollertinskys, 93–94.

p. 59: the sets no longer looked like houses or forests . . . : Meyerhold's mentor was the famous Konstantin Stanislavsky, though Meyerhold's theory of the theater was the opposite of Stanislavsky's "method acting." Stanislavsky believed that every character onstage — even the silent guards and footmen — had to be created by the actor as a full person. Meyerhold believed that even the main characters were just part of a big, stylized design.

p. 59: Every production had a new, futuristic twist . . . : For details and wonderful photos of Meyerhold's productions, see Braun, passim.

p. 59: Meyerhold began one play with a convoy . . . : Fueloep-Miller, 126.

p. 60: One writer slyly predicted . . . : Mikhail Bulgakov, in his novella "The Fatal Eggs." *Diaboliad and Other Stories* (New York: Ardis, 2012), 81.

p. 60: In January 1928, Shostakovich went to Moscow . . . : Fay, *Life*, 45.

p. 60: Meyerhold's nanny . . . took an uncomfortable interest . . . : Shostakovich, *Sollertinskomu*, 31.

p. 60: "Here I am . . . It was brilliant": Bartlett, 68.

p. 61: "Well done, all of you . . .": Shostakovich, *Sollertinskomu*, 25–27; trans. in Bartlett, 68, edited slightly for clarity. The story of Raikh and Meyerhold's children — and their biological father, the poet Esenin — is told movingly in Anatoly Mariengof's memoir, *A Novel Without Lies*, trans. Jose Alaniz (Moscow: Glas, 2000). Reading the details of their difficult circumstances, it is hard to begrudge them praise.

p. 61: "agent in conserving nonliquid property": Volkov, *Testimony*, 205.

p. 64: "very thin and scrawny . . . movements of his hands": Nikolai Sokolov, quoted in Wilson, 77.

p. 64: "I've developed a pain in my hand, too": Sollertinskys, 51; Volkov, *Testimony*, 246. As ever, nothing is certain: there is some disagreement about the number of fingers Shostakovich held out.

p. 65: "Mayakovsky asked me . . . Meyerhold broke up the argument": Volkov, *Testimony*, 247.

p. 65: "as simple as mooing": Fairclough and Fanning, 156.

p. 65: His suits were from Germany . . . : Volkov, *Testimony*, 246.

p. 65: the only reason Mayakovsky had written the play . . . : Mayakovsky, 315n; Jangfeldt, 413, 428.

p. 65: "drummer of the Revolution": Robinson, 146.

p. 65: "wrote revolutionary verses . . . in my opinion a prostitute": Volkov, *Stalin*, 67. Cf. Leon Trotsky's canny discussion of Mayakovsky, whom he both admired and found utterly infuriating, "individualistic and Bohemian," in his *Literature and Revolution*. ("Chapter 4: Futurism," http://www.marxists.org/archive/trotsky/1924/lit_revo /ch04.htm. Accessed August 15, 2013.)

p. 67: driven a teenage girl to suicide . . . : Mayakovsky, 28, 307n16; but cf. Jangfeldt, 375–376.

p. 67: "I can readily say . . . moral law for Mayakovsky" and "fairly lousy": Volkov, *Testimony*, 247.

p. 67: "That'll clean out brains": Fay, *Life*, 51.

p. 68: "We must advise Comrade Shostakovich . . . principles of Marxism": Quoted in MacDonald, "Laurel E. Fay's *Shostakovich: A Life*," http://www.siue.edu/~aho /musov/fay/fayrev1.html. Accessed April 21, 2013.

p. 68: Should "the People" be forbidden to listen to the light music they loved . . . : Jazz was, for all intents and purposes, banned in the Soviet Union from 1929 to 1932. "Even playing jazz records could lead to a fine" (Fairclough, *Credo*, 2). There was an attempt to make the playing of the saxophone illegal (Mikkonen, 68).

p. 68: "The new songs are sung . . . far to the grave": Garros and Korenevskaya, 131.

p. 69: "irrelevant to students . . . textile-workers": MacDonald, 61 (cf. 51).

p. 69: A survey was taken of workers in the audience . . . : Fay, *Life*, 55.

p. 69: Lenin, in his later years, had experimented . . . : This is a reference to Lenin's New Economic Policy, which he launched to ease the nation's economic distress after the Civil War. It allowed people to own modest-size businesses and engage in some higher-level economic transactions. In many ways, Lenin's gamble was a success: by 1927, when the NEP was phased out, the country had finally returned to the levels of industrial and agricultural production it had enjoyed on the eve of the First World War (Service, *History*, 162).

p. 69: the Politburo was sending armored trains . . . : Fitzpatrick, 35.

p. 70: about one and a half million of them starved to death: Service, *History*, 201.

p. 70: roughly 2,200 small rebellions broke out . . . : Montefiore, 46; cf. Gleason, 371.

p. 70: The peasantry fought with sawed-off shotguns . . . : Fitzpatrick, 18–19.

p. 71: "Rubbish, stupid . . . and pretentious": Jangfeldt, 162.

p. 71: On April 14, 1930 . . . : Jangfeldt, 538–539, cf. 563.

p. 71: "What is all this? . . . leader of the new society!": Mayakovsky, 292.

pp. 71–72: "Already people from the town . . . but does not end it": Mayakovsky, 9–10.

p. 72: "sulking and indignant": Ibid.

p. 72: At eight o'clock the evening of his death . . . : Mayakovsky, 47–48; Jangfeldt, 545–546.

p. 72: The rest of Mayakovsky's body . . . : Jangfeldt, 551, 554.

p. 72: "unpleasant Georgian with . . . wicked yellow eyes": Alexandrov, 27.

p. 72: The man called himself Joseph Stalin: His given name was Vissarionovich Dzhugashvili.

LIFE IS GETTING MERRIER

p. 73: "His fingers are as fat as grubs . . . For the broad-chested [Stalin]": Nadezhda Mandelstam, 13. Translations vary widely, given the wordplay in the original.

p. 74: "I didn't hear this . . . I heard nothing": Ivinskaya, 61.

p. 74: Roughly six million people starved to death . . . : Figures vary: See Gleason, 372; Conquest, 20; Montefiore, 84–85.

p. 74: In 1933, more than four million people starved . . . : Overy, 23.

p. 74: "We know millions are dying . . . will justify it": Montefiore, 84.

p. 74: "There are no words to describe . . . could not take it in": Ivinskaya, 71.

p. 74: Mandelstam recited his squib about Stalin to a circle of his friends: But cf. Nadezhda Mandelstam, 149.

p. 74: "committing a terrorist act against the ruler": Volkov, *Stalin*, 87.

p. 74: "There's no place where more people are killed for it": Quoted in Nadezhda Mandelstam, 149.

p. 76: The government's newspaper, *Pravda* . . . "We were born to make fairy tales come true": Fitzpatrick, 68; Tassie, 169.

p. 76: The news that reached the cities . . . : Fitzpatrick, 70.

p. 76: "I think an artist should serve . . . my own fault": *New York Times*, December 20, 1931, quoted in Seroff, 156.

p. 76: "If it is art, it is not for everybody . . . it is not art": Bartlett, 18.

p. 76: "a pale young man . . . a bashful schoolboy": *New York Times*, December 20, 1931, quoted in Schwarz, 83.

p. 76: this was not the best atmosphere . . . : MacDonald, 34.

p. 77: In Shostakovich's ballet *The Bolt* . . . : For a more nuanced view of this piece and its politics, see Simon Morrison's "Shostakovich as Industrial Saboteur: Observations on *The Bolt*," in Fay, *World*, 119ff.

p. 77: They were urged to depict real life . . . : For example, in one of the first definitions of Socialist Realism, we see the contradictory demands for "realism" and for propagandistic optimism: "Socialist realism, being the basic method of Soviet literature and literary criticism, demands from the artist a truthful, historically concrete depiction of reality in its revolutionary development. At the same time, the truthfulness and historical concreteness of the artistic depiction of reality must coexist with the goal of ideological change and education of the workers in the spirit of socialism" (Volkov, *Stalin*, 16).

p. 77: "The main attention of the Soviet composer . . . bright, and beautiful": Schwarz, 114.

pp. 77–79: In a society that was supposed to be understood . . . : Volkov, *Stalin*, 48; cf. Alexander Yashin's story "Levers," in *Soviet Short Stories*, ed. Avrahm Yarmolinsky (Garden City, NY: Anchor, 1960).

p. 79: "engineers of human souls": Montefiore, 96.

p. 79: His friends and colleagues were also working on propaganda symphonies . . . : E.g., Miaskovsky's Symphony no. 12 (*Kolkhoz*), Knipper's Symphony no. 4 (*The Song for the Komsomol Soldier*), and Popov's suite of music for the movie *Communist Youth — The Boss of Electrification*, which later became his Orchestral Suite no. 1.

p. 80: "Either you marry me or I'll stop coming to your house": From Tatiana Glivenko's own account of the relationship, in Wilson, 84.

p. 80: "It's me — Shostakovich . . . in their house": Ibid., 85.

pp. 80–81: "Mitya wants to marry . . . He does not even know how to start": Ibid., 88.

p. 81: "[Shostakovich] was thirsting to recreate . . . for those in love": Wilson, 96–97.

p. 81: We do not know which fiancée . . . : Wilson, 86. In another anecdote, Shostakovich supposedly didn't show up to his own wedding the first time around (Meyer, 143–144).

p. 82: Once Nina and Dmitri got married . . . : Seroff, 183.

p. 82: "No sooner would I arrive . . . when I would get home": Wilson, 161.

p. 83: "the start of the brilliant . . . creativity": Volkov, *Stalin*, 97–98.

p. 83: "a remarkable . . . creative work": Fay, *Life*, 76.

p. 83: Quickly, demands came . . . : Ibid., 77.

p. 83: Leningrad factories staged excerpts . . . : Radamsky, 187.

p. 83: Kirov was one of Joseph Stalin's closest friends . . . : Service, *Stalin*, 294.

p. 83: The dictator demanded quick action . . . : Montefiore, 147.

p. 84: Stalin had always hated the city . . . : Fitzpatrick, 125.

p. 84: People began "masking" themselves . . . : Ibid., 132, 137.

p. 84: Many of the family had been Revolutionaries . . . : Seroff, 19.

p. 84: "Nothing here": Garros and Korenevskaya, 357.

p. 86: Prisoners were usually sent to work-camps . . . : Conquest, 325–330.

p. 86: "I am not sorry for Kirov . . . not be sorry for him": Fitzpatrick, 170.

p. 86: An astounding rumor was making the rounds . . . : Conquest, 33; Service, *Stalin*, 313.

p. 87: As he was being driven to Leningrad Party Headquarters . . . : Conquest, 42.

p. 87: "To choose one's victims . . . sweeter in the world": Service, *History*, 197.

p. 87: the screenwriter of a movie he was working on . . . : MacDonald, 102.

p. 87: "Now, you might ask . . . shot nevertheless": Volkov, *Testimony*, 151.

p. 87: some thirty or forty thousand people . . . : Conquest, 45.

p. 88: After arguing with his wife . . . : Meyer, 145.

p. 88: "Remaining in Leningrad . . . Mitya": Fay, *Life*, 80.

p. 88: "There can be no question . . . how precious to me": Ibid.

p. 89: Easing their marriage even more . . . : MacDonald, 95; Khentova, *Mire*, 53.

p. 89: "white with fear": Volkov, *Stalin*, 101.

p. 89: When most of the audience was seated . . . : Radamsky, 214.

p. 89: He had a bowl of hard-boiled eggs . . . : Vishnevskaya, 93–94.

pp. 89–90: "Melik [the conductor] furiously lifts his baton . . . no impression at all": Volkov, *Stalin*, 101.

p. 90: Every time the brass and percussion exploded . . . : Radamsky, 214. Radamsky claims he was not only present, but sitting right beside Shostakovich. Note, however, that his account differs in several respects from the generally accepted version of events (e.g., Fay, *Life*, 84). Given that Radamsky is sometimes inaccurate, I have taken a few of his details but adhered to the sequence of events as usually narrated.

p. 90: *"Eta sumbur, a ne musyka"*: Radamsky, 215.

p. 90: "Tell me, why . . . will be a bad one for me": Volkov, *Stalin*, 101–102.

p. 90: "with a sorrowful soul": Ibid., 102.

p. 90: On January 28 — the day of his concert in Arkhangelsk . . . : Volkov, *Testimony*, 113.

p. 91: "Coarse, primitive, and vulgar . . . may end very badly": "Muddle Instead of Music."

p. 91: "Hey, brother, you already drunk this morning": Volkov, *Stalin*, 102.

p. 92: While . . . there is no evidence that Stalin actually wrote . . . : Fay, 304n67.

p. 92: "pornophony": Blokker and Dearling, 24.

p. 92: "real art, real science, and real literature": "Muddle Instead of Music."

p. 92: "Balletic Falsehood": "Baletnaya fal'sh," *Pravda*, February 6, 1936, no. 36 (6642).

p. 92: "painted peasants on the lid of a candy-box": Seroff, 207.

p. 92: *"lies and falsehood* . . . the sickly sweetness of *The Bright Stream"*: Volkov, *Stalin*, 112.

p. 93: Stalin's regime fired off a series of similar articles . . . : Ibid., 109.

p. 93: tossing out the old ways of the great composers . . . : These last two accusations, in a record-breaking contradiction, even appeared in the same paragraph in Tikhon Khrennikov's 1948 denunciation of the composer (Slonimsky, 693).

p. 93: "The Devil alone knows": MacDonald, 101.

pp. 93–94: "When I hear Shostakovich's symphonies . . . by all Soviet people": Quoted in the film *A Journey of Dmitry Shostakovich*, dir. Helga Landauer and Oksana Dvornichenko (West Long Branch, NJ: Kultur, 2006).

p. 94: "How Beautiful Life Will Be": This song was from the movie *Alone* (MacDonald, 76).

p. 94: "I was called an enemy . . . enemy of the people Shostakovich": Volkov, *Testimony*, 115.

p. 94: On the way home from his concert tour . . . : Fay, *Life*, 90; Brooke, 406.

p. 94: Tukhachevsky was having an affair: Alexandrov, 166.

p. 94: When Tukhachevsky was visiting Leningrad . . . : Volkov, *Testimony*, 100.

p. 95: "I was a sickly youth . . . he feared prying ears": Ibid., 96–98.

p. 95: the composer sat down at the piano . . . : MacDonald, 106.

p. 95: He stayed in Moscow and waited anxiously . . . : Bartlett, 76; Ross, 251.

p. 95: "Don't worry . . . Don't worry": Khentova, *Mire*, 121.

p. 96: "Even if they cut off . . . writing music": Glikman, xix.

p. 96: The Leningrad Composers' Union held a special session . . . : Fairclough, *Credo*, 25.

p. 96: "One after another . . . opened their eyes": For the account of this meeting, see Radamsky, 216–217.

p. 96: Lev Knipper, spy for the secret police: Knipper had been working for the secret police in some capacity since 1922 (Beevor, loc. 1366). His connections did not protect him and his music from being denounced in terms similar to those used about Shostakovich (Fairclough, *Credo*, 32; Sitsky, 150–151). During this meeting, his comments appear to have been motivated more by his competitive spirit than any darker agenda. It should be noted that in 1948, Knipper was supposedly very vocal in defending Shostakovich and the other "formalists" (Tassie, 273).

p. 96: "You bastard!": Radamsky, 217.

pp. 96–97: "If you are smeared with mud . . . circumstances": Volkov, *Testimony*, 271.

p. 97: We know now from the files of the secret police . . . : Volkov, *Stalin*, 124; Ross, 150.

p. 97: "I can't hear you . . . cut you off": Morrison, 149.

p. 97: Leningrad poet Anna Akhmatova was also being watched . . . : Nadezhda Mandelstam, 17–18.

p. 97: That spring, Shostakovich considered suicide . . . : Volkov, *Stalin*, 124.

p. 97: "What will happen to my son now?": Ibid., 249–251; cf. Ross, 250.

p. 97: "They are driving Shostakovich . . . over the radio": Tassie, 193.

p. 98: "The article in Pravda struck him . . . completely depressed": Volkov, *Stalin*, 115; cf. 116n.

p. 98: The head of the secret police admitted . . . : Fay, *Life*, 97. Gorky died on June 18, 1936. In 1938, when on trial, Genrikh Yagoda, director of the NKVD, admitted to having him killed. It is still unclear whether Yagoda acted independently, whether Stalin ordered Gorky's death, or whether, in fact, Gorky died of natural causes.

p. 98: "paced the room with a towel . . . keeping watch": Volkov, *Stalin*, 124.

p. 98: The government had announced in 1935 . . . : Conquest, 75.

p. 99: "Let me have one night with him . . . England": Lavrentii Beria, quoted in Montefiore, 276.

p. 99: "Better that ten innocent people . . . chips fly": Nikolai Yezhov, quoted in Montefiore, 218.

pp. 99–100: "It was impossible to tell . . . disappeared as well": Jones, 66.

p. 100: "What was he arrested for . . . done anything wrong": Nadezhda Mandelstam, 10.

p. 100: "What for . . . arrested *for nothing*": Ibid., 11.

p. 100: "greater sincerity": Conquest, 85.

p. 100: He saw his earnings diminish . . . : Fay, *Life*, 94.

p. 100: "I was completely in the thrall . . . wanted to disappear": Volkov, *Testimony*, 118.

p. 101: "Speechlessness became my home . . . muteness": Akhmatova, 767.

p. 102: "He is an original among us — for he thinks": Volkov, *Stalin,* 161. Cf. Hakobian, 130; Garros and Korenevskaya, 346.

p. 102: "Dear friend! . . . Do not give in to your sadness": Volkov, *Stalin,* 161. Cf. Fairclough, *Credo,* 26.

p. 102: "said he was incapable of doing anything": Ross, 250.

p. 102: "purely infantile act": Volkov, *Testimony,* 118.

p. 102: The celebration was riotous . . . : Glikman, xix–xx.

p. 102: "I don't write . . . in my soul and mind": Fay, *Life,* 306n34.

p. 102: "After 'A Mess Instead of Music,' . . . my Fourth Symphony": Glikman, 194.

pp. 102–103: Experimental composer Alexander Mosolov . . . : Arrested in November 1937. Brooke, 409; Hakobian, 55; Tassie, 200–201, 221n57.

p. 103: Shostakovich's friend Gavriil Popov . . . : In March 1935 (Haas, 218). The symphony was later rehabilitated, partially thanks to Shostakovich's intervention (Fairclough, *Credo,* 43).

p. 103: The great Sergei Prokofiev . . . : Schwarz, 117.

p. 103: "I sing as I cradle . . . Stalin, Stalin!": Text of Prokofiev's *Zdravitsa* by A. Mashistov; translated by Philip Taylor. Recording booklet: Valeri Polyansky conducting the Russian State Symphony Orchestra. *Prokofiev: Egyptian Nights; Hamlet; Autumnal; Zdravitsa; Flourish, Mighty Land* (Chandos Records CHAN 10056, 2003), 21–27.

p. 103: The whole generation of ultramodern composers . . . : Arthur Lourié had fled for the West and stayed there. Nikolai Roslavets, the Muscovite atonalist, had been banned from working as a composer as early as 1930 and had been forced to publicly renounce his own work (Hakobian, 29). For more information on the fate of this generation of experimental composers, see Sitsky, passim.

p. 104: "step on their own song's throat": Mayakovsky in "At the Top of My Voice," quoted in Hakobian, 29; cf. Fanning, "C Major," 114.

p. 104: "They blow up mines . . . sons of our country": Conquest, 163.

p. 105: wreckers: Ibid., 362.

p. 105: "I demand that these mad dogs should be shot — every one of them": Vyshinsky's final remarks are reproduced in full at: http://art-bin.com/art/omosc22m .html#1. Accessed August 19, 2013.

p. 105: "Long live the cause of Marx, Engels, Lenin, and Stalin": Montefiore, 192.

p. 105: One alleged conspirator confessed . . . : The meeting was supposedly with Leon Trotsky's son. Conquest, 99.

p. 105: "What the devil did you need . . . always there": Montefiore, 191.

p. 105: the musicians of the Leningrad Philharmonic Orchestra were wary . . . : For a much fuller and more nuanced discussion of the incredibly rich Fourth Symphony, see Fairclough, *Credo.*

p. 105: People have tried to hear fanciful scenarios . . . : MacDonald, 110–113.

p. 106: "detected a strong sense . . . formalist tendencies": Glikman, xxiii.

p. 107: "My companion seemed thoroughly downcast . . . symphony": Glikman, xxiii. For variants and discussion, see Fairclough, *Credo*, 28; Fay, *Life*, 95–96.

p. 107: "Composer Shostakovich appealed . . . a long outdated phase": Fay, *Life*, 95.

p. 107: "Meaning in music . . . without any interest": Volkov, *Testimony*, 234.

p. 108: "Listen, workers . . . march with a million feet": Recording booklet, *Dmitri Shostakovich: The Symphonies*, conducted by Bernard Haitink (Decca 475 7413, 2006).

p. 108: "Shostakovich did not like . . . them": Wilson, 62; cf. Fay, *Life*, 40.

p. 108: Russian symphonies and suites spinning tales . . . : Thrilling examples of the barbarian genre are Rimsky-Korsakov's Second Symphony (*Antar*) and his suite *Scheherazade*, Glière's Third Symphony (*Ilya Muromets*), and Prokofiev's early *Scythian Suite*. Examples of Soviet-era symphonies that sketch heroic scenes are Miaskovsky's Eighth (about popular bandit Stepan Razin) and Sixteenth (*Airborne*) and Steinberg's Fourth (*Turk Sib*, depicting the construction of the Turkestan-Siberian railway).

p. 109: There is no need for us to know names . . . : The latter image is conductor Gennadi Rozhdestvensky's for the eerie percussion at the end of the second movement. Fairclough, *Credo*, 165.

p. 109: "Glory, glory, glory! Praise to Queen Jocasta in pestilential Thebes": Volkov, *Stalin*, 137; Fairclough, *Credo*, 221.

pp. 109–110: There clearly is some irony in Shostakovich using this fragment . . . : For a discussion of how much specific defiance might be symbolically encoded in the finale, see Fanning, "C Major," 120–131, and Elizabeth Wilson's review of Fairclough's *Soviet Credo* in *Music and Letters* 90, no. 3 (August 2009), 512, as well as Fairclough's book itself.

p. 110: But we can never be certain exactly what he meant by them . . . : I am thinking here in particular of the Eleventh Symphony, which is overtly about the protests and brutal tsarist repressions of 1905 — but which was also composed as the Soviet government was brutally crushing protest in Hungary, sending tanks through the streets of Budapest. Under those circumstances, the quotation of the Revolutionary song "Death to You, Tyrants" in the symphony, for example, may have had more than one meaning for Shostakovich. For the debate, see Volkov, *Stalin*, 40; Bartlett, 5; Wilson, 317–320.

p. 110: "Pretzels, Buy My Pretzels": Fay, *Life*, 248.

p. 110: At the time, people did not know that this brief motif . . . : For a more in-depth look at the way the DSCH motif and other themes and quotations are used in the Eighth Quartet, as well as the biographical stories surrounding the piece, see Fanning, *String*.

p. 110: "There is more to an artwork . . . bottle": Richard Taruskin, "Shostakovich and the Inhuman," in *Defining Russia Musically: Historical and Hermeneutical Essays* (Princeton, NJ: Princeton University Press, 1997), 493.

p. 110: Shostakovich made a melody out of the name . . . : The discovery of this theme's meaning was due to a couple of incredible feats of musicology. See Fanning, *Breath*, 51–53, and Nelly Kravetz's "A New Insight into the Tenth Symphony of Dmitry Shostakovich," in Bartlett, 159ff.

p. 111: "Shostakovich hated being asked questions . . . what I've said": Wilson, 376.

p. 111: The shadow of the Great Terror . . . : Much more so, in fact, than composers: See, for example, Mikkonen, 18.

p. 111: "I would sing of him . . . sternly kind": From "Lines on Stalin," Osip Mandelstam, 71. Cf. "The Ode" in Nadezhda Mandelstam, 198–203.

p. 112: He never got a chance to say good-bye . . . : Nadezhda Mandelstam, 360–362.

p. 112: He died on the way there . . . : For the fullest discussion of the debated circumstances of his death, see Nadezhda Mandelstam, 376–397.

p. 112: "We were capable of coming to work . . . school": MacDonald, 123; a condensation of Nadezhda Mandelstam, 286 and 304–305.

p. 112: Elena Konstantinovskaya . . . : Wilson, 121.

p. 112: Another one of his ex-girlfriends from his youth . . . : Volkov, *Stalin,* 40.

p. 112: The man who had written the story of Shostakovich's ballet . . . : Adrian Piotrovsky, in Wilson, 121.

p. 112: The head of the Moscow Composers' Union was executed: Tomoff, 23.

p. 113: The NKVD thugs beat her so brutally . . . : MacDonald, 133.

p. 113: Nina's mother was arrested . . . : Fay, *Life,* 98.

p. 113: Shostakovich's uncle was arrested and disappeared: Wilson, 19.

p. 113: Her husband was accused . . . : Volkov, *Stalin,* 139.

p. 113: where he died: See Fay, *Life,*145.

p. 113: Mass rallies were held to celebrate Stalin . . . : Fitzpatrick, 30.

p. 113: "Life is getting better . . . merrier": Stalin first used the slogan in a speech to the Stakhanovite workers in mid-November 1935, but it quickly became a catchphrase of the era. Garros and Korenevskaya, 4; cf. Fitzpatrick, 6–7, 90.

p. 113: Planes spelled out his name in the sky: Montefiore, 165.

p. 113: One night late in the Great Terror . . . : June 1939. This account combines two similar but distinct versions of the story: see Fay, *Life,* 114, and Volkov, *Stalin,* 162.

p. 114: Meyerhold had defended himself and Shostakovich . . . : Meyerhold, *Meyerhold on Theater,* trans. Edward Braun (New York: Hill and Wang, 1969), 248–249, which also gives a sample of Meyerhold's self-defense during the same period.

p. 114: "Where once there were the best theaters . . . eliminated art": Conquest, 306; cf. Robinson, 362.

p. 114: "They beat me . . . whipped by its master": Braun, 301.

p. 115: "If you refuse to write . . . mangled flesh": Ibid., 302.

p. 115: Indeed, they broke his left arm . . . : Conquest, 306–307.

p. 115: "coordinated all anti-Soviet elements in the field of the arts": Braun, 303.

p. 115: "We all had . . . genius": Volkov, *Stalin,* 161.

p. 115: "saboteur": Ibid.

p. 116: "Common Grave Number One . . . inclusive": Montefiore, 324; Braun, 308.

p. 116: A few months after he was arrested . . . : This detail — the call that lured Zinaida Raikh to Moscow — was a rumor at the time recorded in the diary of a friend who ran a puppet theater. Garros and Korenevskaya, 373.

p. 116: She stayed at their old apartment . . . : Braun, 302.

p. 116: According to Russian superstition . . . : Garros and Korenevskaya, 373.

p. 117: "Meyerhold loved her madly . . . they'll survive": Volkov, *Testimony*, 78.

p. 117: Party members were purged . . . : Conquest, 218.

p. 117: Train operators were purged . . . : Montefiore, 239.

p. 117: When the NKVD had finished purging other groups . . . : The NKVD head referred to here is Nikolai Yezhov, tried in 1938, shot in 1940. He himself had been instrumental in the purging of his predecessor, Genrikh Yagoda, in 1936/37.

p. 117: About twenty thousand secret-police officers . . . : There were two distinct purges of the NKVD during the Great Terror; this total covers the whole period (Conquest, 180).

p. 117: Scientists who taught strict Darwinian evolution were purged . . . : Stalin was very much under the influence of so-called Lysenkoism — the belief that acquired characteristics, as well as inherited characteristics, could be passed down genetically. Service, *Stalin*, 307.

p. 117: Collective farmers were purged . . . : Conquest, 283.

pp. 117–118: Meteorologists were purged . . . : Ibid., 295.

p. 118: Stalin purged the other Soviet Republics . . . : Ibid., 233.

p. 118: The government of Ukraine was replaced . . . : Ibid., 227.

p. 118: "Better too far . . . sorting out": Montefiore, 229.

p. 118: In July 1937, Stalin ordered arrest quotas . . . : Ibid., 228; but cf. Fitzpatrick, 127, and Service, *Stalin*, 350–351, which each supply slightly different quotas.

p. 118: Before long, half the USSR's urban population . . . : Conquest, 289.

p. 118: To conceal the unimaginable reach of the purges . . . : Service, *Stalin*, 355.

pp. 118–119: "Everything that divides . . . millennium' ": Fueloep-Miller, 2.

p. 119: "Son denounced father . . . electrolysis' ": Volkov, *Testimony*, 267.

p. 119: One boy who supposedly denounced . . . : Service, *History*, 245. The story of this boy, Pavel Morozov, was almost certainly fabricated.

p. 119: "Look what those enemies . . . *fathers*": Fitzpatrick, 213.

pp. 119–120: "The nausea rises . . . the dead": Garros and Korenevskaya, 352.

p. 120: The final touch of ghastly cruelty . . . : Montefiore, 198.

p. 120: They played pranks on one another . . . : Ibid, 528.

p. 120: "I am a victim . . . dream": Ibid., 273.

p. 120: "Here's to life not getting any 'merrier'": Weinstein, 12:50.

p. 120: One day Shostakovich went to visit a friend . . . : Wilson, 304.

pp. 120–121: As he watched people vanish . . . : MacDonald, 105. Maxim Shostakovich recalls this detail during the period of the 1948 denunciations, too (MacDonald, 32). Cf. Wilson, 183. It's not impossible that the story has been transferred from the one period of denunciation to the other — though it is also not impossible that Shostakovich took these precautions in both periods.

p. 121: Tukhachevsky was a brilliant military thinker . . . : Alexandrov, 73.

p. 121: He also tried to prepare the Red Army technologically . . . : Overy, 9.

p. 121: "What the hell do we need . . . horse-drawn gun": Montefiore, 332.

p. 122: "Tukhachevsky had done nothing . . . justify his arrest": Jones, 62; cf. Watt, especially pp. 60–61.

p. 122: In France, there lived a Russian refugee named Skoblin . . . : This account is based on Conquest, 197–205; Alexandrov, passim; and Watt, 57.

p. 122: They usually worked as sandwich-board men . . . : Alexandrov, 124.

p. 123: Through the staged capture of a spy . . . : Ibid., 107.

p. 123: It seems likely that Stalin knew perfectly well . . . : Conquest, 199.

p. 123: On May 10, 1937, Tukhachevsky received word . . . : Ibid., 193.

pp. 123–124: On May 20, Marshal Tukhachevsky . . . : The precise accounts of Tukhachevsky's arrest vary. I have narrated Alexandrov's, 163. See also Conquest, 199–200.

p. 125: "At the halt . . . supplies": This dialogue is taken from Alexandrov, 163. It should be noted that his dialogue is often speculative.

p. 125: one who had committed suicide: Yan Gamarnik. Conquest, 200–201.

p. 125: Tukhachevsky was allowed to see his wife . . . : Conquest, 200; Montefiore, 223.

p. 125: Shostakovich got an order to meet . . . : This account was supposedly given by Shostakovich to Venyamin Basner (Wilson, 123–125). Basner repeated the story in the documentary *The War Symphonies* (Weinstein, at 23:35), and again in conversation with Maxim Shostakovich (Ardov, 66–68), each time with slightly different details. Solomon Volkov claimed that Shostakovich had also told the story to him, although he did not include it in *Testimony* (Brooke, 407). Ian MacDonald offers some interesting skepticism about the event and Basner's narration of it in " 'You Must Remember!': Shostakovich's alleged interrogation by the NKVD in 1937," http://www.siue.edu /~aho/musov/basner/basner.html (accessed May 24, 2013).

p. 126: "Think harder . . . already": Ardov, 67.

p. 127: "I understood this was the end . . . wouldn't be back": This is from Basner's "word for word" account given to the BBC, quoted in MacDonald's article cited above.

p. 127: On Monday, he took his suitcase . . . : This detail is from Ardov, 67; it differs slightly from Basner's account in Wilson, 125. I have tried to dovetail the two versions.

p. 127: Shostakovich explained he was there to see an investigator called Zakovsky . . . : Basner gives this name in *The War Symphonies* (Weinstein), but note that in Meyer's biography, the name is Zakrevsky (194–195), and in Wilson's version of Basner's account, it is Zanchevsky (125). There was indeed an NKVD officer named Zakovsky in Leningrad who was liquidated at around this time.

p. 127: Tukhachevsky confessed to being an agent . . . : For excerpts of his supposed testimony, see Main, 166 and passim — some of which is clearly Tukhachevsky's real (and quite astute) reading of the international military situation of the time, altered sloppily to prove treasonous intent.

p. 127: He claimed he had cooked up . . . : Main, 166.

p. 127: All of these details were specially tailored by Stalin . . . : Conquest, 195.

p. 128: "I feel I'm dreaming": Montefiore, 225; cf. Conquest, 203.

p. 128: He was scolded for wasting time and money . . . : Conquest, 202–203.

p. 128: "Long live the Party! Long live Stalin!": Ibid., 203.

p. 128: After Tukhachevsky's death, most of his family . . . : Ibid., 204–205.

p. 128: "Tomorrow I'll be put in the same place": Montefiore, 225.

p. 129: "The spies Tukhachevsky . . . will of the people": Garros and Korenevskaya, 29.

p. 129: "It was a terrible blow . . . how bad I felt": Volkov, *Testimony*, 116.

p. 129: "I have known Tukhachevsky . . . on this subject": Brooke, 408.

p. 129: Once Marshal Tukhachevsky was dead . . . : Conquest, 205.

p. 129: The purges hit the tank units . . . : Ibid., 208.

p. 129: In just a few months, the purge liquidated . . . : Alexandrov, 177–178; cf. Conquest, 450.

p. 129: Ninety percent of the generals . . . : Conquest, 450.

p. 130: Shostakovich's acquaintance and neighbor Lyubov Shaporina . . . : Entry for October 22, 1937, Garros and Korenevskaya, 353.

p. 130: on the piano for a musicologist . . . : The musicologist was Nikolai Zhilyaev. See Wilson, 121–123. And note the interesting discrepancies in the story of Zhilyaev's arrest: Fay, *Life*, 99; Volkov, *Testimony*, 121.

p. 132: At the beginning of the fall . . . : There are conflicting reports about when Shostakovich completed the score. See Fay, *Life*, 99.

p. 132: "You don't want to take the mask off . . . carnival begins": Garros and Korenevskaya, 37.

p. 133: "The significance was apparent . . . at stake": Fay, *Life*, 99.

p. 133: "You know . . . I'm afraid of everything": Garros and Korenevskaya, 356.

p. 133: "I wake up in the morning . . . parts unknown": Ibid., 357.

p. 133: "Until this day . . . unhesitatingly": Wilson, 139.

p. 133: "Tiny little fishie . . . how you felt": Volkov, *Testimony*, 266. Though

Shostakovich could not have known it, the absurdist poet and children's book author who wrote that verse, Nikolai Oleinikov, would be executed only three nights later. See Ostashevsky, xx.

p. 133: a stunned, appalled hush: One example occurs at the end of the first movement.

p. 134: "Even before the war . . . suffocated us": Volkov, *Testimony*, 135.

p. 135: "The music had a sort of electrical force": As remembered by A. N. Glumov, quoted in Wilson, 126.

p. 135: "The whole audience leapt . . . close to tears": Garros and Korenevskaya, 356.

p. 135: "A thunderous ovation . . . creator of this work": Wilson, 126.

p. 135: The applause would not stop . . . : Ibid., 134.

p. 135: They whisked him away: Fay, *Life*, 100.

p. 135: The next day, a conductor and friend . . . : Wilson, 134–139.

p. 137: "Unhealthy instances . . . a bad turn": Fay, *Life*, 104.

p. 137: "made a constant stream . . . scandalously fabricated": Wilson, 135.

p. 137: "And in the meantime . . . from its audiences": Ibid.

p. 138: "It's very difficult to speak . . . without it": Viktor Shklovsky, *A Hunt for Optimism* [1931], trans. Shushan Avagyan (Champaign, IL: Dalkey Archive, 2012), 53.

p. 138: "I saw man . . . optimistic note": Sollertinskys, 83.

p. 138: "one that particularly . . . just criticism'": Fanning, *Studies*, 33n.

p. 138: Soviet literature and cinema . . . : Fitzpatrick, 76.

p. 139: Shostakovich had just spent years . . . : *The Counterplan* and the Maxim trilogy. For a discussion of this archetype in these films, see Emma Widdis, *Visions of a New Land: Soviet Film from the Revolution to the Second World War* (New Haven, CT: Yale University Press, 2003), 144–146.

p. 139: "He described his music . . . rest of his life": Vishnevskaya, 212.

p. 139: "A work of astonishing strength . . . tragic force": Fanning, *Studies*, 34.

p. 139: "breaks in upon the symphony . . . severe and threatening": Ibid., 38. Several listeners felt that the ambivalence of the ending was not calculated, but a halfhearted attempt at jollity that failed. Composer Nikolai Miaskovsky, for example, wrote to Prokofiev: "The symphony fascinated me regardless of the somewhat hollow ending" (Tassie, 207).

p. 139: "Just think . . . him for it": Volkov, *Stalin*, 156.

p. 140: "I think that it is clear . . . hear that": Volkov, *Testimony*, 183.

p. 140: Solomon Volkov was never able to produce . . . : See Brown, 282n. Brown's book contains several essays weighing the authority and authenticity of Volkov's *Testimony*.

p. 141: On May 10, 1938, Nina Shostakovich . . . : Fay, *Life*, 109.

p. 142: "I would call it 'spring-like'": Ibid., 112.

p. 142: He started it the month Maxim was born . . . : Lesser, 31.

p. 142: he found his plans for a new opera interrupted . . . : Anatoly Mariengof's libretto based on Tolstoy's *Resurrection*, banned on May 10, 1941 (Fay, *Life*, 118).

p. 142: they granted him an award . . . : In 1940, for the Maxim trilogy (Fay, *World*, 48).

p. 142: "not working out": Ibid., 276.

p. 142: "No matter how many . . . never criticized anyone": Bartlett, 168.

p. 142: those who knew him well could tell . . . : Fay, *World*, 280.

p. 142: he supported several of his students . . . : See Fanning, "Shostakovich and His Pupils," in Fay, *World*, 275ff.

p. 143: they played drunk soccer in his living room: Fay, *World*, 281.

p. 143: Shostakovich still loved soccer . . . : Sollertinskys, 94.

p. 143: "He said the stadium . . . all the time": Quoted in *The Red Baton [Notes Interdites]: Scenes from the Musical Life of Soviet Russia*, dir. Bruno Monsaingeon (Idéale Audience/ARTE France, 2003).

p. 143: Once, when Nina was away . . . : In the interest of historical accuracy, I should point out that Glikman (xxix) claims it was the Zenith team, while the Sollertinskys claim it was Dynamo (94). Though Dynamo makes more sense, as it was supposedly the composer's favorite team, Glikman was actually there.

p. 143: "When the last guest . . . top of the stands'": Glikman, xxix.

p. 143: "could cure elephants": Glikman, 14; Wilson, 4.

p. 143: The composer's daily schedule . . . : Khentova, *Mire*, 81–84.

pp. 143–146: "If it isn't singing . . . sits quietly": Siegmeister, 622.

p. 145: once even signed up to train as a referee: Sollertinskys, 94.

p. 146: When Shostakovich finished a piece . . . : Khentova, *Mire*, 81.

p. 146: "Sergei Sergeich, tra-tra-tra . . .": Ardov, 26 and 28.

p. 146: Once, little Maxim thought it would be funny . . . : Sollertinskys, 43–44.

p. 146: "with a kind of abnormal . . . befall them": Vishnevskaya, 223.

p. 146: "The hatchet job . . . been put on him": Ibid., 225.

p. 146: "The Fifth Symphony was a turning point . . . compositions": Ibid., 212.

p. 147: "It seemed to you that he is . . . a catastrophe": Fay, *Life*, 121.

p. 147: Roughly eight million people . . . : Conquest, 485–486.

p. 148: "Anybody who breathes . . . different form with them": Nadezhda Mandelstam, 297.

p. 148: To get away from it all . . . : Wilson, 144–145.

PART TWO

FRIENDSHIP

p. 151: Recent DNA tests suggest . . . : http://www.telegraph.co.uk/history /world-war-two/7961211/Hitler-had-Jewish-and-African-roots-DNA-tests-show.html.

p. 151: "We National Socialists . . . this earth": A. Roberts, 144.

p. 152: During the show trials of the Great Terror . . . : Simmons and Perlina, 95.

p. 152: "Did you hear what happened . . . some skill": Montefiore, 131.

p. 152: "Everything within the state . . . against the state": Applebaum, xxi.

p. 153: Cautiously, Stalin suggested to the French . . . : Overy, 44; G. Roberts, 30.

p. 153: "little Hitler striding across Europe . . . witness to it all": Garros and Korenevskaya, 367.

p. 153: In the summer of 1939, Stalin met . . . : Service, *History*, 255.

p. 154: As if to underline the fact . . . : Montefiore, 307–309.

p. 155: About a week later, the Germans sent . . . : Montefiore, 310; G.E.R. Gedye, "Arrives by Plane," *New York Times*, August 24, 1939.

p. 155: "Of course it's all a game . . . who tricked him": Montefiore, 312.

p. 155: As historians have pointed out, there was some irony . . . : G. Roberts, 43.

p. 156: "All the isms have become wasms": A. Roberts, 10.

p. 156: It had been filmed at great expense . . . : Jones, 263; Robinson, 352.

p. 156: Stalin had loved the movie . . . : Robinson, 357.

p. 157: "The war machine rolled down . . . swallowed up": Hastings, 75.

p. 157: "Stalin was in a great agitation . . . thrash them?'": Ibid., 73.

p. 157: "What has gone wrong . . . us from war": G.E.R. Gedye, "Soviet 'Neutrality' Stressed in Move," *New York Times*, September 18, 1939.

p. 159: "The Führer estimates the operation . . . a pack of cards": Jones, 14.

p. 159: Hitler therefore decided that he would launch . . . : Overy, 94.

p. 159: At dinners, he boasted about his future conquests . . . : Hastings, 146.

p. 159: He called the coming assault on the Soviet Union . . . : Overy, 84.

p. 159: "The purpose of the Russian campaign . . . millions": A. Roberts, 165.

p. 159: In the end, they would not fall far short . . . : Hastings, 152.

p. 160: German newspapers began to run sections . . . : Salisbury, 63.

p. 160: "On the basis of information . . . added to them": Nelson, 89.

p. 160: Secret reports from pro-Soviet spies . . . : This list is from Pleshakov, 86–87.

p. 160: "There's this bastard who's set up . . . believe him too": Montefiore, 353.

p. 160: "folder of dubious and misleading reports": Pleshakov, 86–87.

p. 162: Stalin ignored the warnings . . . : Salisbury, 63.

p. 162: Several loosely connected circles of spies . . . : Nelson, 186, 189.

p. 162: Full plans had already been drawn up . . . : Overy, 132; Reid, 20.

p. 162: "This is not a 'source' but a disinformer": G. Roberts, 67.

p. 162: followed it up with a rude comment . . . : Nelson, 204.

p. 162: The Soviet Ambassador immediately picked up . . . : Nelson, 210.

p. 162: "Stalin and his people . . . snake": Reid, 18.

p. 162: Historians have struggled to understand how Stalin . . . : Historians disagree quite broadly on how deluded, how deceived, and how surprised Stalin actually was. Geoffrey Roberts (64–71) and Constantine Pleshakov (13–14 and passim), for example, are more generous in their assessment of his strategic thinking; others such as Robert Service (*Stalin*, 411–412) and Harrison Salisbury (e.g., 67–81) emphasize the profound depth of his miscalculation.

p. 163: Stalin was entertaining the idea of his own attack on Germany . . . : His foreign minister, Vyacheslav Molotov, remembered 1943 as the planned time for attack (Service, *Stalin*, 406). As mentioned above, this question of Stalin's precise plan is hotly debated.

p. 163: 70 percent of the higher-ranking officers . . . : Pleshakov, 66.

p. 163: "Not to trust anybody . . . was Adolf Hitler": A. Roberts, 539.

p. 163: Shostakovich and his family went on vacation . . . : Sollertinskys, 97.

p. 163: German reconnaissance planes were flying daily . . . : Hastings, 141.

p. 164: "Zhukov and I think . . . planes down": Pleshakov, 89–90.

p. 164: One of the Nazi planes . . . : Ibid., 180.

p. 164: "Please do not worry . . . in the West": Ibid., 90.

p. 164: On June 11, the NKVD discovered . . . : Ibid., 87.

p. 164: "I repeat: Nine armies . . . June 22": Salisbury, 73.

p. 164: At the same time, German ships began to disappear . . . : Ibid., 17.

p. 165: On June 21, the secret police reported . . . : A. Roberts, 155.

p. 165: The commander of the Soviet Third Army reported . . . : Pleshakov, 99.

p. 165: A vast army of Germans, Croats, Finns, Romanians . . . : These numbers vary slightly, according to account. See Montefiore, 359; Overy, 72; Hastings, 137, 141; and A. Roberts, 155–156.

p. 165: "deserter-informant": Montefiore, 358; Alexandrov, 185. Somewhat confusingly, there are similar stories about different deserters; their fates are identical. Cf. Salisbury, 15.

p. 165: "your wise prophecy . . . in 1941": Service, *History*, 260.

p. 165: Regardless, many did not even receive . . . : Pleshakov, 5, 162.

p. 166: "Since I struggled . . . mental agonies": Brinkley and Rubel, 212.

p. 166: General Zhukov and Defense Minister Timoshenko were not so certain . . . : Pleshakov, 5.

p. 166: "discuss important matters": Hastings, 137.

BARBAROSSA

p. 167: Dmitri Shostakovich had clear plans for the day of June 22 . . . : There is a minor discrepancy about the order of events and when exactly Shostakovich heard the news of the German invasion. I follow Fay (*Life*, 122) and Seroff (236) in placing him on the street with Glikman when they heard Molotov's announcement. Volkov (*Stalin*, 170) claims he was at the Conservatory. The teams at the soccer doubleheader are faithfully recorded by the Sollertinskys (97).

p. 167: eighteen Ju 88 bombers . . . : Forczyk, *Leningrad*, 41.

p. 168: Out in the bay, on a Russian pleasure ship . . . : Salisbury, 82.

p. 168: At the same time, up and down the whole Soviet border . . . : Pleshakov, 162.

p. 168: "Yes, yes. We are being bombed . . . staff headquarters": Salisbury, 37.

p. 168: Within a few short minutes of Operation Barbarossa's . . . : Pleshakov, 126.

p. 168: Within a few hours, the Luftwaffe had blasted . . . : Overy, 76; A. Roberts, 156.

p. 168: The Western Front's air force commander . . . : Pleshakov, 126.

p. 169: "You must be insane . . . signal in code?": A. Roberts, 155.

p. 169: At the Kremlin, General Zhukov and Comrade Timoshenko . . . : Montefiore, 364.

pp. 169–170: General Zhukov called Stalin's country house . . . "summon the Politburo": The dialogue is recounted in Montefiore, 363–365, and Pleshakov, 5–6.

p. 170: Stalin still believed it might be possible to avert war . . . : The details given here are from Pleshakov, 6–7.

pp. 170–172: "Men and women, citizens of the Soviet Union . . . Victory will be ours": Amery and Curran, 193.

pp. 170–172: The commissar spoke anxiously . . . : Hastings, 146; Skrjabina, 4.

p. 172: Chaos broke out in the streets . . . : Skrjabina, 4.

p. 172: Leningraders were so intent on responding . . . : Salisbury, 141.

p. 172: The city government was bewildered . . . : To clarify the timeline of Shostakovich's and Fleishman's attempts to join the People's Volunteers, which has (understandably) been a point of confusion: on June 22, the first day of the invasion, Shostakovich and Fleishman supposedly went to sign up for military service (as Shostakovich attested—e.g., Siegmeister, 242). They were among the horde who stated their willingness to serve in any capacity, but at that point were *not* signing up specifically for the People's Volunteers, a quasi-military force that did not yet exist as an organization. Leningrad Party leader Andrei Zhdanov, seeing the hundreds of thousands of willing conscripts in the city, set up the first branch of the People's Volunteers a few days later; the call for members went out on June 30 (Salisbury, 146–147, 174). Shostakovich may have tried to enlist in the Red Army on the 22nd, as he later suggested in a somewhat scrambled account (Martynov, 102–103). We know that he tried again to volunteer for service on July 2 (Fay, *Life*, 123), which would have been his attempt specifically to sign up for the People's Volunteers. In between Shostakovich's two attempts to present himself for military service, he was swept up in the general levy of civilians working on local defense efforts. The People's Volunteers, having made spectacular sacrifices near the Luga Line in August, were absorbed into the Red Army in late September 1941, a few days after Fleishman's death (Reid, 88).

p. 172: "Until now I have known . . . destruction": Vulliamy, 1, though this is taken from Shostakovich's People's Volunteers application at the beginning of July (Salisbury, 174–175).

p. 172: He and one of his students . . . : The story of Shostakovich's attempted conscription is from Sollertinskys, 98; Seroff, 236.

p. 172: "The population . . . for Mother Russia": Gleason, 398.

pp. 172–175: "Very few families . . . country was another": Reid, 74.

p. 175: As people all over Leningrad . . . : Writer Lidiya Ginzburg has talked about how this desire to put aside the egotism of self and join the masses was particularly seductive to intellectuals of the period (Ginzburg, 91).

p. 175: "sitting on a tall trunk . . . smile irritates me": Skrjabina, 5.

p. 175: The branches of the State Savings Bank . . . : Salisbury, 127.

pp. 175–176: "People were writing . . . on the sills": The conditions at the recruitment centers on the first couple of days of the invasion are recorded in Adamovich and Granin, 219.

p. 176: When they got up to the front of the line . . . : The city government took several days to organize the Volunteers and called up their first three divisions between July 4 and 18 (Reid, 76).

p. 176: "You will be called when required": Seroff, 236.

p. 176: It is likely, however, that his application . . . : Blokker and Dearling, 29.

p. 176: "a mighty weapon which could strike the enemy": Tomoff, 80.

p. 176: On the first day of Operation Barbarossa . . . : Grigoryev and Platek, 86.

p. 176: Thus began a national campaign . . . : Details of this effort can be found in Tomoff, 81.

p. 177: "Everything for the front, everything for victory": Hakobian, 183.

THE APPROACH

p. 178: The Russian fighter planes and bombers . . . : Overy, 90; Pleshakov, 112–113.

p. 179: The Red Army's tanks were in no better situation . . . : Montefiore, 359; Jones, 86.

p. 179: The whole of the Soviet Tenth Army simply disappeared . . . : Pleshakov, 130.

p. 179: German Army Group North was making sickening progress . . . : Jones, 23–24.

p. 179: "spontaneous self-cleansing action": Ibid., 23.

p. 180: Their Panzer divisions were already a hundred miles . . . : Ibid., 20–21.

p. 180: "The war against these subhuman beings . . . German soldier": Hastings, 145.

p. 180: "The troops must be aware . . . conquered territories": Nelson, 212.

p. 182: "This war with Russia . . . Russian-Bolshevik system": Jones, 24.

p. 182: On June 27, Leningrad's city council announced . . . : Ibid., 83.

pp. 182–183: "I thought of Tukhachevsky when I dug trenches . . . start from scratch": Volkov, *Testimony,* 103. Note that Shostakovich's assessment of the tank situation (if these are indeed Shostakovich's words) is not precisely accurate. The Soviet Union did not lack for tanks. They in fact had more tanks, in terms of sheer numbers, than the rest of the world's armies combined. The problem was, instead, the quality of the tanks, their deployment, and their supply of fuel and ammunition (A. Roberts, 139).

p. 183: When Shostakovich was not knee-deep in mud . . . : Fay, *Life,* 124.

p. 184: When the Nazis captured the town . . . : Overy, 123.

p. 184: "The Nazi barbarians seek . . . destroying it": D. D. Shostakovich, "Nazi Desecration of Russian Cultural Monuments," *VOKS Bulletin* no. 3/4 (Spring 1942), 83. As with most of the composer's public utterances, we have no particular proof that this article was actually written by him.

p. 184: One of the purposes of the music troupes . . . : Tomoff, 78.

p.184: Leningrad's musical corps staged . . . : Ibid., 76.

p. 184: "I visited front-line units . . . real heroes": Siegmeister, 243. It is, of course, impossible to say whether these words are actually his, as they appeared in a newspaper article.

p. 184: Eighty percent of the buildings in the city . . . : Pleshakov, 233.

p. 184: "Even the parks were in flames": Ibid., 144.

p. 184: For a few days, the Red Army held up . . . : Ibid., 212.

p. 186: The Nazis took four hundred thousand prisoners: Montefiore, 372; cf. Overy, 86.

p. 186: They told him the truth at risk to their lives . . . : Pleshakov, 10, 12. He notes that it would take the Russians three hard-fought years to reclaim the territory lost in the first ten days of the German invasion.

p. 186: Slowly, he walked out of the room . . . : This anecdote varies in translation and in several of its details. See Amery and Curran, 78; Pleshakov, 218; A. Roberts, 157; Montefiore, 374.

THE FIRST MOVEMENT

p. 187: On July 2, he went again to try to enlist: Fay, *Life,* 123.

p. 187: His ditchdigging lasted for about a week . . . : The chronology of these activities is not exact. They are summarized under "July" in Sofia Khentova's "Timeline" at the conclusion of *Shostakovich in the Years of the Great Patriotic War [Voynï].* He himself wrote many articles about this period (or signed them after they were passed to him by appointed propagandists), but he rarely cited specific dates.

p. 187: His family was still off at a cottage . . . : Siegmeister, 243; Martynov, 103.

p. 187: The Leningrad City Council had created . . . : Salisbury, 144.

p. 188: there were no Luftwaffe air raids during the month of July . . . : Reid, 42.

p. 188: In the streets, however, feverish preparation . . . : Adamovich and Granin, 237.

p. 189: "We'll come back for you" . . . conceal it: Reid, 119.

p. 189: "It is with a feeling of admiration . . . Leningrad's defenses": Seroff, 238.

p. 189: The golden spires now were painted a camouflage gray . . . : Salisbury, 145.

p. 191: Then, like grazing beasts, barrage balloons . . . : The barrage balloons were in place by mid-July. Citizens remarked on their striking appearance (Reid, 54–55; Salisbury, 168–169).

p. 191: "Then you lead us, Vyacheslav! We will follow": Accounts of this incident can be found in Pleshakov, 220; Overy, 79; Montefiore, 376; Service, *Stalin,* 415.

p. 193: He returned to the Kremlin . . . : On July 10, 1941 (Service, *Stalin,* 415).

p. 193: "Comrades! Citizens! . . . my friends": Ibid., 449; Pleshakov, 260; Reid, 39–40.

p. 193: He had never before called his people his family . . . : Adamovich and Granin, 242.

p. 194: He warned his citizens that this was not an ordinary war . . . : Overy, 79.

p. 194: "All the strength of the people . . . victory". . . Moscow by August: Hastings, 145.

p. 194: It could not have been long into July . . . : They launched their offensive into Karelia on July 10, 1941 (Forczyk, *Leningrad,* 29).

p. 194: Wary of the risk, Shostakovich fetched his family . . . : Ardov, 15.

p. 194: They all drove back to the apartment in Leningrad . . . : L. Mikheeva, *Zhizn Dmitriya Shostakovicha* [The Life of Dmitri Shostakovich] (Moscow: Terra, 1997), 221; Sollertinskys, 98.

p. 196: For example, the Germans took Pskov . . . : Reid, 44. Pleshakov (246) puts the conquest of Pskov even earlier, on July 2.

p. 196: Then, ominously, they stopped mentioning Pskov . . . : Reid, 45.

p. 196: "We're winning, but the Germans are gaining ground": Ibid., 51.

p. 196: the city government was starting to demand . . . : Salisbury, 143.

p. 197: "insufficient warehouse space": Jones, 76; Reid, 161–162. Cf. Hastings, 165.

p. 197: "the patter of iron rats . . . rat catcher": Nicolas Slonimsky, "Dmitri Dmitrievitch Shostakovich," *Musical Quarterly* 28, no. 4 (October 1942): 435.

p. 197: The Leningrad city government was daily shipping . . . : Simmons and Perlina, xii.

p. 198: They stumbled out of cattle cars into scenes . . . : Salisbury, 179.

p. 198: In just the first few days of fighting, the Eighth Panzer division . . . : Reid, 59.

p. 198: The delay from early July until roughly August 8 . . . : Salisbury, 190.

p. 198: Military resistance along the Luga Line . . . : Reid, 59.

p. 200: As the Germans crawled closer . . . : Ibid., 52.

p. 200: "One can judge the time . . . smile amongst them": Inber, 9.

p. 200: The workers had little reason . . . : Reid, 96.

p. 200: Even more ominous than the evacuations . . . : Ibid., 96–97.

p. 202: "For a long time my husband . . . leaving Leningrad": Siegmeister, 623.

p. 202: "viewed citizens' refusal . . . people to remain": Reid, 103.

p. 202: On August 10, the city government announced . . . : Jones, 96.

p. 202: Shostakovich kept working on the new symphony . . . : I. Rudenko, "Razgovor s kompozitorum" [Conversation with a Composer], *Komsomolskaya Pravda,* June 26, 1973, p. 4.

p. 203: "It was a steel-gray . . . savagery was raging": Glikman, xxxiv.

p. 203: Late in the summer of 1941, the German propaganda ministry . . . : Howard K. Smith, "Valhalla in Transition," in *Reporting World War II, Part One: American Journalism 1938–1944,* ed. Samuel Hynes and others (New York: Library of America, 1995), 223.

p. 203: We don't know, however, if Shostakovich knew . . . : Volkov, *Testimony,* xxxiv; Mishra, 136–138; MacDonald, 159.

p. 203: "They often beg their father . . . quiet as mice, all ears": Seroff, 240.

pp. 203–204: "We were both extremely agitated . . . piece will be": Glikman, xxxiv.

p. 204: "By chance, you might . . . in the commercial stores": Skrjabina, 23.

pp. 204–206: "Now we realize that we were travelling . . . a remote area": Jones, 97.

p. 206: "We worked out where everybody . . . towards us": Adamovich and Granin, 246.

p. 206: "There are Nazi paratroopers ahead": Jones, 98.

p. 206: The adult chaperones scrambled . . . : Reid, 99–100; Jones, 97–100.

p. 206: "Just imagine . . . hungry and exhausted": Adamovich and Granin, 246.

p. 206: "The children had started to board the train . . . It was dreadful": Jones, 98.

p. 206: "Suddenly, I heard a terrible cry . . . a giant hand": Jones, 99.

p. 206: "The nursery school teacher . . . immediately explode": Adamovich and Granin, 99.

p. 208: "What rubbish . . . what he was bombing": Ibid., 247.

p. 208: "A plane circled . . . totally impassive": Jones, 99.

p. 208: "When they began shelling the coaches . . . blankets over them": Adamovich and Granin, 249. There appears to be some understandable confusion about whether this testimony (by Alexandra Arsenyeva) applies to the same attack at Lychkovo or a subsequent one at Mga. See Jones, 99; Reid, 99. Arsenyeva herself mentions Mga, but the circumstances resemble Lychkovo.

p. 208: "When I got back to Leningrad . . . never happened": Jones, 100.

p. 209: Shostakovich's friend Ivan Sollertinsky . . . : MacDonald, 152.

p. 209: "Dear Ivan . . . two days": Sollertinskys, 100.

p. 210: This was the last train to make it out of Leningrad: There are several dates cited for the shutting down of Mga, presumably due to the fact that the battle for the town lasted for five days. See Jones, 101–102; Reid, 104; Forczyk, *Leningrad*, 30.

p. 210: About 636,000 people in all had been evacuated . . . : Reid, 95–96.

p. 210: "Leningrad is surrounded . . . mousetrap": Skrjabina, 23.

THE SECOND MOVEMENT

p. 211: "I wrote my Seventh Symphony, the *Leningrad* . . . engrave it in music": Fay, *Life*, 124; cf. Volkov, *Testimony*, 154.

p. 212: Shostakovich, toiling away at his symphony . . . : Glikman, 6; Shostakovich, *Facsimile*, 7; Shostakovich, *Works*, vol. 7, 258.

p. 212: Though the Soviets did not know it yet . . . : Salisbury, 373.

p. 212: People looked up; their windowpanes . . . : Adamovich and Granin, 297.

p. 213: "It has made quite an impression . . . destroyed houses": Skrjabina, 25.

p. 213: An even more devastating Luftwaffe assault was to arrive two days later: On September 8, lasting into the morning of the ninth. There is considerable confusion about the date of the destruction of the Bedayev warehouses; as Adamovich and Granin point out (44), there is a tendency among survivors to smear together two air raids: one on September 6 (which was the first airborne assault on Leningrad) and one on the eighth (which destroyed the warehouses and which is, to add confusion, sometimes dated to the ninth). These mistakes are common. Skrjabina, for example, who was supposedly writing her diary day-by-day, nonetheless records the September 8 bombing of the Bedayev warehouses as if it happened on September 12 (27), an odd mistake that suggests she may have constructed some of the "diary" from memory.

p. 213: On September 8, Shostakovich began work . . . : Shostakovich, *Works*, vol. 7, 259–260.

pp. 213–214: "I looked out the window . . . but a massive onslaught": Adamovich and Granin, 43; cf. 44.

p. 214: Twenty-seven German Ju 88 bombers . . . : Forczyk, *Leningrad,* 42; Salisbury, 291.

p. 214: "They flew at low altitude . . . rising higher and higher": Jones, 44.

p. 214: "High in the sky . . . that it was fire": Simmons and Perlina, 23.

p. 214: The Leningrad city bosses had decided . . . : Reid, 140; Jones, 43.

p. 215: "[Leningrad Party bosses] Voroshilov and Zhdanov . . . city to famine": Jones, 79.

p. 215: "It was an immense spectacle of stunning beauty": Simmons, 23.

p. 215: At around ten thirty that evening . . . : Reid, 140.

p. 215: "Whole new squadrons flew over us . . . Sheer hell": Skrjabina, 26.

pp. 215–216: "We were all deafened . . . crying with fear": Adamovich and Granin, 284.

p. 216: "Down there were many people . . . is forgotten": Skrjabina, 26.

p. 216: "Everyone thinks . . . several times a day": Reid, 143.

p. 216: "A few scenes have etched . . . and a lamp": Skrjabina, 26.

p. 216: Another lone wall stood with its house . . . : Adamovich and Granin, 286.

p. 218: The streets . . . smelled of ham and butter: Inber, 17; Skrjabina, 27.

p. 218: "It is not worth risking the lives . . . a single German soldier": Hastings, 166; cf. Jones, 40, 43.

p. 218: "We shall not trouble ourselves . . . scientific method": Adamovich and Granin, 40.

p. 218: "to spare the troops . . . on civilians": Jones, 128.

p. 219: "It is the task of the artillery . . . civilians themselves": Ibid., 129.

p. 219: "Even then a large part . . . of our eyes": Reid, 136.

p. 219: By mid-September, after the destruction . . . : Ibid., 167.

p. 222: Their ration cards were death sentences . . . : Ibid., 169.

p. 222: "didn't believe that the inhabitants . . . From starvation": Ginzburg, 59.

p. 222: The Nazis shelled the city every day . . . : Overy, 106.

p. 222: "This way . . . morale of the Leningraders": Jones, 3.

p. 223: "Even during air raids . . . into the shelter": Seroff, 239.

p. 223: When Shostakovich got up from his desk . . . : M. Dolinsky and S. Chertok, "The Heroic Orchestral Act," *Sovetskaya Kultura,* January 26, 1964.

p. 223: All night the building burned . . . : Sollertinskys, 100.

THE THIRD MOVEMENT

p. 224: "What are our tanks doing in this area . . . wooden dummies": Jones, 113.

p. 224: Zhukov was stunned . . . : The use of decoys, though bizarre sounding, was occasionally quite a successful strategy — most famously in Operation Fortitude and the D-day invasion of Normandy, in 1944.

p. 225: "Get another hundred . . . tomorrow myself": Salisbury, 324.

p. 225: "You have yourself to blame . . . generals killed": Jones, 80.

p. 225: Voroshilov picked up the platter . . . : Hastings, 165.

p. 226: The air force commander at the time . . . : Montefiore, 536.

p. 226: "because you're making us fly in coffins!": Ibid., 345.

p. 226: General Zhukov was reorganizing the city's defenses . . . : Forczyk, *Leningrad,* 32; cf. Hastings, 166.

p. 227: This protocol, originally issued in Leningrad . . . : Hastings, 148.

p. 227: This was simply an extension of Order No. 270 . . . : G. Roberts, 98; Overy, 80–81; Service, *History,* 264.

p. 227: He threw Red Army units against the Germans . . . : Forczyk, *Leningrad,* 33; for a more complete discussion of the strategic situation, see Jones, 118–122.

p. 227: "It's time to assemble . . . banks of the Neva": Hastings, 166.

p. 227: Then the German guns would start roaring . . . : Jones, 122.

p. 227: Hitler released Secret Directive No. 1a 1601/41 . . . : Released on September 22, 1941. Amery and Curran, 197; Adamovich and Granin, 28.

p. 228: "pulverized brick and melting iron": Vishnevskaya, 26.

p. 229: "You begin to realize with astonishment . . . like a waterfall": Ginzburg, 24.

p. 229: route to Radio House: At this point, Shostakovich and his family were living on Bolshaya Pushkarskaya Street (Khentova, *Mire,* 79), in the Petrograd Side. Radio House was located across the Neva, closer to the center of town, on Nevsky Prospect.

p. 230: The building was in some disarray . . . : Fadeyev, 27ff; cf. Salisbury, 460–461.

p. 230: Shostakovich's acquaintance poet Olga Berggolts . . . : Salisbury, 323.

pp. 230–232: "An hour ago I finished scoring . . . bound up with Leningrad": Transcript in Sollertinskys, 101.

p. 232: "I am moved . . . warms the heart": Inber, 25.

p. 232: The night of the broadcast, Shostakovich and his family . . . : Sollertinskys, 102–103.

p. 233: "[Shostakovich] told us . . . large form": Schwarz, 177.

p. 233: He had ideas for the third movement . . . : Shostakovich, *Facsimile,* 8.

FABLES, STORIES

p. 234: "that he had a piece of metal . . . be removed": Wang, 347.

p. 234: "in the temporal horn . . . cerebrospinal fluid": Ibid., 348.

pp. 234–235: "since the fragment . . . when composing": Ibid., 347.

p. 235: "After all, a German shell . . . produce more music": Ibid., 348.

p. 235: The Sovinform Bureau flooded the airwaves . . . : Morrison, 218.

p. 236: "Ivan Pupkin killed five Germans with a spoon": Reid, 45.

p. 236: "No firebombs . . . put one out": Lind, 15. Translation by Ellen Litman.

p. 236: A Conservatory official, Aron Ostrovsky . . . : Fay, *Life*, 123.

p. 236: We cannot really tell, given the swirl of contradictory accounts . . . : In one account, supposedly by Shostakovich (Lind, 14–18), he explicitly says he was living at the Conservatory and watching on the roof in September, during the blockade. Anecdotes by others, however, place him at his home by this time, and both his official Soviet biographer and the late head of the Shostakovich Family Archive presumed that he was barracked at the Conservatory primarily in the summer, at which time he was writing the first movement of the Seventh Symphony (Khentova, *Voynï*, "Timeline" for July 1941, unpaginated; Shostakovich, *Symphony no. 7*, 7). Until more reliable documentation is produced, it will be impossible to speak authoritatively about the specifics of his service.

p. 238: "The war became a terrible tragedy . . . Millions": Volkov, *Testimony*, 103.

p. 238: One of his soccer buddies claimed . . . : Sollertinskys, 99.

p. 238: One composer even claimed . . . : Volkov, *Stalin*, 178.

p. 238: "Morale is the big thing . . . enthusiastic": Bierman and Smith, 249.

p. 239: "He is a really courageous person . . . sense of belonging": Jones, 151.

p. 239: "Any violence which does not spring . . . outlook": Conquest, 446.

p. 239: "The reputation for horror . . . what it will": Overy, 73.

p. 240: In many of the Soviet satellite states . . . : Pleshakov, 172; Hastings, 143; Service, *History*, 276.

p. 240: Ukrainians and Cossacks came out of their villages . . . : Overy, 127; Service, *Stalin*, 418; Pleshakov, 237; A. Roberts, 162.

p. 240: No sooner had they moved in than they began . . . : Service, *History*, 287–288.

p. 242: "Can you imagine . . . my very own eyes": Wilson, 188.

pp. 242–243: "Sometimes I'd wander . . . its stern grandeur": Lind, 16. Translation by Ellen Litman.

p. 243: On September 19, the Luftwaffe launched . . . : Inber, 23, 205; Amery and Curran, 195.

p. 243: Gostiny Dvor burned quietly . . . : Salisbury, 298.

p. 243: "We're giving you a respite . . . the past twenty years": Simmons and Perlina, 24.

p. 244: On September 25, Dmitri Shostakovich turned thirty-five . . . : Sollertinskys, 103.

p. 245: "I kept working day and night . . . but I kept working": Martynov, 104.

p. 245: He was done with the third movement . . . : Glikman, 6.

p. 245: "I confess that I used . . . road open to me": Akhmatova, 570.

p. 245: Anna Akhmatova later claimed . . . : Ibid., 576n, 580n.

p. 245: Is this simply one of the stories people told . . . : See MacDonald, 273–274. Akhmatova claims that she departed Leningrad with the Seventh Symphony on her lap on October 1, 1941. If this were in any way corroborated, it would make sense, as it could mean she was evacuated with Shostakovich and might well have been handed the manuscript to hold. Unfortunately, Akhmatova scholars claim she was evacuated on September 29 (Akhmatova, 580n), a few days before Shostakovich.

p. 246: "This telephone is disconnected until the end of the war": Inber, 19.

p. 246: "Leningrad? . . . Winter Palace and the Hermitage": Salisbury, 341.

p. 246: But Comrade Kalinnikova was calling with good news . . . : Glikman, 3.

p. 246: Shostakovich made the arrangements . . . : Sollertinskys, 103.

p. 246: "beloved home town": Glikman, 3.

FLIGHT

p. 247: Shostakovich was startled . . . : Ardov, 16.

p. 247: Shostakovich apparently asked about the fate . . . : Fay, *Life*, 126.

p. 247: It was a small aircraft . . . : Ardov, 16.

p. 248: the Wehrmacht's lines . . . : Jones, 126–127.

p. 248: "Someone explained to me . . . our aeroplane": Ardov, 17.

p. 248: Behind them, the pilots dragged tree limbs . . . : Ibid.

p. 249: They even took Maxim and Galina to a toy store . . . : Ibid.

p. 249: Food, however, was still hard to come by . . . : Morrison, 220.

p. 249: Air raids on Moscow were frequent and devastating . . . : Overy, 97.

p. 249: To confuse bombers, the medieval walls of the Kremlin . . . : Montefiore, 395.

p. 249: Perhaps the most striking evacuee was the corpse . . . : Overy, 96.

p. 251: "Oh, Wright brothers . . . What have you wrought": Ardov, 17–18.

p. 251: On October 5, a Soviet Pe-2 . . . : Overy, 93; Forczyk, *Moscow*, 39–40.

p. 251: The Soviet general in the area did not know . . . : Forczyk, *Moscow*, 43.

pp. 251–252: "I thought I'd seen retreat . . . hundreds of meters wide": Hastings, 155.

p. 252: Stalin was bewildered by the German successes . . . : Forczyk, *Moscow*, 25; Hastings, 155.

p. 252: Ninety million Soviets . . . were now living . . . : Hastings, 155.

p. 252: "Comrade Stalin is not a traitor . . . been created": On October 3, 1941. Service, *History*, 263.

p. 252: Recently, his secret plans have come to light . . . : Adrian Blomfield, "Stalin Planned to Destroy Moscow if the Nazis Moved In," *The Telegraph*, December 5, 2008.

p. 254: Shostakovich's colleague composer Lev Knipper . . . : Beevor, loc. 2577.

p. 254: On October 11, Shostakovich went into the offices . . . : Brown, 159; Shostakovich, *Facsimile*, 8.

p. 254: "Shostakovich takes a monotonous . . . German Nazism": Brown, 159.

p. 255: "The situation around Moscow has deteriorated": Braithwaite, 245.

p. 255: Shostakovich and his family were told . . . : Fay (*Life*, 126) puts the date of his evacuation on October 15; Wilson (149) on October 16.

p. 255: *bolshoi drap:* G. Roberts, 108.

p. 255: "their rubber plants and chests of drawers": Braithwaite, 249.

p. 255: People blocked exits so the Party elite . . . : Ibid., 247–248.

p. 255: Government officials were destroying . . . : Montefiore, 395.

p. 255: "Black snow flew . . . the Apocalypse": Volkov, *Stalin*, 6–7.

p. 256: "Inside the station writers . . . Bolshoi Theatre": Wilson, 150.

p. 256: "He looked completely bereft . . . by their owners": Ibid.

p. 257: "Allow Shostakovich and his children to pass": Ibid.

p. 257: It was holding more than one hundred: Khentova, *Zhizn*, 41–42; Ardov, 19.

p. 257: At ten at night, the train set off: Fay, *Life*, 126. Sokolov appears to suggest that it left in the morning (Wilson, 151).

p. 257: "It travelled very slowly . . . soften and show kindness": Wilson, 151.

RAILWAY CAR NO. 7

p. 258: "A wet snow . . . for reassurance": Wilson, 151.

p. 259: Two of Shostakovich's suitcases had disappeared . . . : Wilson, 151; confirmed by a letter from Shostakovich (Glikman, 3) and Galina's memory of the trip (Ardov, 18). Maxim Shostakovich was told a slightly different story (Ardov, 19), but his account was based on the memories of Aram Khachaturian some years later.

p. 259: Even worse, he now discovered that the score . . . : Khentova, *Zhizn*, 41–42.

p. 259: "I saw Shostakovich getting out . . . a state of great agitation": Wilson, 151.

p. 259: Dmitri and Nina worked out a system . . . : Sollertinskys, 104.

p. 259: The train did not move quickly . . . : Sollertinskys, 104; Gruliow and Lederer, 3.

p. 260: "There was almost . . . a spirit of defeatism": Gruliow and Lederer, 3.

p. 260: Stalin assembled a temporary office . . . : Service, *Stalin*, 438; but cf. Montefiore, 399.

pp. 260–261: "People are saying things . . . where such moods prevail": Braithwaite, 250.

p. 261: On the fourth day of the clattering voyage east . . . : Nina recalled, "The blanket, resting in the puddle, was in such a shape you'd be afraid to touch it. I'll spare you further details." Daniil Zhitomirsky, "Shostakovich," *Muzïkal'naya akademiya* 3 (1993): 27. Translation by Ellen Litman. Note that biographer Sofia Khentova tells two contradictory stories about the loss of the manuscript of the Seventh, neither of which involves the bathroom. In one (*Zhizn*, 41–42), she wrote that the manuscript was found after four days, when the train stopped in Ruzayevka — though Nina seems to imply that it was found earlier. In another version (*Voynï*, 58), Khentova says that when the train got to Kuibyshev, the family found the manuscript stacked with cargo to be sent off to Siberia. As Shostakovich's official biographer, Khentova might have been euphemizing the story to avoid discussing one of Russia's great masterpieces floating in toilet water. Nina's own narrative obviously takes precedence.

p. 262: "Why not continue . . . how about . . . ?": Wilson, 152.

p. 262: "The impression when the train . . . foam far below": Sollertinskys, 104.

KUIBYSHEV AND LENINGRAD

p. 263: The lampposts were plastered with desperate notes . . . : Beevor, loc. 2692.

p. 263: Description of Kuibyshev and Nameless: Chris Bellamy, *Absolute War: Soviet Russia in the Second World War* (New York: Knopf, 2007), 296–298.

p. 263: Shostakovich and many other refugees on Railway Car No. 7 . . . : The details of this incident are from Wilson, 152–153.

p. 264: It appears that after a few days, the Shostakoviches . . . : Khentova, *Zhizn*, 42.

p. 264: "You know, as soon as I got on that train . . . losing their lives": Wilson, 153.

p. 264: the temperature dropped below zero: Fahrenheit. Jones, 162.

p. 264: Even if trains had been able to get through . . . : Braithwaite, 234.

p. 265: People blocked up the empty window frames . . . : Adamovich and Granin, 9, 73.

p. 265: "The temperature is really dropping . . . dying from malnutrition": Jones, 133.

p. 265: "From one point of view . . . even three times": Adamovich and Granin, 122.

p. 265: The Leningrad authorities were running out . . . : Jones, 142; Reid, 164; Salisbury, 370.

p. 266: By November 20, the bread ration had been reduced . . . : Reid, 168.

p. 266: "In those days . . . have seen those eyes": Adamovich and Granin, 17.

p. 266: "Finish your bread; you'll soon be dead": Ibid., 65.

p. 266: "There have been cases . . . Petersburg": Reid, 191.

p. 267: "As everybody knows . . . Then you let it cool": Fadeyev, 36.

p. 267: Some people garnished it with bay leaves: Jones, 4.

p. 267: A mother, desperate to feed her family . . . : Ibid., 210.

p. 267: "I witnessed a scene . . . looked like executioners": Ibid., 169.

p. 267: One man rapturously remembered the day . . . : Adamovich and Granin, 90.

p. 267: "Protein — meat — we hardly see at all . . . 'We eat them'": Inber, 34.

p. 267: "Before the war, people adorned . . . wanted to seem": Reid, 185.

p. 268: "The city is literally flooded with corpses . . . not firewood": Skrjabina, 41.

p. 268: And around the same time, she noted . . . : Ibid., 38.

pp. 268–270: "You know, Nikolai . . . unfortunately I can't work.": Wilson, 153.

p. 270: At the beginning of December, their living arrangements . . . : Ibid., 155–156.

p. 270: "Today (2 December) I heard the piano . . . three jolly friends": Ibid., 156.

AN OPTIMISTIC SHOSTAKOVICH

pp. 271–272: As the Germans prepared to snap . . . : Braithwaite, 304.

p. 272: It was so cold that when a man spat . . . : Hastings, 162.

p. 272: Winter clothing had been issued . . . : Forczyk, *Moscow,* 23.

p. 272: "We have blundered . . . against us": Hastings, 176.

p. 272: "The frontal attacks puzzled me . . . flank attacks": Ibid., 370.

p. 272: When the Germans were within seven miles . . . : Braithwaite, 297–298.

p. 273: Slowly, painfully, with the loss of more than a third . . . : Forczyk, *Moscow,* 89.

p. 273: "The Collapse of . . . German Forces": Braithwaite, 309.

p. 273: During a devastating air raid . . . : Ian W. Toll, *Pacific Crucible: War at Sea in the Pacific, 1941–1942* (New York: Norton, 2012), 159.

p. 275: Roughly a thousand German tanks . . . Almost half of them . . . : Hastings, 157; Forczyk, *Moscow,* 89.

p. 275: Twenty-four thousand Wehrmacht soldiers . . . : Forczyk, *Moscow,* 89.

p. 277: "As soon as the news came . . . energy and excitement": Wilson, 154.

p. 277: "He was very distraught . . . go and fetch her": Ibid., 169.

p. 277: "He never asked for anything for himself . . . of doing so": Glikman, 27.

p. 277: The composer almost fell to pieces with gratitude . . . : Wilson, 182.

p. 278: While he wrote the fourth and final movement . . . : Ibid., 171.

p. 278: "We took pencils from our father's table . . . stick there": Ardov, 24.

p. 278: "What we need is an optimistic Shostakovich": Wilson, 171.

p. 278: "In the finale . . . been defeated": Fay, *Life,* 127.

p. 279: "There is only good vodka . . . bad vodka": Ardov, 134.

p. 279: They were eating some sausages . . . : Wilson, 156–158.

p. 279: "And, d'you know. . . my Seventh": Ibid, 158.

p. 279: Even more astonishingly, he had written . . . : Siegmeister, 622.

p. 279: "Everybody spoke at once . . . a great success": Wilson, 158.

p. 279: "Of course . . . the bondage of spirit": Ibid., 158–159.

p. 280: "The Seventh Symphony had been planned . . . finished off": Volkov, *Testimony,* 155–156.

p. 280: "I wrote my Seventh Symphony . . . Victory Over the Enemy": Ibid., 154.

p. 280: "the 'invasion' episode": Shostakovich, *Facsimile,* 8.

p. 281: "'theme of evil,' which was absolutely . . . definitions": *Novyi Mir* 3 (1990): 267.

p. 281: But Shostakovich himself does not seem to have restricted . . . : See, for example, Flora Litvinova's revelation that when Shostakovich got to know her and trust her, he told her the Seventh was about "any form of totalitarian regime" (Wilson, 159).

p. 281: "All that I wrote into it . . . against fascist oppressors": Schwarz, 177.

p. 282: "Things are not good with me . . . directly from here": Glikman, 8.

p. 282: One day he got a smudged, rumpled letter . . . : Feuchtner, 142.

THE CITY OF THE DEAD

p. 283: "The city was quiet and empty . . . realm of some sea king": Adamovich and Granin, 69.

pp. 283–284: "The city of death greeted me . . . strength to write": Ibid., 200.

p. 284: "dirt, snowdrifts, snow, cold, darkness, starvation, death": Ibid.

p. 284: *"Kholod, golod, snaryady, pozhary":* Reid, 234.

p. 284: "At present our nights are indescribably quiet . . . never wake up": Inber, 42 (slightly altered for clarity).

p. 284: Just within the limits of besieged Leningrad . . . : Amery and Curran, 200.

p. 285: "We are all ill . . . for a dead body": Reid, 232–233.

p. 285: often down to twenty below zero . . . : Ibid., 208.

p. 285: "and the frost, the cold, were frightful": Adamovich and Granin, 79.

p. 285: "Yes. I came home . . . go to work": Ibid., 80.

p. 286: "was wrapped in a white shroud . . . a man or a woman": Reid, 189.

p. 287: "I recall one truck that was loaded . . . glassy eyes": Jones, 241.

p. 287: "[At first] I was afraid of dead bodies . . . our turn, perhaps": Adamovich and Granin, 102.

p. 287: At the entrance to one cemetery, some comic gravedigger . . . : Jones, 242.

p. 287: "Within a single family . . . children last": Reid, 212.

p. 288: In the case of the family Shostakovich left behind . . . : Glikman, 11.

p. 288: "Hunger changes the appearance . . . swollen": Skrjabina, 63.

p. 288: "hunger tan": Reid, 213.

p. 288: "People were discovering . . . bone": Ginzburg, 9.

p. 288: "It was roughly the feeling . . . you've no voice": Adamovich and Granin, 37.

p. 290: "Everybody is now walking . . . here starving": Jones, 206.

p. 290: "There is much that is revolting . . . three children": Adamovich and Granin, 201.

p. 290: "The brain is devoured by the stomach": Ibid., 32.

p. 290: "Human beings showed . . . on the other": Fadeyev, 59.

p. 291: Corpse-eating was far more common . . . : Salisbury, 478.

p. 291: The NKVD files are unspeakably macabre . . . : Reid, 289.

p. 291: The criminal profile of corpse-eaters was surprising . . . : Ibid., 290. We should remember, however, that these are the demographics of those who were caught, and it is unclear whether the figures are therefore accurately representative. People with a fixed address would have had an easier time hiding their crime. Cf. Salisbury, 447.

pp. 291–292: "felt that something was horribly wrong . . . what a fatty child": Jones, 216.

p. 292: "looked like a beast": Ibid., 218.

p. 292: A woman named Vera Lyudyno recorded . . . : Ibid., 4.

p. 292: a mother whose child disappeared went to the police . . . : Ibid., 218.

p. 292: A young couple, for example, went to the Haymarket . . . : Salisbury, 480–481.

p. 293: "Wait for me here . . . blue veins": Ibid., 480.

p. 294: there really were a few organized cannibal bands . . . : Jones, 216; Reid, 288. Reid appears to think that the first example was actually one of theft, not of cannibalism.

p. 294: There were nine arrests for cannibalism . . . : Jones, 217.

p. 294: A year later, the final figure . . . : Reid, 288.

pp. 294–295: "After the blockade . . . morbid depression": Adamovich and Granin, 341.

p. 295: The Nazis asked carefully about when precisely . . . : Jones, 185.

p. 295: "Countless tragedies are taking place . . . with cold curiosity": Ibid., 175.

p. 295: "A kind of polarization seemed . . . stiff test": Adamovich and Granin, 148.

p. 296: "We moved . . . helping others": Jones, 200.

p. 296: A young nurse named Marina Yerukhmanova . . . : Reid, 217–218.

p. 296: Brigades of factory workers . . . : Simmons and Perlina, xvii.

p. 296: A group of schoolteachers took it upon themselves . . . : Jones, 170.

p. 296: "Everyone had a savior": Adamovich and Granin, 148.

pp. 296–297: "Helping others was crucial . . . gave strength to people": Jones, 5.

p. 297: "People came to the library . . . left in the snow": Ibid., 247.

p. 297: The building itself had been seriously damaged . . . : Simmons and Perlina, 168. All of the following description comes from the memoirs of librarian Lilia Solomonovna Frankfurt (Simmons and Perlina, 163ff).

p. 297: practical questions posed by the city government . . . : Salisbury, 508.

p. 298: A Red Army lieutenant reading an early sci-fi novel . . . : Reid, 244.

p. 298: "We warm ourselves . . . to make our tea": Ibid., 245.

p. 298: In the vaults and crypts beneath the Hermitage Museum . . . : Salisbury, 431–434.

p. 298: During the day, some of them walked the nearly ten miles . . . : Jones, 247; Adamovich and Granin, 62.

p. 298: For a while, they even managed to arrange for a fluctuating flow . . . : Salisbury, 433; Overy, 108–109. N.b.: Jones (182) claims the power source was a naval submarine.

p. 298: "Here, the Muses speak together with the guns": "Shostakovich and the Guns," *Time*, July 20, 1942, 53.

p. 298: Leningrad's Musical Comedy Theater remained open . . . : Jones, 178.

p. 300: Leningrad's radio station also kept broadcasting . . . : Reid, 256; Jones, 233.

p. 300: "Through the hallucinations . . . everything herself": Adamovich and Granin, 23.

p. 300: One night, faint with hunger, Berggolts . . . : Salisbury, 466–467.

p. 301: "Why spread such doom . . . some music": Fadeyev, 32.

p. 301: "Is it possible . . . Shostakovich's Seventh Symphony?": Ibid.

p. 301: "By any means . . . as soon as possible": Vulliamy, 2.

p. 301: "The first violin is dying . . . near death": Salisbury, 462.

pp. 301–302: "Just think . . . sing our Russian songs": Fadeyev, 15.

p. 302: "But Mother . . . need less food": Adamovich and Granin, 169.

p. 302: "Not counting the old people . . . long for this world": Maria Konstantinova Tikhonov, quoted in Fadeyev, 14.

p. 302: "I found in my work . . . morale": Jones, 232.

p. 302: "Something else . . . we don't understand": Ibid., 236.

pp. 302–303: "What saved us all . . . how we survived": Zoya Yershova, quoted in Adamovich and Granin, 148.

p. 303: "The hatred felt . . . defense": Adamovich and Granin, 218.

p. 303: "If anyone . . . labor of their hands": Fadeyev, 64.

p. 303: On the artillery shells produced in Leningrad . . . : Jones, 284.

pp. 303–304: "However did you hold out . . . ration": Adamovich and Granin, 39–40.

p. 304: "talked of faith . . . 'research'": Ibid., 42.

p. 304: "Our life here . . . giving way to my tears": Glikman, 7.

MY MUSIC IS MY WEAPON

p. 305: It took the orchestra in Kuibyshev . . . : Weintraub Papers, "Some Notes on the Shostakovich Seventh Symphony," 4.

p. 305: "the musicians . . . would be fed better": Geoffrey Norris, "Symphony in Shorthand: Geoffrey Norris Talks to Vasily Petrenko about Shostakovich's Leningrad Symphony," *Gramophone* 91 (June 2013).

p. 305: "There they sat . . . taken home": Seroff, 240; cf. Ardov, 21.

p. 306: "The word 'America' . . . ever-falling shares": Ilf and Petrov, 15.

p. 306: "the most advanced . . . social order": Ibid., 127.

p. 307: "Stop acting like . . . Stalin in return": Herring, 85.

p. 307: "They simply walked . . . to it": Ibid., 37.

p. 307: "Surly, snarly . . . their own lives": Reid, 313.

p. 308: They eventually suffered . . . : Hastings, 427, 316. Roughly five million German soldiers died in the war; of these, about 4.5 million were killed by the Russians (Hastings, 427).

p. 308: "God knows we paid . . . in Russian lives": Ibid., 287.

p. 308: "We've lost millions . . . send us Spam": Herring, 95.

p. 308: "one hell of a people . . . like Americans": Ibid., 94.

p. 309: "He was in and out . . . get her in": Seroff, 240.

p. 309: "He's always like . . . a flop": Wilson, 159.

p. 309: "He seemed . . . rigid and unsmiling": Seroff, 241.

p. 309: "My music is my weapon": Weintraub Papers, f. 2.8, telegram from Vladimir Bazykin to Am-Rus Music Corp., July 18, 1942; cf. Lind, 16–17.

p. 309: "We are struggling for . . . Leningrad": Fay, *Life,* 131. This statement originally appeared in *Pravda* but was also translated and adapted for the American premiere of the work several months later.

p. 309: it is at this point that the symphony itself is "invaded": Shostakovich literally sets up an "invasion" of traditional symphonic form. The first movement begins in an absolutely routine sonata-allegro design, with an exposition of two themes, the first of which is even in a traditional C major. Just at the moment, however, when a symphony would normally transition into the development section, Shostakovich drops this material entirely. Instead of a development, we get a non-development: the obnoxious repetitions of the so-called invasion theme. It is quite literally as if a structure had been set up that would have gone on its own way happily—if its whole course and purpose hadn't been utterly trampled by that march.

p. 310: "War and Hitlerism . . . down upon you": "Shostakovich's Seventh, Symphony of War in Russia: Muscovite Reporter Tells His Impressions of Work at Rehearsal," *Boston Globe,* April 4, 1942. Yevgeni Petrov was half of the Ilf and Petrov duo, two of Shostakovich's favorite comic writers.

p. 310: "I kept on hearing . . . getting louder and louder": Ardov, 22.

p. 310: a trumpet playing . . . offstage: Weintraub Papers, "Some Notes," 4.

p. 312: "Never in my . . . verging on tears": Ibid.

p. 312: "Nobody who saw . . . his movements": Wilson, 169.

p. 312: Perhaps more important to Shostakovich was some good news . . . : Shostakovich heard about this development at a rehearsal on February 14 (Fay, *Life,* 130).

THE ROAD OF LIFE

p. 313: It had frozen in November . . . : The last waterborne food shipments reached the docks at Osinovets on November 15 (Reid, 201).

p. 313: By late November, the ice was thick enough . . . : Salisbury (412) suggests that the first truck convoy went across on November 22.

p. 314: Once the Road of Life became fully active . . . : Reid, 203.

p. 314: Road of Death: Jones, 229.

p. 314: "Having dragged . . . managed to leave": Simmons and Perlina, 80.

p. 314: Shostakovich's relatives had dysentery: Sollertinskys, 109.

p. 314: Security forces wouldn't allow the sick to travel: Simmons and Perlina, 80.

p. 314: Once the train reached the processing centers . . . : Reid, 274; Salisbury, 494.

p. 315: "this worn-out, bombed . . . wrecked vehicles": Inber, 66.

p. 315: At first, especially, drivers made the trip . . . : Jones, 220.

p. 317: By January 1942, two thousand tons of food were being delivered daily: Jones, 220.

p. 318: Drivers on the Road of Life liked to boast . . . : Fadeyev, 50–51.

p. 318: "During the blockade . . . before the war": Jones, 227.

pp. 318–319: There was a rash of deaths before a doctor . . . : Adamovich and Granin, 436.

p. 319: Many, weakened by the voyage . . . : Reid, 278.

p. 319: "Got away . . . love to all Grandma": Glikman, 10.

p. 319: "How will . . . state they'll be in": Wilson, 167.

p. 319: On March 19, 1942, the three finally arrived . . . : Sollertinskys, 109.

p. 319: "nothing but skin and bone": Glikman, 11.

p. 319: only a few days later, in Moscow . . . : Fay, *Life*, 131.

p. 319: "Vasily Vasilyyevich . . . have come to be with me": Glikman, 11.

p. 319: There were now nine people . . . : Wilson, 167n14; cf. Glikman, 10–11.

p. 320: "was churned up . . . against the table": Wilson, 167.

p. 320: "You know, once we ate a cat . . . little Mitya": Ibid.

p. 320: A quarter of Shostakovich's colleagues . . . : Reid, 258.

p. 320: Fleishman died in combat . . . : Sollertinskys, 109.

p. 320: "He went into . . . guardsman, no": Volkov, *Testimony*, 225.

p. 320: "Everybody in my family . . . other words": Glikman, 17. This letter was written much later but seems representative of the conversation around the Shostakovich table for quite a while.

p. 320: "We hadn't the heart to shoo him away . . . like his name": Ibid., 9.

p. 320: "He was lively and undemanding — a typical mongrel": Ardov, 20.

p. 321: "It seems to . . . thirty-five thousand of them!": Glikman, xli.

p. 321: The initial printing of three hundred copies . . . : Shostakovich, *Works, Volume 7*, 264.

p. 321: "in the not-too-distant future": Shostakovich, *Works*, vol. 22, 341.

pp. 321–322: The copy for North America was supposed to travel . . . : Memorandum, May 25, 1942; Loy Henderson, U.S. State Department Central File (1940–1944), National Archives, Record Group 59, doc. 861.4038/1.

p. 322: Meanwhile, Shostakovich wanted the piece to be sent . . . : The saga of the journey is beautifully described by Glikman himself (xxxvii–xlii).

p. 322: "in which case . . . sleeping berth": Glikman, xxxviii.

p. 322: "Horror of horrors! . . . like poppy-seeds": Ibid.

p. 322: "Speaking as a doctor . . . perfectly edible": Ibid., xxxix.

p. 322: "The two of us dined together . . . Central Asian ant": Ibid.

p. 323: "No material hardship . . . performed": Ibid.

p. 323: On May 23, an anxious Soviet diplomat appeared . . . : Memorandum, May 23, 1942; Loy Henderson, U.S. State Department Central File (1940–1944), National Archives, Record Group 59, doc. 861.4038/2.

p. 323: The Department of State made inquiries . . . : Memorandum, May 25, 1942; Loy

Henderson, U.S. State Department Central File (1940–1944), National Archives, Record Group 59, doc. 861.4038/1.

p. 323: "the greatest musical event of the year . . . generation": "Sensational New Work Composed Under Battle Fire," *Capital Times* (Wisconsin), July 19, 1942, 14.

p. 324: The score of the Shostakovich Seventh Symphony . . . : The Soviets had a neutrality pact with the Japanese, but America was at war with Japan; Russian shipments to the United States across the Pacific Ocean were always in danger of being detained and seized.

p. 324: It was stowed in a diplomatic pouch and flown to the Middle East . . . : For details of this flight, see Anderson.

p. 324: Tires that lasted eighty thousand miles . . . : Simon Rigge, *War in the Outposts* (Alexandria, VA: Time-Life Books, 1980), 84.

p. 325: At tony clubs like the Kit Kat . . . : Bierman and Smith, 40. I'm thinking here particularly of Hekmat Fahmy, a Kit Kat Club belly dancer who acted as a spy—see, for example, Hastings, 402.

p. 325: On May 30, the diplomatic pouch was delivered . . . : Handwritten note on memorandum, May 30, 1942; Loy Henderson, U.S. State Department Central File (1940–1944), National Archives, Record Group 59, doc. 861.4038/1.

p. 326: "I wouldn't care . . . vast headache": "Symphony," *The New Yorker,* July 18, 1942, 9.

p. 326: "the most thrilling experience of my musical career!": Weintraub Papers, "Some Facts," 15.

p. 327: "this hot baby of a Seventh Symphony": Weintraub Papers, "Some Additional Notes," 2.

p. 327: "a pale, slight . . . streets of Petrograd": "Shostakovich and the Guns," *Time,* July 20, 1942, 53.

p. 327: "The climax of joy . . . favorite team": Ibid., 55.

p. 327: The first performance of the *Leningrad* . . . : Pauline Fairclough, "The 'Old Shostakovich': Reception in the British Press." *Music and Letters* 88, no. 2 (May 2007): 275n36.

p. 328: "People who had no interest . . . name of Shostakovich": Weintraub Papers, "Some Additional Notes," 3.

p. 329: "tells the man who hears it . . . mother are the same": Seroff, 6.

p. 331: "It was universal war music . . . boundaries": Ed Ainsworth, "Soldiers Hear Shostakovich," *Los Angeles Times,* October 12, 1942, A1.

p. 331: It was broadcast on almost two thousand radio stations . . . : On October 18, 1942. Both shows are preserved by the J. David Goldin Collection at the University of Missouri–Kansas City.

p. 331: Stokowski, who had conducted the music for Disney's *Fantasia* . . . : Leopold Stokowski to Dmitri Shostakovich, June 16, 1942, State Archive of the Russian Federation (GARF), f. 5283, op. 14, d. 132; cf. Anderson.

p. 331: Director Howard Hawks, best known at that point . . . : Anderson.

pp. 331–332: "You will hear . . . buildings pulverized": From Faulkner's treatment. Faulkner, 44.

p. 332: She takes a break in her letter writing . . . : In the second draft of the script (Ibid., 234).

p. 332: "It was our music . . . my son!": Ibid., 44.

p. 332: "We were inclined . . . his music": Eugene Weintraub, "Battle of the Conductors," *Music Journal* 34, no. 3 (March 1976): 16. In the final extant version of the Faulkner script, Shostakovich is described as writing the symphony "with one blistered hand still on the pulse of that city which endured" (Faulkner, 235).

p. 332: "At first it seemed . . . On the contrary": Volkov, *Testimony*, 136–137.

p. 332: "I was just uneasy . . . must have irritated Stalin": Ibid., 137; cf. "Willkie and the Bear," *Time*, October 5, 1942, 27.

p. 332: "By now it is almost unpatriotic . . . Russian allies": "Shostakovich's Seventh," *Life*, November 9, 1942, 99.

p. 333: By January 1943, polls showed that 90 percent . . . : Herring, 90.

p. 333: U.S. donations to the Russian war effort . . . : van Tuyll, 54.

p. 333: The jeep became a favorite vehicle . . . : Herring, 118.

p. 333: "one pound of concentrated . . . Army": van Tuyll, 117.

p. 333: In 1942, Russian War Relief donated . . . : Gruliow and Lederer, 1. For a more general discussion of the role of Russian War Relief in the history of the symphony, see Anderson.

SYMPHONY FOR THE CITY OF THE DEAD

p. 335: Later that night, the opera's tenor had died of hunger: Reid, 361.

p. 335: "Rehearsal did not take place . . . not working": Vulliamy, 1.

p. 335: "All Leningrad musicians . . . Radio Committee": Sollertinskys, 108.

p. 335: The acting conductor of the Radio Orchestra . . . : Reid, 361.

p. 336: "I grabbed my instrument . . . took it as it was": Weinstein, 38:00.

p. 336: Eventually, she brought it to a repairman . . . : Vulliamy, 2—in which she is called "Edith." Cf. Simmons and Perlina, 148.

p. 336: All the musicians who could stir themselves . . . : Vulliamy, 1; but cf. Jones, 256.

p. 336: "Dear friends, we are weak . . . start work": Vulliamy, 2.

p. 336: "He lifted his hands . . . he didn't fall": Weinstein, 38:00.

p. 336: The pianist had to warm bricks . . . : Jones, 256.

p. 336: "It's your solo. Why don't you play?": Vulliamy, 2; cf. Jones, 257.

pp. 336–337: "I'm sorry, sir . . . It was hopeless": Vulliamy, 2.

p. 337: The score for the Seventh was flown into Leningrad . . . : Sollertinskys, 108.

p. 337: "When I saw the symphony . . . volumes of music": Vulliamy, 2.

p. 337: It called for a huge orchestra . . . : Ibid. Note that the precise timeline of these events is slightly unclear. There seem to be two reasons for this: First, most of the information is taken from interviews and oral histories, and is therefore somewhat imprecise about dates. Second, in retellings, the mythology of the Seventh tends to blot out the other performances the Leningrad Radio Orchestra gave that spring. This obscures questions about when and how often the orchestra's numbers had to be supplemented by the military bands, at what points Eliasberg had to request more players, and so on.

pp. 337–338: "When we finished . . . work would continue": Simmons and Perlina, 148–149.

p. 338: "On May 1, under heavy shelling . . . Tchaikovsky": Schwarz, 177.

p. 338: "Listening to music . . . classical concert": Jones, 253.

p. 338: "The hotel is dead . . . 40 degrees": Salisbury, 493.

p. 338: Adolf Hitler, predicting that he would take Leningrad . . . : Reid, 361.

p. 338: "not really soup . . . wheat germ": Vulliamy, 2.

p. 338: This kept them from death, but during the rehearsals . . . : Ibid.

p. 339: "Rehearsals in the morning . . . next day": Ibid., 1.

p. 339: "You should have seen it . . . drag their legs": Fadeyev, 9.

p. 339: "Grass, grass, grass . . . were rabbits": Jones, 249.

p. 339: City employees pasted lists of edible wild plants . . . : Salisbury, 535.

p. 339: In the nearby forest, small boys perched . . . : Jones, 252.

p. 341: "As they worked . . . Leningraders": Ibid., 248.

p. 341: "'Look, here comes spring!' . . . remained alive": Vulliamy, 1.

p. 341: In the margins, they have doodled . . . : These copies are now on display at the museum "The Muses Were Not Silent," in St. Petersburg.

p. 341: "To be honest, no one was very enthusiastic": Vulliamy, 2.

p. 342: "It was a very complex piece of work . . . not music": Ibid.; Jones, 257.

p. 342: "It's no good . . . No complaining!": Vulliamy, 2.

p. 342: "This must not happen again . . . be at the rehearsal": Ibid.

p. 342: "The event was unmissable . . . power of that?": Jones, 259.

p. 342: General Govorov of the Red Army . . . : This is a reference to the Wehrmacht's aborted Operation Northern Light.

p. 343: That evening, as the orchestral players tuned up . . . : Jones, 265; Volkov, *Stalin*, 180; Stolyarova, 3.

p. 343: "First we hit the enemy's . . . Seventh was made possible": quoted in Lind, 143. Translation by Ellen Litman.

p. 343: "We played our instrument . . . you know": Vulliamy, 2; cf. Simmons and Perlina, 151.

p. 343: "I awoke that morning . . . since the blockade": Ibid.

p. 343: "I'll never forget that . . . light was like": Ibid.

p. 343: Many soldiers came straight from the front . . . : Schwarz, 179.

p. 343: In the audience was an eleven-year-old boy . . . : Wolfgang Teubner, liner notes for the Yuri Ahronovitch recording of the Seventh (Hänssler, 2006).

p. 344: "It had been an everyday job . . . play as best we could": Vulliamy, 2.

p. 344: "We were dressed like cabbages . . . on my instrument": Ibid., 1, 2.

p. 344: "On the night . . . the meaning of war": Ibid., 2.

p. 344: "It was so meaningful . . . in our lives": Weinstein, 39:50.

pp. 344–345: "One cannot speak . . . about themselves": Schwarz, 179.

p. 345: "It had a slow but powerful effect . . . stay human": Jones, 8; cf. Simmons and Perlina, 151.

p. 345: "We listened with such emotion . . . Leningrad's": Weinstein, 39:10.

p. 348: "It's what we lived with . . . when I die": Vulliamy, 1.

p. 348: "It was so loud and powerful that I thought I'd collapse": Jones, 260.

p. 348: "willing [the orchestra] to keep going": Ibid.

p. 348: "It felt like a victory . . . whatever happens around us": Ibid., 8.

p. 348: "The rumbling approach . . . is still to come": Inber, 101–102.

p. 348: "When we had finished . . . that's all": Vulliamy, 2.

p. 349: "On the table . . . beginning of the siege": Ibid.

p. 349: "No one could feed us . . . our feast": Weinstein, 40:00.

p. 349: "They never had their party . . . Leningrad was saved": Vulliamy, 1.

p. 349: "People just stood and cried . . . Nazi war machine": Jones, 261.

p. 349: "Dear Edith . . . more beautiful than ever": Vulliamy, 1.

p. 349: "So many years have passed . . . life after death": Ibid., 2.

PART THREE

COLD WAR AND THAW

pp. 353–354: "In connection with the improvement . . . just 56": Hastings, 306.

p. 354: "By the beginning of January . . . our own offensive": Jones, 272.

p. 354: "Troops of the Leningrad . . . blockade of Leningrad": Salisbury, 549.

p. 354: "This snowy moonlit night . . . we will never forget": Ibid.

p. 354: "The cursed circle is broken": Hastings, 307.

p. 355: "We were determined . . . trying to reach": Jones, 278.

p. 355: In just three weeks, food and other supplies . . . : Forczyk, *Leningrad*, 76.

p. 355: Crews had to repair the tracks twelve hundred times . . . : Simmons and Perlina, xxiii.

p. 355: Dmitri Shostakovich spent several months . . . : Glikman, 18; Fay, *Life*, 135.

p. 355: "The Seventh Symphony of Shostakovich . . . struggle and victory": Schwarz, 180.

p. 355: "Let us try to create now . . . Seventh Symphony": Volkov, *Stalin*, 177.

p. 356: "He was only a man . . . when it concerned others": Lesser, 12.

p. 356: "too scared to refuse": Wilson, 181.

p. 356: "May I compose the music . . . a funny man": Ibid., 182.

p. 356: The NKVD's enthusiasm for soccer . . . : Montefiore, 505, 553.

p. 357: He fled through the countryside . . . : The heart-rending, harrowing tale of Weinberg's flight from the Nazis is described in detail in David Fanning's biography of the composer, *Mieczysław Weinberg: In Search of Freedom* (Hofheim, Germany: Wolke Verlag, 2010).

p. 357: For the first several months Shostakovich was in Moscow . . . : Wilson, 105.

p. 357: The tide had turned . . . : Ziemke, 21, 27, 35.

p. 358: On January 14, 1944, the last vestige . . . : Simmons and Perlina, xxiv.

p. 358: "The city of Leningrad has been entirely liberated": Jones, 285.

p. 358: "Suddenly Leningrad emerged . . . enough on it": Ziemke, 99.

p. 358: Now that they were on the offensive, the Red Army . . . : Overy, 257.

pp. 358–359: "Estates, villages . . . first days of the war": Hastings, 595.

p. 359: As the Red Army drove deep into German territory . . . : For an example of a powerful early report, see Vasily Grossman's "The Hell of Treblinka," in *The Road: Stories, Journalism, and Essays,* trans. Robert and Elizabeth Chandler with Olga Mukovnikova (New York: New York Review of Books, 2010).

p. 359: "They were simple and cruel . . . without resisting": Hastings, 583.

p. 359: Of the 5.8 million Soviet soldiers captured . . . : Pleshakov, 9; Nelson, 214.

p. 359: In April 1945, three Soviet army groups . . . : Hastings, 600.

pp. 359–360: On April 12, the German Philharmonic Orchestra . . . : Ibid.

p. 360: "A ghost town of cave dwellers . . . hardly anything was left": Ibid., 603.

p. 360: "without electric light . . . fallen masonry": Ibid.

p. 362: "Again from the black dust . . . my Leningrad": Salisbury, 568.

p. 362: Historians now estimate that about 27 million Soviet citizens . . . : A. Roberts, 556. Cf. Overy, 287–288.

p. 362: About 13.6 percent of the Soviet population had died: Pleshakov, 9–10.

p. 362: The Siege of Leningrad alone cost approximately . . . : Hastings, 165. Forczyk (*Leningrad*, 91) estimates roughly 1.5 million deaths on the Leningrad-Volkhov fronts; Simmons and Perlina (ix) estimate 1.6 to 2 million.

p. 362: a higher death toll, in fact . . . : Simmons and Perlina, ix. (The total death toll for Americans in military contests is roughly 1.3 million.)

p. 362: "Both Hitler and Stalin . . . higher bidder": Hastings, 307.

p. 363: Seventy thousand villages . . . : Gleason, 409.

p. 363: Forty thousand miles of railroad track . . . : Overy, 291.

p. 363: The epic battles had destroyed forty thousand hospitals . . . : Pleshakov, 10.

p. 363: "It was the Russians . . . defeat Germany": A. Roberts, 603.

p. 363: "The real reason why Hitler lost . . . he was a Nazi": Ibid., 608.

p. 364: "The ultra-authoritarian features . . . war effort": Service, *History*, 277.

p. 364: He wanted to make sure the Soviet Union's western border . . . : Overy, 311–312. The awful story of that period is told movingly in Applebaum.

p. 364: Within the Soviet Union, anything that reminded . . . : Service, *History*, 280.

p. 365: French bread was renamed "city bread": Volkov, *Testimony*, 173n. U.S. citizens should not laugh: in 2003, when the French condemned the American invasion of Iraq, the U.S. Congress boldly responded by renaming the "French fries" in the congressional canteen "freedom fries." Take that, France!

p. 365: In February of 1948, Leningrad Communist Party boss . . . : For a chronology of this series of meetings, see Fanning's *Weinberg*, 59–60. For extensive excerpts from the 1948 "anti-formalist" meetings, see Slonimsky, 684–712.

p. 365: "a piercing road drill, or a musical gas-chamber": Wilson, 209; Volkov, *Stalin*, 247.

p. 365: He was quietly removing the heroes . . . : Salisbury, 579–580.

p. 365: The success of the Seventh Symphony . . . : Volkov, *Testimony*, 140.

p. 366: "A close study . . . our work": MacDonald, 192.

p. 366: Natalya's father, a famous Jewish actor . . . : Montefiore, 573; a slightly different story was heard by Rostislav Dubinsky (6).

p. 366: "I envy him": Fanning, *Weinberg*, 60.

p. 366: "and he told me to tell you . . . anything": Ibid.

p. 366: Around the same time as this murder . . . : Morrison, 5–7; Vishnevskaya, 156; cf. Robinson, 474–475.

p. 366: Shostakovich wrote letters to the authorities . . . : Wilson, 400; Morrison, 250.

p. 366: "My father is pacing . . . asking questions": Ardov, 63.

p. 367: "I do not understand . . . collection of sounds": Tomoff, 143.

p. 367: The Shostakoviches pulled Maxim . . . : Ardov, 63; Fay, *Life*, 162.

p. 367: "a peculiar writing in code . . . pathological phenomena": Slonimsky, 693.

p. 367: *Well, I'll muddle through somehow*: Wilson, 294.

p. 367: "Take this, please . . . read it out": Ibid.

p. 367: "And I got up on the tribune . . . a Soviet composer": Lesser, 86.

p. 368: "I shall work on the musical . . . collective singing": Sixsmith.

p. 368: "I read like . . . on a string": Wilson, 295.

p. 368: "What else . . . made me do it": Sixsmith.

p. 368: There is still a great deal of bitter argument . . . : Khrennikov is implicitly defended, for example, in Tomoff's history of the Composers' Union; indictments appear in Vishnevskaya, passim; Hakobian, 143; Dubinsky, 221; Robinson, xv; Tassie, e.g., 322; etc. The matter of his culpability is still exceedingly unclear, and may well remain so.

p. 368: "My word was law . . . Commissar": Sixsmith.

p. 368: "They say Shostakovich . . . a cheerful man": Weinstein, 56:50.

p. 368: In 1948, Shostakovich's music was banned: Tomoff, 275–277; Fay, *Life*, 162.

p. 369: They called him a formalist . . . an American spy: Dubinsky, 114.

p. 369: Maxim sat up in a tree and defended . . . : Ardov, 68–69.

p. 369: Shostakovich wrote several works on Jewish themes . . . : Wilson, 229.

p. 369: He also, in his silent fury, wrote a piece . . . : The title is untranslatable and is often given in the original Russian: *Anti-Formalist Rayok*. See Manashir Yakubov, "Shostakovich's *Anti-Formalist Rayok*: A History of the Work's Composition and Its Musical and Literary Sources," in Bartlett (135–158).

p. 370: (His own doctor was being tortured at the time): Montefiore, 640.

p. 370: Comrade Stalin never regained . . . : Ibid., 640, 649.

p. 370: the psychopathic head of Stalin's secret police . . . : Ibid., 642.

p. 370: "Now those . . . to the camps": Grossman, 189.

p. 370: "Our home was sometimes . . . came back": MacDonald, 212.

p. 370: "Bonfires blazed . . . to their heart's desire": Vishnevskaya, 188.

p. 371: "I AM DMITRI SHOSTAKOVICH! I AM DMITRI SHOSTAKOVICH": For a full technical discussion of this symphony, see Fanning, *Breath*. It should be noted that Shostakovich's use of his monogram in the symphony is not straightforward: there are several times, for example, that his motto sounds actively oppressive.

p. 371: Shortly after, Shostakovich, together with many others, was rehabilitated . . . : Via the decree "On the Correction of Errors in the Evaluation of *The Great Friendship, Bogdan Khmelnitsky* and *From All My Heart*" (May 28, 1958) — see Wilson, 292.

p. 372: "Loyal Stalinist or Scornful Dissident": The cover of Ian MacDonald's *The New Shostakovich*.

p. 372: He wrote so many letters to the government . . . : Wilson, 401.

p. 372: He secretly paid for the son of an executed . . . : Ibid., 220.

p. 372: "I showed lack of courage, was faint-hearted": Brown, 114.

p. 372: "I'd sign anything . . . left alone": Wilson, 183.

p. 372: "But their efforts . . . ready for signature": Ibid., 429–430. This is his third wife, Irina. Nina had died of cancer in 1954.

p. 373: "Just be thankful . . . allowed to breathe": Vishnevskaya, 398–399.

p. 373: "the story of his soul": Lesser, 3.

p. 373: "Play it . . . sheer boredom": Wilson, 470.

p. 373: A piece by Shostakovich was the first . . . : Fay, *Life*, 180.

p. 374: "The quartets are messages . . . messages to mankind": Lesser, 278.

p. 374: "Shostakovich's music . . . Russian people": Vishnevskaya, 460.

p. 375: "The majority of my symphonies . . . for them": Volkov, *Testimony*, 156.

p. 375: "Looking back . . . I'm grieving all the time": Ibid., 3, 276.

p. 375: "His face . . . we call 'progress'": Walter Benjamin, "Über den Begriff der Geschichte," IX. http://www.mxks.de/files/phil/Benjamin.GeschichtsThesen.html. My translation.

pp. 375–376: "His work . . . his country": *Red Baton*.

p. 376: "What made Shostakovich's music . . . draw out": Bartlett, 7.

p. 376: "I believe that Shostakovich's music . . . a kind of exaltation": Wilson, 307.

p. 376: "It creates miracles . . . into speech": Akhmatova's poem "Music" (1958). MacDonald, 271; cf. Akhmatova, 476.

p. 379: "although in the empty . . . cautious": Ardov, 37.

AUTHOR'S NOTE

p. 381: "*Testimony* may . . . but true": Quoted in David Fanning, review of *Shostakovich Reconsidered, Music & Letters* 80, no. 3 (August 1999): 490.

p. 382: In the light of recent scholarship, Shostakovich's anti-Stalinism . . . : Hakobian, 57; cf. 60.

p. 382: "*Testimony* . . . isn't a genuine one": MacDonald, 246. MacDonald later changed his mind and became a champion of Volkov's book.

Adamovich, Ales, and Daniil Granin, eds. *A Book of the Blockade*. Translated by Hilda Perham. Moscow: Raduga, 1983.

Akhmatova, Anna. *The Complete Poems of Anna Akhmatova*. 2nd ed. Edited by Roberta Reeder. Translated by Judith Hemschemeyer. Brookline, MA: Zephyr, 1992.

Alexandrov, Victor. *The Tukhachevsky Affair*. Translated by John Hewish. Englewood Cliffs, NJ: Prentice-Hall, 1964.

Amery, Colin, and Brian Curran. *St. Petersburg*. Photographs by Yury Molodkovets. London: Frances Lincoln, 2006.

Anderson, M. T. "The Flight of the Seventh: The Journey of Dmitri Shostakovich's *Leningrad* Symphony to the West." (Forthcoming. See: http://independent.academia .edu/TobinAnderson.)

Applebaum, Anne. *Iron Curtain: The Crushing of Eastern Europe, 1944–1956*. New York: Anchor, 2013.

Ardov, Michael. *Memories of Shostakovich: Interviews with the Composer's Children and Friends*. Translated by Rosanna Kelly. London: Short Books, 2004.

Barron, Stephanie, and Maurice Tuchman, eds. *The Avant-Garde in Russia, 1910–1930*. Los Angeles: Los Angeles County Museum of Art/MIT Press, 1980.

Bartlett, Rosamund, ed. *Shostakovich in Context*. New York: Oxford University Press, 2000.

Beevor, Antony. *The Mystery of Olga Chekhova*. New York: Viking, 2004.

Bierman, John, and Colin Smith. *Alamein: War Without Hate*. London: Penguin, 2003.

Blokker, Roy, with Robert Dearling. *The Music of Dmitri Shostakovich: The Symphonies*. London: Tantivy, 1979.

Braithwaite, Rodric. *Moscow 1941: A City and Its People at War*. London: Profile, 2006.

Braun, Edward. *Meyerhold: A Revolution in Theatre*. Iowa City: University of Iowa Press, 1995.

Brinkley, Douglas, and David Rubel, eds. *World War II: The Axis Assault, 1939–1942*. New York: Times Books, 2003.

Brooke, Caroline. "Soviet Musicians and the Great Terror." *Europe-Asia Studies* 54, no. 3 (May 2002): 397–413.

Brown, Malcolm Hamrick, ed. *A Shostakovich Casebook*. Bloomington: Indiana University Press, 2004.

Conquest, Robert. *The Great Terror: A Reassessment*. New York: Oxford University Press, 1990.

Dubinsky, Rostislav. *Stormy Applause: Making Music in a Worker's State*. New York: Hill and Wang, 1989.

Fadeyev, Aleksandr Aleksandrovich. *Leningrad in the Days of the Blockade*. Translated by R. D. Charques. New York: Hutchinson, 1946. Westport, CT: Greenwood, 1977.

Fairclough, Pauline. *A Soviet Credo: Shostakovich's Fourth Symphony*. Burlington, VT: Ashgate, 2006.

————, and David Fanning, eds. *The Cambridge Companion to Shostakovich*. Cambridge: Cambridge University Press, 2008.

Fanning, David. *The Breath of the Symphonist: Shostakovich's Tenth*. London: Royal Musical Association, 1989.

————. *Mieczysław Weinberg: In Search of Freedom*. Hofheim, Germany: Wolke Verlag, 2010.

————. *Shostakovich: String Quartet No. 8*. Burlington, VT: Ashgate, 2004.

————, ed. *Shostakovich Studies*. Cambridge: Cambridge University Press, 1995.

————. "Shostakovich: The Present-Day Master of the C Major Key." *Acta Musicologica* 73, fasc. 2 (2001): 101–140. http://www.jstor.org/stable/932894.

Faulkner, William. *Battle Cry*. Vol. 4 of *A Comprehensive Guide to the Brodsky Collection*. Jackson: University Press of Mississippi, 1985.

Fay, Laurel E. *Shostakovich: A Life*. New York: Oxford University Press, 2000.

————, ed. *Shostakovich and His World*. Princeton: Princeton University Press, 2004.

Feuchtner, Bernd. *Dmitri Schostakowitsch: "Und Kunst geknebelt von der grossen Macht"* [Dmitri Shostakovich: "And Art Made Tongue-Tied by Authority"]. Kassel: Bärenreiter, 2002.

Fitzpatrick, Sheila. *Everyday Stalinism: Ordinary Life in Extraordinary Times: Soviet Russia in the 1930s*. New York: Oxford University Press, 1999.

Fleming, Candace. *The Family Romanov: Murder, Rebellion, and the Fall of Imperial Russia*. New York: Schwartz & Wade, 2014.

Forczyk, Robert. *Leningrad, 1941–44: The Epic Siege*. New York: Osprey, 2009.

————. *Moscow, 1941: Hitler's First Defeat*. Oxford: Osprey, 2006.

Fueloep-Miller, René. *The Mind and Face of Bolshevism: An Examination of Cultural Life in Soviet Russia*. New York: Harper, 1965.

Garros, Veronique, Natalia Korenevskaya, and Thomas Lahusen. *Intimacy and Terror: Soviet Diaries of the 1930s*. Translated by Carol A. Flath. New York: New Press, 1995.

Ginzburg, Lidiya. *Blockade Diary*. Translated by Alan Myers. London: Harvill, 1995.

Gleason, Abbott, ed. *A Companion to Russian History*. Malden, MA: Wiley-Blackwell, 2009.

Glikman, Isaak. *Story of a Friendship: The Letters of Dmitry Shostakovich to Isaak Glikman, 1941–1975.* Translated by Anthony Phillips. London: Faber, 2001.

Grigoryev, Lev, and Yakov Platek. *Khrennikov.* Translated by Yuri Sviridov. Neptune City, NJ: Paganiniana, 1983.

Grossman, Vasily. *The Road: Stories, Journalism, and Essays.* Translated by Robert and Elizabeth Chandler with Olga Mukovnikova. New York: New York Review of Books, 2010.

Gruliow, Leo, and Sidonie K. Lederer. *Russia Fights Famine: A Russian War Relief Report.* New York: Russian War Relief, n.d. [Summer 1943]. Accessed March 3, 2014. http://babel.hathitrust.org/cgi/pt?id=coo.31924013759117;view=1up;seq=17.

Haas, David. *Leningrad's Modernists: Studies in Composition and Musical Thought, 1917–1932.* New York: Peter Lang, 1998.

Hakobian, Levon. *Music of the Soviet Age, 1917–1987.* Stockholm: Melos Music Literature, 1998.

Hastings, Max. *Inferno: The World at War, 1939–1945.* New York: Knopf, 2011.

Herring, George C. *Aid to Russia, 1941–1946: Strategy, Diplomacy, the Origins of the Cold War.* New York: Columbia University Press, 1973.

Houghteling, James L., Jr. *A Diary of the Russian Revolution.* New York: Dodd, Mead, 1918.

Ilf, Ilya, and Yevgeni Petrov. *Ilf and Petrov's American Road Trip: The 1935 Travelogue of Two Soviet Writers.* Translated by Anne O. Fisher. New York: Cabinet/Princeton Architectural Press, 2007.

Inber, Vera. *Leningrad Diary.* Translated by Serge W. Wolff and Rachel Grieve. New York: St. Martin's, 1971.

Ivinskaya, Olga. *A Captive of Time: My Years with Pasternak.* Translated by Max Hayward. Garden City, NY: Doubleday, 1978.

Jangfeldt, Bengt. *Mayakovsky: A Biography.* Translated by Harry D. Watson. Chicago: University of Chicago Press, 2014.

Jones, Michael. *Leningrad: State of Siege.* New York: Basic, 2008.

Khentova, Sofia. *D. D. Shostakovich v godï Velikoy Otechestvennoy voynï* [Shostakovich in the Years of the Great Patriotic War]. Leningrad: Sovetsky Kompozitor, 1979.

———. *Shostakovich: Zhizn i tvorchestvo* [Shostakovich: Life and Works]. Leningrad: Sovetsky Kompozitor, 1985.

———. *V mire Shostakovicha* [In the World of Shostakovich]. Moscow: Kompozitor, 1996.

Kovtun, Evgueny. *Russian Avant-Garde.* New York: Parkstone, 2007.

Lenin, Vladimir Ilyich. *To the Rural Poor: An Explanation for the Peasants of What the Social-Democrats Want.* 1903. Accessed May 10, 2013. http://www.marxists.org /archive/lenin/works/1903/rp/1.htm.

Lesser, Wendy. *Music for Silenced Voices: Shostakovich and His Fifteen Quartets.* New Haven, CT: Yale University Press, 2011.

Lind, A. E. *Sed'maya.* [The Seventh.] St. Petersburg: Gumanistika, 2005.

MacDonald, Ian. *The New Shostakovich.* Boston: Northeastern University Press, 1990.

Main, Steven J. "The Arrest and 'Testimony' of Marshal of the Soviet Union M. N. Tukhachevsky (May–June 1937)." *Journal of Slavic Military Studies* 10, no. 1 (March 1997): 151–195.

Mandelshtam, Osip. *Selected Poems.* Translated by James Greene. New York: Penguin, 1991.

Mandelstam, Nadezhda. *Hope Against Hope: A Memoir.* Translated by Max Hayward. New York: Modern Library, 1999.

Martynov, Ivan. *Shostakovich: The Man and His Work.* Translated by T. Guaralsky. New York: Philosophical Library, 1947.

Mayakovsky, Vladimir. *The Bedbug and Selected Poetry.* Translated by Max Hayward and George Reavey. New York: World Publishing, 1960.

Meyer, Krzysztof. *Shostakovich: Zhizn. Tvorchestvo. Vremya.* [Shostakovich: Life. Works. Times.] St. Petersburg: Kompozitor & DSCH, 1998.

Mikkonen, Simo. *State Composers and the Red Courtiers: Music, Ideology, and Politics in the Soviet 1930s.* PhD diss., University of Jyväskylä, 2007. Jyväskylä Studies in Humanities no. 78. Accessed January 2, 2014. https://jyx.jyu.fi/dspace/bitstream /handle/123456789/13463/9789513930158.pdf.

Mishra, Michael. *A Shostakovich Companion.* Westport, CT: Praeger, 2008.

Montefiore, Simon Sebag. *Stalin: The Court of the Red Tsar.* New York: Knopf, 2004.

Morrison, Simon. *Lina and Serge: The Love and Wars of Lina Prokofiev.* Boston: Houghton Mifflin Harcourt, 2013.

"Muddle Instead of Music" [*Sumbur vmesto muzïki*]. *Pravda,* January 28, 1936. Translation at http://www.arnoldschalks.nl/tlte1sub1.html. Accessed January 27, 2013.

National Archives and Records Administration (USA). Record Group 59. State Department Control File, 1940–4. 861.4038/1-2.

Nelson, Anne. *Red Orchestra: The Story of the Berlin Underground and the Circle of Friends Who Resisted Hitler.* New York: Random House, 2009.

Ostashevsky, Eugene, ed. *Oberiu: An Anthology of Russian Absurdism.* Evanston, IL: Northwestern University Press, 2006.

Overy, Richard. *Russia's War: A History of the Soviet War Effort, 1941–1945.* New York: Penguin, 1997.

Pleshakov, Constantine. *Stalin's Folly: The Tragic First Ten Days of World War II on the Eastern Front.* Boston: Mariner/Houghton Mifflin, 2006.

Radamsky, Sergei. *Der verfolgte Tenor: Mein Sängerleben zwischen Moskau und Holly-wood* [A Tenor Pursued: My Singing Life Between Moscow and Hollywood]. Munich: Piper, 1972.

Reid, Anna. *Leningrad: Tragedy of a City Under Siege, 1941–1944*. New York: Bloomsbury, 2012.

Roberts, Andrew. *The Storm of War: A New History of the Second World War*. New York: Harper, 2011.

Roberts, Geoffrey. *Stalin's Wars: From World War to Cold War, 1939–1953*. New Haven, CT: Yale University Press, 2006.

Robinson, Harlow. *Sergei Prokofiev: A Biography*. 2nd ed. Boston: Northeastern University Press, 2002.

Ross, Alex. *The Rest Is Noise: Listening to the Twentieth Century*. New York: Picador, 2008.

The Russian Diary of an Englishman, Petrograd, 1915–1917. New York: Robert McBride, 1919.

Salisbury, Harrison E. *The 900 Days: The Siege of Leningrad*. 2nd ed. Cambridge, MA: Da Capo, 2003.

Schwarz, Boris. *Music and Musical Life in Soviet Russia, 1917–1970*. New York: Norton, 1973.

Selby, John. "Dmitri Shostakovich Portrayed by His Charming Aunt Nadejda." Associated Press. *Palm Beach Post-Times*, July 23, 1944, 13.

Seroff, Victor Ilyich, with Nadejda Galli-Shohat. *Dmitri Shostakovich: The Life and Background of a Soviet Composer*. New York: Knopf, 1943.

Service, Robert. *A History of Modern Russia: From Tsarism to the Twenty-First Century*. 3rd ed. Cambridge, MA: Harvard University Press, 2009.

———. *Stalin: A Biography*. Cambridge, MA: Belknap/Harvard University Press, 2005.

Shostakovich, Dmitri. *New Collected Works*. Vol. 7, *Symphony No. 7, Op. 60*. Edited by Manashir Iakubov. Moscow: DSCH, 2010.

———. *New Collected Works*. Vol. 22, *Symphony No. 7, Op. 60. Arranged for Piano (four hands)*. Arrangement by Levon Atovmian. Edited by Victor Ekimovsky, with note by Larisa Miller. Moscow: DSCH, 2013.

———. *Pisma k I. I. Sollertinskomu* [Letters to I. I. Sollertinsky]. St. Petersburg: Kompozitor, 2006.

———. *Symphony no. 7, op. 60: Leningrad* (1949). Facsimile edition of the manuscript. With a commentary by Manashir Yakubov. Tokyo: Zen-On Music, 1992.

Shukman, Harold, ed. *The Blackwell Encyclopedia of the Russian Revolution*. Cambridge, MA: Blackwell, 1994.

Siegmeister, Elie. *The Music Lover's Handbook*. 1943. http://www.unz.org/Pub/SiegmeisterElie-1943.

Simmons, Cynthia, and Nina Perlina. *Writing the Siege of Leningrad: Women's Diaries, Memoirs, and Documentary Prose*. Pittsburgh: University of Pittsburgh Press, 2002.

Sitsky, Larry. *Music of the Repressed Russian Avant-Garde, 1900–1929.* Westport, CT: Greenwood, 1994.

Sixsmith, Martin. "The Secret Rebel." *The Guardian,* July 14, 2006.

Skrjabina, Elena. *Siege and Survival: The Odyssey of a Leningrader.* Translated by Norman Luxenburg. Carbondale: Southern Illinois University Press, 1971.

Slonimsky, Nicolas. *Music Since 1900.* 5th ed. New York: Macmillan, 1994.

Sollertinsky, Dmitri and Ludmilla. *Pages from the Life of Dmitri Shostakovich.* Translated by Graham Hobbs and Charles Midgley. New York: Harcourt Brace Jovanovich, 1980.

Stern, Ludmila. *Western Intellectuals and the Soviet Union, 1920–40: From Red Square to the Left Bank.* New York: Routledge, 2006.

Stolyarova, Galina. "Music Played On as Artists Died." *St. Petersburg Times,* January 23, 2004. www.highbeam.com/doc/1P1-89778318.html.

Tassie, Gregor. *Nikolay Myaskovsky: The Conscience of Russian Music.* Lanham, MD: Rowman & Littlefield, 2014.

Tomoff, Kiril. *Creative Union: The Professional Organization of Soviet Composers, 1939–1953.* Ithaca: Cornell University Press, 2006.

Trotsky, Leon. *The History of the Russian Revolution.* 3 vols. Translated by Max Eastman. New York: Simon and Schuster, 1932. Accessed May 16, 2013. http://www .marxists.org/archive/trotsky/1930/hrr/index.htm.

van Tuyll, Hubert P. *Feeding the Bear: American Aid to the Soviet Union, 1941–1945.* Contributions in Military Studies 90. New York: Greenwood, 1989.

Vishnevskaya, Galina. *Galina: A Russian Story.* Translated by Guy Daniels. San Diego: Harcourt Brace Jovanovich, 1984.

Volkov, Solomon. *Shostakovich and Stalin: The Extraordinary Relationship Between the Great Composer and the Brutal Dictator.* Translated by Antonina W. Bouis. New York: Knopf, 2004.

———. *Testimony: The Memoirs of Dmitri Shostakovich.* 25th anniversary ed. New York: Limelight, 2004.

Vulliamy, Ed. "Orchestral Manoeuvres." *The Observer,* November 24, 2001. http:// www.theguardian.com/theobserver/2001/nov/25/features.magazine27.

Wang, Dajue. "Shostakovich: Music on the Brain?" *The Musical Times* 214, no. 1684 (June 1983): 347–348.

Watt, Donald Cameron. "Who Plotted Against Whom? Stalin's Purge of the Soviet High Command Revisited." *Journal of Slavic Military Studies* 3, no. 1 (1990): 46–65.

Weinstein, Larry, director. *The War Symphonies: Shostakovich Against Stalin.* Documentary. IdtV Cultuur, 1997.

Weintraub, Eugene. Papers. New York Public Library for the Performing Arts, Music Division. JPB 12-02, Boxes 1 & 2. Telegrams relating to the microfilm transfer are in folder 2.8; later memoranda relating to the transfer and premiere are in folder 2.9. The full titles of these memoranda are as follows: "Shostakovich: Seventh Symphony: Some Facts Relating to the NBC Broadcast July 19, 1942" (fol. 2.9); "Some Additional Notes About the Shostakovich Seventh Symphony" (fol. 2.9); "The Shostakovich 'Seventh Symphony' in America" (fol. 2.9); "Volkov's 'Testimony'" (fol. 2.9); "Letter to the Editor," MS, dated 1990 (fol. 2.16). Another document cited, "Some Notes on the Shostakovich Seventh Symphony," is missing its first page in the New York cache (fol. 2.9) but exists in a complete version in the VOKS archives in Moscow (GARF, f. 5283, op. 14, d. 132).

White, James D. *The Russian Revolution, 1917–1921.* London: Edward Arnold, 1994.

Wilson, Elizabeth, ed. *Shostakovich: A Life Remembered.* Princeton: Princeton University Press, 1994.

Ziemke, Earl F. *The Soviet Juggernaut.* Alexandria, VA: Time-Life, 1980.

PHOTOGRAPHY AND IMAGE CREDITS

AKG-Images: 124 (top left), 192 (top), 269 (top right)

Anna Akhmatova Museum: 101 (top)

AP Photo: 151, 211, 241 (bottom)

Bundesarchiv, Bild 101I-020-1268-36/Johannes Hähle: 181 (top)

Bundesarchiv, Bild 146-1981-149-34A/o.Ang: 201 (top)

Bundesarchiv, Bild 183-B17220/Hugo Tannenberg: 275 (top)

Collection of Charlotte Douglas, New York: 38 (bottom)

Deutsches Filminstitut, Frankfurt: 51 (all)

DSCH Journal: 231 (bottom), 258, 374

DSCH Publishers (Moscow): 66 (top), 136, 144 (top and bottom), 145 (top and bottom), 311 (top)

Eric Shaal/The LIFE Picture Collection/Getty Images: 1

Library of Congress: 22, 85 (bottom), 199 (top), 275 (bottom), 276 (bottom)

Margaret Bourke-White/The LIFE Picture Collection/Getty Images: 250 (bottom)

Mary Evans Picture Library/Alexander Meledin: 29 (bottom), 173, 286 (bottom), 340 (top)

Mary Evans/Iberfoto: 185

Mary Evans/Sueddeutsche Zeitung Photo: 158 (top)

Mayakovsky Museum: 41

The Museum "Muses Were Not Silent": 231 (top), 346 (top)

National Archives: 3, 158 (bottom), 276 (top)

M. T. Anderson: 378 (top)

RIA Novosti: 62 (bottom), 73, 78 (top), 187, 190 (top), 195, 201 (bottom), 207, 220 (bottom), 221 (top), 224, 234, 247, 250 (top), 253 (bottom), 269 (bottom), 274 (bottom), 289 (top and bottom), 299 (bottom), 335, 353, 378 (bottom left)

RIA Novosti/Lebrecht Music & Arts: 346 (bottom)

Richard Southern Collection/University of Bristol Theatre Collection/ArenaPAL: 63 (top)

Shostakovich Association (Paris) & DSCH Publishers (Moscow): 15, 55 (bottom), 85 (top), 237, 347 (top)

Sovfoto/Universal Images Group/Getty Images: 101 (bottom), 124 (bottom)

Time magazine, July 20, 1942 © 1942 Time Inc. Used under license: 328

The initials DDS indicate Dmitri Shostakovich. Illustrations, maps, and captions are indicated with *italic* page numbers.